THE
CITY OBSERVED:
BOSTON

THE
CITY OBSERVED:
BOSTON

A GUIDE TO
THE ARCHITECTURE
OF THE HUB

DONLYN
LYNDON

PHOTOGRAPHY BY
ALICE WINGWALL

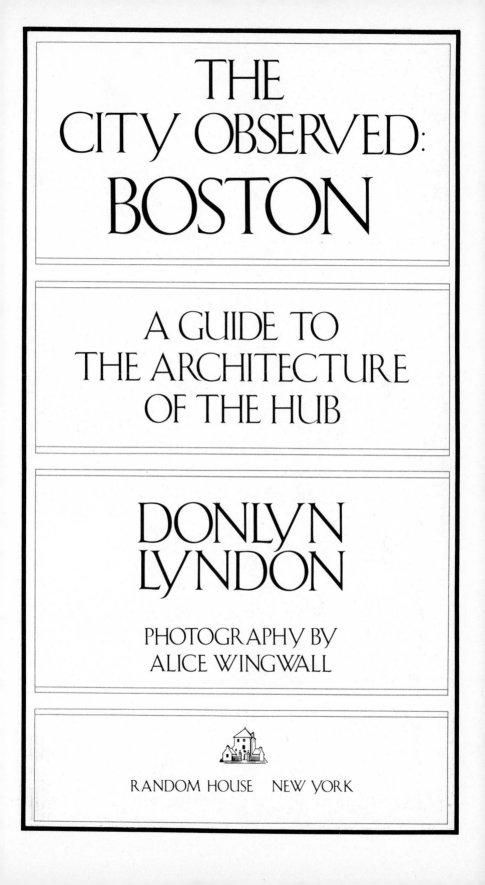

RANDOM HOUSE   NEW YORK

Text Copyright © 1982 by Donlyn Lyndon
Photographs Copyright © 1982 by Alice Wingwall

All rights reserved under International and Pan-American Copyright Conventions.
Published in the United States by Random House, Inc., New York, and
simultaneously in Canada by Random House of Canada Limited, Toronto.

Library of Congress Cataloging in Publication Data

Lyndon, Donlyn.
The city observed, Boston.

Includes index.
1. Boston (Mass.)—Buildings—Guide-books.
2. Architecture—Massachusetts—Boston—Guide-
books. 3. Boston (Mass.)—Description—Guide-
books. I. Wingwall, Alice. II. Title.
NA735.B7L96   1982   917.44′610443   81–48292
ISBN 0–394–50475–5   AACR2

Manufactured in the United States of America

3 5 7 9 8 6 4 2

FIRST EDITION

Cartography by David Lindroth
Designed by Carole Lowenstein

*The text of this book is dedicated to
Maynard Lyndon and Dorothea Zentgrebe Lyndon,
who taught me to care about buildings
and about words*

ACKNOWLEDGMENTS

There are many people without whom this book would not have been possible, friends who have labored generously to help me bring forth both fact and opinion. Seth Schweitzer has done everything that could be done—coaxed ramblings into sentences, checked facts in the field, organized files, and even rescued the stolen manuscript from a junk heap. David Bonetti and Gary Garrels have also been patient, resourceful and insightful collaborators, assembling information for each entry, verifying observations and sharpening the text. Kay Barned was first to be involved in this way, helping to set the whole process in motion. The final version of this text was measurably improved by Gail Winston's editorial insistence on clarity, Jonathan Galassi's thoughtful review and Paul Goldberger's criticism and encouragement. Rupert Davis and the staff of the Bostonian Society have aided with research; Cynthia Panlilio offered timely assistance; Liz Strange, Eileen Hardy, Kitty Steiner and Ginger Temple have been typists for the enterprise. Jean Paul Carlhian has offered wisdom and facts with studious precision; Pamela and Belden Daniels, Sonya and David Sofield have proferred friendly criticisms that nurtured both insights and phrasing. Lu Wendel and Maynard Hale Lyndon have given generously of their hospitality and observations and of their enthusiasm for Boston. The Massachusetts Institute of Technology, the American Academy in Rome, the Graham Foundation for Advanced Studies in the Fine Arts, and Lyndon Buchanan Associates all helped to make time available for the project.

Throughout it all Alice, named Wingwall, has been not only photographer but coauthor of the vantage point from which I write.

CONTENTS

Foreword by Paul Goldberger   *xiii*
Introduction   *xv*
A Note on Architectural Terms   *xxiii*

I / **THE SYMBOLIC HUB**

    A / SPRING LANE PRIMER   *3*
    B / THE STATE HOUSE AND COMMON   *21*
    C / GOVERNMENT CENTER   *32*
    D / FANEUIL HALL AND THE MARKETS   *43*
    E / THE WATERFRONT   *51*

II / **THE NORTHERN RIM**

    A / NORTH END AND WEST END   *73*
    B / BEACON HILL   *90*
    C / BEACON HILL WEST AND THE ESPLANADE   *110*

III / **BACK BAY**

    A / COMMONWEALTH AVENUE AND RESIDENTIAL
        BACK BAY   *121*
    B / NEWBURY AND BOYLSTON STREETS   *142*
    C / COPLEY SQUARE   *161*
    D / BACK BAY WEST   *173*

IV / **THE SOUTHERN SECTOR**   *185*

    A / THE HIGH SPINE   *187*
    B / THE SOUTH END   *205*
    C / BAY VILLAGE AND THE THEATER DISTRICT   *223*
    D / SOUTH STATION   *240*

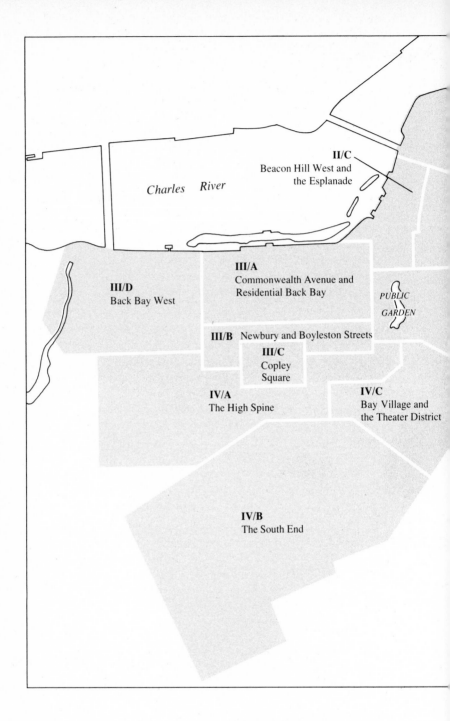

II/C
Beacon Hill West and
the Esplanade

Charles River

III/A
Commonwealth Avenue and
Residential Back Bay

III/D
Back Bay West

*PUBLIC
GARDEN*

III/B Newbury and Boyleston Streets

III/C
Copley
Square

IV/A
The High Spine

IV/C
Bay Village and
the Theater District

IV/B
The South End

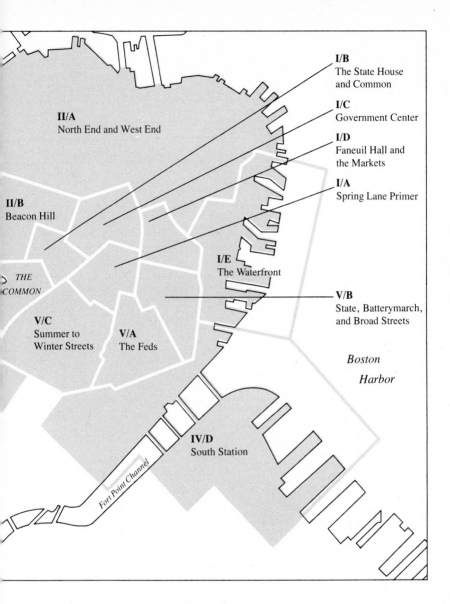

I/B
The State House
and Common

I/C
Government Center

I/D
Faneuil Hall and
the Markets

I/A
Spring Lane Primer

II/A
North End and West End

II/B
Beacon Hill

I/E
The Waterfront

*THE
COMMON*

V/B
State, Batterymarch,
and Broad Streets

V/C
Summer to
Winter Streets

V/A
The Feds

Boston

Harbor

IV/D
South Station

Fort Point Channel

V / THE HUB OF BUSINESS

A / THE FEDS   *255*
B / STATE, BATTERYMARCH AND BROAD STREETS   *266*
C / SUMMER TO WINTER STREETS   *281*

VI / BEYOND THE HUB

A·/ THE RIVERSIDE LINE   *299*
B / THE EMERALD NECKLACE   *302*

Index   *307*

FOREWORD

Donlyn Lyndon is under the impression that he has written a single book, but he has in fact written three. *The City Observed: Boston* is at once a description of the architecture of Boston, a history of that city, and an introduction to the art of appreciating buildings in general. None of these are easy tasks, but all have been done successfully here. The choice of buildings is both thorough and logical, the criticisms pungent and knowing (how deft to describe I.M. Pei's Boston work as representing "an elegantly fashioned emptiness that is presumed to be a rekindled vision of civic order"). The concerns are always with the evolving shape of the city, not with the building as an object isolated in either time or space. And the connoisseurship comes out of a deep respect and love not only for architecture, but for the art of seeing itself. Take, for example, Lyndon on the classical column: "a splendid upright: not just a post but a presence."

The City Observed series, which began with the publication of a guide to Manhattan in 1979, was conceived as a goup of books that would merge a personal outlook with an ample collection of facts. These are meant to be both carried about the city as guides, and to be read at home as references; *The City Observed* works equally well at both functions, and brings this series forward with distinction.

PAUL GOLDBERGER

INTRODUCTION

This is a book of opinions, embellished with some facts. It's not meant to be about the opinions, however, or for that matter about the facts. It's meant to turn your attention to the buildings of Boston, to initiate an exchange between you and the buildings around you, an exchange that can be instructive, rewarding and fun.

Though it is genuinely hoped that the observations recorded in this book will prove useful with or without the building present, reading the book is in no sense meant to be a substitute for the real thing: for standing in the presence of a building, wondering about its form and how it fits with its neighbors, considering the tools available to its builders and the range of decisions made, and rendering judgment—not Judgment of the Last sort, but judgment of whether the building fits, how it feels, whether it speaks of life and invention and initiative.

As an observer's guide, this book is necessarily limited to that which is publicly accessible. It does not attempt to establish a critique of the internal workings of private spaces or to consider what it takes to finance and maintain the structures it examines. It does not speak about everything that matters in architecture. But the public realm that it observes is, after all, the world that surrounds us, the one which Bostonians have chosen to construct in place of the landscape they came to. That realm is therefore accountable and its well-being remains a public charge, subject to deliberation and debate.

To encourage examination of all sectors of central Boston, the book is organized in five divisions, each with several chapters. The text consists of separate labeled entries that each describe and comment on a building, group of buildings or open space. The chapters cluster buildings into roughly geographic locales, organized, with one exception, into a sequence that can be followed on foot. The exception is the first chapter, "Spring Lane Primer," in which the sequence of buildings is chronological, comprising a brief review of the history of Boston's architecture—all to be found within 600 feet of Spring Lane, the approximate location of the first settlement.

The chapters themselves follow a path circumscribing the city, reviewing first the buildings of its symbolic center, then moving out to the waterfront, around the northern rim to Beacon Hill and Back Bay, next through the southwest quadrant of the city to Massachusetts Avenue and back through the South End, Bay Village and the Theater District to the water again at Fort Point Channel near South Station. This loop around the perimeter surrounds the commercial hub of the city. The fifth division of the book describes the remaining central area in three excursions, each dominated by a different phase of Boston's commercial development. "The Feds" begins at the new Federal Reserve Bank opposite South Station and pursues a path through the financial district back to the Old

State House, a path marked out by tall buildings. The second chapter, "State, Batterymarch and Broad Streets" follows a course back to the waterfront among buildings mostly associated with Boston's maritime days. The final chapter, "Summer to Winter Streets," begins again near South Station at the foot of Summer Street and proceeds up to the Common along a route that loops to either side to examine the various forms of commercial structures built since the Great Fire of 1872. The book ends a few hundred feet from where it started—in the Park Street subway station, to be exact.

For those who would carry their investigations a bit further, there are several useful books. A few especially bear noting, for without them this one could not have been written. Walter Muir Whitehill's *Boston: A Topographical History* is an indispensable source for understanding the general flow of events and the successive shapings of the land that underlie what we now observe. Similarly, Bainbridge Bunting's *Houses of Boston's Back Bay*, while more limited in scope, is an immensely valuable work, fundamental to any subsequent study in the area. The bibliography listed at the back of Douglass Shand Tucci's *Built in Boston: City and Suburb* is itself a great resource, and the text offers illuminating essays on building types and architects that have been formative in the city's development. *Beacon Hill: A Walking Tour* by A. McVoy McIntyre surveys that domain practically door to door, and Joseph Eldredge's text in *Architecture Boston*, edited by the Boston Society of Architects, offers summary essays on each of the areas covered here plus others, such as Charlestown, Roxbury and Cambridge, that are amply endowed with architecture of note, but simply lie beyond the scope of this book.

THE GEOGRAPHY OF THE HUB

Boston is fond of calling itself the Hub, in reference both to some fundamental facts of its geography and to the belief that it is centrally important to the world.

Searching the map of Boston for the Hub will not get you very far if you look for the geographic equivalent of a carriage wheel hub with a prominent center point and clearly radiating spokes. Like most major cities, Boston has a path system that is fundamentally radial. But the spokes are pretty wobbly and there is no single focal point. Initially only one road, Washington Street, went across land, traversing the neck of the peninsula to the south. The other paths started as ferries, then became bridges or, much later in some cases, railways reaching out north, south and west into the hinterland for goods that could then be transported east by clipper through the harbor to the world beyond and vice versa. Today, highways plow through the center of town and the airport lies to the east.

The center of all this is a matter for some debate. Oliver Wendell Holmes dubbed the Boston State House "hub of the solar system." This book, with a more limited scope in mind, however, starts with the Old State House, which is in any case a better contender geographically. There are several other places that could be considered as center point. Those more enamored of the recent past might opt for City Hall, while some would hold that Faneuil Hall, "cradle of liberty," was focal, or at least that the markets that have taken its name are certainly the present lodestone of the tourist trade. To add to the confusion, the Boston Stone, one-time starting point to measure distances, is lodged in an alley in the Blackstone Block; the corner of the Common at Park and Tremont streets, clearly marked by the spire of Park Street Church, is a point of great visual importance; and the intersection of Summer, Winter and Washington streets forms the focal point of downtown shopping.

The subway map confirms our ambiguity and suggests a means of resolution. It shows a square at the center, marked out by four stations. Each is the intersection of two subway lines. Nowhere do more than two come together at a single point. The four stations are Government Center, opposite City Hall; State Street, under the Old State House; Washington Street, at the intersection of Summer and Winter streets; and Park Street, opposite the Park Street Church and in sight of the State House. Drawing diagonals between these stations on a street map produces a center point directly in front of the Old City Hall. It is in this vicinity that the first chapter of this book is set.

Boston is many places, and as you pass among them, you will discover that it has become absorbed in its own reconstruction. Everywhere there are signs of reinvestment: refurbished civic structures, previously abandoned office buildings cleaned and gutted and restructured for present-day use, an extraordinary outpouring of investment in new forms of residences within the city—in former warehouses and factories as well as in reconstituted town houses and apartments. Boston, it would seem, has once again discovered its center.

And there is much to discover. Past jostles with present in a particularly boisterous manner. Simple brick boxes that were several generations old when they heard the intemperate voices of revolution stand inconveniently and majestically among elaborate steel-and-concrete structures heralding another form of dominion. Tough granite buildings of uncompromising rationality are interspersed with terra-cotta fantasies and with the splendors of the Renaissance that have been urbanely refashioned for Yankee enlightenment. In the center of Boston, buildings seldom align, so the structures of various periods are more distinct here than they would be in a city constructed on a grid, where differences in architectural style are absorbed in an ambience of uniform layout.

Many of Boston's major streets have their origin in paths that once followed the shape of the land, and they still exhibit the casual adjustments in direction that typify a foot trail. These characteristics are dramatized in the skyline, where the size of large buildings accentuates the differences in orientation and the towers of the recent past stand about like oversize chessmen deprived of a game plan. At street level, where smaller buildings often make subtle shifts in alignment to accommodate the angles, the vistas ahead are constantly changing; major buildings are thrust into view, and the intersections occasionally border on the bizarre.

The street walls of Boston are more shapely and eventful than our conceptions, more fuddling to the systematizer. They have a rich, sculpted and episodic order, made mostly by buildings that are more staid than the ensembles of which they are a part.

There are straight streets in Boston, of course, but they are of limited extent and usually of distinct purpose. Most date from the nineteenth century. Almost always these were constructed on filled land, of which there is an abundance. Straight streets to the east of the old center result from successive programs of wharf building, each designed to extend the town toward the sea and to make the loading of ships a more orderly affair. Beacon Hill has straight, almost parallel streets, also the result of land speculation, though straightness was achieved here by paring down the hills rather than by filling the tideland. Only the north and south boundary streets, Beacon and Cambridge, run the length of the area without interruption. The area inside is a network of T intersections that defies casual recollection, and the streets traverse a series of inclines that enforce a constantly changing variety of building form and outlook.

The greatest concentration of straight, parallel streets lies west of the Common, in Back Bay, on land rescued from the tidal mud in the last half of the nineteenth century and doled out for speculation in a highly ordered orthogonal grid. Broad Commonwealth Avenue forms a very memorable center line, with two parallel streets on either side. Westward progress is measured by the cross streets, labeled in alphabetical sequence: A for Arlington, B for Berkeley and so on, ending incongruously with I for Massachusetts. Beyond Massachusetts Avenue the system is abandoned. Beacon Street and Commonwealth Avenue, parallel in the Back Bay, cross and diverge at Kenmore Square, as though to contain Back Bay's gridlike clarity.

The geography of Boston is the foundation of its uniqueness, but it is the way its citizens have built that captures our imagination and gives occasion for reflection. We are accustomed to thinking of our cities as real estate. We recognize that land has exchange value based largely on its location, that buildings require a great investment of capital and that the services necessary to make our buildings work, the utilities and drainage and transportation networks that make our cities livable, are an extensive public commitment, one that is held and passed from one generation to the next, usually in a modified condition.

The stewardship that each generation exercises over this estate determines its viability for the next generation. We have seen in all our cities that the opportunities for waste and exploitation are boundless. It has been more in the nature of recent times to reap immediate benefits than to cultivate and maintain the inherited estate or to establish places that would serve the future in ways that are not calculable in present exchange.

But the city embodies another estate as well. The buildings and open spaces that make up our cities also represent a tremendous imaginative investment, an estate of the mind, in which we all have a share. That estate is there, waiting to be sought out and claimed as one's own, to be observed.

Each step in the evolution of the city's form involved someone imagining that a window, a wall, a building, a street or a sector might be a certain way, involved making the leap from what is to what might be. Many of these leaps are not great: They are routine imaginings that simply bring to bear the ways of building that are common to a period. Others are great indeed, calling forth a new understanding of what it means to build or, more rarely, what it is to be. A city the age of Boston and one that is as proud of its history contains an extraordinary chronicle of the wanderings of the human imagination. In walking the streets we can recover that chronicle, noting how builders have spent their energy and where they have invested their most intense imaginings. We can, indeed, learn to care.

A NOTE ON THE SELECTIONS

Why, you will probably ask, did the author pick these particular buildings? Is there a hidden agenda, a set of issues that these buildings illustrate more clearly than other ones would?

These are quite frankly the buildings that interested me. They were selected by walking the streets of Boston and paying attention. There was no hidden agenda, at least not one that was consciously contrived, yet a number of themes recur.

First, it is a clear premise of the book that the street is a place that matters and that each building must play a role in establishing the public environment of the street. Buildings, streets and parks have replaced the landscape. Ideally, they should provide opportunities for exploration and enjoyment as enriching and illuminating as the forests and meadows and mud flats they have displaced. But architecture is the organization of social, not natural, space and it is inescapably bound up in issues of property and control. The character of the street is for the most part determined by the actions of those who own property and live or work in the buildings that face that street. The walls that border the sides of a street are the walls of a public room—they owe as much to the public places that we pass through and live among as they do to the private spaces inside. Many buildings give generously to the street, offering examples of craft and imagination that we can live with and enjoy. Often the elements we notice are simply decorative devices, little more than jewelry, that bedeck each house or office in baubles that signify stature as much as or more than they offer enjoyment. But sometimes the shapes and forms displayed on the street are genuinely instructive, and these are most interesting, most rewarding to our attention.

There are three types of insight that we may rightly expect from the streets and buildings of a city: clues regarding the uses of spaces inside and what it's like to live there; understanding of the way buildings have been made; and most subtly, intimations of a common social purpose, reflections on our heritage. Entwined among these there is yet another—the presence of imagination. Traces of that rare facility that lets things be seen afresh are finally the most precious, for they bring us close to the heart of the matter, the force that has led us from there to here, sometimes in error. Imagination is wily and it serves many masters. We must learn to recognize its presence and refocus attention on the places that belong finally to all of us, the places that offer nurture and play to our minds and that will be our trust for the future.

Writings about architecture sometimes do a disservice by leading us to believe that there is one set of right purposes, one way of doing things in architecture. Observing a city like Boston makes that nearly impossible. The Boston of today is the result of many processes; of social, economic and technological developments that have often seemed to be inexorable and blind. It is also a record of thought, a transcription of decisions made by public bodies, landowners, tenants and their architects. The city shows us that architects, like other people, have intentions of various sorts, use their imaginative energies in differing ways and, yes, have unequal portions of talent. Much of the record is obliterated, as Jane Holtz Kay has documented in her book *Lost Boston,* but much of it remains, gloriously or ignominiously or plainly present. It is there in the buildings for us to observe; to see, to read with the eyes, to be next to or inside, to enjoy or disdain. The city is a resource for testing values, for understanding ourselves and our ancestors, for assessing our present state and judging what we may wish for the future.

BOSTON'S ARCHITECTS

A dozen or so architectural firms dominate this record, and the following summary view of their works can provide program notes for the changing conceptions of building that this book intends to help the reader explore.

Charles Bulfinch (1763–1844) was the first person in Boston to practice architecture as a profession. He was a man of extraordinary energy and vision who imagined not just individual buildings but whole segments of the town. His name crops up often in this text, and for the most part his architecture illustrates a change from the consideration of buildings as simple, single accommodation to coordinated elements of civic design. A well-established hierarchy of importance is reflected in the amount and type of decorative elaboration on the buildings, but there is a persistent attention to investing even the most modest buildings with carefully modulated windows shaped to strict rules of proportion and sized to make the relative public significance of each floor of the building discernible from the street. For further discussion of Bulfinch's work, see page 22. For examples of his work, see the State House (I B 4), Massachusetts General Hospital (II A 16), St. Stephen's Church (II A 6), the first (II A 15), second (II B 6) and third (II B 15) Harrison Gray Otis houses, and a row of houses on Chestnut Street (II B 12). He was responsible for dramatically altering Faneuil Hall (I D 1) and for creating large segments of the early-nineteenth-century waterfront on India Wharf (I E 3), Central Wharf (V B 10) and Broad Street, but little of the latter remains in a recognizable form.

Alexander Parris (1780–1852) was the most notable successor to Bulfinch, and indeed he executed some of Bulfinch's work after the master was called to Washington to be architect of the National Capitol. At Massachusetts General Hospital you can already see his hand at work in the rigorous use of granite. The stern, radiant rationality of his designs for St. Paul's Cathedral (V C 22) and for the buildings of the Faneuil Hall Markets (I D 5) combines an admiration of Greek forms with very adroit use of large pieces of granite to make the construction process—the art of placing stone upon stone—evident in the building's appearance.

Gridley J. Fox Bryant (1816–99) absorbed the granite tradition and turned it into the foundation of an astonishingly prolific career that included the construction of warehouses and government buildings in Boston and elsewhere, a number of commercial structures that were destroyed in the Great Fire of 1872 and many of the buildings that replaced them. In the course of Bryant's career the large blocks of granite and simple, rugged structures came to be embellished with forms and details that were borrowed from the academic traditions of architecture then prevalent in France. The large volumes and plain walls of these stone structures are relieved by carving that measures the face of the building not only with blocks of stone, but with vertical pilasters, horizontal stringcourses, elaborated cornices at the top and corners emphasized by rustications. The buildings remain austere blocks elaborated by the use of architectural conventions that are intended to have us think them made up of smaller parts. Familiar and respectable pavilions that capture the mind's eye are inscribed onto stone structures that store the goods.

Mercantile Wharf (I E 9), the State Street block (V B 9), the Boston Transcript Building (I A 9), a row of houses on Arlington Street (III A 2), the Charles Street Jail (II A 17) and Old City Hall (I A 8) summarize the import, if not the extent, of Bryant's career. By far the most sumptuously conceived and fully sculpted of these buildings is the Old City Hall. Presumably this is due not only to its civic preeminence but to the talents and inclinations of *Arthur Gilman* (1821–82), Bryant's collaborator for the project.

Gilman, apparently something of a *bon vivant,* was more widely traveled than Bryant, less ensconced in the business of architecture and a far more flexible stylist. The Arlington Street Church (III B 1), a group of houses on Commonwealth Avenue (III A 3) and, indeed, the plan of Back Bay (page 121) are what we can still see of his work. Together with the Old City Hall, they reveal a wide-ranging mind that was more inquiring than determined and a sensibility that could guide building materials into fully sculpted form. There is no formula evident in Gilman's work; the shape and style of each building reflect a particular judgment about appropriate appearance.

The somewhat later work of *William Gibbons Preston* (1844–1910) is of a similar sort, and there is more of it. Preston's practice grew out of that established by his father, Henry. William was the architect for many projects throughout the city, a number of them buildings of distinction, both in purpose and form. The Museum of Natural History (now Bonwit Teller) (III B 5), the First Corps Cadet Armory (IV C 5), the Chadwick Lead Works (V B 19), the Claflin Building (I B 5) and the International Trust Company Building at 45 Milk Street (V A 13) are each in a different style, and the grace of each has recently encouraged their renovation and reuse.

Into this maelstrom of conventions and styles entered *Henry Hobson Richardson* (1838–86), a Southerner by birth, educated at Harvard and the first of leading Boston architects to study at the École des Beaux-Arts in Paris. His brief but heroic career left an indelible mark on the city and on the nation's architecture. Richardson was singularly able to breathe life into form, to capture the elements of a program and the materials of buildings and meld them into a single integrative vision. His buildings have a presence that derives equally from the massive serenity of Romanesque forms bound together in composition and from the profuse invention of incident within these masses. Trinity Rectory (III B 11), Trinity Church (III C 1), the Crowninshield House (III A 19) and the Hayden Building (IV C 19) are the Boston buildings that remain. They reveal only aspects of his genius. Visits to Sever and Austin halls at Harvard, the Ames Town Hall and Library in North Easton, Massachusetts, and the Allegheny County Courthouse in Pittsburgh are necessary to fill out the most rudimentary picture of his achievement.

McKim, Mead & White of New York used similar talents in the next generation (between 1879 and 1906, the year of White's death) to embody an altogether different vision rooted not in images of monastic individualism but in the propriety of the Classical orders, the grandeur of Rome and the ambitions of the moneyed establishment. The Boston Public Library (III C 4) and Symphony Hall (IV A 15) say it all, but the Algonquin Club (III A 30) and houses on Commonwealth Avenue (III D 8) repeat the themes in various stages of development.

The work of *Peabody & Stearns* between 1870 and 1915 bridges the work of Richardson and of McKim, Mead & White, managing at the same time to be more pedantic than either. Their competent and successful houses in Back Bay are ubiquitous (III A 17), (III A 28), and their progress down State Street from the Boston Stock Exchange (V B 3) to the Cunard Building (V B 5) to the Custom House Tower (V B 8) charts the transformation from Richardsonian to Classical detail on forms that are determined more by their ability to construct high on tight land than by any commitment to style.

The literal successors to Richardson's practice were *Shepley, Rutan & Coolidge,* whose Ames Building (I A 11) of 1889 marks the beginning of a distinguished practice continued through successive firms to the present in *Shepley, Bulfinch, Richardson & Abbott.* In this succession *Coolidge & Shattuck* (1915–1924) made buildings of special distinction, such as 7-11 Beacon Street (I B 9) and the Samuel Appleton Building (V B 15).

Clarence H. Blackall (1857–1942), a skillful stylist, was responsible for the first steel-frame building in Boston (I A 12), for several of its most distinguished theaters (IV C 13) and for the curiously anomalous Tremont Temple (I A 13), which, when properly rediscovered, will be a favorite of Post Modernists.

Parker, Thomas & Rice inherited the McKim, Mead & White penchant for Classical grace and used it in the service of the Boston Establishment, as in the first John Hancock Building (IV A 7) and the early Boston Five Cents Savings Bank (I A 19), each of which has witnessed additions of startling demeanor.

The John Hancock Tower (IV A 7) by *I. M. Pei & Partners* stands opposite the Parker, Thomas & Rice building, glistening with reflections on its ever-so-smooth glass skin. In this it is unlike the other Pei buildings in town, the Christian Science complex (IV A 12) and the Harbor Tower Apartments (I E 1). It bears in common with them ingenuity in site plan, simplicity of volume and precision of detail; an elegantly fashioned emptiness that is presumed to be a rekindled vision of civic order.

Kallman & McKinnell, on the other hand, have taken the empty volumes of Pei's Government Center urban-design plan and filled them with tangible structure, concrete elements of building that make evident how part rests on part and what each has to do with the whole. The City Hall (I C 2), the Government Center Garage (I C 10) and the Boston Five Cents Savings Bank addition (I A 19) are each examples of construction made manifest.

The civic work of *Arrowstreet* in the Washington Street Arcade (V C 14) and the Park Street subway station (V C 24), fill volumes with people and things, engaging our attention with seemly frivolity, often using materials of less enduring scope. An earlier work by the senior partners Ashley and Myer placed the Boston Architectural Center (III D 10) in an articulated framework of concrete, different from, but responsive to, the scale of Back Bay buildings.

The most vivid gatherings of people and things have been wrought by *Benjamin Thompson Associates* at the Faneuil Hall Markets (I D 5). Here the splendid spare rationality of the granite forms designed by Parris has been restored, then augmented by great glass sheds, and filled with shoppers and eaters of every description; all these enshrined in an ambience of smooth graphics and rich colors uncomplicated by nuance.

With the reclamation of Old City Hall (I A 8) and a string of buildings along the waterfront (I E 6, 7, 12, 16, 19) *Anderson, Notter Associates* have shepherded much of the city's historical fabric into the present.

In many cases, buildings in Boston result from the work of more than one architect, with successive generations of modification and renewal. In the entries that follow the original architect is listed, if known, and successive architects are listed for "reuse" when there is substantial alteration.

A NOTE ON ARCHITECTURAL TERMS

Over the centuries, the elements with which buildings have been conceived and composed have developed traditional names. Sometimes clusters of names distinguish subtle differences among building parts that play a similar role in the construction or appearance of buildings. A few of these are described below.

Aedicula

Aedicula   This is a Roman term for a diminutive part of a building that is shaped to appear as though it were a miniature of the whole building. The most obvious aedicula is a niche with columns on either side, a roof overhead, a base underneath and a sculpted saint inside. More commonly, it is the framed surrounding for a window, or a porch that makes a personal place of shelter on the face of a building. An aedicula is used to capture the imagination, to make it possible to understand the larger building as being made up of parts that you can imagine being in.

The *temple front* is like a grown-up aedicula; a specific form that is used to

Temple front

Temple front

Pediment

Pavilions with Pediment in center

focus attention on one part of a larger building. It simulates the well-established and codified frontal appearance of a Greek or Roman temple, with steps at the base and four, six or eight columns supporting a *pediment*. The pediment, triangular or sometimes arched, is derived originally from the shaped ends of a sheltering roof. Its form has been used extensively throughout the history of architecture and at all sizes from the top of a window to a whole building front. The pediment has been so thoroughly imbued with connotations of entry and importance that the placement of a pediment, with or without associated columns and doors, signifies a focal point.

Pavilions perform a similar function, often at a larger scale, generally involving a group of rooms on several floors made to seem like an independent, clearly formed part of the building usually in the center and/or at both ends of a larger structure.

Arches   Arches make openings in masonry walls, with the masonry pieces shaped or placed so that they press against each other to transfer the weight of the wall from directly overhead to the wall on either side. Arches are *round,* with their bottom surface shaped as the top half of a circle, or they can be *pointed,* with the curved segments rising smoothly from either side to a point at the center.

Pointed arches   Round and segmental arches

There are also *segmental* arches with a low flat curve that rises only slightly at the center and butts abruptly into either side of the opening. Round arches were used in Roman and Romanesque architecture and in the architecture of the Renaissance. In the Renaissance and later, round arches happen most often atop upright openings and may be imagined as geometrically ideal forms shaped around the head of a body. Pointed arches are associated with Gothic architecture and were used in Boston principally on buildings of medieval derivation, presumably as aids to spirituality. Segmental arches provide the widest opening for the least height and are frequent among nineteenth-century buildings built

*Cast-iron arches with
small-pane casement windows*

Arches

for commercial and industrial purposes, especially those parts that were deemed not to need adornment.

Arches are used structurally in walls that are made of masonry. They occur generally as incidents in a larger continuous surface. Sometimes arches are used to transfer weight to either side even when the opening beneath them is a simple rectangular window or door. Then they are called *relieving arches.* The center piece of a round arch is the *keystone,* which presses down on the adjoining blocks on either side and is often emphasized or elaborated. Segments of masonry shaped to form an arch are called *voussoirs,* and the *spring line* of the arch is the point at which it begins to curve inward from the vertical surfaces on either side.

Axis   An axis is the centerline around which the parts of a building are arranged, apportioning objects and events to the left and right. There are sometimes multiple axes with a hierarchy of primary and secondary importance. Axes guide the alignment of window to window, room to room, door to entry to building, and sometimes building to building. Most importantly, axes provide the opportunity for an observer to align with any of the above and to experience the place accordingly. Sometimes, however, it's good not to be aligned, to relate to the building more loosely. Buildings of little pretension or of Romantic aspiration or of insistent modernity employ axes sparingly or not at all. An axial walk bordered by trees qualifies as an *allée.*

Bay windows

Bow windows   *Chamfered bay with pedimented dormer*

Bay, Bay Window, Bow Window   A bay is a unit of measure, the space
between points of support. Bays are the spatial components of which a building
is made. In large structures they are often marked out by piers on the face of
the building. *Bay windows* are units of a somewhat different sort, small pockets
of space that project forward from the wall of a building to provide additional
space, with views up and down the street. Bay windows have the power to grasp
our attention and they are especially pleasant to be in; light, close-fitting and
endowed with outlook. Boston has an abundance of *chamfered* bay windows,
projections that have their two sides set at an angle, as though their corners had
been chopped. *Bow windows* are grander still. The whole face of the house swells
forward on a shallow curve to give a graceful expansion to the ends of the
principal rooms.

Beam, Truss   Holding the roof aloft or a floor overhead takes a special kind
of ingenuity. For simple shapes and short spans, beams will do, straight single
members of wood, steel or concrete that carry loads from side to side while

resting on walls or, if walls are inconvenient, on piers and columns spaced appropriately. When specially large spaces are to be spanned in wood or steel, comparatively small pieces are assembled into large interconnected networks of trusses, which can develop greater strength than individual members.

Column, Colonette, Colonnade   The column is a splendid upright: not just a post but a presence. In its Classical form the column is a carrier of culture, its base, shaft and capital formed by over 2,500 years of tradition. During this time the column has been shaped, reshaped, refined, ingeniously transformed, distorted, vulgarized and born again. The great power of the Classical column is that it forms a part of a larger system of proportions and relationships. Three major types, Doric, Ionic and Corinthian, first developed in Greece, have guided the development of Classical architecture. Each has a range of acceptable proportions of height to width, ranging generally from stalwart and husky in the Doric to attenuated and elaborate in the Corinthian. Each type also has a prescribed shape for the base, for the capital and for the entablature that links columns together across the top. Together these elements establish an *order.* For each of the orders there are specified moldings and carvings that establish a distinct dress code. *Doric* is the simplest of the orders. *Ionic* is the most easily recognized by spiraling volutes in the capital, and the *Corinthian* capital is richly embellished with carved acanthus leaves. *Tuscan* is a simple, somewhat rustic order that was used often in the English Renaissance but that lacks the austere power of the Doric. *Composite* is a lush mutant of the Ionic and Corinthian types. The spacing between columns is the *intercolumniation;* its proportion is also governed by convention.

When columns are not literally structural, but are rather a representation of structure or a means for modulating the building surface with traditional measurable units, they are often only *half-round* or flat projections from the building's surface. The latter are called *pilasters.*

The *colonnade,* a linked row of columns providing shaded and protected passage, is a noble civic device that appears all too infrequently in northern

Columns

Colonette

Colonettes

climates, and then most often with insufficient civic purpose. A *loggia* is a roofed passage of limited extent set into the main volume of the building, often at the upper levels. Loggias combine the advantages of colonnade and aedicula.

Colonettes are diminutive columns, vertical pieces which are more likely embellishment than structure and which are thinner and smaller than the body. In line with their more frivolous nature, colonettes are less rigorously codified than columns.

For a full and eminently instructive account of the Classical orders, see Sir John Summerson's *Classical Language of Architecture.*

Cornice   There are many terms relating to the visible tops of buildings because the top of a thing plays such an important role in forming a memorable image in our minds. The cornice is the top of a wall or of a building element made evident by an assembly of projecting moldings which strikes a definitive limit to that section of the building. In the Classical order the cornice is the uppermost element of the *entablature,* which consists usually of three parts, the others being a *frieze,* often with decorative motifs or sculpted figures, and an *architrave* of flat moldings that sits directly on the column capitals. In the case of a door or window frame, the architrave may wrap around the opening.

Cornice

The cornice often marks the intersection of wall with roof, but may instead be drawn horizontally across the building at a lower level to establish a reference line with which to visually measure the building's scope. In instances where the building's walls are meant to be more dominant than the roof, the wall is often extended above the cornice with a *parapet.* In architecture inspired by the Renaissance the parapet is often formed as a *balustrade,* with vigorously contoured uprights that support a rail, as they more commonly do on stairs and balconies. In the most extravagant versions, urns or sculpted figures surmount the balustrade, punctuating the skyline at each vertical division in the building's face. When the building is meant to have medieval overtones, the parapet is sometimes made with *crenelations,* with the height of the parapet alternating between high sections and low, as in the silhouette of a fortified castle. Parapets, incidentally, also keep people from walking off the edge of flat roofs.

Eave   When the roof is intended to be dominant, the underside may project out over the wall to form an eave. The eave may sit directly on top of a cornice, overhang a modest distance or be held forward on *brackets* or *struts* that carry the overhanging weight back to the wall surface. Brackets are also used to support balconies, door heads and various other projections from the building wall. They frequently provide occasion for whimsical decorative treatment.

Lantern, Cupola, Dome   Three means for emphasizing the center of a place. The lantern shelters a source of light; in the lantern at building scale, the source of light is not a flame, as in a gas lantern, but an opening in the roof that lets natural light into the space below. A lantern, then, is an assembly of columns and glass, often designed with considerable elaboration, so that the light plays among the columns outside as well as penetrating to the inside. Very often lanterns open into *domes,* large hemispherical coverings that are for the most part reserved for places of very special importance. The most splendid dome in Boston resides, suitably, above the State House. Domes often have an outer shell that keeps out the weather and is shaped to be noteworthy, and an inner one to form the space. The two are not always of the same shape. The inner shell is sometimes termed a *cupola,* as are the diminutive domes often found atop lanterns, towers and aediculae. A *canopy,* or umbrella, held over an important spot or person is likely the root source of all these symbolic forms.

Dome

Lantern

Masonry Vault   Vaults are three-dimensional extensions of the arch—whole spaces covered by stones, tile or brick, shaped so that they press against each other and span between walls or piers. *Barrel vaults* are arched in one direction and form long tunnels of space. *Groin vaults* are arched in two directions, usually with pointed arches; their intersection overhead forms a diagonal cross. The dome is a special form of vault with all arches radiating from the center. Many vaults in Boston, however, are made of plaster to simulate the original masonry forms.

Terra cotta

Pudding stone, brownstone, limestone, granite, terra cotta   A roster of familiar building materials in Boston. *Pudding stone* is a comparatively hard tan conglomerate stone quarried originally in Roxbury. *Brownstone* was the ubiquitous building material of the last half of the nineteenth century; it is a dark workable sandstone. *Limestone* is a lighter, finer stone, used principally on buildings of pretension. *Granite* is the glory of Boston's architecture, appearing first as large, tough slabs that served as bases for the brick walls of the eighteenth century. Then during the nineteenth century, it came into its own as crisp, precise slabs in the almost skeletal architecture of the mid-century, and was used subsequently as a fine surfacing on buildings of distinction. More recently it has returned once again to a workable mode in the tough granite curbs, benches and paving blocks scattered through the city. The most rugged, widely used granite came from quarries in Quincy, just south of Boston. They provided the solid gray variety that is most in evidence. The whiter, more refined granite of the Boston Public Library came from Milford, to the southwest. More recently a pink granite has come into fashion, fetched from more distant places to surface the sleek office blocks of downtown.

Terra cotta is a baked tile product that was used extensively in the first decades of the twentieth century. Terra cotta became an extraordinarily versatile material, since it could be cast in complicated shapes emulating the carved decoration of previous periods of architecture, and it could be used to clad the steel frames of tall buildings with relative lightness and ease. Its colors and textures could also be made nearly indistinguishable from the stone surfaces it supplanted. With any masonry, the *coursing*—that is, the layout of stones—has been a matter of much concern and of great consequence for the appearance of buildings. A single row of stones or bricks is called a course, and there are many patterns that can be developed by altering the spacing, size and disposition of bricks and stones. A *stringcourse* is a specially inserted row of stone molding that is used to delineate one part of the structure as visually separate from another.

Quoin, Rustication, Basement   A trio of devices for emphasizing the huskiness of buildings. *Rustication* refers to stonework that has been deliberately carved to emphasize its blockiness, usually in large solid rectangles with the joints between them deeply cut. Rustication was usually used to emphasize the *basement* level of a building, meaning the entire level of the building that joined the ground, sometimes half above ground, sometimes a whole level above the ground, but with service functions inside. The basement level of a building was often of a differing material rendered as a sturdier form and made subservient to the upper floors. The *grade* of a building site, that is, the level of the ground surrounding, might vary from one side of the basement to the other, and emphasis of the basement level often established a level starting point for the building's composition. *Quoins* are a special form of rustication that was used in buildings of the Renaissance to delineate the corners of buildings or of elements of the buildings, such as pavilions.

Roof   Roofs come in a few basic shapes. The *gable* is the roof of every child's dreams, peaked at the top and sloped to either side; the pitch may vary from steep to shallow, depending on the materials used and the space inside, but each side slopes in a single plane, casting the water and snow to one side or the other. Occasionally, mostly in the seventeenth and eighteenth centuries, a double slope was used, steeper at the bottom, shallower at the top to form a *gambrel* roof. *Mansard* roofs are a nineteenth-century version of the double slope, with the upper portion almost flat and the lower portion so steep as to be really a wall in disguise. The use of large roofs often requires *dormers* to let light and air into attics and upper floors. Dormers are mini-roofs inserted in a direction counter to the main roof to shelter windows and form pockets of head room in the eaves.

The *hip* roof is the grandest and most demanding, with surfaces sloping in four directions from a central peak or platform. When high enough to be visible, a hip roof establishes a strong sense of centrality for the building it covers; often, however, hip roofs are concealed by parapets.

Dormers

Dormers

All roof forms are subject to elaboration and complication by smaller intersecting wings, dormers and extensions. An abundance of such devices provides fodder for the picturesque.

Skeleton steel frame

Skeleton Steel Frame   Really tall buildings were made possible by the development during the 1890's of a construction type using large steel members to create a skeleton of beams and columns that could carry the many floors of a tall building without depending on the walls for support. This then made it possible for the walls to be hung on the steel frame, to be treated as a thin skin enclosing the surface of the building. This in turn paved the way for buildings clothed entirely in glass or in combinations of glass and light panel, such as those that have become the predominant features of the present skyline.

Transept, Nave, Apse   Traditional elements of a church, the *nave* being the main hall, often with lower aisles to either side; the *transept* the cross arms when the plan is in the shape of a cross; and the *apse* a round-ended termination of the nave, where the altar is generally placed. That part of the church holding the altar and reserved from general use is called a *chancel.* In some instances space to the side of the church is surrounded by arcaded passages, *cloisters,* which shelter a garden. Few of these elements are present, however, in the meeting houses built by the early settlers whose faith demanded strictly regulated communal worship and who viewed the traditional forms of Catholic worship with intense hostility.

Window   Windows are the decisive elements in architecture, the principal points of exchange. They let in light and air and their placement determines the quality of the light in a room as well as the nature of the views from the room to the outside. On the face of a building the windows establish a pattern of solid and void that is one of the architect's basic compositional tools; placed effectively, they also indicate much about the disposition and type of rooms located behind the wall. Windows are actors on the street's communal stage.

The names of windows are often related to the way that they're made: *Casement* windows are windows that are hinged on one side. Any one casement can be of only limited width or the window will sag, so casements are usually vertically proportioned and arranged in rows to make larger openings, or are placed next to fixed panes of glass that let in additional light. *Double-hung* windows slide up and down in vertical tracks, the top segment set forward of the bottom one so that they can pass. They are held in place by sash weights on cords hidden inside the window frame. Exceptionally tall, elegant windows can be made in this way by having three segments that are *triple-hung.* More recently, *sliding* windows have been popular, with large, horizontally proportioned panes of glass arranged similarly on horizontal tracks. *Awning* windows swing out from a hinge point at the top and are likely to be roughly square in proportion.

Small-paned windows are any of the above frames filled with small pieces of glass. The sections of wood or metal that hold the glass in place are called

Windows

Palladian motif

muntins, and the sections of metal or wood frame that divide the window into operating sections are called *mullions.* Recently very large windows have been made with single sheets of glass and have no muntins, and in some cases involving fixed glass there are not even mullions; rather, the sheets of glass are held together with clips and epoxy.

To make any window requires more than glass and frame. There must first be an opening in the wall, which requires an arch or a horizontal *header* or *lintel* spanning from side to side, and there must be a *sill* at the bottom to collect water running down the face of the window and throw it out away from the surface of the building. If the opening framed for the window is larger than the glass area, the solid section above and below the glass is termed a *spandrel.* Windows placed very high so that they let light in but do not afford views out are called *clerestory* windows. Windows surrounding a door are called *lights, fanlights* if they are above the door and their muntins are arranged in a radiating pattern, *sidelights* if they are beside the door.

Quatrefoil windows occur mostly in churches and are round openings inscribed with round windows in a pattern reminiscent of a four-leaf clover; a *trefoil* window is like a clover you can find. *Oriel* windows are miniature bay windows that bracket forward from the wall. *Palladian* windows consist of a large arched window in the center with smaller vertical windows on either side, the heads of which come only as high as the spring point of the arch for the center window. The frame is usually adorned with columns or pilasters and entablature. Windows of this sort are called *Serlian* by those who wish to demonstrate superior scholarship and *Venetian* by those who consider that neither Serlio nor Palladio can be said to have invented a form that was relatively common in the architecture of Venice and its dominions. In any case, the whole assembly is almost as potent an emblem of human presence as an aedicula.

I/THE SYMBOLIC HUB

Old State House, from Washington Street

A/SPRING LANE PRIMER

Spring Lane is the starting point, the source of Boston's existence. It marks the place where fresh water issuing from the ground made settlement possible. Within a short distance from here were the first houses of John Winthrop and his band, who were drawn to the Shawmut Peninsula in 1630 from Charlestown across the river, where they could not find adequate fresh water. They were not

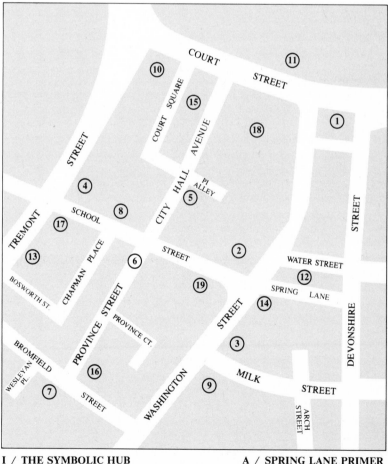

I / THE SYMBOLIC HUB

A / SPRING LANE PRIMER

the first Europeans to settle here; they came, in fact, at the invitation of William Blaxton, who nonetheless continued his hermit's existence above the town on the slopes of a cluster of three hills then called Trimountain (hence today's Tremont Street). The hills have since been so shaped, leveled and built upon that only Beacon Hill remains.

The peninsula had more than spring water and hills. It was an easily protected bit of land with a clear outlook to the sea beyond and a natural cove for landing close by. A narrow neck of land connected it with the rest of the area. The outlook to the sea is now blocked by buildings, the neck has become Washington Street and what was formerly Town Cove on the waterfront has been filled by almost two and a half centuries of construction. Yet the area remains an important locus in the city, and within 600 feet of this spot are telling examples of virtually all the principal stages of the development of architecture in Boston. This section, therefore, will be organized as a primer to set in chronological order the parade of changing conceptions of building, neighboring and civic pride that have taken root in Boston's ground. To walk the sequence literally would require circling through the area several times, but that's not necessary—a little judicious skipping around and thumbing of pages will save steps.

I A 1 · OLD STATE HOUSE
Intersection of Court, Washington and State streets
William Payne, builder, 1712–13
Rebuilt 1748
Alterations: Isaiah Rogers, 1830
Restoration: George A. Clough, 1882, Joseph E. Chandler, 1910

What is now referred to as the Old State House symbolizes Boston—its complicated heritage, its topography, its topsy-turvy development and its stubborn pride. What's more, it is indeed very old and has a subway station tucked underneath. The first building on the site was a town house constructed in 1658 of timber, open at the ground floor for merchants. Its reincarnation in brick in 1712, with an enclosed ground floor, became the meeting place for the provincial governor as the crown strengthened its hold. Later it became the first meeting place for the Commonwealth's government after the crown was discarded and before the present State House (I B 4) was built.

When affection for the building and its Colonial connotations paled in the middle of the last century, it was leased out as a commercial building and festooned with mercantile signs. Later still, demolition was actively considered until the city of Chicago offered to buy it and move it to the shores of Lake Michigan. Postcentennial sentiment probably accounts in part for its restoration, which was directed by George Clough in 1882. The building now houses a meeting room and a lively little museum containing artifacts that help one to imagine the life that has taken place around it.

Like many buildings in Boston, this one has needed to come to terms with its sloping site. Thus it involves three different relationships to the ground. At the upper Washington Street end, a few steps and a carved stone entry lead directly into the first-floor room. Along either side, midway down the slope, a larger set of stairs spills into the sidewalk and a vestibule inside is still a few steps below the main floor. These lead to a circular room on the first floor, where a beautiful spiral stairway winds up to the meeting room on the second floor. This room and

I A 1 · *Old State House, from State Street*

stairway date from the 1882 restoration; they unwittingly reproduce not the original layout but the Rogers floor plan of 1830. On the east at State Street, the basement is several feet above the ground and now accommodates, improbably, an entrance to the State Street subway station.

At the State Street end, however, is an imposing overhead balcony, a perfect setting for pronouncements and decrees. This full-fledged window of appearances opens off the meeting room on the second floor and commands a straight view down State Street to the far reaches of Long Wharf. With the Washington Street ground-floor entrance firmly placed on the road crossing the neck to land, and its second-floor balcony overlooking the principal route to the sea and England beyond, the Old State House was itself the figurative crossroads of Colonial Massachusetts and the logical place for conflict to surface. Not surprisingly, it is perhaps best known from a Paul Revere engraving of the Boston Massacre, which took place in the street beneath this balcony.

Among the features of the building least admired by citizens of the newly formed republic were a lion and unicorn embellishing the gable at the State Street end, emblems of the power of the British throne. Removed in a bit of patriotic censorship, they have since been restored, to the everlasting credit of resurrectionists. Shorn of their threatening implications, they provide a wonderful air of fantasy; two preposterous animals benignly surveying our scene. Between them at the top of the center panel sits young Science, incarnate in a sundial.

Supporting all this symbolism is a long, narrow building of remarkable straightforwardness: brick walls with a regular pattern of openings, steep gable roof with dormers, a three-stage tower in the middle with large windows, parapet and cupola, and at the ends two lovable but ungainly façades. At each façade the brick wall steps up in front of the roof twice, effectively shielding the steep and un-Classical slope. Above the second step there is a small pediment shaped to acceptable Georgian proportions and independent of the actual roof shape behind; an early false front.

The building is now leased to the Bostonian Society. It has known fire, massacre, commercial exploitation, degradation and the threat of demolition, and has survived numerous remodelings and two restorations. The Old State House of today includes exterior walls mostly from 1712, roof trusses from 1748, an interior approximating that of 1830, a tower shaped as it was in 1748 but rebuilt in 1882, doorways carved in 1909 and a slate roof from 1936. The present sundial dates from 1957.

I A 2 · OLD CORNER BOOK STORE
285 Washington Street, NW corner School Street
1711, 1833

The Old Corner Book Store is the most vivid existing piece of eighteenth-century streetscape, even if it has been much reworked, prettified and encumbered by a nineteenth-century tail along School Street. A close look at its dormered gambrel roof reveals the domestic clustering of rooms for warmth and protection in a village whose streets were not yet more than minutes away from an outdoors greater and more mysterious than any we have ever known. Bay windows added around its ground floor capture light to read by and attest to its transformation from a private residence into a bookstore, publishing house and, more recently, museum and office of the Boston *Globe*.

I A 3 · OLD SOUTH MEETING HOUSE
NE corner Washington and Milk streets
Robert Twelves, 1729

Old South is a venerable Boston landmark, with a fine tower and a barn of an interior. All accounts lament the insolence of the occupying British, who during the siege of Boston stripped the meeting house of its pews and used the space for a riding stable. Arrogance, indeed; unwarranted desecration—but the soldiers understood pretty well the real nature of this space. Its most endearing quality inside is a shallow barrel-vaulted ceiling, which betrays the influence of shipbuilder craftsmen. Its 67-foot width is even now a span of impressive dimension.

A great pulpit stands against the middle of the north wall—a long wall of the rectangular space—so that the congregation, arranged in stall pews and balconies around the other three sides, are all close to the preacher, in the best New England meeting-house tradition. It served well also as a place for revolutionary rhetoric, if the inception of the Boston Tea Party is any measure of success.

The tower, with a lovely attenuated spire, stands on the face of the short side of the church, powerfully marking its place along Washington Street. The outside of the building has always accumulated various stands and shelters, like many medieval churches. The basement now houses a branch of Goodspeed's Bookshop.

When the congregation of this church moved to more fashionable quarters in New Old South Church (III C 3) in 1875, the loyalties of Bostonians were put to the test. Happily, the building has been saved and is open to the public. No horses or roller skates allowed.

I A 4 · KING'S CHAPEL
58 Tremont Street, NE corner School Street
Peter Harrison, 1750

King's Chapel has always been different—classy in a Puritan town. Initially the home of the Anglicans, the building brought to Boston its first really noble Classical pretensions, with columns larger and more skillfully used than would be found again until the work of Charles Bulfinch at the end of the century. The interior is all grace and recollection, two generations removed and an ocean away from its Baroque precedents, but formed with skill and an awareness of the delights of the senses.

The plans were commissioned from Peter Harrison of Newport, Rhode Island. A gentleman-architect of real distinction, Harrison took some time to prepare the plans and called for building the church in granite, a warmer, more textured variety than generally found in later Boston buildings. Although part of the plan, the beautiful portico, ringed with Ionic columns, was not constructed until 1790, and then in wood. The planned steeple never materialized.

The tenor of religious and political life in eighteenth-century Boston was such that by 1787 King's Chapel had been transformed from an Episcopalian to a Unitarian congregation.

I A 4 · *King's Chapel*

I A 5 · *Kirstein Business Branch, Boston Public Library*

I A 5 · KIRSTEIN BUSINESS BRANCH, BOSTON PUBLIC LIBRARY
20 City Hall Avenue, at Pi Alley
Putnam & Cox, 1930

This pocket parade of Boston's architectural development would be severely wanting if it did not include a building by Charles Bulfinch, the remarkable architect and civic leader who ushered Boston into the nineteenth century. As chairman of the selectmen, chief of police and architect, he worked hard to implant clear, well-fashioned urban spaces and buildings in a town that was still shedding its provincial status. For examples of Bulfinch's work, we could turn to the State House (I B 4) just up the hill, to the successive Otis mansions on Cambridge (II A 15), Mount Vernon (II B 6) and Beacon streets (II B 15), to Massachusetts General Hospital (II A 16) in the West End, to St. Stephen's Church (II A 6) in the North End or to remnants of his warehouse buildings at Central Wharf (V B 10). But to keep within the adopted confines of this chapter, we must look to a copy.

Ironically it is in the Kirstein Business Branch of the Boston Public Library that we will find an introduction to the style of Bulfinch. The façade of this building, built in 1930, is nearly a replica of the central feature in the Tontine Crescent, an elegant arced row of houses built by Bulfinch in 1794 to create Franklin Place, then an enclosed private green space, now a widening in the pavement of Franklin Street. The Crescent was a great work, the first of many efforts by Bulfinch to make clear, urbane spaces for the town that would rival in dignity and sophistication the Georgian squares of London. Bulfinch also served as developer for these buildings and adopted a financing scheme, called the Tontine, that was then fashionable and productive in London. In Boston the speculative scheme failed and Bulfinch lost his inherited wealth.

The center of the Crescent buildings was a pavilion with a great arch in its bottom, through which Arch Street passed. Above the passage was a large room that housed the Boston Library Society and the Massachusetts Historical Society. The arch in this copy has been filled and used for display, but the handsome Palladian motif inscribed in an arched window above does open into a reading room. The big window, the paired pilasters on either side and the entablature above them all follow their exemplar; the windows on either side are conveniences not present in the original. It's a wonderful design that offers fine details to examine carefully when you are close and that conveys proud order from afar.

What this copy lacks, of course, is the crescent sweep of its neighbors that gave significance to the original pavilion, row-house wings with restrained façades that stretched over 200 feet in either direction, curving inward to embrace the space before them.

The Crescent was torn down in 1858 to make way for commercial buildings. They in turn were destroyed by the Great Fire of 1872 and replaced by others. Franklin Street still follows the curve, but the buildings, even charming ones like 89–93 Franklin Street (V C 6), bear no resemblance to the urbane dignity that once prevailed. Under the circumstances we can be grateful for the library's silly little bit of historicism that lets us sense ever so dimly the presence of a dear departed.

I A 6 · PROVINCE STREET
School to Bromfield streets

Province Street follows the path of Governor's Alley through the one-time gardens of Province House, the luxurious home of the provincial governors that faced down the hill to Washington Street and the Old South Meeting House. Nothing remains but some bits of wall and steps that lead up to Bosworth Street. In the nineteenth century the area was very densely built, but remained a narrow little alley. Well into the twentieth century, Boston guides could still refer to "quaint little Province Street." First a street widening and then a 13-story parking garage built by the city fixed that.

I A 7 · 22, 30 BROMFIELD STREET
between Wesleyan Place and Washington Street
c. 1848
· WESLEYAN ASSOCIATION BUILDING
36 Bromfield Street
Hammett & Joseph Billings, 1870

These neighboring buildings on Bromfield Street serve as an introduction to Boston's granite architecture of the mid-nineteenth century. The pair at 22 and 30 Bromfield Street are as spare, intelligent and fine as any to be found. They embody the Classical minimalism which thrived in Boston before the middle of the nineteenth century and which resurfaced in American architecture before and after World War II. The building at 36 Bromfield Street shows the same material marching to a different, later beat. Its antecedents are somewhere in France, and its prodigal cousin, Old City Hall (I A 8), sits just at the other end of Province Street.

The top two floors of Nos. 22 and 30 have piers made with granite blocks, about the width of a person, slightly narrower than the width of the windows. Each pier consists of three simple slabs terminated by a very strong, shapely

I A 7 · *22 and 30 Bromfield Street*

I A 7 · *Wesleyan Association Building, 36 Bromfield Street*

capital. The capitals support granite blocks that span between them, with the joint centered on the pier. Another row of granite blocks steps out beyond that as a simplified cornice.

These forms are a reduction of the Classical order, but they are not brute simplifications; the proportions are pleasing and there's a remarkable elegance and economy to the way in which the spandrels are made different from the piers by a simple projection at top and bottom. The capitals have no carved decoration whatever, simply a carefully studied curve that brings forth the sinuousness of the Classical order, but in a strong, spare and lovely way.

Fine octagonal dormers project from the gable roof almost to its edge, announcing their presence in an entirely different mode, each rather like a pilot-house on a boat.

36 Bromfield Street is a fairly conventional Victorian building with special markings on the second floor and a central axis emphasized by a dormer, almost a projecting tower, at the very top. It is reminiscent of Beaux-Arts planning, with a strong central pavilion, but in this case the relief is extraordinarily thin. The center is projected only a few inches, and the granite trim, while more complicated than its neighbors', is still very simply done. Much is accomplished with simple changes in plane rather than with detailed carving, which is difficult to execute in granite. The window heads make the point. Only the second-floor level has pediments, and of those only the central arched one actually has a full set of carved moldings; the other six all have a shadow molding with a simple little triangle set on top, relieved by an inset rosette, probably drilled. All in all, an intelligently economical search for stylishness.

I A 8 · OLD CITY HALL
45 School Street, between Tremont and Washington streets
Gridley J. Fox Bryant & Arthur Gilman, 1865
reuse: Anderson, Notter Associates, 1969–70

The French hardly ever made it as well. To describe this building as French Second Empire is only to draw in breath before beginning. The building has fared extraordinarily well over the years. It bears the grace of its ancestry in the partnership of Gridley J. F. Bryant, the prodigious native architect whose father brought granite to Boston, and Arthur Gilman, the fine gentleman-stylist of Arlington Street Church (III B 1), who studied architecture in Europe. Abandoned as city hall in 1969, the building has fared almost as well by adoption. Although what's left inside are offices with no grandeur of space, they have been carefully tended, and the mix of state agencies, private uses and a restaurant makes excellent use of the site, which still retains some sense of civic purpose.

The scale of the building, that is, the relative size of the parts to one another and to observers, is fine. The columns that make the entry portico are at least two and a half persons high. They rise up in three stages on either side of the portico. At the top is a diminutive temple front. A central pavilion is pushed forward from the middle of the building. Beautifully made large windows at the second level are accompanied by full-height pilasters thick enough to seem like real columns. The restoration has carefully kept the mezzanine floor arched back so that the building scale reads as originally intended. Subsequent changes have also cut into the mansard roof with a whole series of windows that make the top floor usable. These windows are simply cut in an unobtrusive fashion, exemplary

I A 8 · *Old City Hall*

in their restraint. The three stages of the wall are distinctly different. The base is predictably heavier than the rest, with piers articulated as a rusticated wall. At the second level, an implied colonnade and arched windows are in balance with each other, the wall seeming to slide behind the colonnade. The third level is more inventive. It has squat pilasters augmented by brackets on either side of segmental arched windows. The wall at this point is thick and eventful, a more definitive top than just a cornice could be.

Arthur Gilman later became a consultant to A. B. Mullett, the Federal Architect, and may have had a hand in the design of many wondrous granite monuments, most notably the State, War and Navy Building (now the Executive Office Building) west of the White House in Washington, D.C.

To the left and right of the Old City Hall entrance preside Benjamin Franklin and Josiah Quincy, each incarnate in bronze atop stone pedestals. The sculpture of Franklin, by Richard S. Greenough in 1855, is the more interesting figure. Its base is adorned by a set of four bronze reliefs depicting telling events in his career. One shows Franklin in a barn holding the end of a kite string with a key on it and a gigantic flash of lightning in the sky. Another, the finest, is set in the printing shop, with a stool marking out the center of the plaque and a very finely cast, sharply cut piece of paper that Franklin holds in his hands in front of the press, while someone else sets type. Be sure to stand about ten feet away from these reliefs to get the perspective right. They are really cast pictorial illusions of space, not sculpture.

Josiah Quincy, on the other side, may be less familiar to most, though he was a major figure in the urban evolution of Boston and for sixteen years (1829–45) was president of Harvard University. As mayor (1823–29), Quincy was responsible for building the Quincy Market (I D 5), and his statue, by Thomas Ball, has an appropriately far-seeing, forthright look to it.

I A 9 · BOSTON TRANSCRIPT BUILDING
322–28 Washington Street, SE corner Milk Street
Gridley J. Fox Bryant, 1873
· BOSTON POST BUILDING
17 Milk Street, between Arch and Washington streets
Peabody & Stearns, 1874

If the Old City Hall represents the fusion of granite building technology with a developing sophistication and stylishness, these two publishing buildings are exuberance running amok, spurred on the one side by newly adopted cast-iron technology and on the other by the competitive rebuilding that followed the Great Fire of 1872, which destroyed much of downtown.

The Boston *Transcript,* located here for over fifty years, was a large circulating daily that described its politics as "Independent Republican"; the Boston *Post,* smaller and around the corner, was known to circulate among "businessmen and Democratic families." The *Transcript* is granite, the *Post* cast iron. Both were housed in extremely vigorous buildings with a profusion of piers and moldings. Those of the *Post* were embellished with cast-iron decoration that is genuinely bizarre.

The *Post* had the extra good fortune of having been built on the site of Benjamin Franklin's birthplace. Stand and stare awhile at the bust of Franklin mounted in the *Post* building's navel, and a Bostonian will stop and tell you a fanciful story.

I A 10 · HEMENWAY BUILDING
42 Court Street, SE corner Tremont Street
Bradlee, Winslow & Wetherell, 1883

For all its seven stories there's a definite aura of smoking jackets about this building, an Edwardian gentleman's building. Perhaps the aura is just a lingering aroma of the old S. S. Pierce store that once occupied the ground floor and below. King's *Handbook of Boston* described it so:

> *Below is a spacious and well-lighted cellar crowded with goods, and communicating with the cigar storage-vaults on one side, and below with the lofty sub-cellar where slumber scores of pipes and puncheons of old Duff-Gordon sherries, Madeiras of 1820, ports and Malmseys, gins and whiskies, and other choice old liquors.*

More likely the aura we note stems from the red-brick-and-brownstone trim that speaks more of residential Back Bay Boston than of commercial districts generally built of granite, metal and glass. The upper floors were originally occupied mainly by lawyers. This was the urban equivalent of the lawyer's row that can still be found adjoining the courthouse in many small American towns —individual, polite, professional chambers all in a row, here stacked as well.

It's really very straightforward, with a façade that's practically a grid. The walls of the building are divided into three major sections: three stories with a stringcourse cornice, another three stories with a more elaborate cornice and an attic story topped by a still-heavier cornice and a parapet. At the top of the second section (the seventh floor) there is a turret swelling out on the corner with little windows looking out over the street intersection—the only overt flight of fancy. It's a real wall with measurable parts and windows that seem handsomely large.

The remodeled ground floor is devastatingly dull, a routine high-cost, low-maintenance front applied to the building face with total indifference to the genuine quality of the original building.

I A 9 · *Bust marking the birthplace of Franklin, Boston Post Building*

I A 11 · *Ames Building*

I A 11 · AMES BUILDING
I Court Street, between Cambridge and Congress streets
Shepley, Rutan & Coolidge, 1889

At 13 stories this was once the tallest office structure on the Eastern Seaboard, and proud of it. Proud, too, of its vigorous cornice, its massive base, of the piers, arcades, carvings and mosaics that adorn its surface. H. H. Richardson's successors used virtually every device available to take command of this great building and they succeeded. Richardson might have knocked it off with a conceptualizing pen stroke, but it's reassuring to see mere mortals work at it and win.

The Ames family figured prominently in the expansive mood of Boston in the late nineteenth century. Heirs to a family fortune built first on manufacturing shovels and then on the Union Pacific Railroad, Oliver and Frederick Ames used their wealth as conspicuous patrons. Oliver was for a time president of the Boston Art Club and built a vast mansion on Commonwealth Avenue (III D 15). His son Frederick, who is reputed to have headed 60 railroad companies, was a major donor of the Arnold Arboretum and commissioned this building. He was a friend of Richardson's, and had asked him to design many buildings, including the town hall and library in North Easton, Massachusetts, and the Ames Monument in Sherman, Wyoming.

On Richardson's untimely death in 1886, Shepley, Rutan & Coolidge took over his practice, continuing it with distinction.

Only a few years later, buildings the size of the Ames would be constructed with lightweight steel frame, but the outer walls of the Ames Building are masonry nine feet thick at the bottom. They remain the second highest wall-bearing structure in the world; second only to the Monadnock Building in Chicago. This building not only looks solid, it is. Its Congress Street and Court Street elevations are virtually identical. They are designed to make the building appear to be a single block, with solid corners, a base strong enough to hold the mass above and a definitive top. The base is four stories high with three very large, very thick arches on each side. The top is a lacy arcade running continuously across the face of the building, capped by a large overhanging cornice supported on a row of thick stone brackets, with windows tucked between them. In the middle section the corners are simple stone walls with a single person-sized window at each floor; the major part of the wall is an eight-story panel of four bays with bands of windows between piers. The piers of the lower four floors are more massive than those above, with giant Romanesque capitals and arches spanning between them at the fifth level to provide both visual measure and horizontal bracing. The remaining three floors of the panel are triple windows between piers that are made to appear like clusters of colonettes. At the edges of almost everything there is judicious carving, mostly derived from Romanesque architecture. Mosaic patterns in the upper spandrels are used to make them seem lighter.

All this may be viewed in one sense as a brave effort to give an imprint of people and the sizes of things that they are familiar with to a structure of unprecedented height. Viewed in another sense, it's a ridiculous assembly of efforts to pretend that the building is a set of things that it is not. In either case it's done with great style. From either Congress or State Street, it looms up in a commanding way, and the strong base combines with tiles, carving, sun and shadow in the upper levels to make a building which registers clearly from afar but which is layered and rich as you approach it. Up close it has a strong presence, a towering capacity, even though in present-day terms it's not a very tall building.

I A 12 · WINTHROP BUILDING
276–78 Washington Street, bounded by Spring Lane, Washington, Water and Devonshire streets
Clarence H. Blackall, 1893

The Winthrop Building is an exquisitely narrow building that stands by the side of Spring Lane. It has nearly everything right. It's easy to imagine being inside, its relation to the site is immediately clear and the nature of its structure has influenced its form in quite evident ways.

It is, furthermore, the first instance in Boston of a construction process that would change forever the shape of the city. Previous buildings had been built with thick masonry walls and piers as primary structure, sometimes supplemented by occasional columns, broad lintels and beams of cast iron or steel. In the case of the Winthrop Building, caught between Spring Lane and Water Street as they taper toward each other, the narrow plot of land posed a special problem, as the dimensions of the site could ill afford the thick masonry walls required to support nine floors of shops and offices. To make the building light, thin and airy, Blackall used a skeleton of steel to support the structure, a technique that architects had already used with success in Chicago and that would subsequently be used to make the much taller buildings that now loom over this and nearly every other city.

All this is anticipated but hardly foretold in the narrow, high shape of the building and in the startling openness of its lower two floors. The frame is directly evident here, dressed up in decorated panels and bracket capitals inspired by the architecture of Asia Minor. Above, the building is much more conservative, with banks of double-hung windows and walls made with alternating bands of buff brick and terra-cotta scrollwork. An attic floor at the top prepares the way for a splendid broad projecting upper cornice.

Around the side along the curving line of Spring Lane, all this is dropped after one bay, and there is a plain painted brick wall with segmental arches in standard industrial masonry form.

On the Water Street side the metal-frame base is interrupted once by a stone entrance that nicely singles out that piece of the otherwise regular bay system to make a palace entrance—the main entryway for the office spaces thus distinguished from the streetfront entries of each little shop.

At the Devonshire end the building is only one bay wide, a marvelously appealing stack of rooms with light on three sides—the most singular office space in Boston.

I A 12 · *Winthrop Building*   I A 15 · *Old City Hall Annex*

I A 13 · TREMONT TEMPLE
88 Tremont Street, between School and Bosworth streets
Clarence H. Blackall & George F. Newton, 1895

Commerce below, an auditorium for the Baptists in the middle and offices up above. What to do? There's no single building type that fits this program. Make storefront spaces on the lower level (with some pretty staid entrances intervening). Have a stair that climbs from the large central entrance directly up to a bold box of auditorium space inside with a lavish ceiling and enormous organ, then cover the front of the auditorium with a blank wall in the Venetian patterned-stone manner. And yes, that's right, place a temple front across the top, a heavy temple front with a cornice deep enough to be proportioned to the whole building, over squat columns that are limited only to the top two floors, where they are spaced out between the office windows.

In the very center of the building face is a large arched opening with a projecting balcony of papal proportions. On either end, closer to the street, are elaborately sculpted balconies that seem more attainable. Clarence Blackall was anything but repressible.

I A 14 · OLD SOUTH BUILDING
294 Washington Street, opposite School Street
A. H. Bowditch, 1902–04

As a piece of the city, this building is ingenious. As architecture, it is stodgy and dull. It is sited at the end of School Street, and from far enough away it looks terrific—a broad bold closure for the street with a clearly marked entry. It is a building to go through, a casebook in making sense out of a snarled and sloping site. Its architect does this by imagining ways to engage people along the street and bring them into its center. Entrances from Spring Lane, Milk Street and Washington Street, each at a different level, lead into a three-tiered series of passages and shops that thread through the building, intersecting at the middle in a spacious elevator lobby. Street, alley and building intertwine to the benefit of them all. Too bad the exterior has no charm, despite all the carved festoons, rustications and moldings. The work of a great problem-solver who hadn't learned about singing.

I A 15 · OLD CITY HALL ANNEX (Boston School Committee Building)
26 Court Street, at Court Square
Thomas P. R. Graham, 1912

In Rome it's not surprising to come on a Classical colonnade embedded in the fabric of the medieval or modern town. In Boston it is. Especially when it's a sign of history being played backward. This rather breathless piece of grandeur is the annex to the more modest Old City Hall (I A 8) and anticipates by fifty years the scale of the new one (I C 2). Since, however, the new one was not built on an adjacent site, these six-story Corinthian columns retain an air of imperial loneliness.

The site has long served civic purposes, first as the jail, later as the county courthouse. The colossal columns sitting on a high blank base may have been an effort to upstage the memory of Solomon Willard's severe granite Greek Revival courthouse, which the annex replaced. In any case, the columns thoroughly disguise the steel-framed loft inside that provides well-lighted office space.

Entering its portals every day may have been a little too heady for the Boston Redevelopment Authority folk. The Government Center redevelopment project they spawned in here has a similar scale, uncharacteristic of Boston.

I A 16 · HUTCHINSON BUILDING
52 Province Street, between Province Court and Bromfield Street
Ralph Harrington Doane, 1925

If I was commissioned to design a nice little three-story commercial building, this is just what I'd like to do: streetscape Regency. Then I'd personally strangle each one of the sign salesmen who mucked up the bottom. High buildings in the city are usually improved by the scruffy ad hoc signs pasted onto their bases; they offer reassurance that street life can still claim its own place in the world. But this little wonder is so integral to the street, its steel frame so lightly and deftly clad with Classical trappings, that it deserves an affluent ballet school for its tenant.

I A 16 · *Hutchinson Building*

The whole face of the building is large arched windows with small pane glass. The floor of the third level has been shaped so that it can be covered by a thin spandrel the size of a pane of glass. In this way there is no change in the surface of the arched window as it passes from one floor to the next. The entire block is a row of these beautiful double-story windows facing out onto the street. Entries to the building are marked by two temple fronts inscribed over this rhythm. The windows in the center of each temple front are really the same size and shape as the others, the relief around the arch an inch thicker, with capitals at the spring point. The differentiation is made by a pair of pilasters at either side that hold a flat carved pediment overhead and, more importantly, by windows made rectangular between them. These vary the rhythm somewhat; a motif similar to that used by Alberti in San Sebastiano at Mantua early in the Italian Renaissance.

I A 17 · PARKER HOUSE HOTEL
60 School Street, SE corner of Tremont Street
Desmond & Lord, 1927

The Parker House has existed on this site since 1855, taking various ever-expanding forms since its start as a tavern. The present building dates from a time when hotels were thought to be real pieces of the city, not the wonderland extravaganzas of the recent past that finally belong to nowhere.

The hotel lobby is disarmingly straightforward, reached from the Tremont Street side by a wood-paneled passage lined with sofas, wing chairs and potted palms, something like a domestic concourse. From the lower School Street side, entry is via an internal collection of steps that negotiates the change of level between streets.

The coherence of the Tremont Street entry has been flawed by the recent remodeling of the Home Owners Federal Savings Bank that occupies commercial space between the concourse and the corner. In an excess of enthusiasm for transparency, the bank has made window walls to the concourse as well as to the street, exposing the inner passage to all the commotion of a heavily trafficked street. Being a part of the city here, as in most cases, was furthered more by a little decorous concealment than by transparency.

Outside, the Parker House does very little but maintain urban decorum. In this, it is a welcome exemplar. It is not in itself very interesting, and indeed, why should it be? Across the street King's Chapel and the Old City Hall offer ample rewards for our attention.

I A 18 · BOSTON COMPANY BUILDING
One Boston Place, corner of Court and Washington streets
Pietro Belluschi and Emery Roth & Sons, 1970

How can one possibly be sympathetic to a building with the contrived address of One Boston Place? Unfortunately, the architects haven't made it any easier. Unlike its predecessors in the neighborhood, the building appears to care not a whit about the streets from which it draws the distinction of its address. Rather than supporting and drawing shape and life from the streets around, it treats them as an unseemly annoyance, to be held at bay by an ungainly red granite fortress wall. Above this, set aloof from the street, the very sleek, very black tower thrusts its prestigious address into the skyline with a pretty little cap—a miniature of itself set so high in the air that it doesn't help us imagine ourselves into the place. We are, however, treated to a view of the structural forces in the building, as they are traced by black metal panels that cover both vertical columns and angled struts braced diagonally against the wind. Such lateral forces are treated in most high-rise buildings as visual unmentionables.

I A 19 · *Addition to the Boston Five Cents Savings Bank*

I A 19 · BOSTON FIVE CENTS SAVINGS BANK
24–30 School Street, between Washington and Province streets
Parker, Thomas & Rice, 1926
Addition: Kallman & McKinnell, 1972

The two parts of this building offer a study in contrasting attitudes as to how a building may be adjusted to fit its site. For the earlier building, street face is all. The bank provides solid, polite Renaissance walls bordering the corner of Province and School streets, gracefully absorbing their angled intersection and a change of level along the edge of the site into a regular, if uninspiring, pattern. The building deals with adversity as a well-mannered servant of the period would have, with an absolute minimum of visible stress. Inside, the seams come apart a bit, as the irregular plan creates some skewed beams in the ceiling but, again, with total aplomb.

For the addition, on the other hand, structure is all, and the building becomes a startling exposition of the shape of the site translated into building parts. Beams and columns are visibly placed one upon the other in a pattern derived from the curving site. A five-story colonnade makes the curving face that joins School Street to Washington Street. The whole colonnade stands six feet forward of an all-glass curtain wall that encloses the banking hall and offices above and makes the entire exposed structure evident from the street—the acts of building made manifest. Most remarkably, the beams fan out from the rear corner of the triangular site to this colonnade that forms a bent hypotenuse. As a consequence, wherever you face the building the profile of the structural system is seen from several different angles, making it seem at once uncommonly active and logically related to its site.

The Boston Five Cent Savings Bank addition resulted from a competition, this one limited to three firms. It takes its place among a distinguished list of competition winners in Boston, including the Athenaeum (I B 8), the First Baptist Church (III A 12), Trinity Church (III C 1), the Boston Architectural Center (III D 10) and, of course, Boston City Hall (I C 2), also designed by Kallman & McKinnell. The competition program for this building, as for City Hall, was written by Lawrence Anderson, then dean of the MIT School of Architecture, who summarized the design conditions this banking hall would need to meet: "to come to terms with colonial tradition while extending a building conceived in a quite anti-colonial spirit and scale, and to cope with a site whose distorted and curtailed form is the by-product of a traffic adjustment." The traffic adjustment in question was a new linkage between School and Milk streets that formed the boundary of the site; this road happily has since been abandoned to make a small park. The building's intelligent forcefulness, however, has not been curtailed.

B/THE STATE HOUSE AND COMMON

In Boston not even the Common is formally simple. Only after you have comprehended its roughly pentagonal shape will directions in the city make sense.

Within it there are a number of meandering paths, some landmarks and an *allée* or two. It's a wonderfully rich place, with promenades, bandstands, monuments, wading pools, graves and walks shaped to a skateboarder's dream. And no grand plan. Yes, there is a formal bit that takes off from the State House and ends in a fountain near Tremont Street; a flat, treeless section lies over the parking garage on the far side; the Frog Pond is near Beacon Hill; and the rest more or less circles "The Genius of America" figure atop the Army and Navy monument on the highest hill in the center. But there is no grand plan, no secret

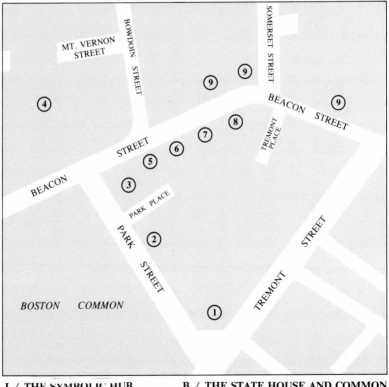

I / THE SYMBOLIC HUB   B / THE STATE HOUSE AND COMMON

perceptual order of events. Its parts just *are,* and they merge imperceptibly into each other. Cows, which used to graze here, would still fit in perfectly well. Indeed, one of the pleasures of the place is that there are dogs and horses about.

It was Charles Bulfinch who, at the end of the eighteenth century, guided most of the efforts to define the Common as a place of resort with a distinct civic form, making pasture into park by fronting its edges on Park and Tremont streets with row houses of distinction. Bulfinch, here as elsewhere, always worked with specific bits of urban form, comprehensible pieces that linked building, street and landscape in a particular configuration, not an abstract scheme. In this sense the Common is heir to his thinking. Each of its parts has a coherence and dignity of its own and there are no universal commands.

The impetus for all this was construction of the Bulfinch State House (I B 4) above the Common on Beacon Hill. It remains the dominant landmark in the area, though Park Street Church (I B 1) runs a close second and the Athenaeum (I B 8) around the corner on Beacon Street is the preeminent repository of culture.

I B 1 · PARK STREET CHURCH
Zero Park Street, NW corner Tremont Street
Peter Branner, 1809

· MINISTRIES BUILDING ADDITION
1 Park Street, between Tremont and Beacon streets
Stahl/Bennett, 1974

· GRANARY BURIAL GROUND
Tremont Street, between School and Park streets
1660

Peter Branner, it would seem, was a brilliant and self-effacing purveyor of urban scenery. His Park Street Church displays elegance, restraint and judicious formal invention. Branner disposed conventional elements in a way that is eminently suitable for this very special site. A tall and elegantly tapered spire rises in four successive stages from a square brick tower that sits just at the intersection of Park and Tremont streets.

Rounded colonnades at either side of the entrance at the base of the tower gently accommodate the change in direction from Tremont Street to Park Street and initiate the picturesque ascent to the State House on the hill. Grandly simple, high, arched windows along Park Street quietly lend dignity to that studied passage up Park Street.

The expanded ministries of the church have been housed in the only building that breaks dramatically with the solid brick walls of Park Street. An addition that succeeds in highlighting its parent by being decidedly different, it is slickly designed and innocuous despite its radical departure. Broad bands of mullionless glass stretch across the narrow façade, higher and grander at the top. Everything else is covered with a deep-blue-red brick, which is set in vertical soldier courses on the cantilevered spandrels and coursed normally for the stairwell. Its color is handsome, but uncharacteristic in this locale. The ground floor is entirely clear glass and looks directly out into the Granary Burial Ground beyond.

The Granary, which initially occupied this site, has interred its name in the Granary Burial Ground around the corner. A splendid granite retaining wall and iron fence designed by Solomon Willard around 1830 edges Tremont Street. The entrance is through a small but potent granite gate carved in a sepulchral mode probably thought to be Egyptian Revival. Step inside for a pleasant interlude of gravestone meditation among the remains of Peter Faneuil, John Hancock, Samuel Adams, Paul Revere and their peers.

I B 2 · PARK STREET
between Tremont and Beacon streets
No. 2: Snell & Gregerson, 1877
No. 3: Thomas James, 1918
No. 5: Maginnis & Walsh, 1956
Nos. 7–8: 1830–40. No. 7 remodel: H. B. Ball, 1896

Park Street, adjacent to the Common, started life as an outlying area for town services. When the State House was constructed at its top, Park Street was still bordered by an almshouse, a workhouse and a granary. Within a few years it was transformed, mostly by Bulfinch, into an elegant residential approach to the Commonwealth's pride. First in the series of rebuildings was the exceptionally grand Amory Mansion (I B 3) at the top of the street, followed by a lower row of four brick houses, also by Bulfinch. Transformation of the street was completed with the construction of Park Street Church fifteen years after the State House was begun.

Only the church remains unaltered; the rest have been transformed or replaced. No. 2 Park Street is a curious and clumsy brownstone set atop a pink granite base. The present structure was designed by Snell & Gregerson in the nineteenth century and extensively altered in the twentieth century. Large but not well articulated triple windows occupy the center on the second and third floors, and a crudely carved cornice underneath a mansard is almost totally eaten

I B 3 · *Amory-Ticknor Mansion*

I B 1 · *Park Street Church, with 1 Beacon Street behind it*

away by blunt dormers. No. 3 Park Street is eight stories high, executed in an ostensibly polite but dreary neo-Georgian style by Thomas James in 1918. No. 5, the 1950's Holy Ghost Chapel of the Paulist Fathers, is even worse, a broad building with crudely carved stone frames and dim recollections of a Classical order, nothing that really engages the attention. Nos. 7 and 8, now combined, make a building of some interest. Brick, with five stories plus an attic, stone window trim and a broad stone entry, the former Abbot Lawrence Mansion is now the Union Club. The major level is on the second floor, where very handsome, wide and high double-hung windows look out on the Common. They reach from the floor almost to the ceiling, topped with a simple rectangular lintel projection and fronted by a continuous metal balcony. The building bends to follow the street, and at its top the two sections are differentiated. The section to the right has a mock balustrade and Tuscan columns with glass set between them; that to the left has a pitched roof with dormers and a large gable on the uphill corner, where a Palladian window appears, as though to announce imminent arrival at the State House.

I B 3 · AMORY-TICKNOR MANSION
9 Park Street, SE corner Beacon Street
Charles Bulfinch, 1804
Alterations: c. 1885

Fulmination is generally thought to be in order when describing the state of this mansion, a once mighty and noble Bulfinch block distinguished by its scale, severity and proportion, now altered to house shops and offices. But it has been a truly marvelous desecration. The old block still remains, but it has been given an additional layer: a set of black metal shop fronts that reach out and down to the falling sidewalk, and a phalanx of witty bays in its upper reaches. The bays, also black, with a flat face, elegant curved sides and small-paned windows, expand the severe narrow windows of the original into capsules of English manor-house comfort. Finally, the house has been indecorously capped on one side by a triplet of gabled penthouse dormers. If only all severity could support this very cheerful invention. As it stands, the mansion shows the charms of simple, pure form elaborated by secondary additions, each of which has a purpose.

The present name, Amory-Ticknor, recalls both the profligate original owner, Thomas Amory, and a later resident, the great Harvard professor and bibliophile George Ticknor, who guided the foundation of the Boston Public Library as an "apparatus that shall carry this taste for reading as deep as possible into society."

I B 4 · STATE HOUSE
Beacon Street, between Bowdoin and Joy streets
Charles Bulfinch, 1795–98
Charles E. Brigham, 1889–95
William Chapman, R. Clipston Sturgis & Robert D. Andrews, 1914–17

Splendor of a genuine sort: government as we would like to know it. The State House is knowledgeable and shapely, possessed of a quiet maternal dignity as it presides over the Commonwealth from atop its hill, hemmed in by residences that have set limits on its growth.

It wasn't originally atop the hill. Beacon Hill rose up behind the State House until 1811, when the crest was removed. And it wasn't originally hemmed in. The State House took its place on the hill among a few stately farmhouses, most notably that belonging to John Hancock's widow, from whom the property was purchased. The subsequent speculative success of Beacon Hill filled the slopes with housing, and the growth of the state inflated the seat of government, first into the yellow brick pile behind, second into the self-effacing white wings to either side and finally, in 1965, into the State Office Building over the hill on Charles Street, the dreariest version of what we expect state bureaucracy to build. If the Bulfinch State House is an emblem of what we wish government to be, the State Office Building could serve well on the letterhead of a campaign for tax reform.

I B 4 · *State House*

The Bulfinch design for the State House is a surprisingly fine work. It was built early in his career as a gentleman-architect, yet it is confidently grand, the portico a sensual assertion of its commanding importance. To fully realize the majesty of its conception, it is necessary to imagine it surrounded by pasture and to envision it among its predecessors and contemporaries—to compare it to the modesty of the Old State House (I A 1), Old South Meeting House (I A 3), the first Harrison Gray Otis House (II A 15), or even King's Chapel (I A 4), predecessor in the use of tall columns. The sovereignty of its form was clear, even when the dome was finished not with gold but with whitewashed shingles.

The gold leaf, first applied to the dome in 1874, was a brilliant stroke of forethought, for its gleaming surface has allowed the building to remain a landmark long after the dome's preeminence on the skyline was usurped.

It's hard now to envision Harrison Gray Otis, for instance, who presided over the state senate chamber in the eastern end of the building in 1805–6, looking

down from there to the harbor, while ruminating over his speculative development of a residential district on open land behind him to the west; or that in 1811,
at the end of his second term as senate president, he could watch out the windows
to the north as the summit of Beacon Hill was carted away in horse carts, to be
dumped into Mill Pond between Cambridge Street and the North End.

The windows to the north no longer exist. They were covered up by an
addition designed by Gridley J. F. Bryant in 1856—an addition that, in turn, was
removed thirty-five years later to make way for Charles Brigham's grandiose
extension, which replaced both it and a granite water reservoir that then occupied the flattened summit.

The Brigham extension, in yellow brick, since the Bulfinch building had for
some years been painted yellow, multiplies many-fold the size of the original
building. It is really fantastic, an enormous mass that extends off the back of
Beacon Hill and is all dressed in Bulfinchian motifs, updated to reflect the more
fully sculpted understanding of Classical precedent that was characteristic at the
end of the nineteenth century. The extension is placed on a much-elaborated
granite basement that gets larger and larger as the land falls away until on the
Derne Street side the basement is a full three stories. The rear façade, though
it emulates the brick arcade and Corinthian colonnade of the Bulfinch front,
becomes quite genuinely and splendidly Baroque as it towers over Derne Street.
Heavily, fluidly sculpted stairs rise up beside it from Temple Place, twisting
finally into a pair of stairs formed with elliptical curves that provide for grand
escalations off the carriage entrance, now a parking lot.

The Brigham extension crosses right over Mt. Vernon Street, which passes
through great arches in the stone basement, one large arch for the street, two
small ones on either side for the sidewalks. Underneath the extension the structure is forthrightly exposed, the riveted bottoms of large steel girders tracing out
a tartan grid and steel beams and shallow tile vaults holding the floor above.
Husky, round steel columns hold the structure aloft and form rows on either side

I B 4 · *Stairway, Brigham extension of the*
State House

of the street. From this underside portico, one steps into the building and directly onto a floor of polished white marble on the north. Ahead lies the very broad base of white marble stairs leading impressively to the principal floor above, then winding back around again on their decorated steel frames to the level of the House of Representatives, which marks a cross axis for the addition.

This was not, however, the last transformation of the State House; its aspect was altered dramatically once again by the addition of wings that bracket forward around courts to either side of the Bulfinch building, framing it in isolation from the Brigham extension, as though embarrassed by the ambitions of the latter. The Sturgis additions are white marble and emasculated. They are, mercifully perhaps, an almost entirely reticent backdrop, making it easy for us to isolate the splendor of the original. The red brick, yellow brick and white marble are all quite distinct from one another, and happily so.

The former House of Representatives, located under the dome in the Bulfinch building, is now the Senate Chamber. It is a beautiful room, covered by a broad inner saucer dome embellished with plaster relief. Of the galleries all around, only two are original; the north and south sides opened through windows to the outside. As the galleries were filled in at roughly mid-nineteenth-century, plaster rustication was added to the lower walls, lending a curious and discordant sense of the outdoors to a room that is very much inside, majestically located and furnished.

The former Senate Chamber, now the Senate Reception Room, occupies the east side of the Bulfinch building. Originally lit by sets of three large arched windows on each of three sides, it is an altogether noble room, formed by a plaster barrel vault that descends, to the north and south, onto columns that delineate shallow galleries on either side, ideal places for a little sideline negotiating next to the windows.

To reach these splendidly elegant rooms, it is necessary to encounter first an array of empty halls on the floor below them, beginning with the Doric Hall of the Bulfinch era, then the Senate Staircase Hall and finally the Hall of Flags. The latter two are exercises in *fin de siècle* marble opulence. The Hall of Flags, built to house the battle flags of Massachusetts regiments that served in the Civil War, is a ponderous, suffocating room. The Senate Staircase Hall fares somewhat better, with various marbles elaborating the stairs as they climb up either side of the space. Throughout, there are several statues and busts, including a rather sweet memorial to nurses of the Civil War by Bela Pratt, some stalwart military figures in relief on either side of the door to the Hall of Flags, and a most upright and righteous Civil War figure by Daniel Chester French in the passage leading to Doric Hall.

The present House of Representatives in the Brigham Extension is a paneled chamber under an elliptical dome of two stages topped by a large stained-glass skylight. The chamber is replete with wall paintings, by Albert Herter, of momentous scenes marking the progress to freedom in Massachusetts, a frieze made up of the names of a select group of Massachusetts super-achievers, and the much-hallowed codfish. The sleek, stiff cod, carved in pine, graced first the Old State House and then the original House of Representatives before taking its place across from the speaker's chair here. Facing the speaker's chair and rostrum, which bear an inordinate measure of pomp, it makes a nice polar opposite.

I B 5 · CLAFLIN BUILDING
20 Beacon Street, between Park and School streets
William G. Preston, 1884

Some buildings simply get better the more you look at them, and that is definitely the case here. Built for Boston University, this was the work of a designer plying his craft at a moment when Industry and Art were still exchanging vows. It's not really a noble or profound building, just well loved and cheerful.

Four rusticated stone piers with glass-and-metal infill made the bottom; a three-arch arcade at the second level has voids filled with glass, the arches springing from Romanesque colonettes above the piers. The same piers, now expressed as wall, rise four floors to be capped by a molded cornice. On either end the void between piers is filled by a shallow triangular metal bay, pushing just forward of the wall. At the top on either side are little florid pediments suggesting that all the while it's really been two towers standing next to each other with a void in between, a suggestion abetted by simple areas of glass between the middle piers.

A storefront renovation for Goodspeed's Bookshop on the ground floor is uncompromisingly stern but crafted with steely affection; it is the work of G. Holmes Perkins, in 1936, who later reshaped much of Philadelphia as chairman of the City Planning Commission and dean of the School of Architecture at the University of Pennsylvania.

I B 5 · *Claflin Building*   **I B 8** · *Boston Athenaeum*

I B 6 · CHESTER HARDING HOUSE
16 Beacon Street, between Park and School streets
Robert Fletcher, builder, 1809

Beloved by historians because it housed the painter and by lawyers because it is now the headquarters of the Boston Bar Association, this house induces affection from the rest of us by being totally anachronous. Its size, normal for 1809, is now puny on a street of hefties. The elegance of its later porch and first-floor windows are totally out of keeping with the simple brick wall into which they are set, and the oversize bay stepping out above the porch roof seems awkward and clumsy but endearing. Sometime after 1910 a zealot removed the third-floor bay, which held mysterious little turrets at either end that seemed imported from an Islamic palace. It was replaced with a cornice that is white and dubiously Georgian.

I B 7 · CONGREGATIONAL HOUSE
14 Beacon Street, between Park and School streets
Shepley, Rutan & Coolidge, 1898

About this edifice there is little to be said. It's a pretty dry result of the wish to render an office block Colonial. It has brick- and stone-trimmed arches below the attic, some deft theatricality in the original storefront windows along the street and a set of carvings for your edification along the top of the stone base. You may detect a family resemblance to the Ames Building (I A 11), which is earlier, taller and Romanesque, but designed by the same office. In fact, the pair make a striking study in the uses of styling to cast a building in the image of its users: humble Congregationalists here, macho railroad baron there.

I B 8 · BOSTON ATHENAEUM
10 ½ Beacon Street, between Park and School streets
Edward Clarke Cabot, 1847
Henry Forbes Bigelow, 1913–14

A fusty private library that has ruled over Boston's image of itself for a century and a half shouldn't be a wonderful place. But it is. Not out front, to be sure, where its Palladian origins are obscured by soot, pale north light and a general meanness of profile; but inside it would be worth the trip to Boston, though only a small gallery in the second floor is open to visitors.

It's really two buildings, one attached to the other. The first, fronting on Beacon Street, resulted from a competition in 1846. It represents the level of erudition available to a gentleman of the time, since it was only after winning the competition that Edward Clarke Cabot established a practice as an architect. Twenty years later he became the first president of the Boston Society of Architects, a position he held for thirty years more. The building is correct, at points elegant.

The second building has no front. It stands behind the first, higher but out of sight. On the opposite side its shape follows the edge of the Granary Burial Ground (I B 1) and endeavors to be no more than background for that hallowed place. Inside, the central room of the older building serves as foyer, inhabited only by sculpture and the slight chill familiar in repositories of the Classical. Another layer beyond, however, it's all magic. Doors open onto a reception desk framed in a handsome white arch. This turns out to be the end of a double-height space that is surrounded by a beautifully molded Classical arcade. A similar central hall is repeated on floors above, with variations to suit different uses.

The power of this organizing space lies not only in its patrician heritage but, more poignantly, in the relaxed, thoughtful secondary forms that are used to adjust this clear space to the irregular site, the demands of book storage and the pleasures of reading, all at once.

On the ground floor, the bay of arcaded space through which you enter is separated from the other three by a partition with glass doors and, above head height, a sheet of thinly mullioned glass panes that let you see the arches marching into the room beyond. The grandeur of these arches is given punch by a delicate but frankly utilitarian mezzanine balcony that weaves behind them, providing access to books. It is supported on small steel beams cantilevered from the wall, with an obscure glass floor and a lovely latticed rail made of steel bars and articulated at the joint to the beam by a row of four-inch steel rings. It is direct, yet lacy and careful in its sharp contrast to the heavy moldings of the arcade. In the larger room, reading tables are covered with journals and periodicals. The floor extends beyond the arcade on the Beacon Street side into another section of the older building that is a simple, big reading room with windows that are perfect to sit by: sill at side-table height, window approximately seven feet high, an ample pool of light. On the Granary side, the wall beyond the arcade is dark green with full-height windows. Following the outline of the burial ground, the building envelope pulls away from the white arcaded enclosure to make a fabulous irregular alcove inhabited by artifacts, plants, stuffed chairs and sun. An incomparable place to read.

The clarity of these central rooms—their ideal order existing in counterpoint with comfortable distortions to meet circumstance—is the stuff of which the architect Louis Kahn's inspiring dreams were often made.

I B 9 · 15 BEACON STREET
between Bowdoin and Somerset streets
William G. Preston, 1903

· 7–11 BEACON STREET
NW corner Somerset Street
Coolidge & Shattuck, 1922

· 1 BEACON STREET
between Somerset and Tremont streets
Skidmore, Owings & Merrill, 1972

Seventy years of office-building development all in a row. No. 15 Beacon Street is the standard turn-of-the-century formula, executed, one suspects, with one eye on the Winthrop Building (I A 12): steel frame revealed by the bottom two floors of shop front, the joints highlighted by a tensile decorative motif; stone covering of the third floor to remind us that this is all a base, surmounted by five floors of striated brick and two floors of stone-covered loggia capped by an overhanging cornice at the top. Solid, sculpted ordinary stuff; we'd expect more of the Claflin Building's architect.

Next door, Coolidge & Shattuck, successors to the architects of Congregational House (I B 7), began to call a spade a spade: regularly spaced piers with carefully proportioned windows and clever little adjustments to the skin for relief, a slight projecting cornice and a vestigial three-story base that is recognized for what it is—an eye-level front for the building that makes no pretense of being sat upon. Very cool, very uptown. At the corner a stylish cartouche acknowledges our presence in the street by giving the passer-by something to

I B 9 · *Nos. 15, 7–11, and 1 Beacon Street (left to right)*

look at. Farther along Somerset Street a perfectly straightforward well is notched into the side of the building to give it light and air.

Fifty years later, at 1 Beacon Street, there's no pretense to anything but power. The steel frame is set forward from the building skin, fully revealed and clad in deep-purple precast concrete panels. A high floor entered off Beacon Street accommodates a pleasant restaurant, banking offices and a terrace that caps the underground parking garage. It's all very easygoing and clear and unabashedly uninterested in its neighbors'—or anyone's—point of view.

C/GOVERNMENT CENTER

Periodically, agglutinative Boston gets to be too much for its visionaries and they seek a new and smoother order. Shortly after the Revolution, Bulfinch took to Beacon Hill and the Common to erect fragments of the gracious ensemble that he imagined to be possible. Later, in the middle of the nineteenth century, a

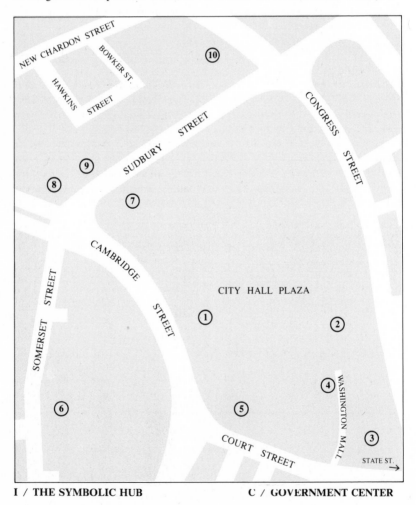

I / THE SYMBOLIC HUB   **C / GOVERNMENT CENTER**

massive landfill project directed development energies from the overbuilt and jumbled city to the orderly rows of Back Bay. In the early 1960's, yet another massive clarifying venture was started, this time not on the edges of open ground or water but in the thicket of the city. Mayor John Collins, Edward Logue, the powerful director of the Boston Redevelopment Authority, and I. M. Pei, their urban-design consultant, evidently set out to make a world of their own, one that would protect selected bits of the older fabric but allow them to intrude on the new order ever so slightly. As a consequence, the Government Center project has totally changed the face of a substantial segment of downtown Boston, creating great new open spaces of a scale previously unknown in these parts. In so doing, Government Center gives visibility to the vast enterprise of local, state and federal governments, and screens from view those elements of the city that did not correspond to the vision. What they've wrought is certainly grand and shapely; much of it is also arid.

I C 1 · CITY HALL PLAZA
bounded by Cambridge, Sudbury and Congress streets and the former Cornhill Avenue
urban design: I. M. Pei & Partners, 1964
execution: Kallman & McKinnell, 1968

The essential shape of City Hall Plaza results from an urban-design plan prepared by I. M. Pei for the Boston Redevelopment Authority. Its scope, the views into and from it, and the basic volumes of the buildings that abut it were essentially determined by that plan.

To the right as you face City Hall are remnants of the "Walk to the Sea," a path proposed in the 1950's by Kevin Lynch and Jack Myer that would have run from Beacon Hill down through the courthouse area, alongside the Sears Crescent and City Hall, on down past Faneuil Hall, through the Quincy Market, and over a sunken Southeast Expressway to the harbor. A bridge extending the plaza

I C 1 · *City Hall, looking toward the Custom House* (V B 8) *and Faneuil Hall* (I D 1)

across Congress Street to the foot of Faneuil Hall was an essential element of the scheme that never came to pass, although the plaza stays high on that side to meet the intended bridge and accommodate underground parking. The view from this high corner of City Hall Plaza past Faneuil Hall to the Quincy Market and beyond shows that many of the connections are yet to be made but that the framework is there. It shows as well how bold was Quincy's 1820 scheme for the markets (I D 5).

To the left of City Hall, the plaza dips down to street level at Congress Street, unintentionally revealing an authentically jumbled little bit of old Boston, the Blackstone Block (I D 2), meant by the urban-design plan to have been curtained by a sleek new slice of hotel. Further to the left, the neatly packaged order is reestablished in the high and low blocks of the John F. Kennedy Federal Building (I C 7). Behind and across Cambridge Street lies the abstracting curve of One Center Plaza (another of those new names that substitute commercial advantage for legitimate historical context). Its architects may have thought that One Center Plaza was somehow going to be like arcaded monumental streets in Europe: a covered passage below with uniform window patterns above. In place, it looks more like a monumental construction barricade, though there is a two-story shopping arcade on the ground floor animated often by bright and skillful banners that act as signs. Ironically, most of this—the only sheltered outdoor space fronting the plaza and not part of City Hall—faces away from the sun and is isolated from the pedestrian place by the arterial traffic of Cambridge Street.

The plaza itself is a vast sloping brick surface broken occasionally by steps, its edges terraced to meet adjoining buildings and streets. At the southwest corner it mounds up to accommodate a subway entrance, at the northwest corner it steps down to form a hollow sunken fountain area that the city seems not to manage to keep running and on the east it reaches over to City Hall, climbing on one side to become the base of the building and descending on the other to reach the level of Congress Street.

I C 2 · BOSTON CITY HALL
City Hall Plaza
Kallman, McKinnell & Knowles, 1968

Conceived in response to an infatuation with the power and splendor of government and completed just in time to be subjected to the derision of street demonstrators determined to hobble big government, Boston City Hall had the worst of both worlds. It's more grandiose than it need be and much more intelligent and hopeful than its detractors contend. It is, after all, an astonishing building, an elaborate structure of concrete parts that rises above the sweeping brick surface of City Hall Plaza to command its surroundings. No doubt it was helped through the bureaucracy not only by the strong hand of Mayor Collins but also by the prestige accorded the design as winner of a much-publicized national competition. Which is not to say that the building is a paper scheme. It is an imaginatively contrived, thoroughly worked-out building of enormous power. It's just not friendly.

As with the Boston Five Cents Savings Bank (I A 19), the architects have filled volume with tangible structure, here more completely. General volumetric limits established by the Pei urban-design plan had been incorporated as constraints in

I C 2 · *Boston City Hall*

the competition. The great strength of the Kallman, McKinnell & Knowles design is that the architects took those volumetric constraints neither as a bureaucratic limit of only negative consequences nor as a geometric volume to be elegantly gift-wrapped, the way Pei himself might have done. They took it as a site to be filled with the dramatized acts of building. In so doing, they perforated the volume of space in ways that segregated the building into Classic constituent parts: base, supporting piers and a three-story mass above that is loosely recollective of entablature and cornice, serrated and stepped out at the top. Lodged within the great rows of piers are special, individually expressed ceremonial rooms the size of small buildings. Each of the compositional parts has a functional connotation: The base, covered with brick and continuous with the plaza, holds a concourse for departments that require a great deal of public contact. The uniformly expressed top floors contain the more aloof bureaucracy ringed around a central light court. In between, in the symbolically articulated blocks, are large offices for the accountable agents of government—the mayor's and the councillors' offices, the council meeting chambers. These are grouped toward the south end of the structure, making it compositionally denser there, an addressable head for the building.

The main entry from City Hall Plaza is under the council chambers and then into a tall space filled with ceremonial stair platforms, most effectively cavorted upon by dancers. The upper parts of this space reach up through the building to clerestory windows above, but the light, sifted past large areas of exposed concrete, is gray when it reaches the floor. From the intermediate lobby, glass doors (now locked) lead sideways into the bottom of a great light court. Here the building is most like a Piranesi fantasy. You stand on top of the brick platform base with its concourse underneath, below a concrete framework that supports stepped terraces of office space overhead, and between mammoth piers and quadrupled columns that hold the whole thing aloft in the open air. Ramps lead up to this space across the plaza face of the building, and a narrow stair plummets down the other side to Congress Street. In principle the populace can clamber over and through the building even when it is closed. It is an amazing place, but in practice it's pleasant only when some exhibit or event is installed there, which is not often because it's so windy. Colored sails do wonders for it.

C / GOVERNMENT CENTER · 35

The public-access concourse in the base is perhaps the most easygoing of the interior spaces. It is split on several levels and amply wide, but dark despite a skylight from the court above that makes a focal point for the stairs. Paradoxically, this spacious area of the building, designed for easy access and passage, is the least inviting from the exterior. Its solid walls of brick, cast in the role of base, open only on the north, and then with little ado.

On the Congress Street side the brick plaza that climbs up into terraces to house the public-access functions of City Hall meets its Waterloo. Where it abuts the street with the land fallen away, the brick mass forms a drear blank cliff almost as large as the rest of the building.

At the south end of the Congress Street elevation, the mayor's office steps out over a gap in the cliff. The gap provides an entrance for the building that is directly accessible to automobiles and is the real place to catch a sense of the life at City Hall. It's probably the most spectacular back door in the history of architecture, with concrete piers easily 65 feet high bracketing the entrance.

Schools of architecture often set as a beginning design problem the carving of space within an established cube, the point being to develop a sense for interweaving spaces within an established set of limits. This is anything but a beginner's building, but the constraints were similar to those involved in such a design problem. The spirit of City Hall is vested in the remarkable way that space penetrates it in all directions, lodges in its coffers and thick edges, and celebrates the ingenuity, passion and knowledgeable care with which its architects directed the assembly of its pieces. There are few buildings to match it in architectonic daring and spirit.

I C 3 · NEW ENGLAND MERCHANTS BANK BUILDING
Washington Mall, between State Street and City Hall Plaza
Edward Larrabee Barnes and Emery Roth & Sons, 1969

Unequivocally the best high rise in Boston. It scores on almost every count. It's a clear statement of speculative office-building construction, it meets the ground in an intelligent and appropriate way, it has an imaginable top and it's a beautiful color. Most remarkably, it manages to be at once a landmark and a quiet neighbor to City Hall.

It is without hesitation a steel-frame building wrapped with a curtain wall. The surface is smooth and unremitting glass and handsome pink granite. At the top the slab notches once to make a terrace facing the harbor, and the windows on both sides are set back from the skeleton frame to suggest a colonnade, in a simple, elegant gesture that is much more telling and memorable than the array of screens, roofs, hats and machines that cap the other high buildings downtown.

At the bottom the slab notches once again to let the frame come to the ground as a full colonnade facing Washington Mall and the path to City Hall. The slab is set back from the corner of Congress and State streets to allow views of the Old State House and the Ames Building, well worth the accommodation. The slab slides into the landscaped, sloping ground of this corner without any effort, saving our attention for its neighbors. Through the colonnade you enter directly into the elevator lobby and a mezzanine overlooking a handsome two-story banking hall that occupies the lower floor where the ground slopes away toward the harbor. The room is filled with eastern light from high windows along Congress Street.

Direct, undogmatic and considerate, this building is genuinely urbane.

I C 4 · 1 WASHINGTON MALL
between State Street and City Hall Plaza
Eduardo Catalano, 1972

Boston reticence executed with Argentine finesse. There's no upstaging here: Catalano's building fits quietly, painstakingly into the space between the Ames Building (I A 11) and City Hall (I C 2). Its volumes are limited out of respect for the office-building ancestor to the north; the materials are like those of the concrete City Hall to the south.

It mimics neither. Where each of the others gains its force from deep hollows and heavy, sculptured surfaces, this building is taut and reflective, its main mass a continuous surface of glass and concrete. The glass is made especially reflective by being meticulously set forward from the concrete surface in delicate metal frames. The concrete is enlivened by the slightest bit of shadow relief at the bottom of the spandrels and a subtle change in size where the columns pass behind. The theme is industrial production; the frame is unabashedly direct, but the flat subtlety of the detailing is reminiscent of early Federalist work on Beacon Hill.

At the lower floors all this is transformed to correspond with the four-story base of the Ames Building. The skin sets back behind the structure for the lower three floors, creating a high colonnade that is comparable to the arches of the Ames Building in scale and that makes a thick, sheltered edge along the mall. This wall is consistent with the character of the commercial ground floor of the city, which is generally more penetrable than the volumes above. Hanging over the sidewalk is a series of picturesque signs, the most interesting being a beehive on a platform, signaling the presence of the Home Savings Bank. Inside, a plaque designates this as the site of Paul Revere's goldsmith shop.

I C 3 · *New England Merchants Bank, behind City Hall*

I C 5 · *Sears Block, with tea kettle*

I C 5 · SEARS CRESCENT
City Hall Plaza, south side
1816, remodeled 1850–60
reuse: Don Stull Associates, 1969

· SEARS BLOCK
City Hall Plaza at Court Street
c. 1845
reuse: Stahl/Bennett, 1969

These two buildings follow the line of what was Cornhill Avenue on its way to Faneuil Hall. They have been selected for inclusion in City Hall Plaza with their ground floors given over to restaurants and shops along its edge. Here the scale of the historical city is maintained, as these buildings offer perfectly imaginable spaces, windows of person size (without the original small-paned glass), and familiar architectural elements—of a size that builders could handle. The scale of city streets remains here also, though faintly marked, where the new subway shelter in the corner of the plaza channels most walkers close to the buildings and offers idlers some respite from the dimensions of the sweeping plaza beyond.

The Sears Crescent is a rather curious building, engaging in a somewhat clumsy sleight of hand. It's really three adjoining buildings shaped by their street into a continuous front and made to appear balanced around a center by providing the middle block with higher floors and arched rather than flat lintels over the windows. The buildings step downhill, each a few feet lower than the rest, but the higher, more fanciful middle obscures that fact. Presumably at one time the top of the middle block, the natural focal point of the set, was more fanciful still, or at least one hopes so.

The Sears Block, on the other hand, ends in just the right way. This delicate little granite-skeleton building tapers to an apex dividing Court Street and the plaza. There, in steaming, gilded glory, is a 227-gallon teakettle hanging over the entrance to a brisk little takeout, stand-up café serving coffee and corn muffins. The kettle is perhaps as much a paean to the bureaucrat's breakfast as to the habit taxed by the British. This fat and splendid object takes its place among the codfish in the State House (I B 4), the unicorn on the Old State House down the street (I A 1), the grasshopper atop Faneuil Hall (I D 1) and the Citgo sign above Kenmore Square as loony Boston objects of affection.

I C 6 · SUFFOLK COUNTY COURT HOUSE
Pemberton Square
George A. Clough, 1895, 1906–9
addition: Desmond & Lord, 1936–39
· **PEMBERTON SQUARE**
between Somerset and Cambridge streets

Poor old Suffolk County. Every time it manages to get up some pride in the form of a vigorous granite building, it gets upstaged and pushed aside by the city. The first county courthouse was on the site of the Old City Hall (I A 8) and initially gave space inside to the newly formed city government. Then the city grew and consumed the county's building.

A new, even prouder courthouse was built by Solomon Willard in 1845 on the site behind. A stern granite Greek Revival courthouse thought by some to be among the best in American architecture, it was torn down to make way for the Old City Hall Annex (I A 15).

The present courthouse, though not thought by anyone to be the best of anything, is a pretty spectacular pile. The bombastic vigor of this work evidently did not appeal to the Government Center planners, however, since it is effectively hidden from view behind the Center Plaza building (I C 1).

Perhaps, in the end, the bland pointlessness of 1 Center Plaza has made us look with new eagerness at the array of rhetorical devices (pilasters, colonnades, dormers, mansards, pediments, balconies and a clock) stacked upon the face of the courthouse. It certainly isn't innocuous. The most endearing device is a round balcony in each of the end pavilions that swoops out over one huge projecting bracket. The building is actually more interesting and amusing at either end than it is in the middle, where it's fairly dry. The corner pavilions have those bays and a profusion of chimneys and piers that project in the perpendicular direction. In these corners, it's sculpted with abandon.

The building as we see it today is actually the result of two successive building campaigns. The upper floors, clad in mansard roofs, were added in 1909. Inside is a very grand, full central-staircase hall and a considerable profusion of sculpture. The courtrooms are high, the large halls suitable for interminable waiting.

The towering 1937 addition next door by Desmond & Lord was once a very dominant Art Deco landmark. Now it has mostly been eclipsed on the skyline.

In fairness, it is to be admitted that the courthouse was itself once a massive intruder in Pemberton Square. The square had been a fashionable descendant of the Tontine Crescent, the space here created by leveling Pemberton Hill in 1835. With one side straight, the other bent in a crescent around a fenced green, Pemberton Square was lined by four-story brick town houses of the sort that still front Louisburg Square (II B 1).

Today, only the elements of the shape remain, the Suffolk County Court House on the straight side, 1 Center Plaza on the crescent side. Each in its own way has obliterated the sense of its predecessors. The present square's best moments are when it tumbles down wide stairs through the Center Plaza building to the

Cambridge Street colonnade. Also from the southeast corner, there's a pleasant view of King's Chapel (I A 4) and the Old City Hall (I A 8).

I C 7 · JOHN F. KENNEDY FEDERAL BUILDING
SE corner Cambridge and Sudbury streets facing City Hall Plaza
The Architects Collaborative with Samuel Glaser Associates, 1966

It's hard to imagine that this building was designed by the firm that was founded and nurtured by Walter Gropius. Or maybe it's not. It was Gropius, whose administration of the Bauhaus in Germany led it to be the dominant educational and intellectual force in modern architecture during the 1920's, who subsequently transformed the Harvard Graduate School of Design into the harbinger of modernism in the United States. For Gropius, modern architecture seemed always to be more about issues of industrial reorganization and professional service than about vision. Suitable expression was considered to be a secondary consequence of good building. It certainly is here, but it's a secondary consequence that marks the skyline of the North and West ends and that considerably dampens the spirits of the Government Center complex.

A well-machined, indifferent grid of concrete and glass clothes both the tower and an ill-proportioned, long, low slab that extends across the northwest boundary of City Hall Plaza. The tower is made up to seem as though it were two rectangular slabs that slide past each other. This arrangement diminishes the apparent bulk of the building when seen from the narrow end and provides more perimeter light for the offices inside than would a square office block of similar bulk. The corners of both high and low slabs are rounded in a rather blunt gesture that injects a bare modicum of elegance to the forms.

The Kennedy Building is thoughtful in detail and obedient to the dicta of uniformity, but it is not governed by any vital sense of visual purpose. It's as though the designers went directly from determining the size and disposition of little wooden blocks that represented the mass of the building in a model to drawing the window details. In between, there was, of course, an endless amount of space planning to do and the usual enormity of technical and regulatory detail

I C 7 · *John F. Kennedy Federal Building with the New England Telephone and Telegraph Company Building* (I C 8) *on the left*

that is required to execute a building of this size according to the demands of the General Services Administration of the federal government, but no vision. The Kennedy Building is instructive mainly in that it illustrates how lackluster City Hall could have been—even in the hands of an acknowledged leader of the profession—if it had tread the conventional paths to governmental approval.

I C 8 · NEW ENGLAND TELEPHONE AND TELEGRAPH COMPANY BUILDING
6 Bowdoin Square, between New Chardon and Sudbury streets
Densmore, LeClear & Robbins, 1930
addition: Hoyle, Doran & Berry, 1970

One of a set of Art Deco buildings in Boston that are detailed with restraint and graphic ingenuity. The United Shoe Machinery Building (V A 4) and III Franklin Street (V A 7) are each more lavish, but this one's no slouch. Vertical piers dominate the form, which is tapered in profile just enough to make it seem an active force on the street, a genuine claim on that spot. Windows fit effortlessly between projecting ribs, and the whole is an integrated statement, albeit a contrived one.

The building was extended in the last decade, using essentially the same wall system, this time with almost no windows; one of the very few examples where the windowless bulk now produced by the telephone company's automated systems is handled with grace.

There are some nice bits of grillwork at the ground floor of the original and a set of bronze plaques proferring historical information. The inescapable Bulfinch turns out to have been born on this site.

I C 9 · CAPITAL BANK BUILDING
I Bulfinch Place, NE corner Sudbury Street
Anderson & Notter, 1972
· RKO GENERAL BUILDING
Bulfinch Place, between Sudbury and New Chardon streets
Fulmer & Bowers, 1969

The Capital Bank Building is almost an architectural parody. The corner of this naughty brick building has been chewed away and filled with glass, making it very clear that there's a steel frame under the brick and that the brick is used as a simple curtain wall, almost as a wallpaper or veneer. It's a mischievous didactic trick that also serves as entrance.

The glass corner is faceted in a way that implies a pyramid of stacked voids, making a very eccentric, high-spirited entry, if not a cultivated one. One would wish that the rest of the building had as much spirit.

Where the Capital Bank Building has compensated for its brick boxiness by flashing its insides, the RKO General Building has set about adding to its box a set of sculpted aluminum teeth. The sculpture was designed by Tony Belluschi and was selected by competition. Its shiny, round metal forms appear like some geared instrument advancing down the path of the colonnade. But it has interesting reflections, both by day and at night under the lights.

The building, itself is very simple and unassertive. In fact, it's downright dreary, almost always in the shadow of the New England Telephone and Telegraph Building (I C 8). The trouble is that except for the sculpture, there's no life along its edges.

The ensemble forms a wholly inappropriate tribute to the street's namesake.

I C 10 · GOVERNMENT CENTER GARAGE
bounded by Blackstone, Sudbury, Bowker, New Chardon and Market streets
Kallman & McKinnell, and Samuel Glaser & Partners, 1970

If you think anything else in Government Center is big, you're clearly not ready for this. Louis Kahn urged architects in the late 1950's to consider parking garages as great constructed harbors for the city, creative elements in the city's regeneration. This is one of the few parking-garage structures made big enough and crafted well enough to begin to qualify for inclusion in that genre.

As with its architects' other work downtown—Boston City Hall (I C 2) and the Five Cents Savings Bank (I A 19)—this is a dramatic assembly of precast concrete elements, here held aloft by columns and beams of great size. The beams become enormous at the eastern end, where the whole structure steps out over the subway and up toward the raised expressway. At its feet a yellow brick structure that was built later to shelter mere bus commuters seems Lilliputian.

Unfortunately, in its Gulliver-like slumber across the north end of Government Center, it has managed to wipe out the apex of still another Bulfinch invention—the triangle of streets that he laid out to fill the Mill Pond.

D/FANEUIL HALL
AND THE MARKETS

Congress Street, behind City Hall (I C 2), is a crazy open seam in the fabric of the city that splits this part of Boston apart and reveals a lot about shifting pressures and sensibilities in the development of downtown. Although the present character of Congress Street is almost fully unintended, it is in some ways much more instructive than City Hall Plaza (I C 1), which has been so carefully packaged.

On the east, where the urban-design plan called for construction of a motel, there is instead an unconvincing little strip of park and a clear view of the perfectly straightforward ramshackle of Blackstone Block (I D 2). Opposite—to the west and high above—are the rear elevations of City Hall.

To the south, the pedestrian bridge that was intended has never been built, and instead there is a remarkably clear vista into the depths of the financial district, with 60 State Street (V B 2) and the New England Merchants Bank Building (I C 3) acting like paired towers at the gate. Their 40 stories dwarf the nearby and similarly paired Worthington and Brazer buildings (V B 1) of the turn of the century. These, in their time, were seen as ominously threatening to the Old State House (I A 1) at their feet. Further behind, the Post Office Building (V A 14) shoulders into view above the cornice line of the lower buildings, and the protuberance of the First National Bank of Boston (V A 6) fills the far end of Congress Street. The north end of Congress is bridged by the Government Center Garage (I C 10).

Faneuil Hall (I D 1) is the fulcrum of the place. It has existed here in one form or another since 1742, and now lends its name to the recently revitalized market area behind it. Dock Square, the paved space between City Hall and Faneuil Hall, is, remarkably enough, the site of the original town dock.

The Faneuil Hall Markets (I D 5), also known as the Quincy Market, originated in a brilliant and bold scheme fostered by Mayor Josiah Quincy in 1823 and executed by Alexander Parris in 1825. Older disorganized buildings along the dock were removed, the land was filled and a startlingly clear composition of three buildings and two streets was projected to the new edge of the water. The middle Quincy Market building was constructed by the newly incorporated city. The North and South Market rows were designed by Parris but built in segments by independent owners.

The Rouse Company development of these buildings into a center-city emporium has been wildly successful. It throbs with people almost all through the day, every day, and it has created a new heart of the city, one that is popular with denizens of the suburbs and tourists, one where petty commerce offers a ready

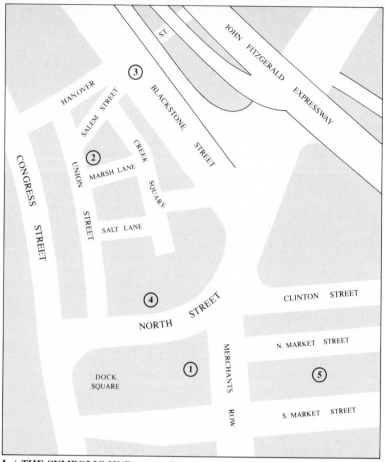

I / THE SYMBOLIC HUB   D / FANEUIL HALL AND THE MARKETS

excuse for being with others. Alas, here it is to no great common purpose—a bauble to add to our store of personal experiences, but little more.

The redevelopment of this place has used a number of its inherent formal characteristics to real advantage. The simplicity of the original plan works as a clarifying support for the myopic confusion created by the jumble of shops, the excitement of beckoning goods and the crowds of customers swimming in the sea of available delights. The name of the game here, as in so many of the popular bazaars that have blossomed throughout the United States within the past decade, is immersion in the goods, the dissolution of boundaries between spectator and scenery. Whereas fashionable commerce used to be encased in proscenium-arched shops and glass cabinets opened only to the worthy and discriminating, now goods are placed among the people, who in turn become absorbed into the ambience of the place. The clarity of the forms and spaces originally established here makes it possible to survive this inundation with some sense of orientation.

The current renovation is not without loss. The city bartered away its interest in the Quincy Market Building to get it developed this way—to shift the burden of maintaining this public place from taxpayer to consumer (in general perhaps a wise move, since one suspects that a preponderance of users are suburbanites and not, therefore, Boston taxpayers).

In the renovations the Quincy Market also lost traces of the scruffy, rugged individualism that had characterized it in the first half of the century when the North and South Market Buildings were no longer simple blocks but were instead adorned by a series of ad hoc adjustments and additions, most notably brick structures (mostly ungainly) that added light and floor space to the attics, and an occasional glorious copper bay bulging from the façade. Inside, too, the cast-iron columns down the center of the main building had acquired a splotchy patina as the fish, meat and cheese shops that it housed built little storefronts and counters that incorporated the columns, sometimes wrapping them in marble or stainless steel, sometimes engulfing them in shingles. The variety there lay not in the type of goods but in the people who offered them and the way they crafted their nests.

The sequence of development that led to the present moment has been somewhat bizarre. Federal grants for restoration were used to remove excrescences (and tenants) and to restore the North and South Market buildings to their original pristine states. Meanwhile, the Center Building, the most carefully considered and specially crafted form, was also emptied and gutted of all trace of the interior (including the inner finish of the dome, a change that seems to radically distort the building), and great glass sheds were added to either side, thus changing its character substantially. As the North and South Market buildings have been further developed, they have once again sprouted modest tack-ons and additions that fortunately enliven them, but in the process we are left with forms that bear the dignity of 1825 and the chic of 1978 and precious little sign that there was ever any life in between.

It's all elegant, clean and wholesome, guided by the hands of gifted designers, with little trace of the struggling common folk. It does speak of the transformation of our society; of crafts, of franchise, of aspiring good taste and of our absorption with our own superfluous pleasures. No meat and potatoes here.

I D 1 · FANEUIL HALL
Dock Square, Congress and North streets
John Smibert, 1740–42
renovation: Charles Bulfinch, 1805–06

Who today would have the bravura to take Boston's Cradle of Liberty, double its width, add a floor and move its cupola from the middle to one end? Harder still, who would come out with a good building? Bulfinch again. He did just that to the original Faneuil Hall, all the while retaining the small, simple orders of the lower floors, simply adding, as if it were predestined, a set of elongated Ionic pilasters to form the third floor. Marvelous arched moldings in the end gables are the one ever-so-restrained grand gesture.

It's important to remember this building in its eighteenth-century context, on the edge of the dock in an area consisting of row houses such as those still to be seen in the Blackstone Block (I D 2). Only a short distance away were large freestanding houses and gardens of a sort that may be imagined as similar to the first Harrison Gray Otis House (II A 15). The ground floor was a market and there was a hall for public assembly above. This hall provided housing for some of Boston's most stirring rhetoric, while the market provided meat and other victuals until very recently when, despite the steadfast opposition of right-minded people, it was reduced to hawking ice cream and trinkets. The meeting

I D 1 · *Faneuil Hall with the New England Merchants National Bank (I C 3), right rear*

room above, one of the great spaces in Boston, remains in public use and is well worth a visit.

The interior two-story volume is roughly square, ringed on three sides by a gallery supported on small columns. The room is very capacious, clearly a place where a number of people can gather to discuss matters, as in a town meeting. The light in the room is particularly beautiful and the large volume of space lends authority to the occasion. On the end wall is a large painting of Daniel Webster addressing the United States Congress in a room of very similar sort and use, although furnished in a more suitably elaborate manner.

Climbing to the meeting hall from the street involves negotiating a set of stairs steep enough to qualify for a Central American pyramid, with enough bifurcations and overlaps on the way to the gallery to be considered Baroque. To confuse the issue still more, the cast-iron columns of the stairs are vaguely Egyptian in form. This entry hall is a wonderful, puzzling place. The present stair probably dates from a late nineteenth-century reconstruction that substituted fireproof materials for wood structure.

I D 2 · BLACKSTONE BLOCK
· UNION OYSTER HOUSE
41–43 Union Street
c. 1715
alterations: 1724, 1790

If Government Center were meant to be a modern living room for the city, and the Sears Crescent (I C 5) and Faneuil Hall (I D 1) its tasteful antiques, then the Blackstone Block would be the family attic. Franklin's childhood was spent nearby, John Hancock owned property here and the young man later to become Louis Philippe, the bourgeois king of France, lived here in the 1820's.

Many generations have left buildings standing about in this attic. Its streets and alleys are the best evidence remaining in Boston of a seventeenth-century

I D 2 · *Blackstone Block*

street pattern, though at present the inner block is unkempt and disregarded. Marshall Street was first recorded in 1652, and Scott's Lane, which now ends in a blank door between 20 and 24 North Street, was established in 1677. Creek Square, which followed on filled marshland, was lined with houses in the early 1800's. In 1833, Blackstone Street itself was made from the part of Mill Creek that had divided the North End from the rest of town (a division much more forcefully achieved by construction of the elevated Central Artery in 1951).

The Union Oyster House at 41–43 Union Street is the oldest and most noted building in the block, actually a pair of simple brick row houses, the first of which was built between 1713 and 1717, the second added in 1724. The ground floor was reconstructed in 1790 and thereafter. In 1742 it became a dry-goods store; in 1826 the present enterprise was established. The Union Oyster House is fond of telling us that its oyster bar was Daniel Webster's favorite haunt. Whatever the tale, the horseshoe-shaped wooden bar and the oysters preferred on it are among the city's most cherished pleasures.

Next door, at No. 37, is another brick row house, this one dating from about 1830 and with higher floors and elegant, elongated windows, a clear example of the power of proportion in determining a building's character. Next again, between Marsh Lane and Salt Lane, is a much larger building, the sole example here of 1860's Italianate with a stylishly articulated if undistinguished masonry façade. Low buildings on either side reveal the bulk of this massive five-story mansarded block.

I D 3 · *"Asaroton," by Mags Harries, in the intersection of Blackstone and Hanover streets*

Midway down Marshall Street is the Boston Stone, a grindstone set up in 1737 as the starting point for distances measured out from the Hub. Also on Marshall Street are the Ebenezer Hancock House, at No. 10, dating from 1767, several handsome, curved, corner buildings from 1835 and a spectacular framed view back up to City Hall (I C 2), the towers of 60 State Street (V B 2) and the New England Merchants Bank Building (I C 3).

I D 3 · ASAROTON
intersection Blackstone and Hanover streets
Mags Harries, 1976

Here, immortalized in bronze, is the only place in town where it's thought to be all right to leave garbage lying about. Bronze castings of squashed fruit and vegetables and discarded papers are embedded in the paving as permanent residue of an incredibly active street market that takes place along Hanover and Blackstone streets and provides ample amounts of the real stuff.

Lest you think the reliefs are some kind of a Pop trick, sculptor Harries will point out that *asaroton* (Greek for unswept floors) is the name of an ancient Roman mosaic-floor genre depicting the aftermath of banquets.

I D 4 · 16 NORTH STREET
Gilbert Miles Ramsey, 1922
reuse: Sy Mintz, 1967
· 24 NORTH STREET
Peabody & Stearns, 1889

The North Street side of the Blackstone Block had been spruced up to face Faneuil Hall even before the markets were redone.

The renovation on the corner of Union and North streets has done little for a 1926 building that did little in the first place, but at No. 16, there is a good, straightforward reworking of a good, straightforward 1922 attempt to stack five stories on a narrow lot. Mintz has simplified the windows and added a glass penthouse that is fully visible without being obtrusive. Fields Butcher, at No. 22, was until recently one of the few remaining holdouts of the meat business that once dominated this place. The building it occupies remained essentially in its 1824 form until 1980, when the dormered gable roof was knocked down by an overzealous demolition crew. The ground floor is now a restaurant. Hark Beef, at No. 24, originally stored six floors of meat above a white-tiled butcher space. Its narrow width for many years resisted economical reuse despite a simple but handsome façade, but the Peabody & Stearns building front is now to be incorporated in the new Hotel Bostonian next door.

I D 5 · FANEUIL HALL MARKETS
between Faneuil Hall and Commercial Street
Alexander Parris, 1825
reuse: Benjamin Thompson Associates, 1976

The three parallel buildings that form the Faneuil Hall Markets were until recently locally known as the Quincy Market, in deference to the mayor who

I D 5 · *Faneuil Hall Markets*

ordered the landfill and construction project that produced the original buildings. The patriarch of the group is a long granite building with finely scaled,
sharply formed, but light-handed Doric porticos at either end and a grand
copper-clad oval dome surmounting a block at the center. To either side are
granite-fronted brick warehouse buildings three stories high, each with a steep
gable roof interrupted by dormers and skylights to light two floors of attic space.

The whole ensemble was a dignified civic intervention in a town of meandering
paths. In establishing a clear edge to this section of the harbor, it followed the
precedent set privately by the Broad and India streets corporations and by the
construction of Central Wharf (V B 10) in 1816, all with Bulfinch as architect. But
the Parris buildings were the first major granite buildings along the waterfront,
and they set a standard for integrated street and building design which exceeded
their precedents and which was never matched by their more massive granite
successors. The wharves built later into the water beyond—Commercial Wharf
(I E 11), the State Street block (V B 9) and the Mercantile Wharf (I E 9)—were
all ambitious projects, but they aspired only to be grand single buildings with
enormous storage and office capacity, standing next to busy wharves. The Faneuil Hall Markets make a piece of the city and they do it with style.

The renovations have been done with skill and imagination. The interior finish
was removed from the central Faneuil Hall Market building exposing brickwork,
the shaggy backs of the granite walls, and timbers. Windows were removed from
the lower portions, and great glass sheds were built out like protective crystalline
wings hanging over the edges of the street and allowing both basement and
upper-level stores to flourish along the promenades. At their outer walls these
glass sheds have great roll-up doors of glass that open the whole building to the
walks on either side. Sidewalk cafés and booths under these roofs make the
transition to the real sidewalks between the buildings.

The streets, bounded on opposite sides by the North and South Market buildings, have been turned into pedestrian ways. The two streets are of different

widths, the one on the south nearly double the one on the north, and they have developed quite distinct personalities. The north street is dominated by the ancient and venerable (in truth, overrated) Durgin Park Restaurant, along with various newcomers and upstart, upbeat establishments. It is long and narrow, a channel of movement reinforced by the shadows and by an elegant and simple canopy over the face of the ground-level stores on the north. The wide, sunny street to the south is filled with trees, benches, cobblestones, light fixtures, telephones and usually more people than it can hold. At its middle opposite the dome is an open space likely to be the setting for some form of ad hoc performance. Much of the fast food peddled inside is eaten out here, even on brisk days.

The uniform walls of the North and South Market buildings were made with such large, narrow slabs of granite and are so filled with windows that they have led historians to surmise that they were among the earliest expression anywhere of the commercial skeleton frame that later appeared in cast-iron façades and became ubiquitous in the late nineteenth century, leading ultimately to the steel-and-concrete skeleton-frame constructions that have come to dominate the skyline of American cities, Boston's included.

In their present reincarnation, the small-paned, wood-framed windows have been replaced by large sheets of glass in dark aluminum; the fine-grained intimacy of the earlier windows has become something approximating a blank stare.

The dome of the middle building, which originally covered a second-floor meeting room, has been opened through to the ground floor, its supporting walls stripped of their finish. The high space serves as a focus for the complex, with tables and benches, a bakery, special events and more fast-food munchers. The middle of the space is ringed by an oval balcony that serves as observing place for the scene below.

A wonderful colonnade of husky cast-iron Tuscan columns marches resolutely down the length of the building, allocating space to left and right and measuring out the bays for each vendor. Signs syncopate their beat.

With a dominant center, clear ends—one facing the landmark Faneuil Hall, the other pointing to the harbor—and readily recognizable spaces to either side, the markets are easily understandable. It makes a difference where you are, whether in the crowded middle corridor or in the high domed space at the center; under the bright glass canopies or out in the promenade; or looking down from the arched windows of upper-level shops on either side. Each part provides a different kind of experience; all parts are quickly accessible from one another. You can choose to walk the length of the place in one domain or another, or you can move across the grain, sampling a variety of goods and changing the scene.

Windows, doors and openings frame views of people at various levels, they focus attention on individuals in the midst of this great street fest. For it is likely, after all, that the presence of other people is the root joy of such places—the same touching of the flesh that makes fiestas so potent and gives politicians their fuel.

E/THE WATERFRONT

The Boston waterfront was formed by busy and boisterous harborside commerce. Its wharfs and warehouses are interlaced with recently converted living spaces, pleasure boats and numerous opportunities to enjoy the blandishments of food and drink in atmospheric settings.

The present line of the waterfront is the result of successive landfill and wharf projects beginning in 1641 and continuing into the twentieth century. It is a built edge, a fabrication that brings hard, flat working surfaces up against water deep enough for boats to use. At the time of settling, the edge was not at all like that. The original joining of land and water was mostly soft and squishy, marshes whose shape varied with the tides. Early maps show the edge of Town Cove, the most regular feature of the shoreline, as an indentation reaching inland as far as Dock Square and Faneuil Hall (I D 1).

The basic form of the waterfront, with fingers of dock and warehouse reaching out into the harbor, was a direct reflection of Boston's role as a major port. Its streets led out, through the ships that departed its docks, to the farthest corners of the world. India Street and India Wharf are mementos now of far-flung paths that once were real. The Hub in this sense included spokes into the harbor as well as across the land.

The transposition of Boston from a hub to a commercial way station accompanied the decline of its port. It was first marked physically by a slashing path parallel to the harbor, connecting North and South stations in 1868. This path, now Atlantic Avenue, literally severed a number of the warehouse buildings in their middle, in order that traffic could move around the city as well as penetrate into it. (Photographs from the 1850's show a jumble of buildings so thick that movement across Boston must have been truly tortuous.)

More recently, the Fitzgerald Expressway, following some of the same path, chopped even more disastrously through the fabric, creating a gash between downtown and the waterfront. For decades, while warehousing foundered and the Boston Redevelopment Authority assembled property, the waterfront existed as a no man's land, with very little public access to, or at least no evident public claim on, the waterfront.

The place has been radically transformed during the last decade, mostly by extensive action on the part of the Boston Redevelopment Authority. The waterfront is now a sporting place for citizens, suburbanites and tourists. It has along its frontage a record not only of the mercantile past and affluent present, but of the transformations in architectural intent that have taken place during its period of renewal. Buildings here range from sensible reinterpretations of industrial tradition to gleaming abstractions.

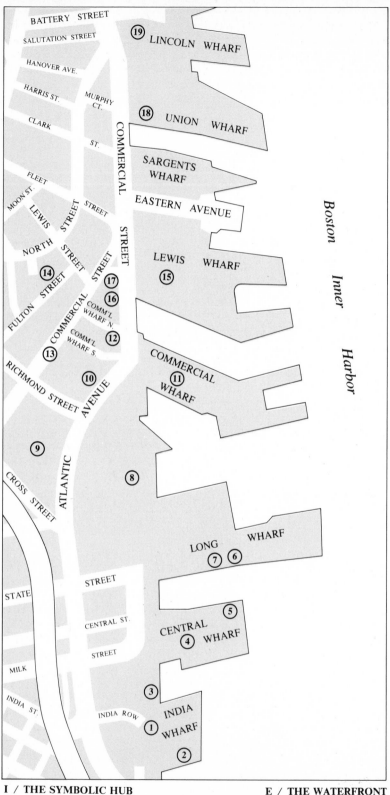

BATTERY STREET

SALUTATION STREET

HANOVER AVE.

HARRIS ST.

MURPHY CT.

CLARK

ST.

COMMERCIAL

FLEET

MOON ST.

LEWIS

STREET

STREET

NORTH

STREET

STREET

STREET

⑭

FULTON STREET

⑰

⑯

COMMERCIAL

COMM'L WHARF N.

COMM'L WHARF S.

⑫

⑬

RICHMOND STREET

⑩

AVENUE

⑨

ATLANTIC

CROSS STREET

⑧

STATE

STREET

CENTRAL ST.

STREET

MILK

INDIA ST.

INDIA ROW

⑲ LINCOLN WHARF

⑱ UNION WHARF

SARGENTS WHARF

EASTERN AVENUE

LEWIS WHARF

⑮

COMMERCIAL

⑪ WHARF

LONG WHARF

⑦ ⑥

⑤

CENTRAL

④ WHARF

③

INDIA

① WHARF

②

Boston Inner Harbor

I / THE SYMBOLIC HUB   **E / THE WATERFRONT**

The final major site along the waterfront became a hotel in 1981. Mayor Kevin White and the neighborhood engaged in a fierce struggle over whether a new hotel at Long Wharf should owe architectural allegiance to the character of its older surrounds or march to the tune of its own abstract drummer. The character of Boston's principal point of linkage with the sea was at stake, and the battle appears not to have been won by either side.

I E 1 · HARBOR TOWER APARTMENTS
65, 85 East India Row, at the harbor end of India Street
I. M. Pei & Partners, 1971

The Harbor Tower Apartments are on the site of what was once India Wharf. What remained of the Bulfinch buildings on the wharf were destroyed in the 1960's to make way for construction of waterside apartments. The new buildings are carefully crafted, earning the kind of stand-off quality that they convey—the sense of being beyond personal experience.

The forms that have been established are very clear; the shape of the towers is handsomely articulated. Their walls are simply but crisply defined: Each is essentially a single planar surface interspersed with engaged half-round piers that run up the entire face of the building. The spandrels below the windows have a heavily in-cut recess; this is curved so that the shadows, though slight, are shapely and give a sense of physical presence to the façade.

In this respect the Pei towers are an antidote to the essential flatness characteristic of so many other buildings of the period. These towers command respect somewhat in the same way that the New England Merchants Bank Building (I C 3), by Barnes, does. Both architects take the characteristics of conventional building systems and work within them—in this case with more push and shove than in the New England Merchants Bank—but both work within the building system to achieve, still, some sense of the craftsmanship and detailed involvement that we admire in other, older structures. But the mode is entirely different, resting in the designer's, not the carver's or molder's, art. The shapes and forms are extremely simple, with interest coming from the modulation of light on the surfaces around the piers, and on that inset recess, and from the curved shadows cast by balconies at the corners.

The balconies at the end are perhaps the least convincing characteristic of these buildings. Their rounded corners do cast an interesting pattern of shadows; at such a scale, however, their projections are so close together that they look more like a zipper than a set of things to inhabit. Their size and location are such that one doubts how intensively they are or can be used. It is also odd to have them uniformly similar up the full height of the building, as though there were no difference between being on a balcony on the 25th floor facing the harbor and being on a balcony two floors off the street, next to a garage.

The analogy to the zipper is telling because a zipper is, after all, a characteristic piece of systematic technology; it allows a single action to take care of a number of closure problems rather than requiring individual attention as a button does. And the same thinking applies to the making of these balconies, where a system of producing balconies along the face of the buildings is established and executed with one gesture of the drawing—zip. To shape balconies pertinent to their particular location and height would take more fumbling and care (and it would count more).

I E 1 and 2 · *David von Schlegell's "India Wharf Project" in front of I. M. Pei's Harbor Tower Apartments*

I E 2 · INDIA WHARF PROJECT
East India Row, between Harbor Towers and the harbor
David von Schlegell, 1972

Between the Harbor Towers at the far edge of the wharf is a large sculpture composed of four bent planes surfaced with stainless steel facing each other in pairs, like oversized book ends from which the books have sprung. They define a space, as the hold of a ship might, between the Harbor Towers and the harbor beyond. The relationship of this space to the surroundings is very hard to understand as anything but a berthing. The brackets block off the harbor view, rather than open up to it, while the space they form is entirely open to the shaggy piers in the south, a view of no particular merit. The orientation is also slightly askew with relation to the two Harbor Towers. If sculpture is, as Suzanne Langer would have it, "virtual kinetic volume," then this one would drift, rather than walk or ride away.

Yet if you attend only to the sculpture and its reflections, it makes an exotic place of its own. Step within the parentheses formed by the sculpture and you will see patterns that are nearly kaleidoscopic—as sunlit and shadowed surfaces of buildings, passing clouds and sky appear reflected in the angled surfaces. You can stand within these tilted and complicated patterns and change them by moving about. With a little concentrated effort, you could probably get seasick.

This great sculpture on the edge of the harbor ought to be very exciting, but it isn't. The combination of these flat, shiny pieces with the bone-gray Harbor Towers and the parking garage beyond is, finally, chilling. Standing among these objects, each of them well considered in its own terms, one has the sense of being hedged in by abstracted things, none of which show much sign of touch or inhabitation by people.

It's rather like one of those innumerable Romantic paintings showing a lonely figure or two framed by fragments of an archaic order, an order that is decaying in the midst of a majestic natural setting. Only here the earlier buildings of India Wharf have been cleared to make way for a fragment that is intentionally minimalist.

I E 3 · INDIA WHARF HARBOR VIEWS

Beyond the sculpture the edge of the pier is made with fantastic newly cut granite slabs sitting atop older pieces of a similar scale. The latter are, no doubt, remnants of what was once one of Boston's grandest enterprises. India Wharf was built as part of an extensive reshaping of the waterfront begun in 1805. The India Wharf buildings were designed by Charles Bulfinch and were the proudest buildings of the complex, with a central two-story arched opening cutting across its middle, marked above by temple-front dormers that interrupted its otherwise simple pitched roof—300 and some feet long. The harbor end terminated in a gabled projection reminiscent of Faneuil Hall (I D 1).

The wharf buildings extended inland as far as India Street on the opposite side of what is now a wretched maze of green steel expressway supports. When India Street formed the land edge of the water, clipper ships were anchored where the Flour and Grain Exchange Building (V B 11) now stands like a turreted castle.

International trafficking now takes place directly across the harbor at Logan Airport; from the tip of India Wharf the planes and terminals are quite evident. On a fine summer evening, there's also a possibility of catching a fleet of sailboats going out through the harbor as well, and almost always a breeze channeled between the towers. It's a splendid spot on a hot night.

To the left lies Central Wharf, once also the site of long rows of brick warehouses (V B 10) and now the location of the New England Aquarium (I E 4). The front of the aquarium, with its additions that have banks of shed skylights, has a sharp, cheerful look. Connecting the New England Discovery Boat to the aquarium really makes the whole thing a waterfront environment, a collection of wharves and boats and loading equipment.

This is quite unlike the Von Schlegell sculpture and the Harbor Towers that face it. They in fact reject any form of attachment, any alteration to their original conception.

What is left of the inlet between the two wharves forms one of the most picturesque spots along the waterfront. The pier edge is terraced at two levels, offering differing degrees of relationship to the water: next to it down low or several steps above it on a tree-sheltered promenade. Moored in front and to the sides, boats make a screen between you and the far harbor, with the Bethlehem dry docks across the way in the middle distance. The whole comprises a range of different-sized elements layered in space. Whereas the end of India Wharf itself, with the Harbor Towers and the sculpture, is composed almost entirely of abstract forms, this inlet is made up of various objects and pieces of building that have scale references to the people who use them—paths and stairs and balconies, little lookouts and rails, seats in the yellow rowboats. It's a much more engaging vista, filled as it is with signs of human occupancy. It's also more Bostonian.

Just at dusk, when you can still see the expanse and scope of the harbor, lights on the buildings and boats begin to go on, and their counterpoint emphasizes the contrast between the great dark expanse of the harbor and the small spots of light that are signs of dwellings.

I E 4 · NEW ENGLAND AQUARIUM
Central Wharf at the harbor end of Milk Street
Cambridge Seven, 1969, 1973, 1979

The aquarium is located on Central Wharf (V B 10), which was built in 1816 and which once had brick stores running down its center for a quarter of a mile. The aquarium took over the wharf in 1969. When first built, it was a simple box with a mildly articulated concrete wall-and-pier system—a reinterpretation in appropriate technology of the simple warehouse structures that had preceded it on the wharves. Interest on the exterior of the building came only from modulations in the pier system, which reflected very quietly some of the differences in space arrangement inside. Subsequently, a more festive entry, ticket and concession place and an extension housing a small auditorium have modified and softened that original appearance, but the original building block stands as the rock against which these other pieces have collected.

Inside, the aquarium is a treat. A great cubic shell of space surrounds what is reputed to be the largest sea-water tank in captivity, a huge three-story, 180,000-gallon ocean tank approximately 40 feet in diameter, buttressed by concrete piers all around and encircled by a spiraling ramp. A large, shallow pool at the very bottom covers most of the floor. The space is architecturally exhilarating in itself. The spiral ramp rises up through the cubic space, with projections and balconies and overhangs that provide a variety of vantage points for the numerous beautifully prepared and instructively labeled exhibits. Two sides of the cube have relatively standard aquarium tanks with various displays of fish. A third wall has a wonderful large neon wave pattern on it, and the fourth has the full-size silhouettes of all manner of sharks. There are several skeletons and shells hanging in the air between the tank and the other display projections. The bottom pool has giant turtles and penguins darting around it. The entire scene is dominated by the fish swimming round and round in the central tank, which can be seen from all angles and from all levels and vantage points within the encompassing room. Meanwhile, the ramps and walks themselves are filled with

I E 4 · *New England Aquarium*

people moving through the place in a kind of pageant. Dim lighting conveys pleasurably the sense of a murky aquatic world, with spots of bright light that pinpoint fish swimming through them.

The tank, of course, is the great feature of the aquarium, whether viewed at a distance, from the surrounding balcony levels, or nearby on the spiral ramp. Few things are more startling than to stand in the niche between columns, snug up against the plate-glass windows of the large tank, and see a shark's teeth glide by, apparently only inches from your face; or to confront head on the great heads and fins of the giant sea turtles that swim around inside this space. The plate glass is so thick it has a magnifying quality that causes the close proximity of the fish to become very dramatic, indeed. The awesomely large fish circling endlessly inside the tank in consort with people spiraling around its edge make this a candidate for a merry-go-round scene in a Lewis Carroll fantasy.

One of the pleasures of the great tank is that you can climb all the way to the top and see the thing from above. There at the top of the pool, where the lights and the diving platform are placed, all illusion is frankly dispensed with, and the simple, pragmatic characteristics of the tank are contrasted with the dreamlike appearance of the big rocks and forms seen through the glass below. The tank itself is cleaned and the fish fed by divers who periodically enter from the very top, after the sharks have been fed, and descend slowly to feed the fish near the bottom.

On the southeast corner of the third level is a small room that allows the only outlook to the harbor. You step out of the main space into a corner room with large windows framing the view and numerous charts and gauges measuring the state of the air and water outside. On the back wall is a photograph of the waterfront when it was still an active port with liners docked along its edges. This connection back to the harbor is a welcome relief—there might even have been more of it.

I E 5 · CENTRAL AND LONG WHARF VIEWS

There is a big paved concrete walk that runs entirely around the aquarium on Central Wharf and has boarded concrete walls, square brick pavers and metal railings along the edge. On this walk you can have the sense that you are really out in the harbor. However, since there are no landings or attachments, it's a relatively uneventful passage and it seems bizarre to need to walk around the empty space that has been reserved for aquarium expansion but is now just an incongruous patch of green occasionally used for specialized meetings and events underneath a summer tent.

As you proceed to the north side of the walk around the pier, you look directly across to the excursion boats and tugs that use Long Wharf. This is the place to watch the departure of Provincetown and Harbor Tour excursion boats, with all the excitement of people getting aboard, maneuvering for position at the rail and wandering off to sea, bands playing and the like. Even though the coming and going is now all touristic, it's wonderful that there is still a life of the pier taking place at this point, which was at one time the center of the commercial life of the region.

The view up State Street from Long Wharf is dominated by the preposterous Custom House Tower (I E 6) with its pointed top and Boston's most visible clock, usually inaccurate. For a while, this was the tallest building in Boston. It is now quite small in comparison with the newer high rises of the Boston skyline, but no less memorable. One can make out where the Old State House (I A 1) is, at the end of the street, but the view of its roof is cut off by the Fitzgerald Expressway. If the plan to recess this highway goes ahead, the connection between the wharf and downtown will become more clear.

I E 6 · CUSTOM HOUSE BLOCK
Long Wharf, at the harbor end of State Street
Isaiah Rogers, 1837
reuse: Anderson, Notter Associates, 1973

The Custom House Block is located on the end of Long Wharf, Boston's first deepwater anchorage. The wharf, built in 1710, extended State Street (at that time King Street) directly out into the deepest part of the harbor.

The Custom House Block, built with more pretension than its predecessors, is attributed to Isaiah Rogers, one of Boston's early and inventive purveyors of granite-faced buildings. It is a warehouse building of four floors capped by a long gable roof that was interrupted on the back by steeply pitched dormers and at the center by a raised but squat, hip-roofed pavilion.

The granite facing is very handsome: huge slabs along the ground floor with more reasonably sized face blocks on the upper floors and finished granite surrounds for the windows. These hold iron brackets for shutters that once covered openings in the building. The uppermost floor, under the roof, has now been transformed into living space by recessed balconies cut into it and sliding glass doors that open out onto those balconies.

I E 6 · *Custom House Block, Long Wharf*

The recently replaced roof is a disappointing flat and gray asphalt shingle. Its silhouette, once very proud, is now compromised by renovations past and present. The central pyramidal block has window balconies cut so close to the hip of the block that the pyramidal character almost disappears. An earlier addition, of the sort often visited upon this kind of warehouse, has an aluminum strip window entirely out of scale with the building, and it is capped by a chunk of unsightly air-conditioning equipment. The final blow to the block's dignity is struck by a graceless elevator penthouse thrusting up aimlessly behind the tip of the pyramid.

The back (north) side is brick above the ground floor and has actually fared better by the various accretions of time than the front. Its face, serrated by steep dormers and measured by large loading doors lined up beneath hoists at each peak, was so intensely picturesque in the first place that subsequent accretions and distortions only frazzle the form a little bit more, adding negligent charm.

Carping aside, however, this renovation is a very important one. It recollects the historic form and character of the buildings that once were along the wharves, and it accommodates a series of shops, offices and apartments in a splendid location on the waterfront.

I E 7 · GARDNER BUILDING
Long Wharf, at the harbor end of State Street
c. 1830
reuse: Anderson, Notter Associates, 1973

Inland from the Custom House Block is the Gardner Building, renovated for the Chart House Restaurant in a clear, direct and careful way. It is a fine reworking of a very simple brick warehouse, the only one surviving of the many that once lined these wharves. Its brick exterior has been restored, adorned only by shutters and granite lintels. It conveys very easily the simple nature of these waterfront buildings, although it is likely more pristine than those buildings were, or became shortly after they were put into use.

Inside, the building has been opened, its stairs connecting several floors through vertical spaces. Chunky bits of exposed wood framing reveal the essential nature of the building and how it was made. With cleaning, some adroit restructuring and very caring attention to detail, the architects have created a place that is both instructive about the past and suffused with that special mix of spatial complexity and wood-crafted surroundings that seems to be *de rigueur* for the swinging tourist-restaurant style that the Chart House offers.

I E 8 · CHRISTOPHER COLUMBUS WATERFRONT PARK
between Long and Commercial wharves
Sasaki Associates, 1976

The core of this park is an elaborate trellis promenade that runs its length, bent in the middle and attended by various sitting places and paved with bricks. It is a particularly successful piece of public-space design. The fundamental scheme of the park is appropriate in that it allows for several kinds of relationships to the water and to the view out in front.

You can choose, if you like, to be near the edge of the water, kept safely back from it by huge bollards and chains. (Would that it were a little bit more like an edge of the water—more precipitous, something with some sense of excitement and hazard to it.) Or, if you prefer, there is the slightly higher, more stately walk behind, and the sloped green, which on any warm day is filled with people sunning. Behind that, in turn, is a granite ledge, which provides a sitting area along the top of the green. There the arbor, with benches along its path, makes a beautifully shaded promenade, bordered by still another set of sitting places —a double row of red oaks paralleling the arbor and divided into a set of outdoor rooms by groups of benches that face each other. These sitting places are three

I E 8 · *Christopher Columbus Waterfront Park, with the Harbor Tower Apartments in background*

layers back from the water but still offer views of both the harbor and the wharves. Back yet another step from the water and behind thick foliage is an open green, which is used for sunning, frisbee and other games.

As the passage bends, there is a very formal square with a different set of trees, dwarf yews. This area is raised slightly, surrounded by feathery locust trees and by a ground cover of firethorn. It has a graveled surface and a splashing fountain throwing water onto the granite cobbles in its middle. Benches surround it. (The only thing that seems not to have been dealt with in it at all is the perennial problem of trash. At present, great green oil drums loom about, badly chipped and without adequate location.) At the Commercial Wharf end of it is a children's play spot with an elaborate wood timber structure that offers clambering adventures of various sorts.

The vaulted arbor is a strong, interesting form, although inherently extravagant. It is made of laminated wood connected with metal straps at all the angles and set on straight, beautifully turned granite columns. The vaulted shape, with its intertwined, lathlike covering, is an appealing idea. After only a short while, roses, wisteria and like climbers at the feet of the granite columns are already well underway, so one can believe that someday this will all be covered with vines. Until it does get covered, it remains unsettling to see that this handsome vaulted structure of bleached wood requires virtually as much steel strap as wood to hold it together; it's a little too much like a Victorian corset.

The lighting fixtures, nicely designed lanterns that are not simply plastic balls on aluminum sticks, are also worthy of note. They have a carefully contoured metal casing that is recollective of the more complicated structure of older gas lanterns without being a trivial copy of previous shapes.

The park was intended to be a mini-arboretum, so there is an extensive variety of plants. The built elements are all well crafted with fine materials that bespeak the city's investment in an area that is meant to serve its citizens for a very long time. It has the determined quality appropriate to the city's most definitive front.

And the people scene here is terrific.

I E 9 · MERCANTILE WHARF
Atlantic Avenue between Cross and Richmond streets
Gridley J. Fox Bryant, 1857
reuse: John Sharatt and Associates, 1976

Mercantile Wharf is another great granite warehousing palace, its exterior more like the originals than any of the others now are. Its large gable roof has been retained, elaborated by projecting ridges and an array of skylight openings to let light and air into the upper floors. From the outside it's a severe, careful building that has been dealt with severely, and it all works.

Inside, the middle has been hollowed to make a six-story atrium space with light filtering down from above, access balconies all around and an elevator in the center. Inherently it's a great space, but one whose designer has simply not had a grand enough vision of what to do with it. The bottom is covered by geometric planting beds that are neither interesting nor appropriate.

I E 9 · *Mercantile Wharf*

I E 10 · COLUMBUS PLAZA ELDERLY HOUSING
Atlantic Avenue between Richmond Street and Commercial Wharf South
Mintz Associates, 1977

Designing housing to fit between two buildings as vigorous and stern as Mercantile Wharf (I E 9) and Commercial Wharf (I E 11) is no easy trick. The architects here have chosen to play it very straight. On the waterfront side, the building is a fully regular block, with large windows filling a brick-faced matrix, interrupted only by equally regular paired balconies and one greenhouse-fronted common room. The sense that it's a warehouse for the elderly keeps hovering on the edge of the mind, but it comes off finally as unassuming, a background building in the sense that our attention turns readily to the earlier buildings on either side. Its red brick and painted metal trim avoid, though, the self-denial that usually characterizes buildings that are slated for a supporting role in the urban scene.

On the Commercial Street side, the building livens up a bit but, again, out of consideration for the site. The corner is left open to make an ample plaza that casts some much-needed light into Commercial Street and allows more extensive views of the Mercantile Wharf building (I E 9) and the similar Commercial Block

I E 10 · *Columbus Plaza Elderly Housing*

across the way. It's not clear, it must be admitted, if the plaza does much more than that, though it may provide a more neighborly meeting and resting place than Waterfront Park (I E 8) across Atlantic Avenue, the latter being almost always filled with people from all over town.

The back side of the plaza is separated from an inner court that is more exclusively the domain of the elderly, for whom this project was built. The separation is made by a change of grade and a big but spare concrete beam over columns that frame the spaces. The inside court is perhaps overwrought, but it does provide for various games and activities and a sense of a special place outdoors.

I E 11 · COMMERCIAL WHARF
east of Atlantic Avenue
Isaiah Rogers, c. 1833
reuse: Halasz & Halasz, 1968–69

Commercial Wharf, like its younger sibling the Custom House block, is two-faced: Charlestown brick on the north side and Quincy granite on the south. The block that now bears the name is only the harbor end of a much longer block that was severed by Atlantic Avenue when it was cut through in 1868. The severed end of the waterside building is marked by a clumsy and disfiguring mansard-roof patch, but the restored granite façade of Commercial Wharf West (I E 12) provides a semblance of continuity for the two ends of the building on either side of Atlantic Avenue.

The sweeping gable roof that runs out along the wharf was originally broken only by small dormers and a row of chimneys at its peak. It was as relentless as the uniform façade. The face of the building simply had no variation save a slightly wider spacing between each set of three windows to mark the presence of bearing walls perpendicular to the face. A stringcourse and larger blocks of granite paced off a wider set of openings at the wharf level. Over time this uniform matrix of building has undergone a number of transformations, principally in the roof and the lower two floors. The roof accumulated an extra story at irregular points along its length, and in several places steel lintels spanning the width of the bay were set into the wall below the third floor to make possible two stories of shop-front infill.

Halasz & Halasz, in renovating the building for residential and commercial use, adopted the syncopated pattern already established by these renovations and added their own modifications. Where roof spaces had not yet been made livable, they cut inverse dormers into the slope, with small-paned French doors set a few feet back from the edge to make a diminutive deck and a low, flat-roofed projection above the roof slope to accommodate the door height. Where two-story sections of remodeled frontage existed, the architects substituted an infill of siding painted white and small-paned casements framing upright picture windows in the center.

I E 11 · *Commercial Wharf*

The spirit of renovation in this building is gentler than perhaps any other in Boston. The architects did not systematically change everything either to its original state or to some new state; there is a very pleasing balance of consistency and special adjustment. This is neither as obsessive as the more conservative renovations nor as totally ragged as wharf buildings have become when left completely to ad hoc development.

Significantly, the building does not have a great deal of presence as a building —it does not announce itself much. It is, rather, a very pleasant, believable bit of inhabited townscape. All the better to live with.

I E 12 · COMMERCIAL WHARF WEST
Isaiah Rogers, 1834
reuse: Anderson, Notter Associates, 1971
· COMMERCIAL WHARF NORTH
1826

The section of Commercial Wharf that is inland from Atlantic Avenue has been renovated more recently and is rather heavier and more systematic than the section to waterside. I think it is therefore less successful, even though very carefully done.

With the Rusty Scupper Restaurant on the ground floor and the Scandinavian Design showrooms on the upper floor, the south face of this building has some long lintels that are actually stucco-faced steel spanning two stories of wood-and-glass infill underneath. The top of the building has a set of wing walls for private gardens and an inset roof deck of the sort that is common in renovations of this kind of building. The original granite façade has a slightly rusticated surface, but is trimmed smooth around the windows. At the top floor the granite window casings run up into a very plain architrave that goes the entire length of the building and serves as the top trim for the windows. At the far end of Commercial Wharf West, the original windows of the second floor are still present. They are nobly proportioned, about eight feet high, and trimmed.

Where Commercial Wharf West meets Commercial Street, the original façade has not been afflicted by any later widenings or enlargements of the openings. It has a very beautiful pilastered entry in the center with a rectangular window above; a clock is set into a square panel above it. To either side are curious and marvelous stripped-down Classical orders, wonderful examples of the Classical vocabulary reduced to the minimal essence of base, upright and cap. These are topped by a very small bit of implied pediment. Quarter circles face out on each end, recollective of the acroteria that graced the corners of Greek porticos. As a final little twist, the north end of this façade has a small, very graceful curved piece that causes the building to face Lewis Street.

Commercial Wharf North, which runs along the north side of the building, has recently had an extensive bit of urban landscaping done to it—of the sort that I think is a great mistake. It has been made rustic, rather than tough and urban, the way this part of town really is.

On the opposite side of Commercial Wharf North is a small brick building that has a very nice alternation of small windows and large openings. The latter, which were originally for bringing in goods, have segmental arched tops to span the larger openings required for the hoisting and loading of bulk, and also have granite sills to resist bumping. These openings have now been made into large windows, some of them still retaining hoists at their tops.

The alternating large and small windows can be read either as a linear sequence or as a series of groupings. A slight variant in the pattern makes it soft and animated as you look down the little street, and the rhythm is particularly beguiling because it is a direct response to the way the building was made and used.

I E 13 · COMMERCIAL STREET
from Richmond Street to Atlantic Avenue

Commercial Street was built to run along the north edge of Town Cove from the Faneuil Hall Markets (I D 5). Many of the buildings along the street today have been preserved and accurately represent early-nineteenth-century commercial architecture in Boston. Mixed in with these are brick row houses, several recently renovated, usually with a granite base that was part of the original system. The tops of these buildings have been modified and adjusted to accommodate sky-lights, decks, bays and other accouterments of middle-class life in the seventies. In the new brick-infill housing beyond them—170 Commercial Street, at the corner of Lewis Street—a set of precast concrete panels that cover beams and the ends of bearing walls attempts to recall the pattern of granite uprights and beams at the lower floor. Curiously, they are limited to the ends of the bearing walls only and therefore establish a quite different rhythm from the granite posts along the original buildings, despite the apparent effort at continuity. And, unfortunately, the exposed aggregate concrete looks rather more like toffee-coated candy than granite.

Otherwise, 170 Commercial Street is all brick-surfaced. It has little insets and reveals that attempt to break it into bays, and there is a jogging of the roof line that recalls the scale of the original units. Yet these are new buildings, built at one time as a unit, and their uniformity is clear despite the embellishments.

A passage runs through this building to the next street. Off the passage is a narrow, deep internal courtyard animated at the bottom by projecting kitchens, with skylights. The space of the court is geometrically cut up by benches and bricks and planting boxes, and surely receives little sun; still, residents have managed to eke out several little gardens.

It's worth turning from the courtyard of the new buildings to look south down the alleyway that exists between the earlier buildings. This has a really handsome irregular shape tapering outward toward the end, with tiny stoops entering it and old light fixtures marching along one edge. It's all a bit derelict at the present time, but it's really a beautiful space, closed by the faces of the buildings. Just the simple distortions on the wall planes, made by the adjustments of various owners over time, render the alley much more animated than the more regularly shaped courtyard of the new building. Few new regulated spaces come across with the vitality that this simple, strangely made alley does.

Continuing north along Commercial Street is a whole series of renovated buildings that are individually owned and therefore show variations in the way they have been treated, both in the level of care invested and in the degree of obsessiveness about the way the building should look.

At 220–30 Commercial Street is one of Boston's punchier signs—HOWE & BAINBRIDGE, INC.—with well-shaped gold letters on a black relief. This building is appealing because it seems to have been well maintained over a number of years and has never gone through the death and rebirth that so transfigured many of the buildings of the waterfront. It is not encumbered, therefore, by as many mannered juxtapositions of building materials and styles.

The next building to the north at 232 Commercial Street is a renovation of a building from c. 1842 that keeps the granite base but places a set of handsome glass French doors behind it—all of them now shuttered for privacy. The second and third floors are made as panels with wood infill and little planting boxes. Above these is a very large overhanging bay, all in painted white wood, with a funny little shaped railing on the edge and a large glass window looking out into the harbor. This in turn is capped by a hood so large that the whole top of the building becomes a kind of overblown dormer. Gerald Cugini designed this remodel in 1967. It's one of the more interesting and memorable pieces of building form along the waterfront, albeit very assertive.

I E 14 · McLAUGHLIN BUILDING
120 Fulton Street, between Richmond and Lewis streets
c. 1850
reuse: Moritz Bergmeyer, 1979

Boston's finest cast-iron-front building, very intelligently and carefully renewed. The façade is uncommonly delicate, worthy of a canal in Venice. The upper stories consist of banks of person-sized, round arched windows set in cast-iron frames; a thin projecting cornice at each level emphasizes the continuity of the rows. The windows almost touch each other, separated by thin, round colonettes alternating with square piers and filled with glass set in very small panes, radiating in the arches. That it's not in fact Venetian is tipped off by the total uniformity of the façade, with not a moment of hesitation or a pause for aberrant detail.

The ground floor is high, with columns at double the spacing and elliptical arches at their tops. The renovation has placed the new ground-floor wall, carefully made in wood, back from the building's face, so that there is a clear separation of materials and evidence of the differing eras of construction—prefab metal in 1850, handcrafted wood in 1979. This sequence of dates should be suitably perplexing for historical determinists, who would expect to have it the other way around, prefab metal replacing wood.

I E 15 · LEWIS WHARF
east of Atlantic Avenue, near the intersection with Commercial Street
attributed: Richard Bond, 1836–40
reuse: Carl Koch & Associates, 1965–69, 1971

North of Commercial Wharf on Atlantic Avenue is another yacht inlet, a good place to watch people tend to their sailing craft. It is bounded on the north side by Lewis Wharf, built between 1836 and 1840. This is the site of a redevelopment project by Carl Koch Associates that has received a great deal of attention, although not all of the project has been executed. The major advantage of the renovation is that the walls of the original warehouse block have been retained; but the form of the block has been drastically altered. It has been topped by a huge mansard roof that is sloped much more acutely than the original gabled or sloped roof common to the area and to that type of building, and the roof has been covered with black asphalt shingles. Obviously this device makes it possible to add more living space to the building without changing the height of the roof peak, but it is a far less attractive form and has little to do with the forthrightness of the original building. The mansard roof, in turn, has projecting windows dictated by the layout of apartments inside. A really obtrusive and unpleasant penthouse sticks out atop the whole block and bears no relation to anything else, either in the historical fabric of the building or in the additions to it.

Occasional balconies jut out from the granite walls below. These balconies, hanging on the granite surface, are very nicely done, placed in a staggered pattern against the building. The lower ones, especially during the summer, hold furniture, plants and other appealing signs of inhabitation. They are a clear addition made with steel brackets that hold a concrete slab aloft. This way of building is very plausible for a wharf building, in the spirit of the original granite blocks.

The granite ground floor of Lewis Wharf, which has been cleaned more than the rest, shows the really handsome color of the original stone and the scale of the strong five- or six-foot-wide openings, with vertical supports to either side of the doors and thick lintels that span across. The ground surface at the edge of the building has been paved with brick and cobblestone. Planted trees offer some welcome summer shade, and a couple of pieces of enclosed grass are appealing, even though it seems incongruous for the landscaping to be suburbanized in this fantastically urban seaside location. Overall the passage along the south face of Lewis Wharf is extremely pleasant. It has the green to the side, the brick surface underneath that café and restaurant tables can be set on, and the cantilevered balconies, light fixtures and signs that hang out overhead. Together these give the granite façade a real sense of accommodating people in a way that would not have been so if the face of the building had been kept entirely bare.

Over by the boats is the actual working wharf, made rather sensibly with a gravel edge bounded by husky granite bollards with chains, which are kept from swinging by steel pieces in the middle. This is much more successful than the similar edge with cast-iron bollards in Waterfront Park. At the far end is a small garden with a peaceful little fountain that consists of a small round slab with water bubbling out onto a polished surface. It bears an inscription in dedication to Ruth Chamberlain Koch. This simple but uncommon investment of care and sentiment adds dimension to the place.

I E 16 · PRINCE BUILDING
63 Atlantic Avenue, between Commercial Wharf North and Commercial Street
1917
reuse: Anderson, Notter Associates, 1966–69

Across from Lewis Wharf, 63 Atlantic Avenue was once the Prince Macaroni Company. It is one of the earliest apartment-conversion projects of the wharf area. Its architects reveal a pleasantly relaxed attitude about the existing order. The whole does not try very hard to establish any rigorous ordering pattern but derives from a combination of the existing ad hoc factory structure with new pieces inserted within and added to the top of it. The earlier structure was based, essentially, on irregular property lines, and the additions in turn take their cue from the internal structure. It knits together quite successfully as a building, even though it has no resolvable form that you can name. It is rather the aggregation of a set of decisions over time.

The Atlantic Avenue face of the original building is dominated by a set of very large fins that hold up balconies on the new top. These must be wonderful places for looking out to sea. Almost all the front walls of these apartments have been set back and aligned with the orientation of the building's back face. Atlantic Avenue, however, is cut at an angle across the property; therefore, almost all of the apartments have a balcony that is inset more on one side than the other, and the balconies are really caves in the building's face. This lends a great deal of animation to the streetfront; even more so because a few of the apartments have been organized differently, with their front walls parallel to Atlantic Avenue, creating an appealing variance in the thickness of the overall building façade.

The base, a very grim one, is made up of a set of parking levels underneath the building, hidden from view behind curving concrete walls. These walls play the same game of moving a surface behind the façade of the original building, except that the face of the parking structure is curved as well as set back from the street. The treatment of the base level is peculiar, though, because it is essentially unfinished and unfriendly and does not leave any clear trace of what the original façade was like; nor does it utilize a new set of forms that seem to be anything but patching.

On the south side, new walls of wood and glass are set into the existing concrete frame, sometimes with spandrel panels at differing floor heights and an occasional jutting balcony. From the back, on Commercial Street, you can see clearly how messed up the original geometry of this building was and that much of its character derives from the overt juxtaposing of planes that align with the back wall of Commercial Street against those that align with Atlantic Street.

Forming a building geometry out of lines that reflect different directions already found in the site is an idea about architectural organization that has been relatively common in Boston architectural circles, but this is one of the most direct examples. It has produced a building that is awkward but rich, both in connotation and visual incident. The Prince building is so much more adventurous than its Lewis Wharf neighbor that it's hard to believe they were initiated at the same time.

I E 17 · SUNOCO GAS STATION
intersection of Atlantic Avenue and Commercial Street
Anderson, Notter Associates, 1970

Next to the Prince Building is what I think must qualify as North America's most distorted gas station, one caught between two very unusual curving brick walls with sloping roofs. It is an elaborate effort to make a place to tank up seem respectable, but it turns out that the curved brick walls are a much more obtrusive part of the street scene than a little old gas station would have been. This twisted shed stands as a monument to the period's efforts to transform everyday life into dramatic geometry—at the cost of disconnection from conventional ways of building or using things.

I E 18 · UNION WHARF
north of the intersection of Atlantic Avenue and Commercial Street
1846
reuse: Moritz Bergmeyer, 1979

This, one of the most recent conversions along the waterfront, includes renovation of the Union Wharf buildings, built in the mid-nineteenth century, and the construction of twenty-three new town-house units as a mixed residential/office condominium out on the piers. The original granite block is immensely powerful; the new town houses are almost equally timid.

The Atlantic Avenue elevation of the Union Wharf warehouse building is a spare granite wall with trimmed pieces around the windows, set almost flush with the rusticated stonework—a very subtle modification of the surface. A sharp gable at the top has two big pieces of granite, out of which "UNION WHARF" has been carved in blocky letters. In this conversion large roof terraces have been cut into the slope of roof along the sides, making an overall form that merges granitic austerity with aspects of the Hanging Gardens of Babylon.

The new condominiums at the tip of the wharf are obsessively Old Boston—two-story, gable-roofed, brick-faced buildings, arranged as though on an inland alley, with occasional telltale sliding glass doors that reveal their true age, or lack thereof.

I E 19 · LINCOLN WHARF
Atlantic Avenue at Battery Street
1907
reuse: Anderson, Notter Associates, 1981

Along Atlantic Avenue there is now a random mixture of renovation and desolation; the area is very much in transition. At Lincoln Wharf, where North Street, Commercial Street, Atlantic Avenue and Battery Street all come together, there is a major renovation of the old Power House, built in 1907. The work involves modernization of the equipment and the powerhouse, and construction of a switching station out back to supply the additional power needed to run new subway trains.

Lincoln Wharf is a huge building. On its front, two arched windows are each five stories high. A third arch is filled by a decorative brick panel, surmounted by a keystone with a vast copper eagle spreading its wings back against a brick attic. The first floor is set off by a brick line simulating rustication, and there are two simple vehicular entries and one pedimented entry for people, diminutive by comparison with the building.

The side elevation to the north was once really magnificent. Behind the great blunt block at the front there is a more articulated block with a roof and dormers and an implied arcade of two-story windows that stroll along underneath an inscription that reads, "LINCOLN POWER STATION 1907." Suddenly out of this large but fundamentally gentle and civilized side block emerged two gargantuan smokestacks; they were startlingly powerful and massive disruptions to the block of a building that is otherwise treated in a conventionally grand manner. The stacks have recently been reduced to stumps.

Right opposite this looming structure, in startling contrast, is a piece of the North End called Powers Court, a very intimate little alley space with stoops adorned by residents and the language of Sicily filling the air.

II/THE NORTHERN RIM

Acorn Street

A/NORTH END
AND WEST END

The areas north of Government Center and the markets reveal a whole succession of development patterns, each with its own brand of architecture and successive overlays of creation, contradiction, destruction and renewal.

The North End, centered on Hanover Street, has been settled since the beginning of Boston. The bending course of North Street indicates approximately the original shoreline, Salem Street was originally laid out as Back Street, and North Cove was beyond. Copps Hill formed the northernmost extremity then as it does now. With its peninsular form, the North End has always been an enclave of sorts. For the past century and a half it has served as an ethnic compound, first Irish, then Jewish and more recently Italian. It's a distinct section of town, a place with its own character.

North Cove was soon converted to a millpond, which in turn was filled beginning in 1807, according to a plan prepared by Bulfinch. The winding streets of the North End were initially formed by paths. In the Bulfinch plan, streets were rows filling a regular triangle formed by what are now Washington, Causeway and Merrimac streets. The apex was once occupied by market buildings still recalled by an abbreviated and desolate stretch of road named Market Street, although the tip of the triangle now lies under the Government Center Garage (I C 10).

Canal Street, in the middle of the triangle, denotes the water path that ran by its side connecting the market to a section of the river now buried under North Station. Later the straight, converging streets made this an ideal area for the arrival of trains from the north, and in the late nineteenth century the area developed large commercial blocks. It is now scheduled for a major renewal program.

The cove to be filled was not quite so regular as the Bulfinch triangle, and between Salem and Washington streets another set of parallel streets was built over the fill, the most easternly being Margin Street, at the edge of the pond. These streets have a mix of residential and industrial buildings that has been made to seem an integral part of the North End by tenements that are common to both areas and by the enormous wall of the Fitzgerald Expressway as it rises toward the bridge and all points north, severing the triangle beneath it.

The West End, on the other hand, between the triangle and Cambridge Street, bears the marks of urban-renewal strategies from the recent past. As a layout it has no character, an aimless set of streets that wander disconsolately among high and alien buildings, with only the barest traces of a previous world and lots of evidence of the 1960's. The West End started out as the gardens of large houses bordering Bowdoin Square and Cambridge Street. They were filled with tenements by the end of the nineteenth century, and the area was almost totally leveled for urban renewal in the mid-twentieth. Renewal involved massive relocation of communities, the results of which have provided casebook studies in the destructive potential of such moves. Indeed, the West End contributed a full share of the pain that caused a reconsideration of urban-renewal policies in the 1970's.

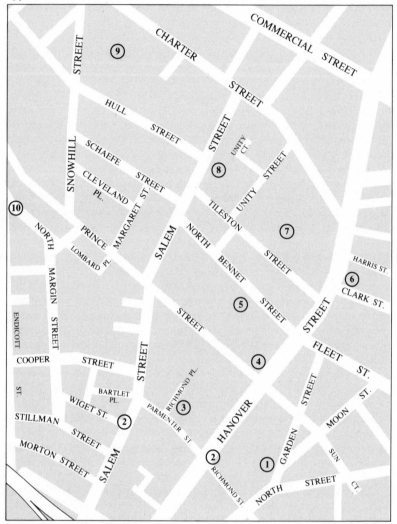

II / THE NORTHERN RIM   A / NORTH END

II A 1 · NORTH SQUARE
· PAUL REVERE HOUSE
19 North Square, between Prince and Richmond streets
c. 1676
reconstruction: Joseph E. Chandler, 1905
· MOSES PIERCE–HICHBORN HOUSE
c. 1711

North Square itself is a perfectly pleasant triangular pocket of space made ridiculous by do-gooders who have surrounded it with heavy chain to proclaim its uselessness and installed a bell, presumably to toll its sanctity as a shrine on the Freedom Trail. The adjoining asphalt playground with trellis and bench is a good bit more appealing. However, the square does provide an important historic comparison in the pairing of two restored structures that show the substantial change in building pattern from the humble type of the early decades of settlement to a more ambitious, clearer pattern in the eighteenth century. Both are open to the public.

The Revere House is no simple seventeenth-century survivor: It had been much deformed by subsequent owners to serve a variety of purposes, including candy manufacturing, we're told. Paul Revere's ownership from 1770 to 1800 led to its reconstruction in 1905. The skin and interior are restored, although the timber structural frame is said to be original. In any case it is our best Boston view into the domestic arrangements of the seventeenth century, with heavy beams inside and mammoth fireplaces. The orderly, visible frame, the small muntin-netted windows and the directly connected rooms vividly convey the sense that in the early years containment against the elements was essential. From the outside the roof overhangs the walls both at the gable and on the street, and the second floor overhangs the first along the street side, with bits of the heavy structural frame exposed underneath. The taut skin of the house is made with narrow boards; heavy shutters stand ready to close the house fully. All the materials are small, crafted with simple tools, and fit together neatly.

The Moses Pierce–Hichborn House is of grander pattern, though still simple, with rooms stacked on either side of a central stair. The rooms on the street side are made very particular and especially pleasant by the angle of the outer wall, which follows the course of the street. The brick walls have segmental arched windows on the lower floors and little windows tucked up against the eave for the attic. The roof is hipped to the two large chimneys along the solid north wall, which perhaps once adjoined other buildings. It's very simple and possessed of genuine elegance.

II A 2 · HANOVER AND SALEM STREETS

The North End is really about streets. It is they more than the buildings that have shape, and the predominantly Italian-American population knows how to use them with verve. The narrow, close-packed streets are heavily peopled, whether in out-of-the-way places, where chairs move out on the sidewalk, or on more trafficked ones, which serve for gathering. Most dramatically, specific streets are commandeered on appropriate dates as the settings for street festivals, each honoring one among many deserving saints. On these occasions the streets are arched over with lights and decoration, and become real public rooms. They are filled with people wall to wall—or, rather, booth to booth—and various festivities and performances take over.

Whereas North Street past North Square curves in a great arc following the original shoreline and sits up just high enough so that you can, when alerted, sense that the land below is fill, Hanover Street runs fairly directly down through the middle of the peninsula that formed the North End and is so densely built now that it's only when you stand in front of St. Stephen's (II A 6) that you can sense the fall of the land at either end of the street and down Clark Street to the

II A 2 · *Hanover Street*

harbor. St. Stephen's plays a dominant role in the streetscape, due not only to its distinguished form, but to its position at the bend in Hanover Street, where it closes the view as you look up the street from the north or south.

The southern reaches of Hanover Street are self-proclaimed Italian, with a string of pastry shops, cafés and restaurants embellished with Italian geographic names and proffering a variety of foods that are indubitably ethnic. There's also an extensive macho scene on the sidewalks outside. There's a bit of pandering to tourism here, but only a very little bit; for the most part it's a scene generated by and for those who live here.

Salem Street marks the other side of the peninsula, and it too curves, though less dramatically than North Street. For most of its southern sections it is lined by meat-and-provisions stores, many of them equipped with roll-down shutters to close up at night as in Italy, though here many of the shutters are painted with scenes of the shop fronts or the goods inside. At the upper end the street is tight, only about 30 feet wide, with four- and five-story buildings on either side. It's an intimate, believable Italian scene inhabited more by older women doing real shopping than by the lounging, wiseacre crowd. At Prince Street, Salem Street jogs sharply and begins to climb uphill. The intersection is an excellent bit of townscape, with the Prince Street buildings closing the view up Salem Street from below or down Salem Street from the hill above. This configuration, combined with the activity of genuine shops all around, makes this one of the most distinctive spots in the city.

II A 3 · BOSTON PUBLIC LIBRARY, NORTH END BRANCH
25 Parmenter Street, between Hanover and Salem streets
Carl Koch & Associates, 1965

There is a string of reasons for visiting this building, not the least of which is that it's so marvelously strange. It is free-standing and singular in a territory of connected, undistinguished buildings, and it is possessed of an exotic air, tinged with the aura of artistic excitement, though clearly within the sober-sided modernism of the early sixties. When the relentless progress of architectural connoisseurship brings enthusiasts to a nostalgic interest in the sixties, this building will be waiting for them. It's a particularly telling example of the efforts to give local character to an architecture that is otherwise rooted in technical determinism.

Like the addition to the Boston Public Library in Copley Square (III C 5), the plan of this branch is nine squares, the middle one serving as focal point. Only here the squares are each covered by a double-curved concrete vault springing like an umbrella from a column standing in its middle. The middle vault is raised up higher than the rest to allow light to penetrate the center. Since the entire structure is internalized, the exterior wall bears no weight, so it is designed as a screen with clerestory windows all around to demonstrate airiness as much as to let light into the vaults and reading areas. The brick wall outside is interrupted periodically by projecting panels and curiously crafted tiles that do much to form the exotic air, even though they seem intended to refer to Classical motifs. They are like the decorative personal treasures sometimes found embedded in the walls of folk architecture. Tiles at the corners of each vault lift the roof silhouette slightly at the ends and lend an oriental tone that is most likely unintended.

The middle space forms a quite nice diminutive inner atrium with a cobbled surface, big plants and a fountain gurgling quietly around the base of the central column. The interior is carefully made, with Philippine mahogany panels and bookshelves that mark subdivisions of the space and line the walls, topped by a simple wooden cornice light piece that throws indirect light up onto the ceiling to supplement that from the clerestory. The original furnishings are still in the children's area—open metalwork Bertoia chairs that are lightweight and shaped from double curves, as the vaults are. It's all very carefully attended to, with real conviction about making things to specific purpose and with fresh technology.

Two other good reasons for visiting the place are a fine marble plaque carved by Luciano Campise and given to the library by the Boston branch of the Dante Alighieri Society in 1913, and a most astonishing 14-foot-long plaster model of the Doge's palace in Venice, animated by painted backgrounds and doll figures depicting, we are told, scenes of the sixteenth century. The model was made by Miss Henrietta Macy, an expatriate spinster, who once taught kids in the North End. Constructing the model was the passion of her later life in Venice. It was presented to the library on her death. The setting and clever figures were made by Louise Stimson of Concord.

II A 4 · ST. LEONARD'S CHURCH
Prince Street, between Hanover and Salem streets
William Holmes, 1891

Set back from Hanover Street behind a "Peace Garden" of flowers and statuary, St. Leonard's may be entered from the side through a door that would be unimportant were it not for this garden approach. The church is startlingly vivid inside, a place that breathes with a sense of immediacy, though not so much through the architecture as through the intensely painted saints, cherubim and trim that are rendered in a manner much closer to popular culture than the refined decorum of ecclesiastical art has generally allowed. The form of the building makes this preeminence of figurative images possible by being itself uneventful. The wide nave and small side aisles are of Renaissance derivation, but the walls of the nave practically dissolve in cross vaults, clerestory windows and an abundance of sculpture around the periphery.

The façade along Prince Street is a very pleasant, modestly scaled assembly of arches and turrets that pile up asymmetrically to a tower on the north side.

II A 5 · NORTH BENNET STREET BATHHOUSE
North Bennet Street, between Salem and Hanover streets
McGinnis, Walsh & Sullivan, 1906

A building of exceptional exterior grace that is surviving severe treatment, the bathhouse sits as part of a complex of schools and a playground amid, it seems, an army of spray-paint graffiti-makers. Unwittingly, perhaps, it's perfectly set up to prevail, even under the circumstances. The red-brick block is organized handsomely into three levels capped by a richly modeled copper cornice. The lowest level is a head-height band of terra cotta that has been appropriated as a billboard for neighborhood notices and inflated autographs. At the south end it is shaped into a set of benches and steps that reach out to frame the approach to a projecting vaulted entry, roofed in copper and faced with a round-arch pediment. The entry seems not to be in use now, but the steps and benches definitely are.

The second level is very simple—brick with windows interspersed easily and virtually no trim. The third level commands the rest, with large windows organized into patterns of Florentine grace by pilasters and bandings of molded terra cotta. These windows are so large and sharply delineated, yet with a delicate hand, that they convey a sense of civic purpose, of the shaping of light and space for common use. They carry a vision that rides literally and figuratively above the petty, angry turfing imposed by the paint-can legion.

II A 6 · ST. STEPHEN'S CHURCH
Hanover Street, between Harris and Clark streets, opposite
  Paul Revere Mall
Charles Bulfinch, 1802–04
restoration: Chester Wright, 1965

Like many other churches in Boston, this splendid brick building has served several congregations. It was built first for the Congregational Society and dubbed New North, was later used by the Unitarians, and finally, in 1862, was purchased by the Catholic diocese in consequence of the major shifts in population that had taken place in the North End. The building was shifted about on its foundations, too—enough to shatter the beliefs of anyone who thinks of brick as immutable. First, for the Catholics, it was raised several feet to allow a lower-level chapel to be placed underneath it, and the whole was refurbished in the ecclesiastical garb of the period. Then in 1965, in a gesture of respect for its early history, it was lowered again to its original level and restored to the Bulfinch design.

St. Stephen's now stands very elegantly in the bend of Hanover Street facing the Paul Revere Mall; it sustains our admiration in either oblique or frontal view. The front of the building is almost a separate building from the gable-roofed bulk

II A 5 · *North Bennet Street Bathhouse*   II A 6 · *St. Stephen's Church*

of the church behind. The front block contains an entry vestibule and stairs and is in the general shape of a Roman triumphal arch, a narrow, high, rectangular volume nearly square in front elevation and measured out by applied Classical orders, pairs of pilasters to either side and a wide panel in the center with a broad arch in the middle of the upper story. The tower rises above this central section. A white-painted wooden balustrade is banded across the whole face of the building, dividing it into two stories and creating a curious, charming ambivalence between the two. Below this band the carved wooden pilasters, capitals and architraves are richly modeled and authoritative. Above in the second stage the forms are much more reticent.

The building is spare, even austere, in the body of the block, then gently complex in the tower, with a grand open cupola sheltering a bell. The broad shoulders of the façade have shallow hip roofs at either end. From the front they are shielded by two big voluptuous wooden volutes atop the cornice, each supporting a large carved wooden urn. These practically steal the show.

The forms of Classical architecture are used here with the casual freedom of the provinces. They lend dignity to the occasion, but do not inhibit invention.

Inside, a delicate two-stage white wooden colonnade holds a balcony on three sides and a very shallow vaulted roof. There's little sense in this broad room of the transfer of weight, but an ample portion of sustained elegance. Most splendid of all, even if they're not original, are chandeliers made of beautifully looped arms radiating out in three stages from a central stalk of graduated globes and rings.

II A 7 · PAUL REVERE MALL
between Hanover and Unity streets
Arthur Shurcliff, 1933

Sometimes referred to as "the Prado," this open space is a perfectly wonderful anomaly. With a clear townscape figure at each end of the space, brick walls and rows of trees that decisively shape the space itself, and a floor articulated in brick paving with concrete banding, this is an outdoor room more definitively independent of bordering building forms than any other in Boston.

St. Stephen's (II A 6) forms the focus at one end of the long narrow space, the tower of "Old North" (II A 8) stands at the other. In joining these two landmarks together, the mall makes life easier for the Freedom Trail pilgrims and establishes a wonderful place of repose, with shade trees, checkerboards and benches, a central fountain (ill-cared for, like others in Boston) and an equestrian statue of Paul Revere cast by Cyrus E. Dallin in 1935. The statute, alas, is a bit comic. Revere stares down at us from his elegantly bred horse high on a marble pedestal as though he had nothing to do but transfix passing tourists with his commanding gaze.

The mall presents the two churches in a mode closer to the spirit of Baroque Rome—with monuments at the end of oblique vistas—than to any effect the churches would have had in their original dispositions freestanding on the hill or in their subsequent enclosure among rows of continuous brick tenements. This viable urban park has added dimension to the place and has itself been made more interesting by the circumstantial adjustments needed to carve this public space out of the irregular building lots through which it passes. As instance of the latter, the mall ends to the north in a small set of stairs that front the Clough House of about 1712 to one side, while a narrow passage leads up past the rear of Old North Church to the entrance on Salem Street. Formalists may consider irregularities of this sort perverse, but the Paul Revere Mall is a place of real character and distinction.

II A 8 · *Christ Church ("Old North")*

II A 8 · CHRIST CHURCH (OLD NORTH)
193 Salem Street, opposite Hull Street
William Price, 1723

The presumption that Longfellow's famous "One if by land, and two if by sea" midnight lanterns were hung in this steeple has led millions of tourists along Boston's Freedom Trail to "Old North." It has a picturesque attenuated spire, and the tale of Paul Revere is surely worth honoring, but the real treat of this church is the quality of light and space inside. A soft, mellow glow fills the white interior with a gentle aura of serenity. This is not all due to the architect's ingenuity; in large measure it is a result of the later close-fitting surrounds. Courtyards bordered by brick buildings on all sides capture the sunlight, filter it through trees and reflect modified light into the space of the church. Once there, the light is well modulated by being reflected off the underside of cross vaults above the balconies, or off the sloped underside of the balcony structure itself.

The lofty main space of the church is covered by a segment of elliptical vault hung from the roof trusses. At the end of the church is a very simple, high, half-round apse. In front and to one side of this a shapely pulpit holds the preacher, his person ennobled and his voice reflected by a gently molded hanging canopy.

Christ Church is the oldest church in town and bears inscriptions that speak more eloquently than most historians of the sea ventures and the tangled loyalties that characterized a colony about to be caught up in revolution. They were especially tangled here because Old North was an Episcopalian parish with strong ties to England and many loyalist parishioners. The inscribed bits of dedicatory chronicle are continued outside on the walls of a beautiful brick courtyard to the north.

II A 9 · COPP'S HILL BURYING GROUND
between Hull and Charter streets
· COPP'S HILL TERRACE
between Charter and Commercial streets

Copp's Hill is the highest and northernmost section of the North End, its summit secured by the second oldest cemetery in Boston (established in 1660). The gentle slopes and modest headstones reveal the natural topography of the place and call to mind the fragility of the first settlements here.

From the north edge of Copp's Hill are views of Charlestown, Chelsea and East Boston. Charlestown is the location that Winthrop and his fellow Puritans forsook for the Shawmut Peninsula. Nonetheless, it became an important settlement and has figured decisively in the history of Boston. The Bunker Hill Monument is its most prominent landmark. Construction of that great granite shaft by Solomon Willard during the years 1825–43 did much to develop the technology of quarrying and transporting granite. It therefore accounts in part for the great number of fine granite buildings constructed in Boston during the same and ensuing years. The Charlestown Naval Yard, now undergoing reconstruction, has a noteworthy group of regimented buildings from the early nineteenth century, when it was an active shipbuilding enterprise.

Copp's Hill Terrace provides a view of these and of the harbor, as well as some pleasant trees and a much beleaguered but graceful loggia. Best of all, however, is a magnificent set of stairs and stone walls that descends in varied stages to Commercial Street. The massive stone walls that frame this stair make it as forceful as a geological feature; the stair's gradual descent dramatizes the slope of the land. It also makes a path filled with opportunities to stop and to be, to survey the surrounds, to linger in conversation or simply to change pace in climbing up or down the hill. It would be a place of exceptional grace if only the hoods would stop vandalizing it.

II A 10 · ALFRED WISNISKI SQUARE
intersection of Endicott and North Margin streets

The odd intersection of streets named Wisniski Square is important as a vantage point for seeing other places and recognizing things about the city. From this point the various street patterns of Boston are particularly clear, and a social history is embedded in the names of the surroundings.

Endicott and Margin streets are part of the landfill. They are outside but for the most part parallel to the triangle of land laid out by Bulfinch, of which Washington Street is the eastern boundary. From Wisniski Square, Endicott Street runs south straight and flat to downtown, bordered on each side by very simple tenement buildings with a regular rhythm of double-hung windows and little else but brick and an occasional bay window tacked on the surface. The tall, prestigious towers of downtown stand in startling contrast to these, separated from them by the Great Wall of the elevated section of Route 1 as it climbs toward the bridges that will take it across the Charles and Mystic rivers. In equally sharp but opposite contrast are the little streets and courts opening directly off the square to the west, north and east. These small pockets of open space and curtailed street, in which every outlook is closed by buildings, are remnants of the intersection of abstract plan with natural topography. There's a resemblance to medieval European townscape, and the short, densely packed and angled streets are not unlike those of eighteenth-century Boston, even though the buildings are taller.

"Margin Street" refers to its position along the edge of the one-time boundary between land and millpond. "Endicott" is one of the early Boston families, with a continuing position of civic preeminence. "MCLAUGHLIN BUILDING 1875," inscribed in stone on a building facing the square, attests to the commercial prowess of a later generation of residents. And most probably there will be a poster in view somewhere, urging support for a current local politician with an Italian surname. The name "Alfred Wisniski" itself, attached to the square as a war memorial, brings to mind the sacrifices of still another group of immigrants, as do many other street plaques throughout the city, mostly bearing names of Central European origin.

II A 10 · *Alfred Wisniski Square*

II A 12 · *170–74 Portland Street*

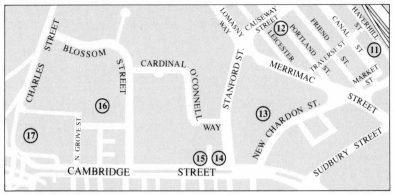

II A 11 · 53–85 CANAL STREET
between Market and Traverse streets
F. A. Norcross, 1916

In the Bulfinch triangle scheme, a canal dutifully followed Canal Street, connecting the markets at the apex of the triangle to the harbor at the base. The canal has long since disappeared and the street now leads forthrightly to nowhere. It is terminated at one end by the hulk of North Station and the elevated, and blocked at the other by wide new roads circumventing the Government Center Garage. Parallel and to the east are rail lines and highway bridges.

This long, low set of buildings remains committed to the street, following it with eye-catching terra-cotta ornament, asking to be reconsidered as the inception of some more lively future for this enclave of streets. The first steps would include new construction that would fill out the boundaries of the street, confining the space of Canal Street to something of more limited size. At present these buildings bring a slim suggestion of human scale to the edges of that special, awful emptiness that is often found next to a transportation corridor.

II A 12 · 170–74 PORTLAND STREET
between Traverse and Causeway streets
Stephen Codman, 1897
· 210 PORTLAND STREET/5 CAUSEWAY STREET
SW corner Portland and Causeway streets
H. W. Hartwell & W. C. Richardson, 1888–92

Two buildings of exceptional merit, each a splendid effort to make stacks of commercial loft space into a building that reads as an integral whole. That on the corner of Causeway and Portland streets is the grander and more suitably emulated; the other is stranger, more peculiarly imagined.

The corner building is magnificent, the most powerful of several buildings in Boston that follow the general scheme made famous by Richardson's Marshall Field Warehouse in Chicago, with beautiful high brick arches gathering several floors of windows in their rise, topped by an attic of rectangular openings. Here, though, the scheme changes on the side, with arches of varying size and disposition reflecting differences in the space use behind. The scale is majestic, the rhythm of openings engagingly varied, the streetscape altogether worthy. Alas, recent brutal renovations on the lower floors and sexpot neighbors have joined with the elevated rail lines to obscure the building's dignity.

The other, at 170–74 Portland Street, is a wonderful rare bird, a curious mix of the tall building verticality that Sullivan championed, also in Chicago, and a hankering for Classical form. Sharply delineated vertical piers rise abruptly from the first-floor commercial base to a deep sixth-floor cornice. At the top floor the piers swell sufficiently to terminate the shafts. In the act the tops acquire the supple rhythms of an upright human body, suggestive of the caryatid figures that sometimes stand in for columns in Greece, but modeled here in abstract rhythms more akin to Art Nouveau. To one side the stair and elevator shaft are marked by a more solid wall with the building entrance at the bottom and a sensuously shaped elliptical window at the top.

II A 13 · HEALTH, WELFARE AND EDUCATION SERVICE CENTER FOR THE COMMONWEALTH OF MASSACHUSETTS
bounded by Stanford, Merrimac, New Chardon and Cambridge streets
Paul Rudolph, coordinating architect; Shepley, Bulfinch, Richardson & Abbott; with Pedersen & Tilney, M. A. Dyer and Desmond & Lord, 1970

This building, or set of buildings, is astonishing in many ways. It is clearly one place, yet it is the work of several firms following the design leadership of one. That in itself is uncommon. It is a building of exceptional architectural ambition built for the state. That makes it exceptional in this century, as the two other state office buildings just up Bowdoin Street will immediately show. It is massive and shapely, imaginative, technically ingenious, sometimes gratuitously graceful, alternately comfortable and overpowering (mostly overpowering). And it is unfinished.

Rudolph earned the leadership of this enterprise; it wasn't ordained. Three firms had been initially hired to do three separate buildings. During the design-review meetings held by the Boston Redevelopment Authority to give some semblance of order to the group, Rudolph brought forth a scheme joining them into one consolidated design with a building that curled around the site to make a great plaza in front of a heavily sculpted tower. The group accepted the scheme and proceeded with a coordinated design effort that bears marks of Rudolph's authorship throughout.

The gaping hole at one end was not part of the scheme. Unhappily the tower, sculptural focus of the complex, could not be built as designed within the budget, and after several tries that section of the project seems to have been abandoned. Here, of course, is the nub of the problem with schemes that attempt a totally unified design on a large scale. Emplanting a singular vision on a whole sector of the city leaves little room for the vicissitudes of economic and political life, for adjustment to changes in priorities and funding, or for the escalation of costs.

The complex is at its smallest and simplest along Cambridge Street, where it plays a rather sedate neighbor to Old West Church and forms a sheltering colonnade for a pleasant set of south-facing benches on a little plaza. It is smallest here because the site narrows and rises to this corner, so the uniform cornice height that surrounds the complex is here a modest five floors above the sidewalk.

It's simplest because the great fluted concrete fins that structure the building and give measure to its form rise on this façade directly to the blank attic wall, with the floors below set back from the face in a simple progression. Each floor bears a different relationship to the pier, the lowest set way back to emphasize the scale of the supporting elements, the highest intersecting the pier near its front. The whole is more comprehensible than intriguing, and appropriately so. The latent Classical order has a comfortably familiar sense and is at this size not more than a little pompous.

The plaza inside is bare in the way that the tops of parking structures almost inevitably become. The building steps away on the west and north, so that mass is low and measurable around the edge. These sections of the building are also held on aggressively textured concrete fins, but between the fins deep concrete sunshades shield walls that are otherwise nearly all glass. The light bounces around among these sunshades in a manner that diminishes the apparent heaviness of the whole structure, but there is a superabundance of concrete. The concrete plaza surface and surrounding buildings make a field of vision filled with a single material variously textured and sunned, but perhaps more comforting to Italian hill-town aficionados than to the unemployed who use the building perforce.

It is at the far northern end that the building becomes unequivocally overpowering. There, where the land has dropped away from the constant cornice line all around, the building is a couple of stories higher, and a large segment of the structure bridges over a void that connects a large, cold, north-facing plaza at the intersection of Merrimac and Stanford streets with the center's plaza inside the ring, several levels above. Passage between the two is via an elegantly attenuated, rhythmically paced curving exterior stair that would serve better in a Fred Astaire extravaganza. It descends through the space among piers, bridges and still crazier stairs heading elsewhere, in a spatial sequence that is at times literally dizzying. If you can keep track of where you're going, you'll almost certainly swing out at the bottom in a gliding step with your fingers snapping —though your clothes may be a bit tattered by the rough concrete.

The building is a genuinely astonishing performance but one that finally and sadly makes the people who use it seem clumsy, frail and incongruous.

II A 13 · *Massachusetts Health, Welfare and Education Service Center*

II A 14 and 15 · *Old West Church with the first Harrison Gray Otis House (left)*

II A 14 · OLD WEST CHURCH
Cambridge Street, opposite Hancock Street
Asher Benjamin, 1806

Old West is in the same genre as St. Stephen's (II A 6): a squarish meeting house with a rectangular block in front that rises up in several stages to a square-plan cupola.

The stages here are indicated in the arrangement of the brick facade, not in the mass. The first two floors are giant-order brick piers, the third is elaborated by wood pilasters and architraves arranged in pairs. The final stage, an attic wall, has an amalgam of windows, clock, pilasters and brick recesses.

The front is more attenuated and less graceful than its predecessor—more the forerunner of all those early high-rise buildings that attempted to deal with height by simply stacking up successive types and sizes of Classical motifs, one upon another. It has a certain charm, but it is entirely possible to imagine that its top and bottom were independently conceived.

Inside, it's a big square hall with a balcony running around three sides, very much a place for congregating. A large circle with a plaster-molded green fret inscribed in the ceiling emphasizes the centrality of the space, and the galleries are held by light-handed columns that have strangely attenuated acanthus-leaf capitals. Greek motifs, Congregationalist sensibility.

The contrast of this simple, fine and comfortable decorated brick box with the complexities of the HWE complex (II A 13) across the street illustrates how vastly different was the scope of their architects' tasks.

II A 15 · FIRST HARRISON GRAY OTIS HOUSE
141 Cambridge Street, opposite Hancock Street
Charles Bulfinch, 1796

This is the first in a series of three houses that Bulfinch designed for Harrison Gray Otis, one of the greatest land speculators in early Boston and a distinguished cultivator of architecture.

The front of the house is a simple block with a shallow hip roof and symmetrically arranged façade, ennobled by a very simple, austere set of architectural devices. The front entry has a shallow elliptical fanlight with narrow sidelights at either side but no sheltering porch. A small Palladian motif at the stair landing, differently proportioned, maintains the central emphasis at the second floor, while above in the attic is another fanlight, this one semicircular. In all, it's a distinguished building, but more a paper design with motifs separately conceived than an integral building of real parts.

Now the headquarters of the Society for the Preservation of New England Antiquities, which runs tours of the interior, this house is your best chance to step inside the last years of eighteenth-century Boston.

It's also worth taking a look at the Otis House—along with its next-door neighbor, the Old West Church (II A 14)—from halfway up Hancock Street. From this vantage point, it is framed by row houses. You get an inkling of an earlier era without being overwhelmed by the new development all around. Of course, you're immediately conscious of the giant blocks in the distance—the West End redevelopment project—but they are so separate and alien that it is easy to conjure up an early-nineteenth-century street scene in the foreground.

The second (II B 6) and third (II B 15) Harrison Gray Otis Houses are nearby on Beacon Hill.

II A 16 · MASSACHUSETTS GENERAL HOSPITAL
N. Grove Street, off Cambridge Street
· WHITE BUILDING
Coolidge, Shepley, Bulfinch & Abbott, 1943
· BULFINCH PAVILION
east of Blossom Street, north of Parkman Street
Charles Bulfinch, 1816–21

To reach the Bulfinch Pavilion in the Massachusetts General Hospital, head first for the White Building, a gray late Art Deco building with towering bays and symmetrical composition that serves as main entrance to the hospital. Then ask directions. The Mass General complex is a city of its own, with a maze of corridors, an incredible array of technological devices and a network of clinics, service rooms and so on. It consists of a string of separate buildings, all interconnected in that endlessly puzzling way that characterizes the modern hospital and makes medicine seem to be a particularly involved branch of traffic engineering, intravenous tubes and all.

It takes a little persistence, but whatever you do, don't miss the Bulfinch building. This, more than most others, is a building that evokes belief.

Stay with it awhile. Ignore the towering disrespect that engulfs it. Attend to its fine proportions, to the sizes of windows and the way the granite is placed, to the parts that are so clear, mostly unadorned and strictly formal.

Walk up one of the paired stairs and sense the portico sheltering entries on either side. Or stand back to absorb the power of its central cubic block that penetrates the gable to hold aloft a shallow dome, with four chimneys standing sentinel at the corners. The whole is so confident, the parts so refined and

II A 16 · *Massachusetts General Hospital, with the Bulfinch Pavilion (lower right)*

rational, the sizes of things so pertinent to the human body, that one can remember the hopefulness of Science, child of the Age of Reason.

The special splendor of this building undoubtedly owes something to the circumstances of its building. It was designed by Bulfinch just before his departure for Washington to work on the United States Capitol. Supervision of the pavilion's construction was taken over by Alexander Parris, and the building shows the attributes of both: the clarity and grace of conception expected of Bulfinch and the intensely rational building sense that Parris later brought to bear on the Faneuil Hall Markets.

Shift focus to the surrounding buildings and you will be brought back to the expedient indignities that attend the delivery of technological medicine. Fortunately, the effects of ether were first demonstrated in the domed operating theater at the top of the Bulfinch Pavilion, and this bit of medical history has probably done more to preserve the building from destruction or alteration than all its visible dignity.

II A 17 · CHARLES STREET JAIL
Charles Street, north of Cambridge Street
Gridley J. Fox Bryant, 1851

The Charles Street Jail was built 30 years after the Bulfinch Pavilion of Massachusetts General Hospital. The difference in spirit is telling.

Bulfinch called forth, in the pavilion, a vision of Reason and Enlightenment, order based on the dignity of human achievement. Bryant's jail is just as firmly related to the utilitarian. It is no coincidence that this work is by an architect who excelled in the design of warehouse buildings and commercial structures. Bryant was acclaimed, though, for his public buildings, including 35 other jails and courthouses and half again as many seats of government, ranging from a set of state capitols to Boston's own Old City Hall (I A 8), where a little help from Arthur Gilman added grace.

The Charles Street Jail is a relatively early work. Like his warehouses, it's a building that does its business—in this case guarding prisoners—in a direct and uncompromising way. A bit of enthusiastic wall patterning that collects windows into great arches is added for civic pride, and to amplify the stern effect the granite is heavily rusticated. A lantern once capped the roof of the bold octagonal middle section, from which wings extend in four directions. The west wing reaches out to Charles Street to hold an entrance; pretty nicely at that.

B/BEACON HILL

Beacon Hill is a place to get lost in. (Some say there are residents who have done so for years.) It's a world unto itself, one that is richly varied, yet uncommonly consistent in scale, materials and building types. It is varied in detail, topography and street layout. Each street has a distinct character, each building type is made in a way that visibly makes sense.

There is a standard set of materials used here: brick walls on a granite base, wood trim in the form of shutters, bays and door surrounds. The wood is usually painted either a cream color or black, and the sidewalk is red brick, like the walls.

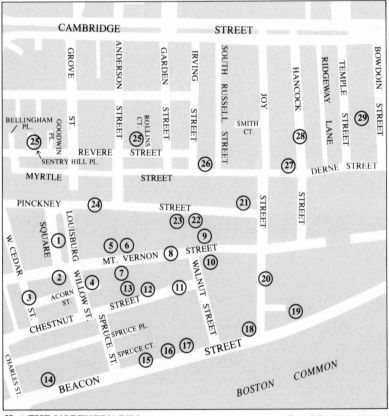

II / THE NORTHERN RIM   B / BEACON HILL

To speak only of the consistency of materials, however, is to miss the point. The real charm of these buildings is that each of the characteristic parts is suited to its particular purpose. Wood is used where precision is required, to fit pieces of glass into the wall for windows or to be carved with the refined emblems of hospitality at the entrance. Often the wood is set back from the surface of the brick, painted and protected from the weather. In later buildings or in bay-window additions, wood is used to create ancillary structures, projecting out beyond the line of masonry walls in shapes that the rigors of brick would not easily allow. Stone is used where the units of brick are too small to be useful, to span gaps in the brick wall as lintels for doors and windows or, most importantly, to join the ground as steps or foundation. Large, tough granite blocks rise from the ground, their tops struck level to create the flatness that floors require, their depths absorbing the slope of the ground around them—eloquent testimony that to build is to give human structure to the land.

In counterpoint, thin, sinuous metal handrails frequently wind out from the porches and inset entries onto the building face, sometimes even extending along a wall to help people negotiate the slope.

The incline of the hill, though treacherous for the pedestrian in winter, has distinct visual advantages, providing telling juxtapositions of view. Close, tight buildings are seen against a far glimpse of the Charles River below or the Common or the State House up the hill. There are middle-ground views of the flat surface of Charles Street at the foot of the hill, an obvious gathering place with its shops, Meeting House and traffic. And fitting each house to the incline establishes a recurrent measure of the scale of ownership and construction, as buildings step down the hill in increments even when their walls are continuously joined.

All this is more true of the south slope; the north slope is mostly narrow streets running down to Cambridge Street. Some, like Joy Street or Hancock Street, are lined with a mix of town houses and apartment buildings; many are closely packed with apartment flats stacked in speculative buildings that use several of the same elements as the town houses elsewhere on the hill but with less affluence and less personal care—landlord territory.

II B 1 · LOUISBURG SQUARE
between Pinckney and Mt. Vernon streets
Various architects, 1834–47

Louisburg Square is an exception on the hill, a place that runs across the hill rather than down it, and that is ample enough to be self-sufficient, for its outlook is contained in all directions. Nonetheless, for many it epitomizes the special wonders of the Beacon Hill environment. This may be because it is so singular that the attributes of consistency and variation that everywhere else run on down the street are gathered together here in a place that can be remembered.

The square is a justly famous piece of privately owned urban design, with an oval park in the center ringed by a cast-iron fence and cobbled streets. Elegant town houses face onto the square from all sides.

On the west, the length of the square is characterized by the gently undulating round brick bays of Nos. 8–22. On the ground level, large windows, reaching virtually from floor to ceiling, rise above the ubiquitous granite base. Between the sidewalk and the buildings there is a narrow gap two to four feet wide that makes room for steps up as it lets light into basement rooms and provides an

II B 1 · *Louisburg Square, west side*

opportunity for small bits of planting or decorative brick paving. These buildings have low, sloping roofs with dormers set back from the front wall. The cornices all roll gently with the bays, while great chimneys join the dormers in a rhythmic, picturesque roofscape that makes an animated contrast to the restrained façades. The entries vary: The one at No. 8 has a full, assertive projecting pediment on full, round columns; the others are more reticent.

On the east side the buildings are taller and more elaborate. The end elevation of No. 1 is a very high brick wall on Mt. Vernon Street, culminating in two massive chimneys with a horizontal band between them. It's a very strong end to the square and the street, almost a dominating one. Here and elsewhere throughout the square, cast-iron screens in front of the windows at the second level imply a balcony rail and provide a net of privacy for these low windows as well as the opportunity for tasteful patterns and ingenious castings. Farther along the street, metal balconies, assorted bays of black-painted wood and copper, screens and entries of greater or less flamboyance add an incredible urban richness; they reflect many decades of maintenance, adjustment and willful invention all lodged in a brick fabric of serenity and grace.

To fully appreciate the cast-iron fence around the park in the center, it's necessary to stand close to it, to sense the size of the vigorous main stanchions, which stand person-high, and to note the provocative spears and fleurs-de-lis that cap the vertical stakes. The elliptical park itself has little sculptures at each end facing out, Columbus to the north, Aristides the Just to the south. A ring of planting around the edges makes for still another layer of privacy inside, with benches facing each other across the green. In summer the trees and shrubs here diminish the impact of the surrounding brick buildings, making a serene place of retreat.

II B 2 · 90–102 MT. VERNON STREET
between Willow and West Cedar streets

No. 90: 1826
No. 92: 1834
No. 94: 1835
No. 96: 1835
No. 98: 1835
No. 100: c. 1837
No. 102: 1832

While the pattern of building on Beacon Hill is constant, there is also persistent invention in the execution, much of it prompted by the slope. For instance, just in the little space of Mt. Vernon Street from Louisburg Square to West Cedar Street, you can see rhythmic variations within the inset entries, each one allowing a set of stairs to make the transition from the sloping street to the level of first floor.

No. 90 Mt. Vernon Street, on an axis with Louisburg Square, is the oldest town house on the block, built on speculation by Harrison Gray Otis in 1826. It has a vaulted entry with window panels at either side of the door and a fanlight above divided into glass panels by delicate muntins that trace most elegant, sinuous patterns. The next five town houses, built almost a decade later, are much simpler, with flat lintels supported on pilasters—Greek Revival in the classifier's mind. Yet each of them is different in initial execution and in subsequent maintenance. The lintel of No. 92 is of brownstone, and the entrance has simple rectangular windows to either side and above the door, the three panels of approximately equal size and proportion. No. 94 has more elaborate pilastered wood paneling on the sides and an arched fan window over the door. The housewright Jesse Shaw, who built many homes on the hill, was likely responsible for the next two, Nos. 96 and 98. They are very plain; 96 has a shallower inset on the first floor and more vigorous rounded moldings but no light over the door. No. 100 has full-length glass sidelights. No. 102 reverses the simplifying trend with a particularly elegant round-arched door that has glass lights all around its edges, filling the shape between rectangle and arch.

Each of these is slightly different in color and pattern, but all work with the same set of transitions: street stairs leading up to the main floor, the penetration through a brick front wall marked by some form of elaboration and arrival at a welcoming chamber, still outside the front door, with finely finished walls and windows.

Near the curb line between these houses and the street there is characteristically still another layer of enclosure made in a variety of ways by trees and cast-iron lamp posts spaced at essentially the same rhythm as the entries. The brick sidewalk itself is interrupted sporadically by insets and iron grills for occasional windows at the lower level and by a granite step projecting into the brick at each entry.

II B 3 · WEST CEDAR STREET
between Mt. Vernon and Chestnut streets

· ACORN STREET
between Willow and West Cedar streets
Cornelius Coolidge, 1828–29

West Cedar is a particularly handsome street. It has a fairly consistent house size and rhythm on the west side and a much more varied and complicated pattern on the east. The two sides play against each other with trees of various sizes in between. The street is terminated on the south by Chestnut Street, and to the north it bends with the contours of the hill so that it has closed views each way.

The most elegantly severe houses on the east side of the street are the two built in 1834 at Nos. 7 and 9, the latter built by Asher Benjamin for himself. At the south end of the street, a courtyard behind 57 Chestnut Street has evoked a charming collection of roof terraces and bays on the adjoining houses that capture light and views into the foliage provided by the courtyard trees.

The scale gets smaller and more distinct in Acorn Street, a straight, short, miniature cobbled street of great intimacy and directness that climbs from West Cedar Street back up to Willow Street. The south side of Acorn is lined by a row of unprepossessing houses, all designed by Cornelius Coolidge, with a pattern of entries and windows staggered down the hill and one magnificent attic bay. On the north, brick-walled courtyards provide open space for the houses of Mt. Vernon Street. Their large trees reach out over the walls to cover the sidewalk and the street. (Watch your step—the pavement is erratic.)

There are smaller passages still: Just a few paces farther south on Willow Street, a person-sized service alley divides gardens of the Chestnut Street houses from those of their diminutive Acorn Street neighbors.

II B 4 · WILLOW STREET
between Mt. Vernon and Chestnut streets

Willow Street has a very particular character because it is so short that it is made up almost entirely of the side walls of houses that front other streets. The walls, therefore, are much blanker, bearing most of the weight of these structures and characterized more by incident than by a regular system of openings. The chief exception is a curious eight-story brick apartment house at 9 Willow Street that probably grew up on the back of someone's lot rather like an oversized, vigorous weed, too energetic to succumb to cultivation. Bays, small medallionlike windows and dormers blossom from the basic brick form to seek light in various directions, and fire escapes fill the air space of Acorn Place behind it.

The most amusing incident along Willow Street is at No. 19, where a door with wooden carvings is set within the granite base, protected by a bay projecting above it on brackets. The bay has outsized windows and a bracketed cornice. The entry door underneath is dressed with architrave and pilasters but only three uprights, spaced irregularly to accommodate the door, and only one side panel instead of the customary two. The wooden architrave and pilasters are finely carved but cut abruptly where they join the granite, hinting that perhaps there is a continuation of the pattern somehow locked within the stone. No. 17 is equally charming, with brick steps that wind up through the small pocket of space otherwise occupied only by a tree. A simple metal rail negotiates the curving ascent with a fine and nimble spirit.

II B 5 · 87 MT. VERNON STREET
between Louisburg Square and Walnut Street
Charles Bulfinch, 1805
· 89 MT. VERNON STREET
between Louisburg Square and Walnut Street
Charles Bulfinch, 1805
reconstruction: Nineteenth century; William Dinsmoor, 1925

The first pair of houses up the hill from Louisburg Square is an opportunity to examine the basic house type Bulfinch used to give coherence to Park Row (now vanished) on the Park Street side of the Common, though these two houses are a freestanding pair and at Park Street they would have been part of a row.

The mansion at No. 87 is the Bulfinch original and a house with a sense of differentiation in its various parts, despite its great simplicity. Its neighbor, No. 89, has been rebuilt twice, once in the last century and once in this, and each time resurfaced, first in brownstone and then again in brick. As a result its walls are now thick and somewhat ponderous, with windows set back from the front surface and proportions that seem cramped.

In the Bulfinch design at No. 87, the windows are set out at the façade except at the lower level, where the wall steps back slightly under relieving arches. Pilasters at either side of the windows at the second level, which was the important one, end in brackets that support little cornice window heads. These windows are very tall and double-hung. The third and fourth levels have windows that are progressively smaller, with simple lintels keyed into the brick.

By contrast, the architect who resurfaced No. 89 the second time to return it from brownstone to a Beacon Hill style made, in the second and third levels, windows that are equal and the relieving arches over the first-floor windows are narrow, cramped and unconvincing. Finally, the porch of No. 87 is held on fine robust columns; those of the later porch at No. 89 seem effete and too broadly spaced by comparison. These are small details, but they reveal a revivalist's piecemeal vision, whereas the Bulfinch original has coherence and scope.

II B 4 · *19 Willow Street*

II B 6 · *Second Harrison Gray Otis House, 85 Mt. Vernon Street*

II B 6 · SECOND HARRISON GRAY OTIS HOUSE
85 Mt. Vernon Street, between Louisburg Square and Walnut Street
Charles Bulfinch, 1800–02
remodeling: Peabody & Stearns, 1882

This, the second house designed by Bulfinch for Harrison Gray Otis, is the most endearing. Whereas the first house (II A 15) is foursquare and stern, this one is foursquare and appealing, with full-height pilasters rising at each end to attract our attention. The third house (II B 15), on the other hand, is thoroughly integrated and mature, where this one is tentative, its paired pilasters only pasted to the front in a civic gesture that is at heart adolescent. But what a gesture; what a thing to do on the top of a pastured hill in 1802!

Designed at a time when people still imagined that Beacon Hill would be spacious, the house is set up on the hill and back from the street behind a granite wall. It's beautifully planned, with tall windows on the ground floor reaching almost from floor to ceiling, set in a row of segmental arches that imply an arcaded base. Above these a stringcourse of stone supports at either end a pair of tall white wooden pilasters with a short stretch of entablature between them. These pronounce the building's aspirations to grandeur with an economy of means worthy of folk architecture. Above the cornice a wooden balustrade stretches around the edges of a hipped roof, and the whole is crowned at the top by a very fine octagonal lantern.

II B 7 · 70, 72 MT. VERNON STREET
between Louisburg Square and Walnut Street
Richard Upjohn, 1847
reuse: Bullerjahn Associates, 1965–70

Nos. 70 and 72 Mt. Vernon Street are a startling exception to the Beacon Hill pattern, built in a dark-purplish stone and in a style that practically defies description.

Richard Upjohn, who did so much to transform and disseminate the Gothic Revival in Episcopalian churches, seems here in the construction of a paired house for bachelor brothers to be on much more tentative, experimental ground. It was later converted to the Boston University School of Theology. The building is like no other on Beacon Hill, with the possible exception of the Boston Athenaeum, which has the same somber tone with its sheer face and the same year of construction. Very fortunately, this anachronistic form has survived still another renovation into condominiums.

There are high-arched entries at either end. Above each of these, the building is articulated into a projecting shallow pavilion and bedecked with a balustraded balcony. In between these the wall is flat, with two pairs of very high, narrow windows at the ground level. Above each pair are equally high but very broad windows that are spanned by an iron lintel with rosettes on its surface, the opening beneath entirely filled with small panes of glass.

It's a tall, looming building. Although it doesn't have a strong sculptural presence, its color, its size and the peculiarly grand windows cause it to cut a distinct figure on the street.

II B 8 · MT. VERNON STREET
between Louisburg Square and Walnut Street

Mt. Vernon Street from No. 83 up is more expansive than the rest of Beacon Hill, since these row houses are all set back about thirty feet from the sidewalk. This makes the street much more spacious and sunny than other sections, even though the gardens that result are seldom anything more than patches of grass. The gardens are set behind retaining walls made of big blocks of granite that edge the sidewalk and that are capped by iron fences of various sorts.

The large open spot of sunshine across these gardens results from a proviso in the original deeds of trust that limited buildings on this stretch of the south side of Mt. Vernon Street to one story.

II B 9 · 51, 53 MT. VERNON STREET
Charles Bulfinch, 1804
· NICHOLS HOUSE
55 Mt. Vernon Street,
Charles Bulfinch, 1804
· 57 MT. VERNON STREET
opposite Walnut Street
Charles Bulfinch, 1804
addition: Cornelius Coolidge, 1838

These houses, designed as a set, were apparently meant to accommodate the daughters of the Mason family, whose mansion they faced. They form an elegant transition from the street-fronting town houses that preceded them farther up the hill to the Mason mansion (since demolished), which was set back from the street. They all have the familiar Bulfinch brick relieving arches at the base.

When the Mason properties were subdivided in 1838, the original west-facing portico of No. 57 was removed and a bank of windows was added with an entry now facing Mt. Vernon Street. The resulting ensemble of houses sharing a garden entry makes a particularly intimate and gracious end for the larger space of Mt. Vernon Street that stretches away from them to the west.

The Nichols House at No. 55 is now a small museum of Beacon Hill historical memorabilia.

II B 10 · 14 WALNUT STREET
SE corner of Mt. Vernon Street
1803

Many of the buildings of Beacon Hill show the results of adjustment of a fundamental house type to meet the conditions of the site and to reflect the means and interests of their owners, often through successive alterations. The original building here is one of the early houses on the hill, and it has endured more change than most. On the north it displays a rare example of an early New England building technique in which rough brick walls were covered with wood siding. There's also a diminutive arched passage to the garden at the rear, a frequent Beacon Hill device.

The end wall on Walnut Street is regularly laced with windows and dominated by an off-center chimney. Uncommonly, the roof has differing slopes front and back, an accommodation to increased demands for space inside that adds to the general sense of ungainliness.

The major change in the building took place because the site changed around it. The city lowered Walnut Street in the nineteenth century, and the resulting repairs and adjustments included a new entry off Walnut Street and the granite retaining wall that holds the rear yard high above the street.

With the original entry removed, the Mt. Vernon Street elevation must have seemed excessively blank. This was alleviated by a projecting bay that appears to have been designed in High Caboose style.

II B 11 · CHESTNUT STREET
between Walnut and Charles streets

Chestnut Street is arguably the prettiest street on the hill. It is short and distinct, butting into Walnut Street at the top and sloping toward the Charles River Basin at the bottom. In between, the street is quite consistently formed, with houses standing close to the sidewalk on both sides, varying ever so slightly as they step down the hill. The distance across the street between the front walls of these buildings is about equal to their height, a proportion that is especially pleasant when the dimensions are small enough to make the space of the street seem like a large room.

The street edge is soft and varied. There is a narrow area three to five feet wide between the building walls and the normal sidewalk. This space is variously filled by stoops, small blocks of granite that hold the sidewalk away from the basement windows and capture miniature gardens of ivy, and occasional sections of cast-iron railing that just march around in the brick sidewalk. There are pleasant trees on either side of the street and, of course, the constant presence of the slope.

Buildings along the street provide a casebook of modest invention, with endless variation in the porches, entries and window proportions, and in the alignments of windows and dormers. Even though these houses use very few design elements, there's a great deal of improvisation in the way they are used, both by the builders and by the people who now live here. The result is gently animated, like a conversation among people with differing views and common interests.

Chestnut Street also offers a wonderfully controlled sense of the world beyond. From the top there's an appealing view of the river below; from the bottom, at West Cedar Street, one can see up to the gold dome of the State House, presiding over everything. As Chestnut Street descends the hill, it crosses Spruce Street, which offers a view south to the Common, and then Willow Street, with its view north into the trees of Louisburg Square.

Topography and architecture combine here to form a magnificent place: an environment that provides both residents and onlookers with a world of intimate personal care and invention, set within the context of a larger, more enduring geographic order. This environment tells of the land falling to the water, of open space reserved for the common good, of nature changing with the seasons, of the proud Commonwealth and of a general consensus among residents. Few urban settings are so profound and pleasant.

II B 12 · *13, 15, 17 Chestnut Street*

II B 12 · 13–17, 18 CHESTNUT STREET
between Walnut and Spruce streets
No. 13: Charles Bulfinch, 1806
No. 15: Charles Bulfinch, 1807
No. 17: Charles Bulfinch, 1808
No. 18: Cornelius Coolidge, 1823

Bulfinch was an urbanist. His concerns were for public order, rectitude and refinement. There are no endearing little bays or crafted witticisms here, only propriety. Bulfinch was, we are reminded, superintendent of police.

He seemed also to make quite a business of building town houses for the daughters of those for whom he built mansions. Hepzibah Swan had three daughters, and their houses, at Nos. 13, 15 and 17 Chestnut Street, are the best surviving Bulfinch row houses.

The whole pattern is there, designed with great distinction: the granite base stepping out of the ground; the ground floor measured by inset arches and capped by a stringcourse; the tall, graceful windows at the first floor, with their taut, fragile wrought-iron balcony screens; the progressively smaller windows above. All very severe, very finely tuned, the domestic equivalent of a Classical order.

The entries especially are exquisite, more like fine cabinetry than the elements of building. Colonettes no more than five inches in diameter, slightly tapered at the top, are set in the plane of the wall. The doorframe, perhaps six inches behind them, is in turn four to six inches deep, with rounded flutes on its front. The door itself is set back in the middle of the doorframe and has windows on either side.

Although graced by fine proportions and elegantly crafted doorways, these houses are the sternest on the street, quite unlike all the others, which have projecting entries or deep recesses or splendid collections of bay windows. Take No. 18, for instance, as an antidote to restraint.

II B 13 · 29A CHESTNUT STREET
attributed to Charles Bulfinch, 1802
addition: c. 1817

· 29B CHESTNUT STREET
c. 1888

· 27 CHESTNUT STREET
near Spruce Street
Bellows, Aldrich & J. A. Holt, 1917–18
reuse: Bullerjahn Associates, 1965

Three more of the aberrations that make the fundamental order of Beacon Hill so appealing.

Like other early houses that still exist on Pinckney Street (II B 21), No. 29A Chestnut Street faces sideways, though this is possibly the first house built here and may well have been the pattern first intended for the hill. Its yard was subsequently used as the site for No. 29B. The present garden, enclosed on three sides, becomes a wonderful respite on a street of brick façades. The other bold feature of this house is a very large bow, probably added in 1817.

The third side of the garden is defined by an aberration even odder: a limestone Gothic chapel built in 1917–18 for the seminary then located behind at 70–72 Mt. Vernon Street. Its large pointed windows are held between projecting buttresses and were filled lately with full glass walls for the condominium spaces behind them.

Originally there were three banks of windows here—large clerestories at the top, a band of triple windows in the middle and two narrower ones in thick walls at the bottom. Renovation has neatly severed the middle pier on the bottom to open large windows for the lower room, a very handsome conversion.

II B 14 · 63, 64 BEACON STREET
between Charles and Spruce streets
Ephraim Marsh, 1821

· 61 BEACON STREET
between Charles and Spruce streets
possibly renovated c. 1920

· 56, 57 BEACON STREET
between Charles and Spruce streets
Ephraim Marsh, 1819

· 54, 55 BEACON STREET
between Charles and Spruce streets
attributed to Asher Benjamin, 1807

Three pairs and a specimen. The specimen, No. 61, has been described as "Beacon Hill's pride." The façade is indeed very elegant, its metal rails exquisitely wrought, its granite stoop finely honed, each detail stamped with an unobtrusive sign of refinement, even the round-topped dormers. In fact, it's a bit cloying.

The pairs are another story. Nos. 63 and 64 and Nos. 56 and 57 were all built by Ephraim Marsh. They differ principally in that one set is paired with adjacent entrances and the other, Nos. 63 and 64, have entrances at either end. As if to emphasize the distinction of address, No. 64 has a porch with Tuscan columns;

II B 13 · *29 A and 29B Chestnut Street*   **II B 14** · *54, 55 Beacon Street*

No. 63 has a more sensuous Ionic order. The brick fronts are continuous, though at slightly different levels, with the wall of each bowing out toward the street.

Nos. 56 and 57 have comely arched doors, each with its own stoop but no portico. They are joined together rather uneventfully, the major event being a fussy but nicely shaped bay window added over the entrance to No. 57.

Nos. 54 and 55, on the other hand, are joined with an eye to making something on a grander scale. The swell-front bays here were the first on Beacon Street, and their high, triple-hung, unshuttered sash windows make them the most gracious still. At street level, these houses are bonded together by a delicate colonnade of the sort found at No. 61, only here it gains greater emphasis by curving around the bays. Most conspicuous, however, are full-height, slender white wooden pilasters that bracket each bay and announce the building's intent to be a noble neighbor to the Common. A wooden balustrade screen that remains atop No. 55 does much to amplify this announcement, though next door on the mate it's been removed.

II B 15 · THIRD HARRISON GRAY OTIS HOUSE (American Meteorological Society)
45 Beacon Street, between Spruce and Walnut streets
Charles Bulfinch, 1805–1808

Under sustained contemplation, some buildings gradually emit radiance. The effects of this phenomenon are mysteriously soothing, its causes not altogether clear.

The phenomenon is invisible to those who view architecture as akin to collecting flowers or as a matter of gathering tangible, identifiable signs of human invention, then bundling them together into a luscious bouquet of observations —with a bay here, some carving there and a finial of exotic profile. No, the quiet radiance is accessible only to those who attend carefully and wait. It's hard to do with the traffic of Beacon Street, but the third Harrison Gray Otis House will definitely reward your patience.

Not that the Otis House is inadequate part by part; rather, the relationships between the parts, the subtlety and grace of their disposition, account for more than the elements themselves. Enumerating the parts won't help; the only appropriate response to this building is to stand still, attend to its proportions and sense its being.

Then later you can think about Harrison Gray Otis, his tremendous impact on this city through his activities as one of the Beacon Hill Proprietors, who developed the hill through speculation, and similar historical thoughts; or you can thumb through the entries on the first Otis House (II A 15) and the second (II B 6). This, the third Otis House, ended his rapid migration across the hill, and he remained here, finally altering his life once again in 1831 by building the abutting house at No. 44 Beacon in what used to be his garden. Not only does the latter house abut the earlier one, it swallows up the projecting bay of an oval dining room, which, like Jonah, remains intact within the encompassing new structure.

It is, after all, worth mentioning that the form of the house was at first a freestanding cube, modified slightly by the dining room bow on the east and by a service court and stables to the north. The beautiful, nearly cubic portico of the Beacon Street entry restates in miniature that conception of house as pure geometric form; only here the cube is hollow, its corners marked by fine shapely columns nearly the size of a person, the finest porch on Beacon Hill.

II B 16 · SOMERSET CLUB
· 42, 43 BEACON STREET
between Spruce and Walnut streets
No. 42: Alexander Parris, 1819
No. 43: 1832

II B 15 · *Doorway, third Harrison Gray Otis House, 45 Beacon Street*

II B 16 · *Somerset Club*

You may recall that Bulfinch doubled the width of Faneuil Hall (I D 1) and added a story. The original David Sears mansion by Alexander Parris has undergone the same transformation. Only here the result is more like a sex-change operation. The building's character has been totally altered, even though all the details are consistent.

The first house, No. 42, had one bay and a hipped roof. It stood free on its site. The second bay was built by Sears in 1832 on what had been a part of the Otis garden. The addition of a third floor after the Somerset Club acquired the building in 1872 completed the transformation, turning a quiet, centralized structure into a stern twin-towered façade that commands the street.

Even granting that the building was never intended to merge with its brick surroundings, the choice of granite was a bold, if not arrogant, first move. In the extended version the manifold increase in surface area, combined with the initially severe geometry, makes the building aggressively different, even though the overall form changed from a singular, distinctive building into the row-house pattern that is now more common on Beacon Street.

II B 17 · WOMEN'S CITY CLUB
39, 40 Beacon Street, between Spruce and Walnut streets
attributed to Alexander Parris, 1818
remodel of No. 39: H. W. Hartwell & W. C. Richardson, 1888

Parris built this pair of town houses a year before the Sears mansion. It is in the archetypal Beacon Hill mode, but bigger. If the Sears house was an affront to the Bulfinch tradition on the hill, this pair could be regarded as an act of homage.

The Women's City Club, at No. 40, and its sister building, at No. 39, are distinguished by strong, nine-foot-high temple-front entrances, with flat architraves supported by Ionic columns and fabulous fanlights that swirl around as though they had the whole world to command.

The tall windows have stone lintels with dynamically carved fretwork. At No. 39 the bow has been remodeled by the simple addition of middle windows, making it almost all glass. Hartwell & Richardson also added an additional floor and extended the stair of No. 39. Both upper and lower cornices would seem to be theirs.

II B 18 · THE TUDOR
34 ½ Beacon Street, NW corner Joy Street
S.J.F. Thayer, c. 1890

Consider, if you will, the possibility of a Beacon Hill resident visiting the château of Chambord and imagining that its wild array of chimneys, turrets and roofs might have some affinity with the traditional Beacon Hill bow front. No. 34 1/2 could be the result. The architect, S.J.F. Thayer, must have been a very resourceful man to have produced such a perfectly astonishing pile. The incongrously tall nine-story apartment house nevertheless continues Beacon Street's undulating face and resolves the angled corner of Beacon and Joy streets. It also provides an abundance of outlooks, nooks and bays for every apartment.

II B 18 · *The Tudor*

The entry is in a rusticated brownstone base on Joy Street, a base that absorbs the slope of the hill, so that there are two stories on Beacon Street and only one on Joy. Above, the building is mostly brick, with generous amounts of brownstone coursing and window trim.

The top two floors, above a powerful brownstone cornice, are absorbed in a mansard roof that keeps appearing and disappearing, dissolving into wall as the chimney pieces and round bays go up or as a dormer is projected forward to the edge, then reappearing around the corner to maintain the notion that it's still the roof.

The building itself wiggles up Joy Street, starting with a round bay on the corner, then a metal-clad quarter-round, then a couple of jogs, one for the entrance, another with a little carved balustrade making the stair, then a round bay, which straightens out, another jog and another round bay. Then suddenly a great right-angled piece rises up to a large arch at the top, embedded in which there's a copper-clad bay. Fantastic.

This splendid eccentric fits into the hill perfectly.

II B 19 · 25 BEACON STREET
adjacent to the State House grounds
Putnam & Cox, 1926–27

At the top of Beacon Street, next to the grounds of the State House (I B 4), is a large building from the twenties built to appear like a continuation of the Beacon Hill pattern. It's higher, though, with a good bit of wrought iron on the front, the top rendered as three gabled dormers similar to those found nearby on Park Street (I B 2). It represents some of the best of that period of work. Putnam & Cox, who built the equally mimetic Kirstein Library (I A 5), here found ways to house new, large organizations in a manner that hardly disrupts the familiar Beacon Hill scale. Indeed, the building's long east face seems an appropriate lead-in to the State House. This side elevation is all very clearly and straightforwardly set out as an overall pattern, but the pieces still break down into forms that are consistent with the scale and type of building of the Beacon Hill area. It faces out onto an empty plot of land, which was once the site of the John Hancock house.

No. 25 Beacon Street houses the Unitarian Universalist Association and is one of a set along Beacon Street that has roofed metal balconies that seem at first to be strays from New Orleans. The other two, Nos. 33 and 34, were designed originally by the ubiquitous Cornelius Coolidge in 1825.

II B 20 · 1–5 JOY STREET
between Beacon and Mt. Vernon streets
Cornelius Coolidge, c. 1825–30
· 6 JOY STREET
SE corner Mt. Vernon Street
Alexander Parris, 1824

The little stretch of Joy Street from Beacon to Mt. Vernon streets is particularly charming. On the west, it has row houses continuously set back about 15 feet from the sidewalk, with little fenced-in yards and trees in front. The group is brick set on a brownstone base, with brownstone trim on the windows, brownstone entries executed mostly in overblown scale and very high, narrow windows at the upper level.

The one at No. 2 is especially amusing, with overgrown scrolls for brackets. It looks like a Maurice Sendak drawing of an entry. The street is mostly offices now, as can be seen from the fluorescent lights and acoustic ceilings that show through the windows.

The window patterns of Beacon Hill tend to be so consistent and predictable that a building such as No. 6, at the southeast corner of Joy and Mt. Vernon streets, becomes very enigmatic. On close examination, it seems to offer evidence that the special needs of the inside have shaped the house to purpose. It is a solid brick box with very few windows, but these few are very telling. The Joy Street elevation is most surprising. It has a beautiful, deeply recessed entry of double doors just a few steps up from the street at the basement level. This is marked by a carved architrave and pilasters. Above is a wrought-iron balcony and a very large, wide window, about six by nine feet, set astonishingly off to the side right above the door, neither free of it nor on top of it, but rather balanced on one corner. Why not? Just adjacent to it is a little narrow window that looks as though it might be a subsequent modification. At the top there is a large round window between chimneys in the end gable. The rest of the fenestration is again fairly casual.

Along Joy Street there's a large yard, which is set up on a granite retaining wall with the standard cast-iron fence around it. The garden fenestration is much more predictable, with beautiful tall windows on the second floor reaching from the ceiling down to a cast-iron balcony that runs the length of the building.

The buildings that line Pinckney Street are unusually varied. On the northwest corner of Joy Street and two houses down at No. 5 are rare examples of wood-frame construction in the city. On the southwest corner is a brick cube from 1803, with balconies and a bay added later. Further down the street are brick houses and apartment buildings of varying sorts, mostly up against the sidewalk. Several, however, are set back, as at Nos. 9 and 11. At 15 Pinckney Street is a nineteenth-century building with nice metal bays sticking out all over the front of it.

Nos. 17 and 21 have handsome, narrow, wood-clapboard faces with corner boards on one, wooden quoins on the other. Both have faceted bays. No. 17 has a brick wall overlooking a court to the side, with No. 19 set back at the rear of a garden: a marvelous sharing of the site.

No. 21 is quite extraordinarily located as a nearly freestanding house. It has a little porch facing the blank brick wall of the next building at No. 23, and it in turn forms a court on the east with the wood and brick houses at Nos. 17 and 19.

II B 22 · *24 Pinckney Street*

II B 21 · *5 Pinckney Street*

II B 22 · 24 PINCKNEY STREET
between Joy and Anderson streets
William Ralph Emerson, 1884

No. 24 Pinckney Street is a wonderful and profound oddball. For this carriage-house conversion, William Emerson took the opportunity to reverse almost every convention that is common in the buildings of Beacon Hill. It's longer than it is high, rather than vice versa; it has a bay window incised in the brick wall rather than projecting forward. It enters at street level, so it does not have the benefit of privacy that results from being slightly off grade, but the lower windows are for the most part quite large and face directly onto the street anyway. And none of the windows is identical.

The central stair is marked by a long, narrow window that sits directly atop a lintel that spans both the narrow entry door and a tiny square side window.

Above the stair is a minuscule eyebrow dormer and on the back a big skylight. Despite all this invention, this is a building that speaks very strongly and with great clarity. The directness of the way the windows are placed is an emblem of what's going on inside, and there is no embarrassment about not adopting a traditional pattern. The house is simply one pair of rooms atop another; it bluntly announces that fact and plays with it wittily all the while.

II B 23 · 36 PINCKNEY STREET
between Joy and Anderson streets
c. 1884

No. 36 Pinckney Street is another exception, a bit of Back Bay suddenly blossoming in the Beacon Hill garden. Like No. 24, it is wider than it is high, even though this one is three stories above a basement. A broad Romanesque arch enfolds the stair as it runs up parallel to the building face rather than projecting out from it. At the top is a residential entry, and at the bottom a passage on the left leads into the garden behind.

The building bends slightly to accommodate differences in alignment between the building on the east set right up against the sidewalk, and the building on the west, set back about four feet from the sidewalk, as the rest of the houses down Pinckney Street are. The bend in the building allows the façade to join each of its neighbors and in the meantime produces a fine brick bay with angled corners.

II B 24 · PINCKNEY STREET
from No. 47 west to Louisburg Square

From this point at the crest of the hill, there is a wonderful view out to the Charles River, framed by the comfortable domestic invention of houses that descend along the way, with various bays popping out to make an alternating rhythm along the sides, punctuated by a fantastic four-story copper bay at No. 58. Stoops reach out to the sidewalk, and the roof line steps up and down on the higher, flatter part of the hill, but then progressively steps down toward the river and the Esplanade. It's a very beautiful stretch of street.

At the intersection of Anderson Street is Bay State Junior College. Built in 1824 as Boston English High School, it's a very high, austere building, curiously proportioned, with heavy Doric columns at the entrance. It has a central projecting pavilion with two symmetrical sides, the central pavilion capped with a gable. There are large classroom windows on each floor, the second-floor ones on the sides nicely lodged in brick relieving arches. The central pavilion front is crude, however, as though the architect had lost some of his tools.

From a spot in front of Boston English, there is a good view down Anderson Street to the building's much more serious predecessor, the Bulfinch Pavilion at Massachusetts General Hospital (II A 16).

The further descent of Pinckney Street is even more picturesque, with slightly angled walls that make adjustments for the irregular intersection of lot lines resulting from the layout of Louisburg Square, which is not quite perpendicular to Pinckney Street. Together they form a rich and gently undulating piece of street scenery.

II B 25 · BELLINGHAM PLACE
· SENTRY HILL PLACE
· GOODWIN PLACE
· ROLLINS PLACE
Revere Street between West Cedar and Garden streets

Off Revere Street are four little places that demonstrate the power of even diminutive public-space design. They're narrow, they provide precious little sunlight, and they would be practically indistinguishable from service alleys on a surveyor's map, but they're strong places with distinct identities, each providing entry for a few families who take pride in their diminutive commons.

II B 26 · BOWDOIN SCHOOL BUILDING
45 Myrtle Street, between Irving and South Russell streets
Wheelwright & Haven, 1895

This clunker fits more easily into the Beacon Hill fabric than one would have thought possible. It fills the head of an anachronistically straight and narrow block, which has been a school site since at least 1848, when Gridley J. F. Bryant built one here. The Bowdoin School, pedantic successor to that earlier structure, has lately been converted into apartments. It shows an intelligent blending of the propriety of the Classical order, the upright seriousness of the schoolmaster and the particular demands of a sloped site.

The Bowdoin School front elevation was a very restrained work for the period, reflecting the new-found interest in Renaissance forms. It has a simple entry beneath a pediment and Corinthian columns on either side. Above, a simple Palladian motif is set within an arch, and a row of arches runs across the building façade between brick piers.

A glance down Myrtle Street to the east will provide an angled view of the very grand north face of Brigham's extension of the State House (I B 4).

II B 27 · 57 HANCOCK STREET
NW corner Derne Street
c. 1875

Given half a chance, practically anyone will tell you this is an Egyptian Revival house. But the traces of Egypt are very light indeed, found mainly in some carved detail.

On the other hand, this is a building that does know how to take command. Situated at the head of Myrtle Street, it is, despite its uncharacteristic form, effectively the entry to Beacon Hill from the east, and it guards the access to Myrtle Street like a fairy-tale watchtower.

The house, though big enough, is really much smaller than it seems, since the entry and twin bay towers are on the long side of the lot, actually the end lot in a row of town houses facing Myrtle Street. With its symmetrical elevation capped by a cupola and a bit of open space on either side, No. 57 looks, however, like the front of a grand establishment rather than the side of a common lot.

II B 28 · THE HANCOCK
36 Hancock Street
Rand & Taylor, 1886
· 34 HANCOCK STREET
John Bennett & James McNeely, 1974
· 33–39 HANCOCK STREET
c. 1860

Hancock Street is short and spatially coherent, with the State House extension (I B 4) at one end and a fine view of Old West Church (II A 14) and the first Harrison Gray Otis House (II A 15) at the other. In between are a number of row houses, some indistinguishable tenement buildings and a group discussed here that marks with clarity three successive stages of development, each inherently at odds with the basic pattern but each forming an effective element in the street.

The Hancock, at No. 36, is an apartment building in cut-rate Richardsonian style. It has a very fine round bay and an arch that protects the inset entry quite grandly. It gets cheaper as it goes up; and the original cornice has been removed.

At No. 34 is an unabashedly contemporary building rebuilt on the lot of a structure that burned in 1974. Its form keeps the rhythm of flat front entry and projecting bay windows by using large windows in the flat part over the entry and a bay that is not round but is instead a skewed polygon with one angle more acute than the other. One side of the bay is blank for most of its height, the other is notched by corner windows. The bay stops two floors short of the top to make a balcony for one floor and to leave the highest floor free for a full-windowed penthouse. It's a modestly eventful brick building and does not fawn on the past; a seemly neighbor.

Nos. 33–39 are a stone-faced group of row houses with wide, bulging bays and a composition that is altogether striated, each level of the building adopting a slightly different rhythm. Most notably, the bays play a syncopated beat with respect to the regular segmental arches at the lower floor that alternate between window and door. This row is similar in some ways to early buildings in Back Bay. The entries have double doors, with glass, which are arched at the top and divided most improbably by pendants. They're not like any others, and I want some.

II B 29 · CHURCH OF ST. JOHN THE EVANGELIST
Bowdoin Street between Derne and Cambridge streets
attributed to Solomon Willard, 1831

A very early example of the architectural division between Church and State. Willard, who otherwise was noted for his beautiful carving of Classical forms for Bulfinch and Parris, and for the construction of the Bunker Hill Monument, here built a Gothic church. Or nearly Gothic. It's really a block, like most other buildings of the period, only built with rough stone and with jagged crenelations at the skyline. The blunt, square tower with its serrated crown and pointed arch windows filled with wooden ribbing seems a bit out of sorts, about as comfortable as a patriot in Tea Party Indian dress.

A new vestibule inside includes stained-glass windows by Gyorgy Kepes.

C/BEACON HILL WEST AND THE ESPLANADE

The area west of Charles Street was developed more recently than most of Beacon Hill; it began as the fringes of a mud flat, deemed suitable only for service buildings, warehouses and the indigent.

After the mid-nineteenth century, as filling and taming of the Back Bay proceeded apace and the Public Garden (III A 1) came into being, this area was gradually transformed, most dramatically along the Charles River frontage that it parallels. Brimmer Street was filled after 1863 and was soon lined with elegant brick town houses. Its respectability was heralded by the spire of the Church of the Advent (II C 7).

The land was pushed farther west in 1903 when a 100-foot-wide promenade was constructed along the Charles River edge, establishing the river as a place of stately resort. The next set of developments virtually coincides with the damming of the river, which relieved the surrounding areas from the stench of the tidal mud flats. In 1930 the embankment finally became the well-fashioned, landscaped and lagooned Esplanade that we know today extending from here all along the shore of Back Bay—only to be severed from the adjoining residential areas in 1951 by Storrow Memorial Drive, a torrent of traffic that limits access to the park to a few narrow and unappealing overpasses. Despite Storrow Drive, it's a great place to walk (or run, if you must).

II C 1 · CHARLES RIVER SQUARE
NE corner Embankment Road and Revere Street
Frank Bourne, 1910

· WEST HILL PLACE
Embankment Road, at Charles Street exit of Storrow Drive
Coolidge & Carlson, 1916

These two development schemes are fundamentally alike; each set of houses surrounds an open space all its own.

West Hill Place has a circular plan; Charles River Square ends in an oval. Each is an enclave of row houses, built all at once, that turns its back on the commerce of Charles Street and opens with framed views toward the river; each is a shapely vestibule linking a group of houses to the Esplanade beyond. Alas, the heavy traffic of Storrow Drive has intervened and the gracious vestibules have become embattled cloisters.

Both places are charmers, with an architectural vocabulary drawn directly from Beacon Hill. The walls, doors and windows, decorative iron balconies and ivy are used here to make urban scenery as much as to provide private accommodation. These are the opposite of the modernist injunction to "design from the inside out." Whatever else these houses do or don't provide, each group forms a distinct, identifiable place.

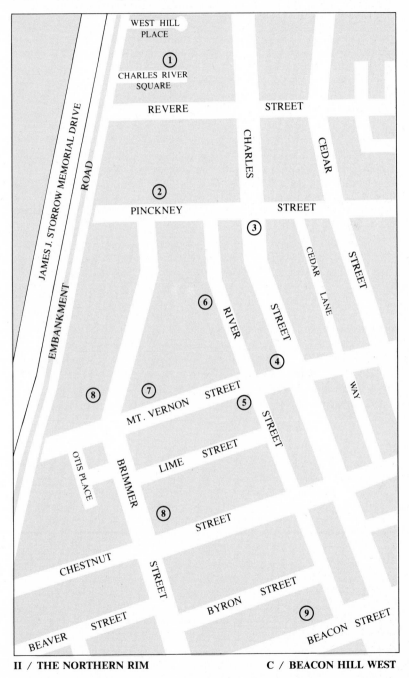

II / THE NORTHERN RIM   C / BEACON HILL WEST

II C 2 · RIVER HOUSE
145 Pinckney Street
Desgranges & Steffian, 1951

The last piece of development in Beacon Hill, and the most radical break with the past. Whereas Charles River Square and West Hill Place (II C 1) staked their investments in the creation of distinct open spaces, each identifiable with a particular group of houses but nearly indistinguishable in materials and building form from the rest of Beacon Hill, River House makes no gesture whatever to simulate the earlier Beacon Hill mode of building. It is organized instead to take advantage of the surrounding space for each individual unit rather than to create any collective form. It takes all and seems to give back little save the opportunity to admire how skillfully the architects spread the building around to capture maximum light, air and exposure for the occupants within.

In an effort to maximize proper exposure, the apartment units on the south side facing Pinckney Street are staggered, with large openings onto balconies. The repetitive breaks in elevation that this produces establish a unit of measure not entirely dissimilar from that of the earlier row houses stepping down the hill, but there the similarity ends absolutely; stepping down is not like staggering sideways. The light-brown brick, the metal mesh rails and the horizontals of this building separate it decisively from its neighbors, as a brief look back up Pinckney Street will attest.

This and 100 Memorial Drive directly across the river in Cambridge are the best of a very few residential buildings in Boston that try such a radical break with the traditional relation to the street, providing wings that are oriented to light, air and view, as though the rest of the world was a free-flowing park. They illustrate the promise that fueled the imaginations of those who created urban renewal programs of the period. To work, however, such designs require a reorganization not only of building form but of land ownership, with collective access to large areas of recreation and open space. What they lack most is the opportunity for immediate social contact that is channeled by traditional streets, or by spatially identifiable enclaves, such as the adjoining Charles River Square. Generally the destruction of existing social and physical fabric required by such total reconstruction has proved to be too high a price to pay for optimum sunshine.

II C 3 · CHARLES STREET
Cambridge to Beacon streets

There are two circumstances that make Charles Street particularly charming as a thoroughfare and as a shopping place. One is that while the buildings all retain more or less the same scale, they differ because they have been developed at different times and with different types of street frontage. To entice shoppers, various tack-on storefronts and bays have become the order of the sidewalk, while the brick walls above, which form the shape of the street, are measured by a steady pattern of regularly spaced domestic windows.

The other condition that makes Charles Street especially engaging is a bend just about midway that makes it a street with visual closure. The street has continuity and scope, jazzy improvisation and a contained vista that makes it comprehensible—perfect for people to meet in while shopping.

Two of the neo-Georgian buildings on the west side merit special notice. On the southwest corner of Revere Street, the lower floors of an apartment building have a handsome colonnade that steps along at an irregular pace, the narrower space between columns making a place for entry, the wider being filled with bays of small-paned glass, inset behind the columns. At the northwest corner of Pinckney Street, another carefully crafted 1924 Georgian building has a copper bay sticking out over arches, with the corner open below for an entry and a Palladian window motif at the very top.

II C 4 · *The Charles Street Meeting House*

II C 4 · THE CHARLES STREET MEETING HOUSE
NW corner Charles and Mt. Vernon streets
Asher Benjamin, 1807

One in a series of block-front churches built in the first decade of the nineteenth century, this is simpler and less pretentious than Old West Church (II A 14) and not nearly as elegant as St. Stephen's (II A 6). The transitions from three-bay porch to square tower to octagonal cupola are forthright and unelaborated.

Built first for the Third Baptist Church, later home for the African Methodist Episcopal Church and later still the Unitarian-Universalist Church, the meeting house has for some years sheltered various community activities. The principal landmark along Charles Street, it now shoulders amicably into the scene, having been moved some yards to the west when Charles Street was widened in 1920.

II C 5 · THE SUNFLOWER CASTLE
130 Mt. Vernon Street, between River and Brimmer streets
1840
remodeled by Clarence Luce, 1878

This visually extravagant house stands as witness to the sobriety of the Charles Street Meeting House, its near neighbor. Originally a perfectly ordinary little gable house, it has been remodeled into the most overtly eccentric building on Beacon Hill, a Queen Anne vision executed with a curious Chinese flourish. The entire gable end of the building facing Mt. Vernon Street has been transformed by a very large bay that projects forward from the wall to create a continuous band of small-paned windows, interrupted only by a carved griffin in the middle panel. The bay is held up by fantastically carved brackets and posts, some of which extend its surface a little to shelter the entry.

The lower floor is yellow stucco, the upper sheathed in scalloped red tile shingles. At the very top, sheltered by a projecting half-timber pediment, is the literal source of the building's extravagant name, a huge sunflower carved in wood, with bright-yellow petals and large green leaves.

II C 6 · RIVER STREET PLACE
· MT. VERNON SQUARE
between Mt. Vernon and Pinckney streets

The converging angles of Brimmer and Charles streets conspire to create an oddly shaped city block. With characteristic Beacon Hill ingenuity, the space between has been captured and shaped into two distinct places. River Street Place opens off Mt. Vernon Street, defined at the end by a handsome little house with a pair of double doors under a wide lintel at the second floor and more conventional domestic arrangements at the ground. Adjoining it is a small sunken garden faced by two more houses, with a very large tree in the middle —a beautiful little pocket of captured space.

River Street leaks past this closure, alongside a carefully reclaimed carriage house, into Mt. Vernon Square, a loose, ambling backyard turned into a square by a little bit of common green, some trees, a few lamp posts and a very spirited little house that enfronts it. Stairs lead up either side of the house to an entry set just to one side of the center line. The other side is filled by a large window divided into two small side panels and one big one in the middle—an effective bit of frippery. In the top bay a large set of windows is treated like a diminutive loggia, with two Tuscan columns and a mock balustrade.

II C 7 · CHURCH OF THE ADVENT
NE corner Brimmer and Mt. Vernon streets
Sturgis & Brigham, 1875–83

At first sight this is notable mostly for a pleasant but unexceptional Gothic spire. On closer examination the church proves to be a composition of real ingenuity, provoked in part by the irregular conjunction of streets at its site.

The large brick volume of the church follows the orientation of Brimmer

Street, but Mt. Vernon and Brimmer streets meet at an acute angle, so the church is at odds with Mt. Vernon Street and sits on a site much wider at the front than at the back. John Sturgis solved this by placing the tower toward the corner and filling the angled space with conically roofed chapels that make for a very bumpy and irregular form, one that modulates the relationship of the large church volume to the domestic scale of the street. Not coincidentally, the resulting ensemble composes well in pictures, too.

A similar ingeniousness inside leads to arrangements that combine the predictable hierarchical form of Gothic nave and chancel with large balconied transepts and a surprising sideways view of space passing on into the Lady Chapel, designed by Ralph Adams Cram and Bertram Goodhue. The interior is richly embellished with carvings and screens.

The church was a center for the promulgation of Episcopalian High Church liturgy in the latter decades of the last century.

II C 8 · 41 BRIMMER STREET
NW corner Mt. Vernon Street
Ware & Van Brunt, 1869

· OTIS PLACE
between Mt. Vernon and Lime Streets, west of Brimmer Street

· 50–58 BRIMMER STREET
between Lime and Chestnut streets
R. A. Fisher, 1912

The intersection of Brimmer and Mt. Vernon streets offers a whole array of peculiar and interesting later versions of the architecture typical of Beacon Hill.

Most distinguished is a house at 41 Brimmer Street, on the northwest corner, by Ware & Van Brunt. Built in 1869, it reveals the ingenuity, thoughtfulness and training of its two architects. (Ware established the schools of architecture at MIT and Columbia University; Van Brunt wrote extensive critical reviews.) Like the Church of the Advent on the opposite corner, this building takes good advantage of its oddly shaped site.

Here a large chamfered bay projects into extra space at the back of the angled lot, forming a corner for the entry porch. The stairs come up along the side of the house to enter at the middle on the Mt. Vernon Street side. This large brick town house sits on a rusticated brownstone base with brownstone pediments, lintels and stringcourses. Much of its visual interest comes from panels of brick set in intricate patterns.

Examine closely the details of this house and you'll find they're often based on careful consideration of the art of building. At the outside corners of the bay, for instance, the angled walls are tucked behind the front panel of bricks to make a better brick joint. Or notice where the tops of windows are set high enough so that the brownstone stringcourse that bands the walls can also form lintels for the window openings.

There are very vigorous brick chimneys as well, and a strong mansard roof atop a rich corbeled brick cornice. This house would be perfectly suitable in Back Bay.

More surprising and varied is a set of houses around the corner in Otis Place that display the full gamut of design attitudes from polite similitude to conservative dreariness, misshapen invention and single-minded daring, the latter most evident in a huge studio window that makes up nearly the whole upper face of a converted row house.

Along Brimmer Street, at Nos. 50–58, R. A. Fisher made a row of housing in the accepted Beacon Hill style. Its entries are set back from the street just far enough to allow a tiny margin of garden space to personalize and care for. Following tradition, they are set up half a level to gain privacy for the rooms inside. At the ends of the row, high windows take advantage of the corners. Behind the group is a private alley that cuts through the block from Chestnut to Lime streets. Nothing dramatic, but worth our attention precisely because it's intelligent, not assertive.

This group fits into the general street scene as skillfully as Charles River Square and West Hill Place make their own settings. They were all built at about the same time, all consciously extending the traditional character of Beacon Hill into the flat, filled land a century after the style developed on the slopes above.

II C 9 · *70–75 Beacon Street*

II C 9 · 70–75 BEACON STREET
NW corner River Street
attributed to Asher Benjamin, 1828

This row, facing the Garden, ranks with the very handsomest houses in Boston. It has clarity in style and materials, yet it has been modified and adjusted over time so that there is variety within that basic context.

Granite-faced, the strongly rusticated base has arches set into it after the manner of several Bulfinch houses. Above, a smooth granite wall has regularly spaced windows. This face has been elaborated, however, by a series of bays and balconies and an incredibly tall wisteria vine that has grown up to the roof of the second in the series, No. 71. The roof line has also been broken by additional floors placed on the second, fifth and sixth houses. On these, a balustraded terrace at the top of the façade shields still another set of rooms set back on the roof.

The wonderful bay on the corner at No. 70, slightly medieval in tone, projects forward from the house as an extension of the room, one that fits snugly to the size of a person.

At No. 75, all of the second-floor windows have diminutive bays added onto them, small faceted oriels of a sort that are more usual in Germany than here. At the ground floor is a bay very like the ones on the Amory-Ticknor mansion (I B 3), with flat side panels and a projecting window in the center.

These variations act in counterpoint with the granite and the basic window rhythm to bond these houses together as a particularly urbane bit of streetscape.

III/BACK BAY

The Patrick Andrew Collins Memorial on Commonwealth Avenue (III A 15) with the John Hancock Tower in the background (IV A 7)

A/COMMONWEALTH AVENUE AND RESIDENTIAL BACK BAY

From the day in 1856 when the City of Boston, The Commonwealth of Massachusetts and the Boston and Roxbury Mill Corporation formed an agreement to fill in the stinking marshland known as the Back Bay, it was clear that this was not going to be just another money-making real estate scheme. No, this project was going to be the most handsome and spacious development imaginable, healthful to live in, a source of civic pride, something positively grand. In fact, Bainbridge Bunting, in his definitive study of Back Bay, notes that the Commonwealth had such high hopes for the area that it was willing to devote more than 43 percent of its land holdings to streets and parks "to achieve the desired monumentality."

The result can be seen today, centered around the Commonwealth Avenue Mall, the *grande dame* of American boulevards. Generous lot sizes (compared to elsewhere), standardized at 26 feet on Commonwealth Avenue and 25 feet on Marlborough, Newbury and Boylston streets, were auctioned off as separate parcels with options to buy adjoining lots at the same price for larger projects, like the Hotel Vendome (III A 16).

These uniform, mostly single-lot sizes establish the steady rhythm of stately

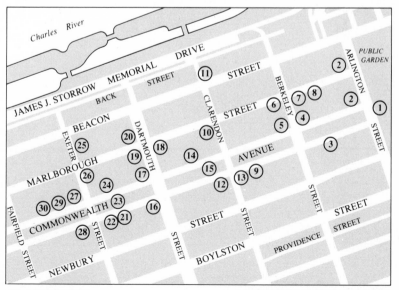

town houses and apartment blocks, each with its fancy brickwork or cut stone, tiny front gardens, bay windows and big elms lining the avenue. A central green space, punctuated with statues, stretches all along the ten long blocks of Commonwealth Avenue from the Public Garden at Arlington Street to Kenmore Square. At this point, the mall runs short of elegance, degenerating into a barren streetcar right-of-way that wends its way past Boston University to Boston College, the suburbs and beyond.

But in the well-tended part, in Back Bay proper, we can still sense the power of this grand scheme. Somehow, Commonwealth Avenue has managed to keep up with the present while holding on to the richness of the past. Despite a general decline in decorum (people aren't always altogether dressed, dogs are seldom curbed), the avenue remains very much alive. Its substructure of decorative forms and motifs and variations on building types lends a certain identity to each individual building, to the pairs and trios they group themselves into, to the entire block they enfront and to the neighborhood. What we come away with is the image of Boston as a setting for civilized urban living.

III A 1 · PUBLIC GARDEN
bounded by Charles, Boylston, Arlington and Beacon streets
George F. Meacham, 1860

Boston Common has its Frog Pond, but the Public Garden has the Swan Boats. It also has meandering paths, beds of flowers that change with the seasons, blossoming trees, Japanese lanterns, a sizable collection of sculpture, a shallow lake overhung with willows, and a cast-iron fence. The area was reclaimed from the mud in 1860 after years of dispute and signaled the beginning in earnest of Back Bay's development.

From the Garden you can see many of the major buildings of the city, or at

III A 1 · *Public Garden*

least those that make it to the skyline. In the Garden you can find segments of Boston's history embodied in bronze, most notably an equestrian George Washington of 1878 by Thomas Ball that commands the Commonwealth Avenue entrance, and a stooped Edward Everett Hale sculpted by Bela Pratt in 1912 that stands large and humble by the side of the main path that crosses Charles Street to the Common. In spite of its mud-flat beginnings, the land of the Public Garden now has a good bit of roll, with the east-west axial path leading up over a bridge to allow swan boats and strolling couples to pass underneath.

The swans in question are large, proud sheet-metal swan bodies that glide along at the back of boats holding about 20 people. These swan bodies shield from view the straining legs of husky young folk who pedal the craft with apparent ease, gliding about on the surface of the lake. The scene has all the thrills of a merry-go-round, but transported to placid water, powered by coolie labor and bereft of calliope. It's an astonishing invention that pulls mysteriously at the heartstrings and has for generations.

III A 2 · 1–12 ARLINGTON STREET
Beacon Street to Commonwealth Avenue
1860–61
· KATHERINE GIBBS SCHOOL
7 Arlington Street, NW corner Marlborough Street
Strickland & Blodgett, 1929

The north blocks of Arlington Street facing the Public Garden are a small microcosm of Back Bay. The buildings closest to Beacon Street—1, 2 and 3 Arlington Street—may well have been designed by Gridley J. F. Bryant. They represent the state of the art of brownstone town-house construction at the beginning of Back Bay's development: simple volumes articulated into discernible parts by slight projections in the wall that make it possible to imagine the end pieces as independent pavilions. All of this is capped by a straightforward mansard roof and elaborate chimneys. The set of town houses bordering Marlborough Street at 8 and 11 Arlington Street is more complicated. These town houses are softer, with more elements, more variation, but still understandable as a group with a similar overall scheme. No. 12 has been combined with 1 Commonwealth Avenue into a stone palace facing the Garden. It represents the loftier aspirations of Commonwealth Avenue, site of Back Bay's most pretentious mansions. Also, like most of the others, it has now been taken over for offices.

In the midst of all this, at 7 Arlington Street stands a dark, stridently linear and higher Art Deco building, a sentinel from a later era. It has a setback profile, black marble, Deco-Baroque entry and a black brick base. Strickland & Blodgett were less conservative here than at the Ritz-Carlton Hotel (III B 2), but not much more interesting.

III A 3 · 20–36 COMMONWEALTH AVENUE
between Arlington and Berkeley streets
Gridley J. Fox Bryant & Arthur Gilman, 1864

Nine houses in a row, with the longest stretch of flat façade on Commonwealth Avenue. Flat, that is, except for nine quite determined bay windows at the second

III A 3 · *Doorway, 28 Commonwealth Avenue*

III A 5 · *Haddon Hall*

floor and as many recessed entries a few stairs off the ground at the first level. Lest you think the units identical, keep track of the entries in relation to the bay windows with which they only sometimes align; there's a very subtle slurring of the apparently regular beat.

In case you've had any reason to doubt Gilman's contribution to the Old City Hall design (I A 8), compare these town houses to the Bryant block on Arlington Street (III A 2). These have style, even if they are slightly dumpy.

The ensemble is very aloof and strong, though unlike what the rest of Commonwealth Avenue has become. These are more suggestive of the hard urban structures of Europe. Since Gilman laid out the plan for Back Bay, these row houses may more closely represent his intentions than the more romantic, variegated houses that now line the street. Luckily, the result is much more amiable than the intent.

III A 4 · 25, 27 COMMONWEALTH AVENUE
NE corner Berkeley Street

At the corner of Berkeley Street and Commonwealth Avenue, there is a pair of particularly grand, mansard-roofed mansions with an unusual corner garden. The group, whose architect is not known, is tied together by compositional patterns: paired bays, continuous horizontal banding and a balustrade that surrounds the corner at the sidewalk line. The Nova Scotia stone balustrade, once splendid, has been victimized by the weather. Originally, the balusters were cut in large panels that neatly fitted together, like chunky blocks with little arches in between. Now they stagger a bit, but they draw the line between private and public space in a very friendly and engaging way.

The entry path to No. 27 passes through the garden alongside the carved stonework of the building's substantial base all the way to a porch at the midpoint of the house. This side entry allows the front room to have windows on two sides. At No. 25, which appears to have been designed jointly with No. 27, the entry is up front, with its own little half-round bay and a balcony above, giving it a sense of its own independence. These are not standard row houses but read as one single complex house composition with the scale of two units. The units are inseparable: their distinctive entries, the pairs of identical bays alternating with triple windows, the flat pediments over the arched ground-floor windows—all these elements are wrapped up by the unifying balustrade. It's a fine work.

The records in this case are unclear; it seems that the two houses were originally in one ownership and were first built in 1861, but then either rebuilt or altered separately, No. 27 by Peabody & Stearns in 1871 and No. 25 by Rotch & Tilden in 1883–84. Chances are good that the present unified composition is a result of the Rotch & Tilden work.

III A 5 · HADDON HALL
29 Commonwealth Avenue, NW corner Berkeley Street
J. Pickering Putnam, 1894

Haddon Hall is a wonderful building that shouldn't have happened—it's 11 stories tall on a 5-story street. Since few others like it were built, it's a fine aberrant object in the cityscape, and there's little enough of it so that, purity aside, no damage is done. Taken, however, as a signal of things to come, it must have been ominous indeed, the portent of a city lined with tall apartments, more like Manhattan than Back Bay.

It was designed as a residential hotel—kitchenless apartments, actually—with a restaurant and other public services provided on the lower floors. It's built in the same style and with the same vocabulary as the rest of Commonwealth Avenue, only taller. Thus, we have the obligatory octagonal grace of a bay window rising the entire height of the building, next to a more delicately scaled triangular bay that does the same thing. At the top, just before the attic story, a strong cornice ties these two bays together, projecting over the gap between —a simple device that makes the form distinct and powerful. The first three stories and the one next to the last are brownstone, just like many of the neighbors. The other floors are all buff brick trimmed in brownstone.

Despite the street address (29 Commonwealth Avenue), the entrance is on the Berkeley Street side, expressed through a colonnade of half-columns and an enclosed loggia above the entrance. Paired, metal-framed bow windows, set into the masonry wall, alternate with the more typical double-hung windows. The result is a composition that is symmetrical and flat only at first glance.

Haddon Hall is now used for offices and professional suites. But its lobby and grand stair still give an inkling of its heroic past, and it's an object of real distinction.

III A 6 · FIRST AND SECOND CHURCH IN BOSTON
SW corner Berkeley and Marlborough streets
Ware & Van Brunt, 1867
Paul Rudolph, 1972

First Church was incorporated in 1630, Second Church in 1649. Both have long histories of burnings and replacement, beginning with a fire that very early

III A 6 · *First and Second Church in Boston*

destroyed the First Church building, which then stood opposite the Old State House on the present site of the Brazer Building (V B 1). When this later Ware & Van Brunt First Church was devastated by fire in 1968, the First and Second churches combined to sponsor an ingenious renewal.

Rudolph managed to use the most identifiable features of the earlier building, the tower and rose window, in making a new church that accommodates significant programmatic changes and fits the street in an understanding and generous way. What was left of the original façade was incorporated in the new structure, and the new parts, the copper sheeting for the roof and the ribbed concrete blocks that have become a Rudolph trademark, simply intersect with the old masonry in a very legible way. Both orders are present. From the Marlborough Street side you can see the backs of the tower and the façade, the various kinds of stone construction in the earlier rubble walls, the steel bracing that's holding the wall in place and the ruined wall itself, complete with charred traceries. These provide embodied memories of the fire's ferocious destruction and they give fresh understanding of the building's initial means of construction.

Along Marlborough Street the new construction dominates, but with a sweeping metal roof that enfolds an exterior court along the street and reaches down to form a broad entry porch supported on simple steel columns and beams. The court is shaped into an amphitheater that on one side joins the street with a low wall in a manner entirely sympathetic to the prevailing street pattern, and on the other climbs up under the roof to bring parishioners to the higher floor level of the new structure, which is necessary to accommodate parking underneath. The stepped court is a brilliant device, though it may be used as an amphitheater only for an occasional wedding or church festival.

The inside is equally convincing. The porch continues within as a large socializing vestibule and meeting space. Stairs lead up a little farther and angle sideways to the main hall, which is ingeniously tucked in at the rear of the site: a high, beautifully lighted space with several balcony levels.

The ribbed block works effectively both inside and out, with none of the nasty connotations of concrete block; instead, it has a light-enhancing texture that graces the walls of the church—simple planes that are joined together in unexpected and interesting ways. The interior unfortunately suffers from a superabundance of rose carpet and red glass, but otherwise the architect invests our attention wisely in the people who gather here and in the light that embraces the space.

III A 7 · FIRST LUTHERAN CHURCH
SE corner Berkeley and Marlborough streets
Pietro Belluschi, 1959

At first glance, the First Lutheran Church would seem to be in the mainstream of New England's brick churches, shorn of the sentimental attachments of spire, portico and whatnot. It sits up against the regulated setback line of Marlborough Street the way Old South Meeting House (I A 3) now sits against Milk Street: sheer, mostly unadorned and in the middle of things, albeit domestic ones here. The entry and the interior, however, reveal a more complicated lineage, a different understanding of church. Entry is from the Berkeley Street side through a walled and trellised atrium. The street here is viewed as alien, if not hostile, and the atrium sets a part of the outdoors aside to create a small place of cloistered repose, as its Latin antecedents did.

Inside, stained glass and natural-wood screens derive more from the Gothic Revival traditions than from those of New England Colonial, but together with the beautiful salmon color of the exposed brick and the gentle radiance of well-balanced indirect light, the place surrounds us with its own quiet authority.

III A 8 · 22–30 MARLBOROUGH STREET
between Arlington and Berkeley streets
1863

These town houses are similar to the Bryant & Gilman group on Commonwealth Avenue (III A 3), but they are a step more polished and borrow more directly from their Parisian antecedents. The spacing here is absolutely regular, the proportions more severe, with solid and void equally attended to. And there are no bays whatever, except those added in later renovations. The beautiful, shaped base of Nova Scotia stone is decaying badly and is now covered with paint, but its regular arches still accomplish their mission of implying an arcade while they accommodate paired entries alternating with windows. The second-floor windows, longer than the rest, are framed with stone carved in elegant but robust Renaissance contours. These have a schooled severity and grace which even Gilman couldn't manage and which was not to return to the Back Bay until the end of the century. It matched neither the naïveté nor the exuberant inventive temper of the time.

III A 9 · 80 COMMONWEALTH AVENUE
between Berkeley and Clarendon streets
1872

One of a very few Back Bay houses that adopts a medieval mode. Here the attenuated colonettes are used to good advantage, turning the central bay occupying most of the façade into a network of glass and structure. It's a light-handed repudiation of the solid bearing-wall architecture that dominates the city.

An entry with a cleverly shaped hood is jammed into the bottom of this three-story bay in an offhand, not altogether charming way. But the dormer at the top is another story—an utterly cheerful bit of invention. Smaller in girth than the bay it surmounts, it nonetheless repeats the basic shape, though here there's a steep little Gothic pediment in intricately cut wood set out in front of the window to mark the central axis. This creates a layered, shadowy eave at the peak.

The architect is unknown, but his dormer anticipates both the exuberance of the J. F. Ober dormers for the Hotel Vendome addition (III A 16) ten years later and the layered affectations and delights of self-proclaimed Post Modernists a century later still.

III A 10 · 270 CLARENDON STREET
SW corner Marlborough Street
Weston & Rand, 1873

A particularly bumpy and interesting building, this displays the architects' inventive enthusiasm for the ornamental possibilities of machine-cut stone, brick coursing, carved wood and cast iron.

The volume is simple enough: a corner house with a faceted bay centered on the Marlborough Street elevation, a gabled pavilion midway on Clarendon Street that marks the entry, and a mansard roof interrupted by dormers. Two large bays are bracketed off these walls on the Clarendon Street side. One is faceted, with wooden brackets that spring from positions at either side of the entry to hold it up. The other is a piquant boxed addition to the front room that is topped by a steep hipped slate roof and supported by delicate little struts that converge on a stone corbel.

Each level of the building is differentiated by brick and stonework, the shapes and details always relating to the task of making openings in a masonry wall. At the first level, the stone window lintels are very simple, with carving reduced to mere notches and a tautly carved segmental arch cut into the face of the rectangular stone block. At the second floor, the top of the stone lintel itself is arched beneath a small brick reveal. At the third floor, there's a combination of stonework and brick voussoirs under a brick molding.

In the same way, brick bands at the level of the window heads are also differentiated, ranging from simple insets to a checkerboard of recessed and projecting bricks at the top. In the brick gable on Clarendon Street, these devices are intertwined in an elaboration of the basic form that is practically Celtic.

The small, sharply pointed dormers display a similarly inventive use of wood brackets to join the shape of the dormers to the roof they intersect. Altogether the building is a study in exuberant detailing.

III A 11 · 180 BEACON STREET
NE corner Clarendon Street
S. J. Kessler, 1965

What is most disturbing about 180 Beacon Street is not the sudden appearance among staid old neighbors of an 18-story tower of handsome brick and dark anodized-aluminum window frames. It's not even the multiple glass-and-metal balconies projecting across the façade. No, the biggest trouble is a massive granite-faced wall along the sidewalk line, which rudely blocks the building's entry court from view.

The wall is even more of an interruption of the Back Bay street pattern than the building's enormous mass. All along the street, there is a buffer zone between the sidewalk and house, between the public and private domains. This space, usually reserved for tiny gardens, special pavings or individualized touches by the owner, animates the street and gives it a living personality. The tradition of the wrought-iron fence invites the passer-by to look in but keep out. But the granite wall, perhaps an overzealous bid for the internal security of the tenants, doesn't even allow the passer-by a look. It denies that there is any community of interest between those inside and those outside the wall.

About the building there is little more to say—a conservatively tailored impertinence.

III A 12 · FIRST BAPTIST CHURCH
SW corner Commonwealth Avenue and Clarendon Street
H. H. Richardson, 1871

A winner on all counts, chosen in competition by the original owners, the Brattle Square Church. In the hands of some architects, most notably H. H. Richardson, a building's walls become energized. Each window and door, each sculpted bit becomes an incident of note. The whole surface of the building becomes an arena of decision, and each decision a confirmation of controlling intelligence and judgment. This is the earliest of Richardson's works with these qualities, a significant turning point in his career.

The overall form of the church is hardly astounding; it's rather humble, in fact. The parts and details, though, show a purposeful clarity that rewards careful observation. They don't fuss or bother to attract attention.

The tower doesn't fuss, either. It just stands there, uncommonly proud, at the corner of Commonwealth Avenue and Clarendon Street, an unmistakably virile announcement. The top is banded by a wonderful set of carved stone reliefs depicting the sacraments, sculpted by Frédéric Auguste Bartholdi with drapery no less appealing than that of his Statue of Liberty, albeit at smaller scale. At the corners angels thrust attenuated gilded horns into the silhouette, trumpeting their messages down to us.

It's an altogether splendid thing to see. In fact, the tower has always been more admired than the church itself. Already in 1881 a group of concerned Bostonians raised a fund to preserve it in a park even if the church proper should be removed or destroyed. And since it's modeled after a detached Italian campanile more than an English parish steeple, it could easily have withstood such isolation from the mass of the church itself.

The rest of the church consists of several distinct parts held together more by the ivy crawling over it than by the initial composition. There's a porte-cochere cut into the base of the tower and a porch sliding out beyond the tower to serve as an entry point off Clarendon Street. The transept, nave and parish house take on an asymmetrical massing as a result of the corner siting. A small chapel—a barnlike attachment with a handsome window—was added by the First Baptist congregation at the Clarendon Street end.

III A 12 · *First Baptist Church, with John Hancock Tower* (IV A 7)

Much of the energy spent on detail is invested in the Clarendon Street porch and plate tracery window above. The window follows a Norman precedent, an eight-petaled floral pattern divided by a cross of carved colonettes. Since the flat pattern requires that the colonettes are directed up, down and sideways, they are shaped at each end into a curious form that is a mutation of the traditional forms of capital and base, top and bottom. The ends here have some of the qualities of base and some of the characteristics of capital and serve with either end up.

The porch is a deep shelter. One enters past vigorously contoured piers that seem carved out of the masonry plane of the wall itself; each pier has details that refer to the main plane of the wall while being modeled into round and octagonal shafts. The whole has a rational eccentricity that comes with careful reconsideration of each part in relation to the whole.

III A 13 · 90 COMMONWEALTH AVENUE
SE corner Clarendon Street
G. N. Jacobs, 1925
penthouse: Halasz & Halasz, 1974

Scanning the surroundings of the First Baptist Church, you might at first think that the tower's angels were trumpeting their messages of grace on deaf ears, for directly across Clarendon Street, G. N. Jacobs, who made a business of designing unseemly apartment buildings along Commonwealth Avenue, did his worst. But step back and gaze skyward. There, closest to the angelic tunes, are a set of penthouse structures and terraces that were added to the roof by Imre Halasz as extensions of his own condominium.

Pointed, crisp and straightforward, they are clearly additive constructions that show wonderfully the potential for rooftop development. The sense of animation and liveliness that they give and the broad stroke of color provided in season by a planter-balustrade are both valuable additions to an apartment structure that is otherwise without redeeming qualities.

For a negative example that is equally convincing, glance down the street at 82 Commonwealth Avenue, where someone has plopped a dismal two-story child's version of a house onto the roof of a perfectly respectable four-story mansard row house. If you have a weak stomach, don't look.

III A 14 · *115–125 Commonwealth Avenue*

III A 14 · 115–125 COMMONWEALTH AVENUE
between Clarendon and Dartmouth streets
No. 115: Cummings & Sears, 1876
No. 117: Cummings & Sears, 1876
No. 119: Bradlee & Winslow, 1879
No. 121: Cummings & Sears, 1872
No. 123: William G. Preston, 1872
No. 125: William G. Preston, 1872

This is the set to remember Back Bay by—the full flowering of their type. Individualized, romantic, not altogether graceful, but of a kind and in agreement.

No doubt they were built on speculation, like so much of Boston, but in a time and place where the pleasures of being inside (and the imagining thereof from outside) were thought to be primary. The architecture of these houses is based on forms that you can imagine being in. They are not absolute. Furthermore, Commonwealth Avenue between Clarendon and Dartmouth streets was no place to demonstrate frugality, so the parts and the materials of the buildings were conceived by the architects as opportunities to invest care and craft, bit by bit.

The house forms, here as in most of residential Back Bay along Commonwealth Avenue, Marlborough and Beacon streets, march along with regular chamfered bays, alternating with entries marked out occasionally by large doors at grade, more often by stairs running up under pediments or sheltering brackets. The type is fundamentally the same; changes are in the details.

The streets therefore have a harmonious sense of continuity, but within them there can be heard many individual voices. Here, for example, at Nos. 121 and

123, the brick bays have similar but hardly identical lintels and cornices of contrasting stone, with cheerfully elaborated caps making towers out of what could have been mere bays. The difference between them is that one has a lavishly fantasized, steep gabled roof and the other, like its twin at No. 125, has a magnificently contoured, octagonal mansard tower. They understood well the power of silhouette.

III A 15 · PATRICK ANDREW COLLINS MEMORIAL
Commonwealth Avenue Mall between Clarendon and Dartmouth streets
Henry Hudson Kitson & Theo Alice Ruggles Kitson, 1908

The bust of this former mayor (1902–05) emerges from the top of a stone shaft placed right on the Commonwealth Avenue axis. The obelisk base is attended on either side by formidable allegorical ladies and surrounded by curved benches and a slightly raised terrace. The assembly physically interrupts the mall down the center of the avenue and visually arrests our attention. The figure serves here as a measure for the building forms around it, reminding us of human size and symbolically invoking a measure of civic accomplishment.

The sculpture is reported by various earlier Boston guidebooks to have been originally placed, perhaps less provocatively, at the Fenway end of Commonwealth Avenue.

III A 16 · HOTEL VENDOME
160 Commonwealth Avenue, SW corner Dartmouth Street
William G. Preston, 1871
J. F. Ober, 1881
Stahl/Bennett, 1971–75

The Hotel Vendome is the somewhat bloodied patriarch of Commonwealth Avenue. In its transformation from a rather modest, elegant hotel facing Dartmouth Street to a splendid grand monster fronting Commonwealth Avenue to a rundown hotel and then finally to a commercial and residential condominium complex, the Vendome has had a rather checkered history. The greatest trauma was a disastrous fire that broke out while the most recent renovations were under way, destroying the roof of the earliest building and the pyramidal peak of its 1881 addition and requiring a total rebuilding of the southeast corner.

Half of the first building, by William Preston, is still visible at the corner of Dartmouth Street and Commonwealth Avenue, distinguished by its colored and inventively elaborated stone trim. The two symmetrical bays there were originally capped by more aggressively shaped roofs, making them appear like corner turrets. The present entrance off Dartmouth Street was then the center and focus of the building, also capped by a mansard tower.

When Ober added the much larger wing to the west, faced in white stone, he began with a huge central peak-roofed pavilion jammed up against the older building to make of it an unsymmetrical wing. He then added toward the west a higher, grander wing with walls modulated by bays and articulated with stringcourses, and with Renaissance window trim varied by floor but generally more routine and restrained than that of the original. Generally, but not always. At the tops of three bays along Commonwealth Avenue, the world becomes rich and fanciful. A strange set of columns and brackets all merged together climbs up off a balustrade and over onto the mansard to support tripartite collections of dormer windows surmounted by metal pediments. On the way up these verticals are joined, on either side, by quarter domes that cover the sides of bay windows below. Hardly routine.

The Commonwealth Avenue entrance is framed by a broad arch and by lights on either side. Above it, a block with three large windows is the base for a round bay that rises up the axis of the center pavilion, where it once also climbed up onto the roof; now, after renovation, the central mass is topped by a truncated pyramid, with stepped bands of view windows set into its form, less fanciful than its predecessor.

The new section at the rear on the Dartmouth Street side is a very straightforward spandrel-and-glass interpretation of the earlier building's spirit. It's broken down into faceted projecting bays, their glass set back in alternate floors to make room for balconies. The bays are executed in an abstracted fashion that, while acknowledging the scale of the original, remains oddly remote from human touch.

III A 17 · AMES-WEBSTER HOUSE
306 Dartmouth Street, NW corner Commonwealth Avenue
Peabody & Stearns, 1872
alterations: John Sturgis, 1882
reuse: Childs, Bertman, Tseckares Associates, 1969

The Ames-Webster House mirrors the early history of the Hotel Vendome (III A 16) exactly, offset by one year. That is, it was originally an elegant, gracefully mansarded symmetrical block, in this case facing Commonwealth Avenue. Ten years later the Frederick Ames family commissioned Sturgis to make it grander. To do so, as Ober had on the Vendome, Sturgis added a massive pavilion large and commanding enough to steal center stage and become the new focus of the composition.

III A 18 · *315 Dartmouth Street*

III A 16 · *Hotel Vendome (right) with view of Dartmouth Street*

In this case the pavilion contains a spectacular reception room and stairway that are often referred to as the most palatial space in Back Bay. In these terms the visible entry on Dartmouth Street is modest enough, a porte-cochere that extends beyond the major pavilion and has a pair of arches and wrought-iron gates. One arch leads to a larger-than-life-size entry for people, the other makes provision for carriages.

Dormers and a chimney of pronounced silhouette animate the skyline of the Dartmouth Street side, while the Commonwealth Avenue elevation remains quiet, restrained and carefully studied, a brick wall of continuous stringcourses and well-proportioned windows. The most singular event along Commonwealth Avenue is a two-story conservatory with copper mullions and spandrels, all glassed in with small-paned windows at the top and larger, double-hung ones below. Formerly these offered glimpses of tantalizing floral displays; now they are joined to offices that one cannot help but covet.

Restoration and conversion of these rooms for elegant office suites have preserved a place of real distinction.

III A 18 · 315 DARTMOUTH STREET
SE corner Marlborough Street
1870

Viewed from the Ames-Webster House, this is an exceedingly picturesque pile, with a few simple elements made, masterfully, to seem many and complex. It rises dramatically from a one-floor pavilion beside the alley to a two-story block, capped by a floor and a half of mansard tower, to a three-story tower block on the corner, capped again by a very high and very shapely square mansard roof. Along the way various chimneys and dormers accompany the ascent. With this view from his windows, it is not hard to imagine that it might have been a quite specific case of mansard-tower envy that led Frederick Ames to make his addition (III A 17).

Along Marlborough Street the massive corner pavilion and its shapely roof are still present, but otherwise the house seems disappointingly uneventful.

III A 19 · CROWNINSHIELD HOUSE
164 Marlborough Street, SW corner Dartmouth Street
H. H. Richardson, 1870

Great oaks from little acorns grow, but not here. If you're looking for the Richardson you know and love, the Richardson of the First Baptist Church (III A 12) or Trinity Church (III C 1), you'll be disappointed. This early work shows signs of repressed talent and an interest in seeing how materials can be used, but on the exterior these traits are only to be found in the details; the mass is uninteresting.

A brick box bay on the Marlborough Street side makes the entry. Over the door is a lovely, tight little metal-and-glass hood. The corners of the brick bay twist unexpectedly at the second floor to make corner windows divided by a spiraling brick pier that is capped incongruously by proto-Richardsonian Romanesque capitals.

The stairs also show a mind at work, a mind with a disposition to plasticity. The sides and base are carved stone, buttressed at the street into blunt, evocative corner posts. Bricks placed on the diagonal are inset like tiles in the stone baluster walls. In the walls of the house, diamond patterns of glazed ceramic tile are spaced at intervals where usually there would be a stringcourse. Similar diamonds are set under the eaves between the cornice brackets—a clever device for sparkling the shadow. Alas, set as they are under the eaves and protected from the cleansing rain, they've become quite grimy.

The imagination here is good solid currency, but invested in accounts too small to earn much interest.

III A 20 · 165 MARLBOROUGH STREET
· 326–28 DARTMOUTH STREET
NW corner Marlborough and Dartmouth streets
Snell & Gregerson, 1871

A very restrained, subtly modulated exterior combines three houses in one composition, yet establishes a distinct identity for each. The façade is carefully paced, with high framed windows mostly organized within projecting bays. Narrow, solidly formed corners shape the edges of each house.

The planning behind this stately face is much more ingenious than you might at first imagine. The three houses interlock in plan, and the middle one is set at a different floor height than the others, as the façade reveals. What is not evident from the exterior is the shape of the plans: The central house is T-shaped, having two spacious rooms along Dartmouth Street and only one at the back. At the rear the two side buildings become thicker to interlock with the T, and the additional space is used for stairs and service areas.

Each house has a stretch of façade, but the one on Marlborough Street has the best of it. A beautiful wide, colonnaded porch has shallow stairs that spread out toward the street. Above these, a cast-iron grill shields the bottom of four narrow framed openings. Three have windows and one is blank in deference to the composition of the offset drawing room behind. The middle two are capped by a centering arched pediment. The high-style ingenuity of these gracious houses renders them both unified and distinct.

III A 21 · 172 COMMONWEALTH AVENUE
between Dartmouth and Exeter streets
J. H. Besarick, 1885

Imagine building next to the Hotel Vendome! J. H. Besarick could, and he set about it with his usual florid magnanimity. The result: a very spirited building with a narrow, almost inconsequential entry. A chamfered bay at the bottom is surrounded by wonderfully abundant Richardsonian vegetable carvings. This turns into a round bay above, with a balcony at the top. Also up there at the top are three arches covering a recessed porch; one that is more like a mysterious cavern than a rooftop outlook. This in turn is capped by another of those prickly, rolling floral motifs, only here we find a head peering out of the center.

III A 22 · 176, 178 COMMONWEALTH AVENUE
between Dartmouth and Exeter streets
Charles Atwood, 1883

A great duo, worthy still of emulation. Both houses are entered at the ground level through a common brownstone arcade stretching across the front with three low arches. You figuratively duck under this arcade to come to the entry doors. The front face of the rusticated base then lurches up to become a faceted bay on one house, a round bay on the other. The round one rises up the full height of the building, ending in a conical roof that is interrupted by a splendidly capped window facing the street. The one-story faceted bay has two windows above and a balustrade. Above these, in turn, is an incredible pediment, Flemish Baroque perhaps, which is the front face of a two-story dormer projecting from the steep slate roof common to the pair. The effect is of two domestic empires bonded together by ridge, cornice and monkish base.

The power of these paired buildings lies more in the disposition of their parts than in materials or decoration, so they commend themselves to our attention more than many others. The scheme might not work so well in the cheap materials we can afford today, but it's worth a try.

III A 23 · WILLIAM LLOYD GARRISON STATUE
Commonwealth Avenue Mall between Dartmouth and Exeter streets
Olin L. Warner, 1885

"I am in earnest—I will not equivocate. I will not excuse. I will not retreat a single inch, and I will be heard!"

So said William Lloyd Garrison, 1805–79, and so his statue sits squarely in the middle of the Commonwealth Avenue Mall in the resolute manner of his speech. It's larger than life, relaxed but attentive, with piles of loose papers and a thick book under a comfortable-looking armchair, as if he were still in his publishing

III A 22 · *176, 178 Commonwealth Avenue*

III A 23 · *William Lloyd Garrison Statue in front of Hotel Vendome (III A 16)*

office, immersed in work, just leaning back for a moment to have a word with a visitor. He has a remarkable profile, with balding head, long straight hair brushing the collar and sharply pointed nose. Nevertheless, he looks rather more kind and avuncular than the steely inscription would suggest. The text is from the opening manifesto in the first issue of *The Liberator,* which he founded and edited.

In the Boston of 1835, Garrison was nearly lynched for his vociferous and uncompromising opposition to slavery.

III A 24 · 165 COMMONWEALTH AVENUE
between Dartmouth and Exeter streets
Cummings & Sears, 1879
· 167 COMMONWEALTH AVENUE
between Dartmouth and Exeter streets
Sturgis & Brigham, 1880

Two houses that are not a pair, showing instead a polarity of conceptions within the fundamental constraints of building in Back Bay. Cummings & Sears invested their attention in animating the brick face of No. 165 with stone inventions. They had a disposition to make things planar and a (perfectly reasonable) infatuation with aediculae, little miniature temple fronts in which saints, doors and windows might appear. Here they are filled with doors and windows.

A pair of doors at the top of an imposing set of stone steps is embraced by an insubstantial stone aedicula of Romanesque persuasion. On the second floor, the center window is framed by pilasters of the sort that only Victorian minds could conceive, supporting a carved stone roof above. The center window of the third floor has something approximating a squashed and flattened Greek pediment over knobby Corinthian pilasters. Surmounting all this, wondrously, are two piers almost standing free of the mansard and holding the front edge of a diminuitive pyramid of colored slate. Not dull.

At No. 167, Sturgis and Brigham show more Classical inclinations. A half-round bay sweeps out in a strong form but is otherwise uneventful—not big enough to become the façade, as some later ones do, not small enough to convey a sense of inhabitation inside. The top is banded by a set of carved garlands and a rather pleasant stone balustrade outlines a balcony that offers its tenants the opportunity for pots, plants and personal objects of the sort that are otherwise missing from the building's façade. Not thrilling.

III A 25 · 199 MARLBOROUGH STREET
NE corner Exeter Street
E. N. Boyden, 1890
· 295–97 BEACON STREET
SE corner Exeter Street
S. D. Kelley, 1885

The east side of Exeter Street between Marlborough and Beacon streets presents an extraordinary array of bay windows rolling across two seven-story apartment blocks.

Those on the Marlborough Street building are varied and inventive, artfully considered in relation to the building surface. By contrast, those on the Beacon Street building, originally the Hotel Royal, are routinely executed and unsympathetic to the masonry of the façade. But at the corner of this latter building, turning the corner of Beacon and Exeter streets, there's a bay that's round beyond all expectation, a tower set out from the corner so that it is a full three-quarters round. It appears almost as a master stroke of afterthought, and judging from the rather shabby details where metal meets stone, it may well have been.

The Marlborough Street building is more fastidiously crafted. Four bays of three heights and three shapes combine in syncopation with two chimneys to compose the Exeter Street elevation. On the lower floors a thin, hard brick, orange in tone with little flecks of burnt material in it, is interlaced with brownstone trim; above, the brick is dark red. Metal-clad bays are detailed so that they appear to be merely set upon the surface of the building. The chimneys start from voluted brownstone brackets and corbeled bricks and climb up the face of the building, incorporating more and more flues as they rise, until they burst through the roofline as wide, strongly molded forms. A metal cornice between the sixth and seventh floors is adorned with a string of discs jutting forward, like so many cymbals nailed to its façade.

The Marlborough Street side is more conventional, with a bay on one side rising the full height and a flat area above the entry holding a metal bay at the third and fourth floors with its own small cornice and a triangular protrusion. This breaks the larger building into pieces that are recognizably akin to its Marlborough Street neighbors. The entry itself is nicely scaled by a brownstone arch that bows low to the ground at each side. Winged griffins hold shields emblazoned with 199's to announce the address.

III A 26 · 196 MARLBOROUGH STREET
SE corner Exeter Street
W. Whitney Lewis, 1886

Prestidigitation. W. Whitney Lewis is faulted by historians for being a lightweight follower of Richardson. Perhaps, but he sure could juggle. This building has more decisions in the air at one time than any other in Boston.

To begin at the bottom, the base is pudding stone, the rest of the structure brick, both trimmed in brownstone. But the base has more glass in it than the brick walls above. The ground is scooped away on the Marlborough Street side to provide light and air to a lower floor of offices, where dentists now look out of their curtained windows at the garden slope. There are entries to both lower and upper floors, neither pretentious, although the upper entry passes through a beautifully carved brownstone arch.

The windows in the base do not, for the most part, align with those in the walls above. In fact, very seldom do any windows in this building align; mostly they take their place according to the room layout inside, sometimes according to the street outside. Those on the softly angled corner bay, for instance, do align with each other at the third and fourth floors, but they are not in the center of the bay when seen head-on from Marlborough Street. As it turns out, their centerline is skewed away from the corner so that when viewed on the diagonal from across the street, these windows match a similarly offset group in a bay on Exeter Street.

III A 26 · *196 Marlborough Street*

III A 26 · *Exeter Street doorway, 196 Marlborough Street*

Together, these bays form a single polygonal bow window on the corner. Their diagonal symmetry is marked by a brownstone shaft in the middle of the bow, at the point where the swelling bays on either side intersect the basic rectangular volume of the house. And lest you miss the cornerness of it all, the names "Marlborough" and "Exeter" are inscribed in the appropriate faces.

The faceted corner bow begins in the ground on Marlborough Street, but on Exeter, where the building is up against the sidewalk, the bow doesn't begin until the third floor. Then it corbels out from the wall above a row of arches just like those holding the entry and windows on Marlborough Street. The arch at the far end is slightly smaller and lower, and projected slightly forward on colonettes to mark the Exeter Street entry. The tops of the arched windows are glazed with large panes of glass, changing at the spring line to a pattern below that has a central clear panel framed by casement windows of very small panes, giving a netted, protected quality to those openings that are closer to the street.

There are other sleights of hand: a beautiful five-window brownstone bay swelling ever so slightly on the Exeter Street side; dormers of various sorts, including an eyebrow; a short stretch of raised stringcourse in the middle of the Marlborough Street elevation to prove that the architect knew where the center of the building was; and a grand gable end with chimney.

It's great entertainment—from bottom to top, and especially around the corner.

III A 27 · 195 COMMONWEALTH AVENUE
NW corner Exeter Street
J. Pickering Putnam, 1881

The Exeter Street side of this building gives us a Flemish vision of a tropical garden. Its brick walls are overgrown with decorative terra-cotta panels, mostly floral, cast with abundant invention, angularity and intertwinement. The entry is a lacy centerpiece on Exeter Street, shaded by a bay window. The centerline is capped by a generous two-story strap-work pediment ending in a finial with a tiny set of windows in the attic. Meanwhile, on the corner an extra-wide bay with almost continuous windows is topped by a copper-hooded roof that bears an astonishing resemblance to Bismarck's helmet. A crocketed copper ridgepiece and a curious cornice of what look like terra-cotta shingles delimit the slate roof. At the north extremity is a fabulous conflation of bay windows, dormer and chimney, all very three-dimensional and solid.

The Commonwealth Avenue side has no entry, but does have, like its opposite number at 25 Exeter Street, a porch lodged in the attic. Built only a year apart on nearly identical sites, the two face each other across Commonwealth Avenue, each projecting a very different sense of the world.

III A 28 · 25 EXETER STREET
SW corner Commonwealth Avenue
Peabody & Stearns, 1882

A powerful form handled more decisively than most. From its corner site this building treats both streets with respect, with a steep roof running parallel to Exeter Street and ending in a gable on Commonwealth Avenue. Gable dormers at each end of the Exeter Street elevation make implied towers at either side of the entry. It's a splendid entry, tucked into the side of the building, with steps that slide up sideways under an arch to the large door and vestibule, lately painted an altogether unseemly green. Between the implied towers above is a syncopated rhythm of large and small windows playing out the internal room arrangements within a fundamental compositional order.

The Commonwealth Avenue gable, meanwhile, covers a large open porch with a single oversized arch springing almost from the porch floor. Below it and off center, most of the street frontage is occupied by an expansive round bay with brownstone trim, a bay worthy of its Commonwealth outlook.

III A 29 · 199 COMMONWEALTH AVENUE
between Exeter and Fairfield streets
James T. Kelley, 1890

Back Bay in Beacon Hill dress, tailored so well that you hardly notice. Elsewhere architects had been using their projects as opportunities to exercise their talent for inventing forms, but the game here was to make personal decision unnecessary, or at least invisible, by adopting the decorous garb of an earlier era.

Sometimes ascribed to McKim, Mead & White, this is one of the first buildings to result from a serious and self-conscious look at Boston's own Classical architecture as a source of inspiration. Yet no mansion on Beacon Hill could be taken as a complete model, and there's an unmistakable expansiveness to the pair of swell-front bays flanking a single gracious entry. The whole is handsomely sedate, entirely abdicating the picturesque incidents of craft and inhabitation, the crocket pediments and chamfered bays that characterize most earlier building in Back Bay, in favor of a controlling conception of dignity that simply eliminates the particular. It now serves, quite suitably, as the home of St. Botolph Club.

III A 30 · *detail, Algonquin Club, 217 Commonwealth Avenue*

III A 29 · *199 Commonwealth Avenue, St. Botolph Club*

III A 30 · ALGONQUIN CLUB
217 Commonwealth Avenue, between Exeter and Fairfield streets
McKim, Mead & White, 1887

You might, with some justice, consider this building oversized, pretentious, even awkward. But it's really very interesting. Where other architects later would simulate the detail of the Renaissance as they went about designing row houses, McKim, Mead & White here made a Renaissance palace for the Algonquin Club out of the stuff of row houses—three, to be exact. There are few buildings in Boston of comparable opulence and scope.

The windows, though comparatively few, are arranged with great purpose, overlarge at the bottom floor and diminishing in size as they rise to blank squares in the attic.

The faceted bays familiar to Back Bay here form pavilions at either end bonded to the rest of the façade by a continuous Classical balustrade at the skyline. The center entry is a mere five steps above the ground, but is emphasized on the building face above by two stories of carefully proportioned colonnaded porch. All three features—the center and the two end bays—are marked at the fourth floor by high, arched windows in their centers. Originally they all rose from a continuous base, a terraced basement that spread across the whole face of the building in the plane of the front wall of the entry and at the height of the present rusticated base. The full-width basement story was in clear violation of Back Bay ordinances, however, and the projection was subsequently removed, its front face pressed, figuratively, into the face of the building.

The top two floors are rendered with great abandon, including a Palladian window, semicircular wreaths, banners and bunches of fruit, to say nothing of eagles, putti and the aforementioned blank windows.

B/NEWBURY AND BOYLSTON STREETS

Newbury and Boylston streets are the segments of Back Bay that have been taken over by commerce. Boylston Street, closest to the now vanished railroad lines that ended in Park Square, early developed sizable parcels of land and larger buildings. Newbury Street remains mostly town-house conversions.

The Arlington-Berkeley block of Newbury Street, though, is infected with a bit of Manhattanitis. Not that that's all bad. Every city needs a little uptown chic, replete with show windows that have mitered glass held in place by bits of metal frame and flat, dull, polite façades up above. The lifeless uppers keep your attention down at the street, where the action is. This outbreak is confined mostly to the south side of Newbury Street, ending at Berkeley Street with F.A.O. Schwartz and Brooks Brothers. On the north side the Ritz-Carlton Hotel (III B 2) was the most seriously affected, but the spirit of Manhattan lurks still in the walls of the new Knoll Showroom (III B 4).

Along Boylston Street, on the other hand, there is enough material for a catalog describing the various ways that five- and six-story commercial buildings have been made during this century. The Berkeley Building (III B 7) is a simple framed structure clad in elegantly elaborated, decorative terra cotta. The Coulton Building (III B 8), in contrast to those around it, is vigorously molded, with

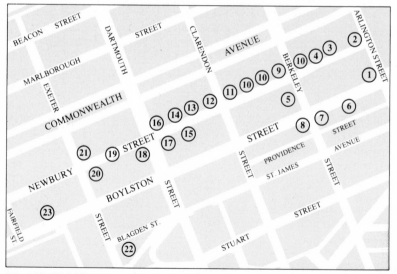

III / BACK BAY   B / NEWBURY AND BOYLSTON STREETS

thick, shiny bay windows and solid brick walls. The rest of the buildings along the street are flat, the more recent ones offering a parade of uninteresting ways to cover a building's front surface. They are a result of the bleak period since 1950 during which many architects of commercial buildings have thought that their formal role should be limited to determining whether horizontal or vertical lines prevail. Sometimes they've wondered whether all buildings should be shiny, but recently they've given up doubting.

Farther west, Newbury Street develops its own very distinctive and appealing character and becomes one of the nicest shopping streets in Boston, or anywhere. Renovated town houses with large glass bays on the ground floor produce a delightful urban landscape. It's a very particular urban environment resulting from an interplay between the original lot divisions, the town-house structures that first occupied them and a fairly consistent vocabulary of renovation and new construction that has transformed the street for commercial use.

Owners and tenants of these buildings have further animated the street by using the 25-foot space between the building and the sidewalk for various purposes. Some areas are paved and used for displays or sidewalk sales. Others have thick planting. During the summer months several cafés move tables out onto the paved areas and give passers-by a place to see and be seen. Some lots have stairs up and down to shops and galleries, others have show windows and display cases for flowers or fashions or other items for sale. But each contributes something extra, and together they make these blocks of Newbury Street genuinely attractive.

III B 1 · ARLINGTON STREET CHURCH
NW corner Arlington and Boylston streets
Arthur Gilman, 1861

This church is a bother to historians. It's 50 years too late to be Georgian and 30 years too early to be Georgian Revival. Perhaps its conservative form was meant to provide reassurance for a congregation that was moving from a Bulfinch church on Federal Street to the edge of a mud flat only recently filled.

Anomaly or not, it's handsomely shaped. One can only wish that more of Boston had been guided by Gilman's hand. He was evidently an accomplished student of form, here working in a very different mode than at Old City Hall (I A 8). The whole church is proportioned with care, with a knowledgeable balance of parts: the piers, capitals, architraves, brackets, everything.

The tower is especially fine, akin to the Park Street Church (I B 1) but more subtly shaped, bearing just a hint of the attenuated proportions of its Gothic Revival contemporaries without for a moment abandoning the Classical vocabulary. Its tower rises from Arlington Street in five carefully modulated stages, all surmounting a powerful pedimented entry block. The sides of the church are measured by giant-order pilasters that reach the full height of the walls. At the entry they become nearly full, round columns engaged to the wall, framing an entry scaled down again by smaller, square, composite columns supporting an arch over the portal.

The tower rises above all this, resting securely, if improbably, on the apex of the pediment. Its first stage is a high square block with quoined corners and simple arches. Next is a block with Ionic pilasters and open arches. Then a short cornerless section, the four faces of which frame four clocks between volutes and

III B 2 · *Ritz-Carlton Hotel, Arlington Street façade*

III B 1 · *Arlington Street Church*

carefully balanced urns. Then above this is an octagonal section in which engaged Corinthian columns frame eight large arched windows. A broken entablature then leads to a small attic piece, the base of an eight-sided conical spire. It all ends in a weather vane. On the second and fifth levels, glass in the openings makes rooms out of the stages of the tower—resting places in your imagination's ascent to the top.

Style sleuths are anxious for us to know that the tower is based on the one by James Gibbs on St. Martin's-in-the-Fields in London. Good choice, well studied.

III B 2 · RITZ-CARLTON HOTEL
15 Arlington Street, Newbury Street to Commonwealth Avenue
Strickland & Blodgett, 1931
addition: Skidmore, Owings & Merrill, 1981

The Ritz-Carlton Hotel is distinctive inside, but has little to recommend its exterior. Its best feature is a row of canvas awnings that reach south in the sunny season to shade large windows at the second level. These set Newbury Street off marching to a quick, urban pace. Otherwise, the Ritz dominates the edge of the Public Garden by bulk alone, like a piece misplaced from a Monopoly game.

The building has a considerable amount of wall dressing: the bottom floors rendered as a high stone base, gray brick corners, red brick middle, stone-framed windows in the base and top three stories, carvings too delicate to read from the street, a miserly cornice. But it all serves only to emphasize the brick blockiness, like clothes drawn on a flat figure, not actually tailored to fit a living person with parts. The only place it fills out is in a penthouse tower at the back, where decorum slipped and somebody remembered the blunt vigor of the English Baroque. And that has now been obscured by the new addition. The extension just built at the corner of Arlington and Commonwealth is an even more graceless affront, its unseemly bulk clad haplessly in what might as well be rented clothes.

The bar is one of the older building's interior charms. Not overdesigned, not lavish, just a good bar appropriately nooked and paneled in a rich wood veneer. Nicely shaped, comfortable chairs are tastefully upholstered in an improbable pattern, and dumb-looking lights do their job well, so the dimness is not blinding. Plate-glass windows on the Arlington Street side let you watch the arrival of high-stylists or, when the taxis are gone, view the Garden. If you are male, wear a tie.

The café at the rear of the building is a few steps down from the lobby level, steps that announce your arrival into a low, squarish room. A large round bay projects out toward Newbury Street, making the room light and cheerful and placing the diners right in the sidewalk. The decor has recently been made more ponderous and the room is not so forthright and pleasant as it once was.

Upstairs, in the original building the dining room has a fine view of the Public Garden, if you can get near the windows. This staid room is graced by a row of great columns marching down the middle. The round piers are robust enough to support the tall building above, yet smoothly contoured in a conservative Art Deco style without any kitsch in the capitals.

III B 3 · EMMANUEL EPISCOPAL CHURCH
13 Newbury Street, between Arlington and Berkeley streets
A. R. Estey, 1864
Allen & Cullen, 1920

Emmanuel Episcopal Church has been altered over the years from a freestanding stone block to a tight urban composition squeezed ingeniously into mid-block. Three portals come out toward the street. The middle one is the transept of the original church, the other two date from additions in 1898 that oriented the church to the street. The middle portal now appears to be the central pavilion of a Beaux-Arts composition, only here it's in a rural English Gothic mode. The ends are then brought back to the line of the adjoining buildings on the east by a town house in the shape of a cool stone castle and on the west by a clumsily placed chapel the width of a town house with a fourth portal of its own in smooth limestone. The chapel, designed in a perpendicular Gothic style, shows neither the selfless humility of its parent nor any very proud spirit of adventure.

Inside, the main church is an expansive space with broad wooden arches and a generally pleasant if uninspiring sense to it.

III B 4 · KNOLL SHOWROOM
37 Newbury Street, between Arlington and Berkeley streets
Gwathmey/Siegel, 1980

High style for the 1980's—which just goes to show how much can be lost in a hundred years. Gray stucco and glass, elegantly spare and colorful furniture inside, a great half-round showroom bay projecting into the setback area with curved glass—all these and glass blocks in the wall are signs of the times, smoothly handled and devoid of invention.

III B 5 · BONWIT TELLER
234 Berkeley Street, Newbury to Boylston streets
William Gibbons Preston, 1863

This fine building for the Museum of Natural History has been occupied by Bonwit Teller since 1947. It is a remarkably serene Classical building with none of the latent boosterism of its near contemporary, Old City Hall (I A 8).

Next door, a sibling building (now deceased) housed the Massachusetts Institute of Technology and particularly its School of Architecture. Together they formed the first bastions of culture in the Back Bay, only to be upstaged later by the original Museum of Fine Arts and the Boston Public Library in Copley Square (III C 4).

Still, Bonwit Teller is more remarkable than it may at first appear; it is a very self-consciously designed object. Giant brick pilasters rise from a rusticated stone basement story all the way to a plain but hefty architrave and cornice. In between, tall pedimented windows and segmental arch windows mark out the second and third floors, respectively. The pilasters are regularly spaced but

III B 5 · *Bonwit Teller, with second John Hancock Building (left rear) and John Hancock Tower* (IV A 7)

doubled at the ends. In a subtle detail the corners are notched slightly and covered in stone, thus avoiding thick columns in angle view and allowing the entire walls to be seen as flat sets laid on the face of the basic block.

The entry façade on Berkeley Street has a full-scale temple front projecting slightly forward, its end pilasters also coupled. Within the additional depth, tiny balconies are set between the pilasters with diminutive freestanding columns, crowned at the third floor by handsome round arches. These balconies, scaled to comfortable human size, help us to understand the size of the building and imagine ourselves within it.

Broad, gentle stairs lead up to the arched entrance in the basement story. On either side are platforms where stone lions or suitably instructive sculpture would ordinarily stand guard. Here mannequins stand in curious *haute couture* poses, under metal-and-glass baldachinos that are silly but amusing. A proud eagle previously poised at the apex of the pediment has long since vanished.

The Rogers Building, once next door on Newbury Street, was also designed by Preston. It was MIT's first building in the area, later to be joined by several others in the vicinity of Copley Square. Most were vacated in 1916, when MIT moved across the river to its more extensive temple in Cambridge.

The New England Mutual Life Insurance Building, which replaced the Rogers Building, is a Cram & Ferguson opus so lifeless that it defies even unsympathetic description, though in fairness the Boyleston Street side was originally much lower and somewhat more in scale with its neighbors. Like the first John Hancock Building (IV A 7), it was consumed by its own addition.

III B 6 · WOMEN'S EDUCATIONAL AND INDUSTRIAL UNION
356 Boylston Street, between Arlington and Berkeley streets
Parker, Thomas & Rice, 1906
restoration: Shepley, Bulfinch, Richardson & Abbott, 1973

This meticulously groomed renovation of a handsome, rather simple building bears extraordinarily elegant overlays. No. 356 was occupied by Schrafft's Restaurant until 1968. Then it endured five years of shoddy alterations by many tenants. Finally it was given a complete restoration and renovation inside and out by Shepley, Bulfinch, Richardson & Abbott, who sensitively joined a new set of uses to the old architectural elements.

The main entrance is a set of the original filigreed colonettes highlighted by a gilded swan that hovers before the lunette of the arched entry. The swan, a new incarnation of the 1877 logo of the Women's Educational and Industrial Union, refers back to the Swan Boats (III A 1), inaugurated in the same year as the union, which was then housed just opposite the Public Garden.

You enter through a beautiful rounded glass vestibule with doors on either side. This makes a delicately formed little room inside, most of which has its original decoration. Inside the larger space a very nice, simple brass-rod-and-white-glass-globe lighting fixture is mounted in the middle, underneath four vaults, each neatly outlined with gold-and-brown paint around the edges. A new mezzanine was added for a luncheon café.

The exterior of the building wears its large windows and elegant framing with unprepossessing authority. The reclaimed storefront has been enhanced by the addition of a sign announcing the union's presence with well-formed, blocky serif letters. With just a little gold leaf, the new sign picks up the theme of the earlier entry without in any way competing with it.

In the right-end bay of the façade, there's a curious three-door entry. Two doors form an entry for offices; the third opens to provide a stand for the florist who sold flowers in front of the union's previous headquarters.

III B 7 · BERKELEY BUILDING
420 Boylston Street, SE corner Berkeley Street
Codman & Despredelle, 1905

High style straight from Paris (via MIT). Despredelle was the Beaux-Arts studio master imported to conduct design classes across the street at the former School of Architecture, and this is his major remaining building in Boston.

III B 6 · *detail, Women's Educational and Industrial Union*

III B 7 · *Berkeley Building*

It's a particularly fine example of a decorated structural frame, a building whose lightweight steel members have been clad in enameled terra cotta, with copper-and-glass walls filling in between. A beautiful building dressed to the teeth, but intelligent, too.

Both the Boylston Street façade and the one on Berkeley Street consist of a series of five-story bays above a ground-floor base of shops. The bays are treated like very tall, narrow proscenium arches, each topped with a sinuous keystone, each divided into a wide space and two narrow ones. The central bay on Boylston Street, marking the main entrance, is wider and taller, rising up beyond the parapet with its own false front and filled by a beautiful bulging glass bay.

The space between the regular bays and the extra-wide entrance arch is taken up by a narrow bay on each side, vaguely similar to the niches on each side of a triumphal arch and directly repeating the scheme of each bay. The top was originally more elaborate, with a high lacy screen-wall parapet and pointy finials for all the piers below, but this has been removed, presumably to forestall its collapse.

On the Berkeley Street façade, some of the bays have been reframed lately. They project slightly over the sidewalk, giving more space and character to the offices behind. The renovation preserves the original terra-cotta frame and the old bay windows at the very top. Even though the simplified anodized-aluminum framing is without any intrinsic character, there's not enough of it to diminish the original charm of the Berkeley Building. There's more of this framing and some copper-colored mirror glass at the refurbished entry, used quite effectively. More still would be dangerous.

Around the corner at the back, the treatment is quite uncommonly elaborate for the rear of a building, but all with direct functional purport. Beyond the terra cotta you can see a large courtyard faced with very light-colored brick that bounces light between the building faces. It makes a bright and airy light trap for the offices looking out onto it. These spaces, too, bow out on one side. On the west side of the courtyard are copper-covered lintels, and on the north some windows that step down in consort with the stairs they light. At the ground floor the columns on the back face of the building are all in their original state, with a simple form of infill stepping back discreetly to allow the structure to be clearly articulated.

Worth a special visit.

III B 8 · COULTON BUILDING
462 Boylston Street, SW corner Berkeley Street
c. 1905

This may be my favorite building in Boston, an astonishing combination of straightforward building construction and sheer willful iconoclasm, the latter in some measure induced by the reuse of walls and foundation from a YMCA building that earlier occupied the site.

The building is a basic brick block. On the Berkeley Street side are four large, quite simple but handsomely framed windows and four rhythmically placed, narrow ones. The Boylston Street façade, though, is made up of alternating brick piers, narrow windows and spectacularly glassy projecting bays. The bays, it seems, were originally glazed with the small panes that can still be seen in their side panels and tops and in the smaller windows inset into the piers. Sometime considerably later the lower parts of the bay windows were reframed with virtually no mullions, so that in angled view the bays are much more reflective now than they would have been in the original building, while viewed from the front they are more open. As you look at the building you look directly into the offices, with various forms of chairs, bicycles, plants and drapery juxtaposed against the architectural patterning. On the back side a little bit of the original strong urban stone base is visible. Along the street it's been covered with crass commercial signs.

There's great visual sturdiness to this building. The volume of the block is

III B 8 · *Coulton Building*

clear, cusped just a bit at the corner. The bays, for all their glassiness, are firm, distinct forms that project beyond the main volume of the building as columns of inhabitable rooms it is easy to imagine being in. Here the building's size is measured with design elements that can really be used, not simply with emblems that lend a rhetorical flourish.

The punch line, however, is the corner. In most buildings of the period, such as the Berkeley Building (III B 7) across the street, the corner is reinforced to make the whole seem to be a solid block. In the Coulton Building the corner quite inexplicably dissolves into a diminutive octagonal glass bay. This bay is made in the same way as the other bays but is only about half the size, and the parapet follows it out around the corner to make a little turret. It very thoroughly befuddles the structural character of the building at a critical intersection. In this it elaborates a theme established earlier in the 1883 YMCA building by Sturgis & Brigham, which had on the same corner a rounded, full-windowed turret at the second floor.

The combination of very strong and rational elements with the shimmering glass bays and the contradictory corner make this a fabulous building.

III B 9 · CHURCH OF THE COVENANT
NW corner Newbury and Berkeley streets
Richard M. Upjohn, 1866

Spiky, knobby, planar, brown, this building uses more formula than feeling. It was designed by the son of Richard Upjohn, the great Gothic Revivalist.

There is a thin, graceful feel to the stone elements here, particularly in the porch, but nothing that compels attention. The spire, 236 feet high, was once the tallest in the city.

Inside, the action is all above, in a thicket of crocketed beams and trusses that make the roof structure. High, dark and intertwined, they add mystery to the space. Some of the stained-glass windows echo this mystery, depicting forest scenes under a similarly entwined tree cover. The windows are Tiffany, added between 1893 and 1914, many with a wonderful luminosity and a color sense that seems based on Impressionist painting.

The elder Upjohn, whose interest in the Gothic was neither merely aesthetic nor only archeological, was an active proponent of Gothic architecture as the ideal setting for religious worship. To him, its adoption was akin to rediscovery of the faith. It is likely no coincidence that the Church of the Covenant, designed by his son, has a touch of this zealotry about it and little of the relaxed deliberation that characterizes Richardson's First Baptist Church (III A 12), for instance.

III B 10 · 45 NEWBURY STREET
Peabody Building, NE corner Berkeley Street
C. R. Beal, 1899
reuse: Halasz & Halasz, 1975

· 77 NEWBURY STREET
between Berkeley and Clarendon streets
Peabody & Stearns, 1874

· 97 NEWBURY STREET
between Berkeley and Clarendon streets
Fred Pope, 1872
reuse: H. B. Allen, 1921

Three types of residential space redesigned for commercial use. No. 45 was changed in 1924 to a florist shop, with high, sunny spaces made by dropping the first floor to ground level and substituting columns for the bearing wall, then filling in between with glass. It was recently converted again into the Magic Pan Crêperie by Halasz & Halasz. Now a sunny outdoor café serves an an introduction to a particularly pleasant group of rooms, each with a distinctive sense. Some are cavelike, one has a raised platform on one edge; the main room rises almost two stories to an airy, wood-slat ceiling that slopes to give shape to the room. Above all this the original residential form remains intact.

No. 77 has been totally refaced, leaving its façade a flat plane topped by absurd little crenelations. On it various bays have been placed: On the first floor an expansive show window has been detailed as a glassed-in marquee; on the second floor a glassy bay is stretched all across the building's width, giving a layered look to display space between the window and the original front wall of the building, still visible as a set of piers behind. On the third floor, right in the middle, a small, square bay window with a copper base and a copper top simply juts forward as an altogether enviable spot.

No. 97 has also been given the full treatment, but with a more light-hearted fancy. Though it's not really Parisian, this building somehow conspires to look like something from a French tourist-bureau ad: mansard roof, round pediment on a wide dormer, window boxes full of flowers, narrow façade with almost continuous windows, small paned. A broad segmental arch brings all this down to the street, with a beautiful show window in the center, recessed entries right and left, and a transom window that steps across the top.

III B 11 · TRINITY RECTORY
223 Clarendon Street, NE corner Newbury Street
H. H. Richardson, 1879
renovated: 1893

This simple, strong Richardson work has survived the addition of a story with a slight but debilitating limp. The entrance is particularly splendid, set back into the surface of the wall on Clarendon Street with a robust stair running parallel to the street under a very grand, low arch. And the endpiece on Newbury Street, with its paired windows and chimney, still bears the master's touch.

A third floor was added in 1893 after Richardson's death. The roof was replaced above it in faithful imitation of the original, but there was enough revision of the fundamental proportions of the structure to take away the lithe forcefulness it once had. The totally bland third floor now intercedes between the eave and the carved panels of the second floor, to which it was once visually joined, leaving a flaccid band in an otherwise energetic composition. It is, however, all covered with ivy.

III B 12 · 109 NEWBURY STREET
NW corner Clarendon Street
Charles A. Cummings, 1871

The gem of Newbury Street, No. 109, at the corner of Clarendon Street, was designed by Charles A. Cummings to be his home only a year before work began on the Cummings & Sears New Old South Church (III C 4). With two swell-front bays and a center entry, this building is kin to 199 Commonwealth Avenue (III A 29), though from an earlier, more picturesque generation.

There have been many changes here, but the overall brick form remains, with its stone trim and copper cornices. The central entry is flanked by two great round bays that are treated like towers, with cones of slate roofing. These intersect a mansard and are themselves intersected by dormers with steep pointed roofs.

Conversion to storefronts in 1923 removed the piers from the bay windows, leaving only the cornice brackets to recall the vertical supports. This makes for a dramatic juxtaposition of the delicate glassiness of the bays against the heavy façade itself. These renovations destroyed the structure's fundamental masonry character but created a vivid new sense, because the glass bays are elegant and dramatic, infused with spirit and sophistication, as the original was.

Recent renovation is more maddening, however. The Lodge, a chain store specializing in blue jeans and casual wear, has covered over the ground-floor bays above and below the five faceted windows with rough-sawn lumber painted white. This effort to achieve an instant neo-rustic look totally denies the elegance of the building, like a jeans label stapled on fine tailoring. It's an infuriating kind of denial: crass, commercial, pandering to the crude in the face of real distinction.

III B 13 · 113–23 NEWBURY STREET
between Clarendon and Dartmouth streets, north side
113–15 Newbury Street
reuse: J. E. Bennett, 1932
117 Newbury Street
S. D. Kelley, 1887
119–23 Newbury Street
F. H. Moore, 1873

On the north side of Newbury Street between Clarendon and Dartmouth, a number of town houses still exist, set back from the sidewalk, their first floors a half level up. In some cases, as at No. 117, they are fully intact: bay, entry to the side, planting between building and sidewalk. Others have been revamped elegantly into combined buildings with tall, voluminous copper bays; still others have been brutalized by decay and carelessness.

No. 121, for instance, has been devastated by paint in an effort, presumably, to make it appear different from its identical neighbors, Nos. 119 and 123. Paint it all cream and white, someone seems to have said. So shingles, copper, brownstone, the storefront, the stair balusters, everything, is all cream and white except for the air conditioner and burglar alarm, which were left as they were when they came off the shelf.

Meanwhile, on all three buildings the brownstone itself is decaying very badly. Only on close inspection can you see that it was once a rather precise set of

III B 13 · *113–23 Newbury Street*

window edges and delicate inscribed carvings. Yet despite the poor condition of the surface, these houses survive. The first and second floors have been eaten away by glass-fronted shops supported by steel columns and beams. But rising undaunted above this are the vigorous dormers that almost conceal the mansard roof in a flurry of profiled pediments.

III B 14 · 137–41 NEWBURY STREET
between Clarendon and Dartmouth streets
H. B. Allen, 1929
· 143–45 NEWBURY STREET
between Clarendon and Dartmouth streets
H. B. Allen, 1927

These two buildings, both by H. B. Allen, represent very different architectural approaches to the context of residential Back Bay now turned commercial.

The six-story building at Nos. 143–45, while stone-faced with neo-Gothic detail, works essentially within the structural rhythm and formal vocabulary that dominates the rest of the street. The bays of the first two floors are especially handsome, shaped in copper, like many of their predecessors, and carefully formed within a larger arched opening. This assembly of bays is one of the most pleasant incidents along Newbury Street, bringing the interior life of the shop discreetly out onto the street.

At Nos. 137–41, Allen used the dimensional freedom allowed by assembling three lots as one property to make a structure that is bigger (nine stories) and more pretentious than its surroundings—quite a sharp break in the pattern of the street. The curious decorative motifs used to elaborate the windows, parapet and piers at the top similarly break with tradition. They seem to be the not-very-happy result of some commingling of Gothic and Mayan sources.

III B 15 · 128–34 NEWBURY STREET

between Clarendon and Dartmouth streets, south side
128 Newbury Street
Peabody & Stearns, 1877
130 Newbury Street
Peabody & Stearns, 1877
reuse: E. B. Stratton, 1927
132 Newbury Street
Peabody & Stearns, 1877
reuse: H. B. Allen, 1927
134 Newbury Street
Peabody & Stearns, 1877

The south side of Newbury Street between Clarendon and Dartmouth is very different than the north. Much of it has been rebuilt in various classicizing styles, mostly tiresome. There is no consistent rhythm of bays, as there is on the opposite side of the street, save in a group of remaining town houses by Peabody & Stearns, which are almost bold enough to carry the street.

The Peabody & Stearns houses are three stories above a basement. Their top floors are behind steep mansard roofs with heavy, fabulously molded cornices that bulge out around the top of half octagonal bays on each house.

No. 130 is an especially good example of how the accretion of small adjustments over time can make a place richer in subtle ways. A renovation by E. B. Stratton in 1927 tackled the problem of providing entry to shops at both the basement level and the first floor. The main stairs head for the original entry, then turn and climb a few steps more to enter into the bay (which now houses a gallery). Below, another set of steps ducks underneath to enter the basement shop. It's all very inventive, if not particularly handsome.

III B 16 · 147 NEWBURY STREET

NE corner Newbury Street
J. Pickering Putnam, 1878

J. Pickering Putnam's house is at the opposite end of the block from Cummings's house (III B 12). These were two prominent locations for the architects' own houses, evidently set out as examples of each architect's taste and ingenuity. The one by Cummings has more sweep, but Putnam's house bears closer scrutiny.

It is filled with craft, a compendium of shaped and carved motifs, each a testimonial to the architect's attention to sculpted detail. Stringcourses and lintel edges are carved with little knobs and slots that give relief to the shadows. If the knobs are carved buds (as they seem to be), then we need only wait till they bloom for a spectacular floral treat. If the wait seems excessive, visit the house in full bloom at 195 Commonwealth Avenue (III A 27), designed by Putnam three years later.

Although built against the side of a row house on Dartmouth Street, Putnam's house is designed to appear as though it were a freestanding château, altogether skillfully. It is topped by a large hipped slate roof interrupted by dormers and turrets, capped by a flat copper piece and exceeded by three great profiled chimneys.

III B 17 · HOTEL VICTORIA
275 Dartmouth Street, SE corner Newbury Street
J. L. Faxon, 1886

Six stories of terra cotta; a massive block of bays, turrets and arabesque tomfoolery. At the top a stepped parapet meanders up and down like the top of a cardboard castle. Windows at the lower levels (where you can see them clearly) are configured with small inset columns at the jambs and pointed arch tops that slide in front of the window sash, their surfaces all frittered with Islamic motifs cast in terra cotta.

Below the very top are two stringcourses, one of small arches holding the parapet slightly forward, the other a wave motif made with bricks stepping forward in a manner that makes the top of the building appear to be dripping down its face.

An altogether pleasant extravaganza, however lightweight.

III B 18 · 270 DARTMOUTH STREET
SW corner Newbury Street
William Ralph Emerson, 1881

William Ralph Emerson's building for the Boston Art Club follows Putnam's house (III B 16) across the way by three years and precedes Faxon's Hotel Victoria (III B 17) folly by five. It represents a heroic moment between the two, a moment in the development of Boston's architecture that was characterized by expansiveness, a liveliness of imagination accompanied by a great appetite for form and most especially by a capacity to see the building whole and to make us feel its presence as something alive.

The moment, of course, belongs mostly to Richardson, but Emerson could

III B 18 · *270 Dartmouth Street*

breathe life into a building more ably than most of his contemporaries, as in the slight but fascinating town house in Pinckney Street (II B 22). Here, for the Boston Art Club, he demonstrated his powers more grandly. There is no mistaking that this is a presence to be dealt with.

If one misses the scope of the whole, it's only because one is so amazed by the parts. And Emerson certainly made no effort to be modest about them. The building is an assembly of artful devices drawn large and made slightly peculiar. Most compelling are the gargantuan floral scrolls that bracket either side of the entry and the Dartmouth Street gables. These and the fruit-bowl plaque on Dartmouth Street are so grand and enormous, larger than life in vigor as well as in dimension, that they must certainly have taxed the limits of the claymaker's art. Coming upon them in the streetscape is like suddenly seeing details through a telescope.

More subtly, the hexagonal tower on the corner makes a remarkable adjustment to the nature of the site, which is long and exposed along Dartmouth Street. It is a near neighbor to the assertive mass of New Old South Church (III C 3), while on its Newbury Street side it has a comparatively narrow frontage, the last of a long row of houses. The tower, then, has one face flush with, indeed emerging from, the sweeping wall of Dartmouth Street, while it sets its point, narrow and sharp, as a distinct termination to Newbury Street. Viewed from Dartmouth Street, the tower enlarges the wall; from farther away on Newbury Street, it appears as a faceted freestanding element. The bottom of the tower is squared by a stone balcony at the second floor, to align with both streets.

Entry from Dartmouth Street is through a large arch scaled to that street and surrounded by a molded facing. Entry from Newbury Street is up a flight of stairs to a wonderfully plump little porch sitting atop pairs of Romanesque columns beneath a slate roof. Windows throughout are large and eventful, located with apparent ease.

The relation of the building to the narrow face of its lot has been somewhat obscured by later developments. In 1884, G. F. Meacham built the Boston Bicycle Club next door with such fidelity to the Emerson scheme that a subsequent merger of the two buildings is practically seamless. With a little careful scrutiny you can see that the western bay is detailed differently, that the original building was not square.

Finally, but not incidentally, the corner tower is capped by a shallow but splendid copper dome.

III B 19 · NEWBURY STREET
Dartmouth to Exeter streets

More than any other section of Newbury Street, the block between Dartmouth and Exeter streets displays a variety of relations between sidewalk and building. Most of the buildings here are converted town houses, with many types of new entries. Show windows, stairs, courts, hollows, bridges and additions reach out across the setback space to seduce shoppers strolling along the sidewalk, enticing them into shops that are both above and below the street level.

This engenders an encyclopedic array of transformations in the standard bay windows that fronted most of the original structures. Two examples, fundamentally similar, yet polar opposites in their attitude toward the existing structures, can be compared at Nos. 158 and 160. The first is outrageous and very funny. A wooden white-painted temple front has been stuck under the stone-faced bay, whose weight is then transferred through the Copley Society show window by two white pipe columns neatly spaced inside the Classical shop front. Proto–Post Modern; a little too tarnished for New York.

Its neighbor at No. 160 has similar columns captured behind a two-story faceted glass bay that approximates, cheaply, the line of the bay above. Elegantly bent pipe rails painted the color of brownstone reach out to encompass the sidewalk and make a recessed entry and display area for Placewares, a store that "specializes in places to put things."

Along the north side of the street, there is a row of shops that demonstrates many ways to go up and down at the same time. No. 161 is the simplest: The stairs simply go down to a brick-paved court and the bay is continued down as an entry to the shop. No. 163 is an elegant variant that has stairs running up to a large arch in a centered bay. Inside the arch a triangular space opens on one side into a shop, on the other to a passage that serves as an entry for a stair to the upper stories. At No. 165, built in 1927, the shop is all at grade level, and the flat area set back from the sidewalk gives a dramatic view of Artisans' show window. Occasionally the space also serves as a stage for musicians and street performers.

The most elaborate arrangement is a triplet at Nos. 171, 173 and 175. Here are a bridge, sunken courts, a fountain, half-level entries, and a variety of stairs and rails that link the three buildings and their art galleries to each other and to the street at several levels.

This is perhaps the most pleasant section of Newbury Street, delicate in scale, full of incident, spatially complex and well cared for.

III B 20 · EXETER TOWERS
28 Exeter Street, SE corner Newbury Street
Steffian Bradley Associates, 1979

Brick-clad, steel-framed, nine stories high, this is one of the first new buildings in Boston to be deliberately scenographic. It's much bigger than its Newbury Street neighbors, but its appearance is almost brought back to street size on Newbury Street by a terrace, four bays and a visual trick.

The apartment terrace parapet on the east end is just at the spring point of the town-house cornice next door. Above this parapet the building is set back, and its face is no longer brick but flat, mostly glass and shiny—to merge visually with the sky (or the John Hancock Tower) behind. But it's just a bit too diagrammatic, especially when the wall turns the corner to become a standard abrupt blank brick party wall above the adjoining building. The reflective upper floors recall the Batterymarch Building (V B 17), where the brick fades in color as it rises to the top; only there it is less abruptly diagrammatic and more compelling.

The terrace and bays stack progressively higher as they approach Exeter Street and views of the tall Prudential Building (IV A 8) beyond the corner tower. The tower, alas, lacks a purposeful silhouette, victim of our century's inhibitions to formal invention.

Black metal window frames of varying sizes inhabit the bays in reasonable proportion as they rise from the street; but on a street characterized by storefront additions that free themselves from their buildings to meet the shoppers passing by, it seems odd that the ground-floor stores here are all locked into the domestically scaled bays.

III B 21 · EXETER STREET THEATRE
26 Exeter Street, NE corner Newbury Street
H. W. Hartwell & W. C. Richardson, 1885
reuse: Childs, Bertman, Tseckares Associates, 1975

Built in a style that we associate with H. H. Richardson, the Exeter Street Theatre is a little tighter, a little more conventional, but not to be slighted. It is a building that lives its own life, even though its debt to Trinity Church is very obvious.

Designed as the First Spiritual Temple by Hartwell and the other Richardson, W. C., this is a solid block of 1880's splendor, with a brownstone base, attic and entry, and rough pudding stone walls. It's topped by a simple hip roof, which is interrupted by proud brownstone dormers that stand up in the skyline, and is modified at the top by copper end gables for ventilation.

The temple was built by a Boston philanthropist to be a place where the Society for Human and Spiritual Understanding could study spiritualism in its various guises, without regard to established dogma. In 1914 the society opened the Exeter Street Theatre in the building in an attempt to bring in income. We owe thanks to the temple for a fine block of a building, fully conceived and executed with care. To its second life as a theater, we are indebted for the best remaining theater signs in Boston—splendid affairs of shaped metal and little light bulbs that add cheer to any evening—rain, sleet or snow.

To the Raymond Cattle Company, we owe its present reincarnation as a cinema, with a bulbous glass shed added on to the Newbury Street side to capture the yard space and incorporate it into a chic lower-level café-bar for the singles set.

III B 22 · *detail, 88 Exeter Street*

III B 22 · 88 EXETER STREET
SE corner Blagden Street
Thomas W. Clark, 1889–91

A very thoughtful building well on its way to an architectural style that is recognizably American, a new form made directly and well, with little allegiance to previous styles. Compare this to the Hotel Victoria (III B 17) on Dartmouth Street, a building of similar bulk also intended as a residential hotel. This one is as serious as the other is frivolous, yet no less endowed with imagination. The visible distinctions here all have to do with something about building, with making many openings in a very high brick wall and with bonding the wall to the structure behind. At the top floor, however, the building celebrates its height with forms designed to make the most of being at the top.

The walls of the building are dark brown and buff. Brown is used for the base, window trim and the vertical shaft of the chimneys, buff for the rest. Brown and buff alternate in a ladder of stripes that scales the front faces of two projecting brick bays on Blagden Street. The windows are organized in vertical stacks, with spandrels set back slightly and iron tie rods clasped to the outer face by lovely, loopy cast-iron brooches. In the middle of each street façade elegant rounded copper bays with small-paned windows drop from a projecting balcony at the top to the dark base. The uppermost floor is much more open than the others, with regularly spaced, high, round-arched windows that open out onto long balconies with wrought-iron rails. The balconies extend across most of the building front, held out from the wall on heroic brick corbels.

III B 23 · 715 BOYLSTON STREET
between Exeter and Fairfield streets

· 739 BOYLSTON STREET
between Exeter and Fairfield streets

· 777 BOYLSTON STREET
between Exeter and Fairfield streets
Kilham & Hopkins, 1902

These three buildings and their renovations document the vital absurdities of commercial architecture.

This section of Boylston Street was originally residential, then rezoned for commercial use. The result was a shift in the setback line. So we have a block-long continuous façade made up of former town houses that stand shoulder to shoulder with more businesslike structures. In front of this there's another layer of construction that attempts, in high kitsch, to establish an atmosphere appropriate for each enterprise. So, for example, La Crêpe Restaurant tacked on a façade of arches and half-timbering and the Seafood Grotto added a whole Viking pediment, complete with fake carved beams and a great ship's mast. Needless to say, these clip-on façades change with some frequency as tenants come and go.

But the architecture remains. At No. 715 is the Driscoll Building, one lot wide. A large set of windows is treated as a single inset panel, subdivided by colonettes into one wide center panel and two narrow ones, and framed with Renaissance-based ornament and a little cartouche richly festooned at the very top.

At No. 739 there's a large, handsome commercial building worthy of Chicago. It is distinguished by a very direct expression of the structural bay and a clear indication of spandrels spanning the vertical piers. Alhambresque motifs over the windows and a diagonal pattern of terra cotta at the top underscore a rather conventional cornice.

Further down the street, No. 777 has a more notable cornice of narrow brick, cast stone and inset medallions. Below, two massive brick arches and two very large arched show windows neatly divide the façade in half for its two tenants, or did. Boston Blue Print remains, as it has for many years, on the right side. But J. C. Hilary's, a tavern of sorts, occupies the left side as well as the two adjoining storefronts. A unifying wall five feet in front of the main building façade aligns with the Boston Blue Print show window and other extensions down the street, adding a layer of syncopated construction that serves as an atmospheric introduction to the eating spaces behind.

C/COPLEY SQUARE

The area of Copley Square merits very special attention. From it one could illustrate the major forces in American architecture since 1850. It is the seat of two of the best and most influential buildings in America: Trinity Church (III C 1) and the Boston Public Library (III C 4). It is adjoined by the John Hancock Tower (IV A 7), an elegant and controversial construction of the recent past, and the present surface of the square itself (III C 7) is the result of a national competition in 1966.

Copley Square exists because of two rail lines that struck out across the mud flats of Back Bay, which had been dammed in 1821 to capture the tidal flow and convert its energy to run mills in the industrial expansion of Boston. The rail lines created major disruptions in the grid plan imposed on Back Bay in 1856 at the start of the landfill program. The lines cross at Back Bay Station just south of Copley Square, one arm dividing Back Bay from the South End as it heads out what is now called the southwest corridor to Providence and New York, while the other cuts diagonally across the grid toward western Massachusetts. The latter is now the path of the Massachusetts Turnpike, the gash that it creates through Back Bay covered in part by the Prudential Center (IV A 8). Huntington Avenue originally started at the corner of Boylston and Clarendon streets on the diagonal, crossing what is now the Plaza parallel to the southwest Boston & Providence Railroad line.

Therefore, the Copley Square area was initially the back end of Back Bay. Since it was as yet unformed, it could accommodate the exceptional. At first it was a site of great expositions. In 1869 it was the locus of a vast truss-roofed temporary coliseum built for the National Peace Jubilee. The area then came to be dominated by MIT, which spread out with laboratories, a gymnasium and classrooms after its first building was erected on Boylston Street adjacent to the Museum of Natural History (III B 5).

The Museum of Fine Arts was the first building to intimate that Copley Square itself might be a cultural center. Designed by Sturgis & Brigham, in 1871 it fronted the square from the south side, on the site of what is now the Copley Plaza Hotel. It was a fine, fussy building, replete with efforts to transform the programmatic and technical requirements of a museum into suitably inspiring brick-and-stone neo-medieval craftsmanship of the sort espoused at the time by Ruskin in England.

Trinity Church followed. The congregation, under the leadership of Phillips Brooks, held a competition for a new church to be built on the odd site bounded by Huntington Avenue, Clarendon, Boylston, and St. James streets. H. H. Richardson won the competition, moved to Brookline from New York and became

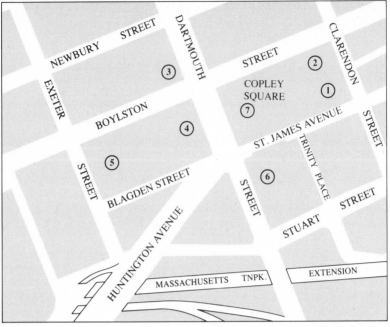

the central force in Boston's (and the nation's) architectural development during the remaining 15 years of his life. Trinity Church set the standard for inventive medievalism in American architecture, a standard that Richardson often exceeded through the analytical willfulness of his imagination, but which few others matched.

Shortly after Richardson's death, the Boston Public Library came to the opposite face of Copley Square with a building by McKim, Mead & White that is equally masterful, a touch more urbane and entirely the opposite in mode. The Boston Public Library set a standard for the American Renaissance that was seldom exceeded by anyone. Among its progeny is an addition (III C 5) out back by Philip Johnson, a grim reminder from 1972 that there's more to the Renaissance tradition than granite and arches.

Meanwhile, the town houses of Boylston Street were gradually replaced by a motley selection of commercial buildings, some early ones retaining the original lot-size modules, while other, more recent ones are indistinguishable from their commercial peers anywhere.

Like MIT, the Boston Museum of Fine Arts later sold its holdings in Back Bay and moved farther out into a Neoclassic temple of the sort thought suitable for cultural institutions in the first decades of the twentieth century. The departure of the museum cleared the way for a major hotel, now called the Copley Plaza (III C 6). Sibling to the Plaza Hotel in New York City and to the Winthrop Building (I A 12) downtown, it manages, surprisingly, to be dull.

Not so the newest kid on the block, the John Hancock Tower by I. M. Pei & Partners. It may be nihilistic, overbearing, even elegantly rude, but it's not dull. As a chunk of speculative real estate exploiting its location and the city services established there, it is brilliantly packaged, its surface smoothly reflecting the changing character of the sky. It's a landmark worth looking at, even when you shouldn't have to. In this book it is treated as part of the insurance-building complex it belongs to (IV A 7), not as a part of Copley Square, though if you happen to view it from the square, facing Trinity Church, note how its skewed angle deftly minimizes the apparent bulk from this crucial vantage point.

III C 1 · TRINITY CHURCH
east side, Copley Square
H. H. Richardson, 1872–77
porch: Shepley, Rutan & Coolidge, 1897
chancel: Charles D. Maginnis, 1938
restoration: Shepley, Bulfinch, Richardson & Abbott, 1974–81

Trinity Church has a presence that is so securely placed in our image of Boston and in our understanding of American architecture that it is hard to imagine it new, to sense its freshness and invention. The powerful spell that H. H. Richardson's church holds over us results from the coexistence of two salient characteristics: a powerful simplifying vision of the whole and a restless, inventive vitality in the parts. These two qualities, in tension with each other, are to be found in all aspects of the building—in plan and massing, in surface elaboration and in the interior space itself. To grasp the full power of the place, you must attend to it, surrender yourself to examination of the details, imagine the making of the parts.

Richardson was selected as architect for the church by competition. The essentials of his early scheme have remained and give the church its fundamental order, but its form was changed and refined in detail during the five years of building, then altered still more by revisions in the west towers and the addition of a porch in 1897 by his successors Shepley, Rutan & Coolidge. More recently still, Shepley, Bulfinch, Richardson & Abbott have supervised extensive restoration with assistance from the Society for the Preservation of New England Antiquities.

The controlling feature of the building is a great square tower that sits over

III C 1 · *Trinity Church, with adjacent John Hancock Tower* (IV A 7)

the center of the church, dominating the rest and establishing a fundamental pyramidal order. The peaked red tile roof of the tower is an irregular octagon, brought to the square by round turrets over the four corner piers, with stretches of richly arcaded, louvered and glazed screen wall in between. The central tower, seen from all around, is virtually identical on all four sides. Beneath it, every face of the building is adjusted. The east end is a round-apsed chancel, the south transept face extends to enclose a subsidiary entrance and stair, and the west portal end is fronted by two smaller towers connected by a very grand screen façade that invites attention from the square before it and commands the broad porch below. On the north side a cloister of alternating columns and piers creates a charmed spot between the mass of the church and a linked parish house and chapel. The parish house occupies the small end of what was once a trapezoidal site, its corner lopped off by Huntington Avenue before the street was closed to create the present pedestrian plaza.

In what is surely one of the smoothest, most carefree gestures in American architecture, the cloister colonnade simply steps up the side of the parish house and merges with the mass. In this spot alone Richardson epitomizes the characteristic that makes his buildings live where others are inert. The great stone mass of the building looks as though it were carved away here by the action of climbing; the body of the building adjusts to the life within. Yet this momentary entwinement of person and stone is hard won.

Elsewhere throughout the building we are made to sense the brute force of the stone. The intractability and coarseness of granite are dramatized by massive blocks with rough-hewed rock faces and irregular stacking. These are held in bondage by red sandstone, coursed in bands across the surface and carved into arches and colonettes at the openings. Yet these bands, too, change and deform as they cross different volumes of the building, acknowledging the force of the three-dimensional masses they clothe.

This is perhaps most obvious at the cornice of the west elevation where it intersects with the west towers. Here there is an extraordinary subtle interweaving of wall plane, patterned stone course, cornice and dormer. The coexistence of the three-dimensional forms and surface patterns makes for a multiplicity of readings here that gives the sense that it has resulted from a layering of decisions over time; the richness of form is built up by the accumulation of design attention.

In this case, it was quite literally so, since the tops of the towers were completed in all their spiky wonderment some years after Richardson's death. But it was inherent in Richardson's way of working that his initial ideas were elaborated and extended by those who worked with him. He was the initiator of schemes, the critic of their development and final arbiter in frequent visits to the construction site. Whole and part, master, draughtsman and builder are all allowed to influence one another. Indeed, the west towers were originally capped by much simpler roofs, which were pronounced unsatisfactory and removed. For some time, the west façade ended at the cornice, though a scheme existed for raising the towers and the west façade another story. The present dormered, conical towers make up in intensity what they lack in height.

The west façade without the porch was sterner than it is now. The added porch is more conventionally lavish and intricate than the rest of the building, an essay in piers and colonettes and columns of graduated sizes. Yet its size is majestic, the hierarchy of the parts clear, its three great arches and deep recesses forming a place of shelter that speaks eloquently to the expanse of space before it.

Inside, the centrality of the tower is again apparent, in a fabulous cubic volume of hovering space. On its four faces, round, cusped arches trace the shape of large, improbably shaped plaster vaults that cover the four short wings of the church, their surfaces ribbed in wood, their cusps tied together with great carved wooden beams encasing iron tie rods. The powerful spatial image of the whole encompasses an extraordinary wealth of murals, stained glass and decorative invention.

If you're planning to dash in and dash out, don't. It's a waste of the serenity of the place. This is one of the few places in America where a full range of talent in the visual arts can be seen at work, and here the creative capacity is writ large. The hand of artist John La Farge is present throughout, most grandly in the painted figures that inhabit the tower walls, most vividly in the brilliant stained-glass figure of Christ in the center window of the west façade or in the depiction of the New Jerusalem in a window over the gallery in the west wall of the north transept.

Carvings, mosaics, stained glass, murals, fittings—all are graced with a sense of tradition; most are informed by a bold sense of opportunity. Living as we do in a world racked by the rejection of precedent, it's a marvelous change to see the works of men who were so intensely interested in their predecessors, yet forceful and imaginative in their own right.

III C 2 · PHILLIPS BROOKS STATUE
NE corner Trinity Church
Augustus Saint-Gaudens, 1907

Only a very good sculpture could stand next to Trinity Church and steal even a little bit of the show. Phillips Brooks does it. But then, Trinity itself was in large part his show. It was Brooks, a man of superlative intellect as well as physical stature, who persuaded his congregation to move from their previous site on Summer Street, cramped by commerce, to the still-barren site in Back Bay.

His statue stands lofty and upright, with eyes peering into yours, one hand raised in exhortation, the other smothering a Bible on the lectern before him. Behind, touching his shoulder, is a figure of Christ. Weathering has added to the drama of this sculpture, creating contrasts of dark and light, most notably between the two faces. Christ has a hood mostly shrouding his face, which has weathered into a great darkness, while Brooks's is washed bright, emphasizing his forthright expression. Likewise, the great sweep of Brooks's coat is brightly oxidized, while his legs, sheltered from rain, are dark, like the deep, dark recesses around the base of the pulpit.

The extraordinarily effective setting was probably designed by Charles McKim. The two figures are framed by a small half dome supported by columns and raised up on a pedestal centered in front of the north transcept façade. From this vantage point, Phillips Brooks commands a small space at the end of Copley Square, bracketed by a set of linden trees and the wall of the parish house. It's certainly the most pleasant place in Copley Square.

III C 3 · NEW OLD SOUTH CHURCH
NW corner Boylston and Dartmouth streets
Cummings & Sears, 1874

Though there are many splendid parts to this building, it lacks the fluid sense of a total, living whole that is so common (and wonderful) in Richardson's work,

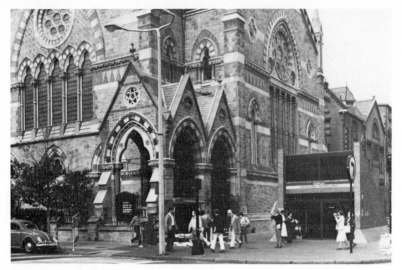

III C 3 · *New Old South Church*

as in Trinity Church at the other end of the square. It is, however, picturesque.

The exterior has a pleasing abundance of invention, generally in a North Italian Gothic style, with polychrome masonry details. But the façade along Boylston Street remains a succession of separate building types: the cruciform church itself, an entry hall marked by a very tall, square tower, a chapel, some communal rooms and, finally, the parish house. It's unified by the pudding stone, but the parts don't coalesce.

The tower is very tall indeed, even though it was rebuilt lower than the original after the first one tilted excessively. There's also a very fine clerestoried cupola and, at the very corner of Dartmouth and Boylston streets, an attenuated porte-cochere that makes an engaging bit of urban streetscape as it serves as backdrop to news and flower stands.

The inside should be compared with the first Old South Meeting House (I A 3), from which this congregation moved. Like the earlier church, this is a squarish meeting hall, but this one is roofed with timber trusses. The stained glass, dark cherry woods and medieval forms of this church trade in mysteries to an extent that would have seemed like witchcraft in Colonial Boston.

III C 4 · BOSTON PUBLIC LIBRARY
Dartmouth Street, Boylston Street to St. James Avenue
McKim, Mead & White, 1888–95

Clear, forthright, impeccably serene, the Boston Public Library has intrinsic grandeur that results from clear assumptions thoughtfully, indeed studiously, executed. In this it is distinct from many buildings that followed, including a number by the same architects, which depend more on elaborate architectonic appurtenances for their claim to Classical status. The library was the first public building in the United States to be throughly imbued with the scale, grace and compositional integrity of the Renaissance.

It is the library, finally, that makes Copley Square an urban space. It stands

III C 4 · *Boston Public Library, from Copley Square Plaza*

as a great white block closing one side of the square, its firm, subtly modulated façade asserting an unmistakable claim on the whole space before it. More than any other wall in the city, this cool, measured arcade belongs as much to the civic room it implies as to the building volume it contains. Indeed, the arches are more civic gestures than face; windows at either end and around the sides are filled with dark marble where glass does not suit the spaces within.

What's really exciting about this building is the way that all the parts of it turn out to be more interesting and thoughtful than one first supposes. The care with which the elements come together is consistent throughout the design, from the way it meets the city to the details of the lamp posts, even down to the stone panels in the upper-level arcade, inscribed with the names of leading cultural figures, which suggests the content of the reading room bookshelves behind them. And the material, Milford granite, is not just white but has a soft pinkish glow to it that makes the stone warmer and more interesting than it at first appears.

The Boston Public Library was characterized by its trustees and architects as a "Palace for the People." In pursuit of the cultural richness that might be associated with the phrase, its benefactors assembled here an uncommonly opulent group of paintings and sculpture. The relief panels over the entry are by Augustus Saint-Gaudens; those on the bronze doors in the vestibule are by Daniel Chester French. Inside are murals by Pierre Puvis de Chavannes, Edwin Austin Abbey and John Singer Sargent, and assorted busts, paintings and plaques. In front of the main entrance, two large bronze seated figures by Bela Pratt attend our approach. On the right sits Art, painter's palette in hand. Inscribed on her throne is a roster of inspiring names. On the left is Science, staring at a globe, her throne similarly inscribed. It may be noted that the figure of Art is peering curiously at the figure of Science, whereas the latter stares intently at her globe, with hood drawn slightly over her brow, shielding her eyes from distraction.

The vertical face of the building is divided strongly into two great bands, a molded and rusticated base and, at the upper level, an arcaded wall with a sculpted cornice and a large hip roof that encompasses the whole. The roof is made of large red pantiles and crested with copper.

All the detailing—from the vigorous contour of the moldings and sharply curved inset frames of the windows, to the metal grillwork at the entrances, to the absolutely sensational lights over the front entry—is executed with great attention, a sure hand in design and an abiding interest in correctness.

The whole block sits three steps off the square on a terrace about 18 feet wide with carefully formed steps all around its edges. The base of the building begins with a large molding shaped as a bench. The rest of the ground-floor façade is smooth to a height of about 8 feet, then rusticated in a sharply cut but flat pattern interspersed with large, broadly spaced windows, placed high enough so that they let large shafts of light and air into the rooms of the lower floors while protecting them from the distractions of the street.

The windows of the upper floors are also placed high, throwing light deep into the reading room that stretches across the full front of the building. These windows are in the top of the arcade of the second story, their surfaces divided by a grid of mullions. They are set back deeply into the wall to reveal its full thickness, and so that strong shadows are cast in the voids of the arcade. Below the windows the arcade is filled by screen walls that shelter bookshelves behind them; these in turn are each punctuated by a very small window in the middle.

The gradation of units of size is very consistently controlled, from the clarity of the block as a whole to its division into two strong bands, each of which then has further divisions of approximately the same size. The windows come in graded sizes, from the little peekaboo windows to the somewhat larger-than-person-sized windows of the lower floor and then finally to the large arched openings of the top of the reading room.

The most subtle transformation of size takes place at the entrance, where three arches slightly shorter than those inscribed in the upper wall open through metal grills and bronze doors into a vaulted vestibule. These strong voids combine on the face with carved emblematic panels in the arches above to mark out a square of the façade that, by contrast to the horizontal mass of the building, seems predominantly upright. In the very center of the square formed by these three entry arches and their mates above is the message of the building, projecting boldly in simple, forceful stone letters: "FREE TO ALL."

As you approach the entry, however, still more is in store: a startlingly vigorous array of lanterns that forms a virtual canopy overhead as you enter and leave

III C 4 · *detail, Boston Public Library*

III C 4 · *detail, Boston Public Library*

III C 4 · *courtyard, Boston Public Library*

the building. The entry arches are bordered on either side by vegetable-form bronze tubes that swoop down almost to head height before twisting up again to sprout bronze-framed, spike-topped glass lanterns in clusters of six. By night they provide a sparkling reception, by day an inspiriting display of bristles.

Stepping into the library, you are immediately enveloped by warmer materials, the square yellowish tiles of the vaults and the yellow marble of the grand staircase that leads to the upper floors and reading rooms. Above, the celebration of authors continues, with the names of Franklin, Hawthorne, Emerson and so on set in mosaics into the vaults of the entry vestibule.

The grand entry stairs start up as a single bank of shallow, wide steps that narrow at the top to accommodate the bases for two very noble lions, then split at the landing to go back up either side of the stair hall. In the middle of the landing, doors open to a balcony looking over the central courtyard. The whole stairway is rather like a grand loggia with, at the top, a full arcade that bounds the main corridor connecting to the reading room. The arcade has a base just the right height for leaning against and a little step to bring one closer to the edge, where you can look down on the bifurcated stair where much is made of the scene of people entering and leaving the library. The other three walls of the stair hall are lined at the upper level by an implied arcade measured out by pilasters and filled with Arcadian landscape scenes, painted by Puvis de Chavannes of Paris, in which the branches of knowledge are personified. Three similarly arched windows on the courtyard side open to the sky.

Bates Hall, the main reading room, is a subdued, very long barrel-vaulted affair that terminates in a half-domed exedra at either end. The light of the large, high windows is supplemented by continuous table lamps, new and ponderous. The little lower windows on the street side provide a special place to return attention to the world outside without having it press in upon you. Such an arrangement is much more thoughtful than either the all-glass or no-glass walls that are presently common.

Adjacent to Bates Hall is the room that was known as the Delivery Room. In this ostentatiously carved hall surrounded by a lavishly colored sequence of

murals by Abbey depicting the quest for the Holy Grail, Boston's readers, great
and small alike, once awaited their books, fetched from the inconvenient stacks
by a toy train that was kept discreetly out of sight.

On the third floor, entered from a gallery over the main vestibule, is a series
of special collections. This hall, with murals by Sargent, is reached by a long,
dark stair that was surely meant to be grand as well, but simply doesn't succeed.
The third floor consequently seems always a place apart.

The ground floor holds special collections and service areas. To either side of
the entrance are passages, frescoed with Mediterranean colors and patterns, that
lead to periodical and reference rooms. The first room on the right originally
housed periodicals and now contains government documents. It is a fine, simple
space with shallow exposed tile vaults spanning from the walls to five Tuscan
columns that stand in a line down the center of the room. The inside walls are
ringed by bookshelves at the upper level, reached by a balcony held on strong
metal strap brackets. General illumination is provided by the large, high windows and dropped half globes hanging on chains from the ceiling. Reading light,
in the best library tradition, is provided by lamps in the center of large oak tables.
These lamps are in pairs, bracketed off a central stand—a quiet recollection of
the fabulous entry lamps.

At the center of the building, reached by the ground-floor passages that turn
and lead unexpectedly into it, is the most thoroughly wonderful courtyard in
Boston: a public living room in the midst of the city. The central court is
embraced at the lower level by an arcade that is based on austere Roman
Renaissance precedent (Bramante's Cancelleria) but is proportioned somewhat
more gently. Throughout most of the year, readers pull the library's wooden
Windsor chairs next to the comfortable round stone columns of this arcade, there
to read by the light of the court, half sheltered by the surrounding vaults.
Landscaping is minimal but effective: gravel, shrubs, a few delicately leafed trees,
and fountains and reflecting pools. The court is deep, but the beautifully scaled
arcade and the intimate uses it supports distract attention from the size of the
surrounding walls.

Alas, much of the peace of this courtyard has been destroyed now that the
arcade serves also as a passage to the new wing.

III C 5 · BOSTON PUBLIC LIBRARY ADDITION
Boylston Street, SE corner Exeter Street
Philip Johnson, 1972

If Charles McKim, doyen of the self-styled renaissance emerging in New York
at the end of the century, was the right choice for the Boston Public Library,
then quite plausibly Philip Johnson was the inevitable choice for its addition.
Johnson, whose urbane wit has been largely responsible for leading many of his
peers out of Modernism and once again onto a Classical path, has produced
buildings of great sophistication, as well as some that are brilliantly naughty. He
could have been expected to produce an addition here that was either irreverent
or very refined. What we have instead is one that is reverent and crude. A palatial
structure, not a palace for the people.

Even though the mass of the addition, the materials, the cornice heights and
the roof form are nearly identical to those of its parent, the scale of the building
is entirely different, driven by the nature of its structural scheme rather than by

III C 5 · *Boston Public Library Addition*

any sense of relation to the people who use it. The structure is organized as nine great squares, the central one hollow, the others trays of space with books and reading interspersed. Each large bay is evident in the façades, with glass and granite walls spanning between husky vertical shafts, which bear the principal weight of the building. Except for a slot, a few projections and a dubious sloped arch, the granite surfacing changes not a bit from top to bottom. The scheme is a creature of the drawing board, not the view from the street.

Along the street at ground level the addition becomes particularly offensive. Where the original library has a welcoming bench incorporated in its base, the bottom of this one disappears behind a blunt fence of upright granite slabs more than head height, which rebuffs any possible sense of connection with the build-ing.

Inside, the central drum, also clad in granite, echoes with hollowness. The stairs that climb up through it are bordered by metal rails and glass screens. In sharp contrast to the older building's stairs, there is nowhere here a surface to enjoy touching or a place to enjoy being in. Only when you pass through the middle of one of the four great column clusters that support the center of the structure does it ever provide something of a size to which you can belong. Then it's quite poignant.

In the book-filled spaces beyond, it becomes clear that this is a building which is about books. The open-stack shelving that lines these reading areas makes them the visible repository of a great store of ideas and associations—books that can be reached, fondled and used without waiting for delivery.

III C 6 · COPLEY PLAZA HOTEL
St. James Avenue, Trinity Place to Dartmouth Street
Clarence H. Blackall & Henry Hardenbergh, 1912

Hardenbergh was the architect of the Plaza Hotel in New York City. Blackall, an accomplished designer of theaters (IV C 13) and of the Winthrop Building (I A 12), was to play the role of local architect. It promised to be the perfect match for a stylish Boston hotel, but it didn't work.

The swell in the center is meant, presumably, to be a brilliant stroke, a much-enlarged version of the bow-front houses of Back Bay and Beacon Hill. But it's more effective in drawings and photographs than in three-dimensional reality. Perhaps this building would fare better somewhere else. Here, surrounded by structures that are masterworks and facing a great square, it just doesn't make it.

III C 7 · COPLEY SQUARE PLAZA
bounded by Boylston and Dartmouth streets, St. James Avenue and Trinity Church
Sasaki, Dawson & Demay, 1968

Urban public space needs to be more than a vantage point for monuments. It should have a firm shape of its own, one that can coexist with the buildings around it; and it must be good to be in. Copley Square does not and is not. Its edges evaporate, despite its designers' efforts to shape them by digging down into the ground and raising the earth around the outside to shield the square from surrounding traffic. The space enclosed is more vacant than eloquent, even if it does proffer undisturbed views of Trinity Church and the library and a clear path to the subway for the hordes of Hancock workers.

Copley Square took its present shape after its architects were selected in a national competition. The diagonal of Huntington Avenue was removed from Clarendon to Dartmouth and the whole space was paved as a pedestrian plaza and ringed by trees.

The Boylston Street edge is where the action is—and understandably so. It has the most sun and fun, the most places for urban play. Along Boylston Street there's a double row of trees and a sloped bank leading up to a thick concrete wall. While evidently not intended to be a seat, it is a very popular one. Here there are real choices: facing the plaza, idlers can dangle their feet over a drop to the pavement ten feet below; or facing Boylston Street, they can keep an eye on the passing scene, far enough removed to be out of it, close enough to make contact. Grass will never survive on this slope; it should be made into steps and platforms and given some spirit of its own.

The best benches in the paved, sunken section of the plaza are against this same wall, collecting the sun. Nearby, a large fountain gushes attractively over an uncommunicative truncated pyramid. The latter is redeemed only by its ability to attract the attention of bare feet anxious to test their agility on its slippery slopes. Because people have taken it over, this corner of the plaza has the sunny festival quality of stage and grandstand, with actors on both. It's an active complement to the quiet, reflective mood established nearby in front of the statue of Phillips Brooks (III C 2), who feigns not to notice.

D/BACK BAY WEST

Since Back Bay took several decades to fill, proceeding from east to west, everything west of Fairfield Street was built after 1870, and along Newbury Street and Commonwealth Avenue the buildings are nearly all post-1880.

Commonwealth Avenue becomes, in this period, the site for a number of pretentious in-town mansions, including several elegant town houses by McKim, Mead & White. Newbury Street, on the other hand, was developed in large sections at a time, with only a few architects—S. D. Kelley, G. Wilton Lewis and George Avery—responsible for almost everything we see between Fairfield and Hereford streets. The architects, as a consequence, looked for simple but ingenious ways to make these long stretches of nearly identical buildings break down into recognizable parts. Newbury Street beyond Hereford Street is a section all its own, with buildings that started out mostly as stables and carriage houses, and are now transformed into shops, small offices and garage buildings. On the

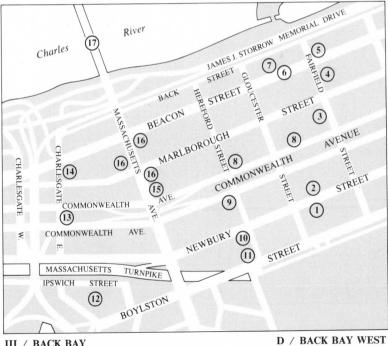

III / BACK BAY   D / BACK BAY WEST

western edges of the section, several luxurious apartment hotels, most notably Charlesgate (III D 14), reflect the growing social credibility of apartment dwelling in the 1890's.

III D 1 · 246–52 NEWBURY STREET
between Fairfield and Gloucester streets
George Avery, 1884

· 254–80 NEWBURY STREET
between Fairfield and Gloucester streets
G. Wilton Lewis, 1882

Virtually all of this block was designed by two architects and built for two land speculators. The set of row houses at 246–52 Newbury Street was constructed four years later than the corner building, also by Avery. The main body of the buildings, at the second and third floors, is quite simple, with continuous windows evenly spaced and a chamfered bay for each house. The bottom of the bay has high, round-arched windows, but the top is where the interest lies. Each bay rises the full height through the attic to a small pediment at the top, the transition between flat pediment and polygonal bay formed by copper-roofed bits of dome in a manner reminiscent of the Hotel Vendome (III A 16).

The longer string of row houses at 254–80 Newbury Street by G. Wilton Lewis displays a greater rhythmic invention, with alternating round bays and chamfered bays, with some that rise only two floors and others that rise the full four floors to a pyramidal roof. They create a continuously changing roof line. These are not the robust variations of houses built individually by different architects, but they do make a difference; they establish a sense that there are possibilities for modification and that there are a variety of ways of doing things within a group of buildings built all at one time. This makes it easier to accommodate the kind of radical changes that have taken place in the project over time, as various uses have occupied the ground floor and modifications have been made on the façades above. The variants also make it easier for each person who lives there to recognize a place in the structure that is distinct and to consider it home.

The rather complicated rhythm that results from these bay variations is played out against a steady, consistent wall to the street. At Fairfield and Gloucester streets, the end lots and their homes face the cross streets rather than Newbury Street. This then makes a break in the building pattern and adds further variety to the street, with generally a longer and more solid wall on the corner building and a rear-yard gap between it and the beginning of those that face Newbury Street. In some cases these have been filled by shops built later.

Across Gloucester Street the corner building at No. 284, one of the nicest in Back Bay, and the row from No. 286 to No. 302 were also designed by G. Wilton Lewis, between 1884 and 1886.

III D 2 · 269 NEWBURY STREET
between Fairfield and Gloucester streets
W. Whitney Lewis, 1881

A witty exception to the standard pattern of alternating bay and entry, each house individually expressed all in a row. These are symmetrical houses on a double lot, with two bays, two entries brought together under a single center arch, and both united above by a great carved floral medallion set in a single, rather flat, round-topped gable.

Recent commercial renovations have opened the basement floor with two large arches and a nicely curved stair on the left side that winds its way down to a restaurant entry. Carefully made new show windows and small bays elaborate but do not really disturb the essential splendor of the building's bold face. This has been considerably diminished, however, by a well-meaning but ultimately insensitive repointing job. The mortar between the bricks is too white; it hurts the appearance of the walls, its own and the neighbors'.

III D 3 · 20 FAIRFIELD STREET
between Marlborough Street and Commonwealth Avenue
W. Whitney Lewis, 1875

· 21 FAIRFIELD STREET
NW corner Commonwealth Avenue
W. Whitney Lewis, 1880

Here are two more town houses by W. Whitney Lewis, architect of 196 Marlborough Street (III A 26). No. 20 is small and determined, with a spunky wooden bay bracketed awkwardly from its brick face. The top floor was added later.

No. 21, the Coolidge House, is another energetic compositional array, unfortunately quite garish now that the stone trim is painted white, in sharp contrast to the brick. But the detail of the design is lavish, including patterned brick, an oriel window, an end gable and chimney that form a picturesque cluster on Fairfield Street, and a strong band of windows between this and the great entry arch. On Commonwealth Avenue a massive chimney-and-paired-window feature is piled up against the wall.

Too bad it has been painted; the architecture doesn't need any help.

III D 4 · 8, 10 FAIRFIELD STREET
between Beacon and Marlborough streets
Sturgis & Brigham, 1879

· 12 FAIRFIELD STREET
NE corner Marlborough Street
Cabot & Chandler, 1879

Buildings that make you love brick. The walls are lively, active surfaces, with just enough relief in their dominant planes to make them vibrate. Nos. 8 and 10 are a pair, but they share with No. 12 a fine sensibility for the use of brick and a continuous front plane, lending the three a cohesive presence.

Nos. 8 and 10 have a recessed entry, with steps divided by an iron rail leading to small glassed-in porches on either side. Ground-floor windows are set in segmental arches; third- and fourth-floor windows are lodged within panels as though they were bays, but they project only a few inches from the main plane of the wall.

On each end at the top, there is a wonderfully supple, rounded brick pediment;

III D 4 · *8, 10, 12 Fairfield Street*

volutes on each side rise to the edges of a semicircle capped with a finial. Venetian Baroque via Flanders, I suppose, but lovely.

No. 12 has more intricate brick patterning, including specially molded shapes and cast decorative elements, but its overall form is much simpler. It meets the sky as a hipped roof with inset dormers and a wonderfully pronounced chimney. The house is vivid without being flamboyant. Cabot, remember, was architect of the Athenaeum (I B 8) and founder-president of the Boston Society of Architects.

III D 5 · 330 BEACON STREET
NE corner Fairfield Street
Hugh Stubbins & Associates, 1959

Stubbins is the only contemporary Boston architect who has dared to disturb the skyline of residential Back Bay. No. 330 Beacon Street, at 17 stories, has a front façade that is faceted as though it were all bays. Window alignments are shifted every third floor to subdivide the face into a surface pattern with units not unlike the scale of adjoining row houses, a relation that is perhaps too subtle to make a difference. The brick walls of the tower are framed around the windows in concrete, loosely recalling the trimmed windows of traditional Back Bay architecture. But since Stubbins's windows are higher and wider, the window pattern becomes texture rather than incident, and the effect is very different.

The plain rectangular grid structure of the building emerges dogmatically at the top and, especially, at the bottom. Here the columns resemble Corbusian piloti, detaching the structure from the ground and its neighbors rather than presenting a face to the street and forming a world of polite social encounter as its neighbors do.

III D 6 · 346 BEACON STREET
between Fairfield and Gloucester streets
Allen & Kenway, 1882
· 347 BEACON STREET
between Fairfield and Gloucester streets
J. H. Besarick 1884
· 348 BEACON STREET
between Fairfield and Gloucester streets
Allen & Kenway, 1886
· 363 BEACON STREET
between Fairfield & Gloucester streets
F. H. Jackson, 1878

This segment of Beacon Street contains an instructive collection of buildings from the optimistic 1880's and an urbanely tidy one from the 1870's. No. 346, by Allen & Kenway, is an ungainly collection of porches, windows and doorways dating from 1882. It would probably feel more at home in the country than here. No. 348—also by Allen & Kenway, but four years later—is an entirely different matter. Built on a comfortably wide lot, it has an exuberant Richardsonian entry and a very wide, very urbane bay. In 1884, J. H. Besarick let loose an incredible profusion of carved brownstone vegetable trim at No. 347, a year before his similar town house on Commonwealth Avenue (III A 21).

Predating all these by several years is No. 363, by F. H. Jackson, the architect who solved the perennial problem of how to have a central bay and a side entrance in a symmetrical façade. What he did was to place a large two-story bay in the center, with a broad stair running up before it onto an entry porch. The visitors ascend, to be greeted by an inset panel with a brickwork relief. They then turn left to the front door, symmetrically balanced by a window placed in the wall at the right. At the same time, a small service stair ducks underneath the porch for basement and kitchen access. A neat handling of up, down and center.

III D 7 · 358-92 BEACON STREET
between Fairfield and Gloucester streets
Ralph Harrington Doane, 1926

This is the way to add density to the Back Bay. An *allée* through a compound of apartments gives both residents and passers-by a midblock view of the Esplanade. Three stories of apartments are placed above entry-level basements, then assembled as groups two deep on each side of a central garden that is open through the block.

It's a very strong scheme all dressed up in architectural detail borrowed from its Beacon Hill ancestors. Alas, it is flawed in execution by a prissy fastidiousness. The common image is so strong that there is no sense of personality in the parts, no feeling of inhabitation in the buildings or the landscape. Entries to each block have no direct connection with the individual apartments. And since the balconies are only decorative metal grills, there is no direct connection between inside and out, either.

These grills, as well as the shallow bow fronts and cast-concrete details, all follow models from the Federal period quite precisely. But the detailing here is a cogent example of how tiresome cribbed décor can be. Somehow you sense that it wasn't this architect's sweat and blood but someone else's that was spent inventing these forms and learning how to make them work.

III D 8 · 247 COMMONWEALTH AVENUE
between Fairfield and Gloucester streets
William Rantoul, 1905

· 303 COMMONWEALTH AVENUE
between Gloucester and Hereford streets
McKim, Mead & White, 1895

· 32 HEREFORD STREET
NE corner Commonwealth Avenue
McKim, Mead & White, 1884

The black-shoe set. All three buildings have bow fronts that take command of the surroundings. The one at No. 247 is an addition, a vestibule-cum-granite-façade that no doubt owes its inspiration to the earlier McKim, Mead & White work down the street at No. 303. You enter directly off the street into the rounded vestibule, then go up inside to the original main floor. It is urbane and demanding, not the sort of place for sneakers.

The bow front at 303 Commonwealth Avenue is the whole façade, a single grand sweep that encompasses the building in a smooth, white, subtly curving granite surface. Entry is at the lower level through a delicately carved doorframe. Between it and the inventive, small, but potent cornice at the top is nothing but stone coursing, six symmetrically placed windows, a stringcourse to mark the attic story, and three very restrained attic windows, separated by two carved medallions. This building in turn refers directly to the local precedent of seventy-five years earlier, the white granite swell front of the Sears mansion by Parris (II B 16). This one is less round, softer and more a part of the street wall, its proportions modulated in a way that points up the bluntness of the earlier Parris work.

No. 32 Hereford Street, which now belongs to an MIT fraternity, has a subtler, more accommodating elegance. This is one of the very first McKim, Mead & White buildings to assume Renaissance detailing, and in this is a precedent for the Boston Public Library (III C 4) as well as for thousands of affluent homes in Boston and elsewhere. It set a precedent also for the other two of this set by having an entry at street level that rises inside to the principal upper floor and by being composed with round swell-front bays, in this case two. The walls are buff brick with a stone base and thin carved-stone window frames spaced with deliberate regularity even as the Hereford Street bow front becomes a three-quarter ellipse to round the corner into Commonwealth Avenue; a quiet, very fastidious design that could, by now, use a little cleaning.

III D 9 · BOSTON EVENING CLINIC
314 Commonwealth Avenue, SW corner Hereford Street
Charles E. Brigham, 1899

Originally the mansion of Albert Burrage, lawyer, mineral and gas baron, and cultivator of orchids, this was built during the same years that he was a member

III D 9 · *detail, Boston Evening Clinic*

III D 8 · *303 Commonwealth Avenue*

of the commission responsible for constructing Boston's subway system. It aspires to be a Vanderbilt mansion on Fifth Avenue or a château on the Loire, but is at least 20 years too late and certainly in the wrong location.

Nevertheless it is exuberant, though more in detail than in configuration. At the ground floor the building starts out simply enough, with two familiar bays on either side of a heavily carved entrance, modeled, we are assured, after châteaux. As the forms climb they become more flamboyant, ending at the skyline in a riot of cupidinous ornament clustered around dormers, chimneys and stair towers. These in turn only hint at the abundance of the interior, replete with stained glass, wood, marble and plaster reliefs, and with iconography that is variously inspiring or a bit lascivious.

At the rear is a splendidly formed glass-roofed adjunct, once the home of the orchids.

III D 10 · BOSTON ARCHITECTURAL CENTER
320 Newbury Street, SW corner Hereford Street
Ashley, Myer & Associates, 1967
mural: Richard Haas, 1977

This is the only serious concrete building in Back Bay, and on its back is now painted the only one that's totally imaginary. The Ashley, Myer firm (now Arrowstreet) was the winner of a competition to house the Boston Architectural Center, a prized Boston institution and one of the few American schools of architecture independent of a university. The design posed the special challenge of being both neighbor and exemplar.

The winning solution is extremely clear about just how the structure is put together. It's a rational system in which infill panels are articulated as separate from their supporting columns and beams of concrete, and specialized spaces are expressed as distinct volumes, as they are in Boston City Hall (I C 2).

Although there are no forms here exactly like the bay windows and projections that are common in the area, the shape of the units of the design bespeaks a similar concern for human size. The overall form of the building is a six-story structural frame into which all classrooms, studios and meeting places are inserted. The ground floor is mostly glass at the corner, making a very public exhibition space and lobby. The second floor holds large and small meeting rooms, but they don't occupy the full frame, leaving the upper part of the exhibition space to fill out the volume. The top floor, housing the library and some offices, is projected forward like a giant cornice.

In 1977 the back wall, which had been necessarily left blank because it adjoined another property, was painted with an illusionistic mural by Richard Haas. His sectional view of a Beaux-Arts dome makes a witty juxtaposition against the modern concrete structure, yet would have been a greater work if it could have given us some additional insight into the building it's painted on, rather than remaining simply a whimsical, one-shot spoof.

III D 10 · *Boston Architectural Center from the west, showing Richard Haas mural*

III D 10 · *Boston Architectural Center, Hereford Street side*

III D 11 · ENGINE AND HOSE HOUSE NO. 33
941 Boylston Street, SW corner Hereford Street
Arthur H. Vinal, 1885
reuse: Arrowstreet, 1971

· INSTITUTE OF CONTEMPORARY ART
955 Boylston Street, between Hereford Street and Massachusetts Avenue
Arthur H. Vinal, 1886
reuse: Graham Gund Associates, 1975

This pair was originally designed for the fire and police departments by the City Architect, Arthur Vinal. During the same year he was authorized to design the Boston Public Library, but was later supplanted by McKim, Mead & White after producing what Ralph Adams Cram is said to have described as "a chaos of gables, oriels, arcades and towers, all worked out in brownstone." Perhaps Vinal's inclinations were better suited to fire and police stations, for these structures hardly have the abundance of chaos.

What we see are two distinct forms, both vigorously Romanesque, joined together by their style of execution. Recently they've undergone renovations, the fire station suitably retaining its original function, the police station becoming the headquarters of the Institute of Contemporary Art. The fire station had only minor alterations in its window pattern, some new doors, a new interior color scheme and a rejuvenated mechanical system. The police station was completely gutted and an all-new interior was carefully slipped in.

Entry to the Institute of Contemporary Art is up a few steps from the sidewalk, bringing the visitor into a two-story space that reveals the café and restaurant dropping down in two stages to the left, while a passage on the right leads to gallery space beyond and stairs that climb up to additional exhibition areas. So on entering, you understand everything all at once—everything, that is, except why the windows in the second-floor gallery have been permanently sealed up on the inside, entombing the works and their visitors.

III D 12 · FENWAY STUDIOS
30 Ipswich Street, off Boylston Street
Parker, Thomas & Rice, 1905

This remarkable building is a collection of artists' garrets rationally assembled and built like a factory building, but embellished with motifs said to be Iroquois. This is one of the last, if not the only remaining, brick artists'-studio buildings from turn-of-the-century Boston. It combines the industrial vernacular with a bit of artistic craftsmanship, as in the patterned brickwork of the spandrel over the entry arch. The entry also features a small balcony and a nicely carved wooden pediment supported by two rather grumpy lion-head capitals that are not so very noticeably Iroquois. Heavily textured handmade clinker bricks are used throughout.

On each side of the central entry, there are five structural bays, the end one projecting slightly. Four levels of double-height studios all have great double-hung, two-story-high windows on the north. An ingenious access system places a corridor along the back on a mezzanine level. You enter each studio from above, with a view of the entire light-flooded room, before stepping down into it. Under this corridor there's a low space for a bathroom and a small work area (with windows for cross-ventilation).

The studios have always been popular with artists, many of them associated with the Boston School, a fairly successful group of academic impressionists active at the time of its construction.

Though the Massachusetts Turnpike now speeds past the Fenway Studios' front door, the building remains popular for its great interior spaces. Lately a group of tenants formed Artists for the Preservation of the Fenway Studios to purchase the building for their use in a move to block its conversion to condominium apartments.

III D 13 · LEIF ERICSSON STATUE
Commonwealth Avenue Mall at Charlesgate East
Anne Whitney, 1885

We don't always seek an explanation for the location of monumental sculptures. But the westward-ho look of Leif Ericsson at the intersection of Commonwealth

Avenue and Charlesgate East invites speculation. Why here, at the terminus of Back Bay? Perhaps the question would not be so insistent if his view were not now blocked by a highway overpass and access ramps. The setting was slightly more idyllic once.

Charlesgate Park is still the path of the Muddy River as it meets the Charles. Before its desecration by the highway it was the carefully landscaped connection between the Fenway and the Charles River Basin, a key link in Frederick Law Olmstead's "Emerald Necklace" (see Beyond the Hub, p. 302). The statue was moved here as part of a beautification program at the turn of the century that also produced the balustrades by Arthur Shurecliffe that now labor so heroically to maintain some semblance of decorum underneath the highway ramps (not to be confused with the indecorous concrete bathtub benches of a still more recent era).

In any case, at least Ericsson was remembered, though he might not be altogether pleased with his fictitious likeness or the fact that his boat is skewered to the ground by a pylon on which he stands and the pool in which it was supposedly afloat has long since dried up. But the best part is a carved frieze of intertwined animals, where the Nordic theme and local contemporary traditions of neo-Romanesque sculpture come together.

III D 14 · HOTEL CHARLESGATE
535 Beacon Street, SE corner Charlesgate East
J. Pickering Putnam, 1891

One of the earliest and biggest in a spate of fashionable apartment buildings that followed the introduction of elevators in the last decades of the century, Charlesgate is also one of the wackiest. Whereas three years later, at Haddon Hall (III A 5), Putnam would design a tall apartment building that comes alive with just one strong gesture at the top, here he has used a multitude of bays, turrets, chimneys and Germanic pediments more akin to his work at 195 Commonwealth Avenue (III A 27).

If the Marlborough Street end of the structure seems even stranger than the rest, it may be because Putnam seems to have swallowed up some prior buildings by Rotch & Tilden and incorporated them in the Charlesgate. The result is a startling pile, clearly reflecting its character as a multiplicity of residences and creating a memorably picturesque skyline to be seen across Charlesgate Park.

III D 15 · AMES MANSION
355 Commonwealth Avenue, NE corner of Massachusetts Avenue
Carl Fehmer, 1882

The Ames family had a considerable impact on the city of Boston, most notably with the Ames Building (I A 11) downtown. Oliver Ames and his son Frederick were patrons of Richardson, but in this case Oliver had Carl Fehmer design his mansion, apparently after rejecting a scheme by the master for which a plan sketch exists.

One wishes for a mite of the vigor that Richardson's scheme might have had. This one is remarkably unprepossessing for a building of its bulk. The brown-

III D 14 · *Hotel Charlesgate*

III D 16 · *The Marlborough*

stone walls, generally flat, are graced with incongruously delicate but highly amusing decorative panels filled with putti and rather thin emblems of floral and vegetable abundance.

III D 16 · THE MARLBOROUGH
416 Marlborough Street, SE corner Massachusetts Avenue
Willard T. Sears, 1895
· 421, 423 MARLBOROUGH STREET
NW corner Massachusetts Avenue
S. D. Kelley, 1889
· 425, 427, 429 MARLBOROUGH STREET
between Charlesgate East and Massachusetts Avenue
O. F. Smith, 1886
· HOTEL CAMBRIDGE
483 Beacon Street, SE corner Massachusetts Avenue
Willard T. Sears, 1898

Two more apartment hotels and a grouping of row houses that pile up on the corner. The Marlborough is a stalwart building that has an organizational scheme for the façade very similar to that of the earlier Copley Plaza Hotel Annex (III C 6), with regular windows, large copper bays and windows leading out onto a thin balcony at the top. It's much more massive, though, and was made to seem even more so by rounded corners and a strong cornice all around, now removed. Remember, too, that most of the windows were once graced with operable canvas awnings that protruded in random array.

The Hotel Cambridge is similar in organization but bigger and heavier, made grotesquely ponderous by a giant two-story mansard roof.

Diagonally across from the Marlborough is a set of houses that makes a particularly pleasing transition from the standard row-house height and form to a more towering section that is two stories taller on Massachusetts Avenue.

III D 17 · HARVARD BRIDGE
· CHARLES RIVER BASIN
Massachusetts Avenue at the Charles River

This bridge will lead you to Harvard, but only after you pass MIT and traverse downtown Cambridge. A walk out onto the bridge in acceptable weather is the best way to understand the topography of the Charles River Basin, with the hills of Newton, Brighton and Brookline visible to the west and the sailing basin directly east, bordered by the Esplanade and closed in at the far end by Beacon Hill. The gold dome of the State House gleams unobstructed and magnificent on the hill, and the buildings of MIT are sprawled out along the other side on still more mud flats reclaimed at the beginning of the century and turned into campus.

A quick survey, left to right, of the Cambridge shore will show you the Hyatt Hotel by Graham Gund, MIT housing towers by Hugh Stubbins, low, new brick terraced housing by Sert, Jackson Associates, the beautiful, long, sinuously bending wall of Alvar Aalto's Baker House dormitory, the pompous gray main buildings of MIT designed by Welles Bosworth, two towers designed by I. M. Pei and Eduardo Catalano, and the model apartment building at 100 Memorial Drive designed by Rapson, DeMars, Kennedy & Brown—all notable works.

IV/ THE SOUTHERN SECTOR

A / THE HIGH SPINE

Just as the shipping industry gradually moved away from downtown, leaving the harbor and wharves to be filled in and reused, the railroads, after their heyday in the late nineteenth century, gradually became consolidated and reorganized, withdrawing from valuable urban real estate as their services diminished and land prices increased.

The area between the original neck and the Back Bay landfill project had been particularly convenient for railroad development. It was new land unencumbered, near the traditional land routes to the south. The railroad yards that were assembled in a swath left an indelible mark on the city, separating neighborhoods in the classic American way. But the vast acreage used for railroad yards has also served as a reservoir of land susceptible to large-scale planning.

The first area to become available was west of Park Square, formerly the site of the Boston & Providence station and its accompanying yards. In this space the business community of the 1920's saw a whole new center developing. Commercial arcades and a string of office buildings were all built conveniently adjacent to the elegant homes of Back Bay. The splendid Peabody & Stearns station of 1872 was replaced by a combined hotel/office building (IV A 1). A large garage (IV A 2) was built nearby. The ripple effect of this new development may be seen in the Manhattanization of Arlington Street and the proliferation of apartment buildings on Commonwealth Avenue. A second great reservoir of space, held by the Boston & Albany Railroad, became the subject of intense study and speculation after the Second World War, ending up as the Prudential Center (IV A 8).

MIT was a lesser but still important reservoir, holding land in the vicinity of Copley Square, now the site of major insurance companies. Even before the railroads, MIT sought cheaper, more expansive space elsewhere.

To these developments may be added the power of a conceptualizing phrase. In 1961 the Committee on Civic Design of the Boston Society of Architects presented the concept of a "high spine." The phrase referred to a proposed line of high-rise buildings that would develop south of Boylston Street on a line already established by the first and second Hancock Insurance Buildings (IV A 7). The intent was to limit high development to a band that would form a comprehensible element of the city and in the meantime protect Back Bay from a disintegration of character. In essence the scheme has been followed, but the actual development has become something of a battle of the Titans, held together more by the phrase than by a visible reality. There are, however, a lot of insurance buildings all in a row.

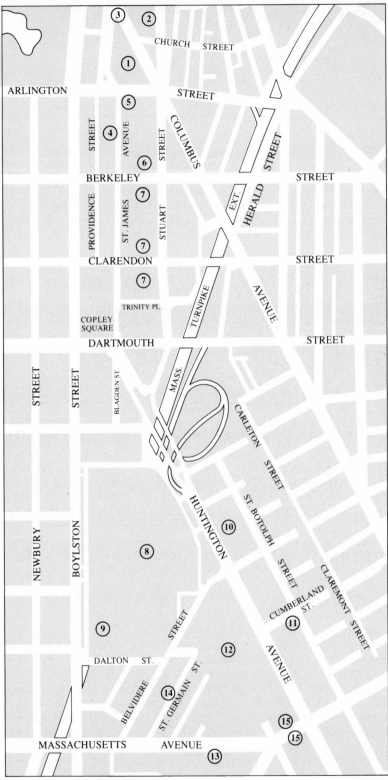

IV / THE SOUTHERN SECTOR   A / THE HIGH SPINE

IV A 1 · PARK PLAZA HOTEL AND STATLER OFFICE BUILDING
64 Arlington Street/20 Providence Street, bounded by Providence Street, Columbus Avenue and Arlington Street
George B. Post, 1927

This building has no independent form whatsoever. It's a marvelously single-minded filler of space, completely determined by the shape of the site. If the lot had been ten feet wider, so would the building be. It was built at a time when streets were thought to be good, especially when well dressed. Urbanity was the thing (and profitable). Inside was thought to have very little to do with outside, and structure even less. But being inside could also be public and urbane, with a variety of passages and spaces worth wandering through.

This would now be called a mixed-use building, with hotel and office spaces jammed together in one structure. The hotel, now the Park Plaza, occupies more than half the site, with shops and public rooms on the lower floors. On the

IV A 1 · *Park Plaza Hotel*

exterior the shift from hotel at one end to offices at the other is marked only by a slight shift in the window pattern, except at the thick Arlington Street end, where hotel rooms finger out around courts to provide light at the upper levels. At the opposite, office, end, Providence Street and Columbus Avenue shape the building into a very powerful, bluntly rounded point.

Inside the Park Plaza Hotel, the main lobby is a simple, good two-story space, not particularly dramatic or wonderful, but characteristic of its period. It does its job, indicating the public nature of the place by making a two-level stage for people to walk around on and see each other. There's a minimum of fuss, a lot of reliance on colonnades of Renaissance derivation to measure out the space. It's not what you would call restrained and elegant, but it has so far been spared much of the plastic redecoration that has beset other hotels of its vintage. It's a simple space that's a pleasure to be in.

IV A 2 · MOTOR MART GARAGE
64 Eliot Street, between Columbus Avenue and Charles, Church and Stuart streets
Ralph Harrington Doane, 1927

Another altogether irregular form determined by the shape of its site. This one is filled with automobiles and made of stuccoed concrete, with Classical overtones.

Ralph Harrington Doane was better at delicate three-story commercial buildings (I A 16), or even apartments in the Federal mode (III D 7). Faced with a much larger scale, Doane's rigid, prettifying decoration turned fascist. The various ordering schemes with which he attempted to gain control of a bulky new problem simply became silly. Forms that started life in Egypt as windows for Pharaohs or their spirits to appear in were not meant, finally, to reveal bumpers and headlights. What's more, the scheme is not that inventive, bearing a resemblance to the elevations of Burnham's building for Filene's (V C 16) downtown. Burnham's is much better.

Still, it must have been hard to do a large garage in 1927, and it clearly amazed his peers. He won the Boston Society of Architects' coveted Harleston Parker Award for the most beautiful building constructed in Boston that year.

IV A 3 · PARK SQUARE
intersection of Charles and Eliot streets and Columbus Avenue
Emancipation Group Statue: Thomas Ball, 1875

Park Square at present is a meaningless, shapeless space surrounding an 1875 bronze statue, by Thomas Ball, entitled "Emancipation Group," a very patronizing homage to Abraham Lincoln with a black slave crouched and humble at his feet. It is inscribed: "A RACE SET FREE AND THE COUNTRY AT PEACE, LINCOLN RESTS FROM HIS LABORS." A little too soon perhaps: Judging from the separation of races in Boston, he needed more energetic successors.

This does, however, make an interesting vantage point, with the gold dome of the State House gleaming from its hill across the Common to the northeast, and Columbus Avenue opening like a corridor southwest to the South End and beyond. To the west the Park Square Building, one block away, shapes the space in front of it as it squeezes Providence Street into a service alley. All of it is dominated by the blunt point of the Statler Office Building.

On a remnant of plaza at the Arlington Street end of Providence Street is one of the enameled cartoon maps designed by the Southworths that are so helpful in finding your way around parts of Boston. There are eleven such maps in the city, showing significant buildings in the immediate area. They were installed as part of a series of programs organized to bring attention to the city's heritage.

A more ambitious experimental information center was temporarily installed on this site by the architectural firm Arrowstreet in 1969 as part of the City Signs and Lights Project. It had great balloons as landmarks and included maps and historical information as well as a primitive but engaging question-and-answer machine. Alas, nothing of comparable interest has replaced that temporary installation.

IV A 4 · PARK SQUARE BUILDING
31 St. James Avenue, between Arlington and Berkeley streets
Densmore, LeClear & Robbins, 1923

The ground floor here has a scheme like that of the Faneuil Hall Markets. It's a long, narrow building with a concourse down the middle and shops to either side. At the center is a spacious lobby opening to St. James Avenue with elevators leading to stacks of offices above. The volume of the building is a simple projection upward of its property lines, a dozen or so floors rendered simply as a long, uneventful, undemanding wall. Shops along the ground floor are reached both from the street and from the internal passage, although the Providence Street side to the north is definitely the back, confirmed as a dark alley by the shadow of the structure's unrelenting hulk.

The building has only recently been rescued from neglect, and that just barely, through rather tinny marquees that thrust out from either end and a general cleaning of the brass storefronts along the passage inside.

High-rise buildings of the 1920's were usually designed to let the city into their bases, which were filled with shops and services and with passages broad enough to stroll in. The covered arcades of Paris were perhaps the indirect antecedents, but even more important, this form of organization required a predisposition to invest in collective forms of passage. These urban passages were not, after all, so different from the train and subway tunnels through which people came to work.

After the Second World War, with the populace fleeing by private car to the suburbs, high-rise buildings became like points of destination on an open plain, their lobbies giving onto nothing. Their image was anti-urban. Offices above, as many as possible; people shuttled to the ground floor as quickly as possible, there to meet the great outdoors in whatever guise it may appear, usually barren. The general result now is that in newer office buildings there is as little intermediate lobby space as possible, and what there is is hard, expensively finished, easily maintained—a place to avoid dwelling in.

The Park Square Building is quite the opposite of this, and judging from the great success of people-filled places downtown in the Faneuil Hall Markets, this building may someday soon come into its own again. But the passage will need more connections.

IV A 5 · PAINE FURNITURE BUILDING
81 Arlington Street, between St. James Avenue and Stuart Street
Densmore & LeClear, 1914
new entry: Charles Hilgenhurst & Associates, 1980

Originally a combined furniture factory and showroom with a large bulk and modest pomposity, the Paine Furniture Building has been deftly revitalized by a new entry at 6 St. James Avenue. The original doors to Paine's Furniture remain on Arlington Street, providing access to the ground-floor furniture show-rooms. That entrance is under a grand suspended canopy and promises passage into the domain of mass-produced opulence. The new entry on the side provides access to a severe building lobby and elevators to offices above, which have replaced manufacturing lofts.

This recent construction substitutes artistry and sophistication for pomposity. It is the first work in Boston that picks up the urbane Classical themes of the first part of this century and continues them in the spare materials and forms of the present time. It gives us hope that neither the studied grace of the past nor the rational directness of the present need be irretrievably lost.

The trick is that the doors are set at the very rear of a glass gable-roofed canopy that is held aloft by steel beams that span between four slender green marble cylinders to make an aediculalike porch. A dark-green grid of steel sash windows intersects this canopy midway, passing above it on the top and bending to wrap around its sides at the entry itself. The front of the canopy is thus a positive form stepping out toward the entrant, while the rear is a negative hollow in the glass-paned wall, with the outside underneath rather than over the roof.

Beyond the entry vestibule is a spacious lobby dominated by the large concrete columns of the original structure. These columns spread gently at the top in the mushroom-cap form that is familar in industrial buildings of the period, a direct and easy way to deal with the forces present in reinforced concrete-slab construction. They are made surprising here by a painted simulation of marble streaking —common among Baroque buildings and their progeny, and wittily arcane in this instance.

IV A 6 · LIBERTY MUTUAL INSURANCE COMPANY
175 Berkeley Street, between St. James Avenue and Stuart Street
Chester Lindsay Churchill, 1937
renovation: Perry, Dean & Stewart, 1974

This must be the most mausoleum-like building in town. If you did not have death on your mind before, passing by Liberty Mutual may quickly induce morbid thoughts of life insurance. If this is what the old order had been reduced to in the thirties, it's easy to see why any young architect of spunk would seek a new way of building, or at least long for modernity.

Everything here is spare of imagination and feeling, though not all the deathli-ness can be attributed to the original architects. In a recent remodeling the windows have all been replaced with a very dark glass that only reflects in a distorted, tinselly way, preventing passers-by from seeing anything within. So the façade has become an absolutely blank interlacing of Portland stone and black glass, with even the window frames reduced to an absolute minimum, according to the contemporary idiom.

Where some architects call for buildings that speak with many tongues, the dark-and-reflective-glass contingent seems determined to silence their buildings altogether.

IV A 7 · JOHN HANCOCK MUTUAL LIFE INSURANCE COMPANY BUILDINGS
· 200 CLARENDON STREET
between St. James Avenue and Stuart Street
Parker, Thomas & Rice, 1922
· 175 BERKELEY STREET
between St. James Avenue and Stuart Street
Cram & Ferguson, 1947
· HANCOCK PLACE
between St. James Avenue and Stuart Street, west of Clarendon Street
I. M. Pei & Partners, 1975

Like Harrison Gray Otis on Beacon Hill, the Hancock Insurance Company, with three distinctive buildings constructed in succession, has played a central role in the development of the area now known as the High Spine.

In 1922, J. Harleston Parker, senior partner in the firm of Parker, Thomas & Rice, made a bequest to the city in honor of his father, Harleston Parker. The Harleston Parker Award has been bestowed ever since by the Boston Society of Architects as its most prestigious design prize. His own firm received it in 1924 for the first Hancock Building, the Cram & Ferguson firm received it in 1950 for the second Hancock Building on Berkeley Street, and in the 1970's Pei's firm received it, not for the third Hancock Building, but for their less controversial Christian Science Center farther up the spine. Nevertheless, the latest John Hancock building, known as the John Hancock Tower, is undeniably a major landmark in the city.

If you stand on the corner of Clarendon Street and St. James Avenue and look directly into the mirrored surface of the third Hancock, you will see reflected there the first two, aligned hierarchically in an ethereal family portrait. Actually, the first building, on Clarendon Street, was once much more elegant than it now appears; traces of it can be seen in the Corinthian pilasters and attic that form the four lower floors of the building. These are the façade of the original low building, which surrounded four light courts and a narrow central tower that was twice as tall and that stood in its middle with a grand loggia at the top and a cluster of hip roofs and dormers. Some years later the present four additional stories were unabashedly piled on top of the outer perimeter, making the looming block that's there now. Judging by the view from the observation floor of the third John Hancock, the earlier tower remains walled up inside the additions like a character in an Edgar Allan Poe short story.

The second building, the tower on Berkeley Street, is an amazement. Built only five years before Lever House in New York City and awarded the Parker Prize in 1950, it sticks in the mind nonetheless as a prewar building and reminds us that it took some years after the war for the "modern" architects who created a stylistic convulsion in American architecture to work themselves into established positions. The Cram & Ferguson firm, however, had been established for some time, even though Cram had retired from active practice in the thirties and died before this building was erected.

For several decades after the beginning of high-rise construction, architects sought valiantly to maintain the fiction that they were dealing with an architecture of walls, and they expended much of their energy attempting to maintain control over the wall surface as a plane that you, the observer, could address and whose size and extent you could measure, as in the Ames Building (I A 11),

IV A 7 · *The John Hancock Mutual Life
Insurance Company towers, 1947 and 1975*

Congregational House (I B 7) and Board of Trade (V B 7). Sometime in the
twenties it became clear that this was a losing battle, that the walls of tall new
buildings were actually screens with virtually no intrinsic limit and that the steel
frames that channeled their forces were too strong and thin to allow much sense
of empathy with the forces coming to the ground. So instead, architects concentrated on the two areas of the building most readily encountered: the top seen
from a distance and distinguishable against the sky, and the bottom edging the
citizens' lives in the street and shaping the nature of public access to the building.
Walls became a field of transition between the two, often, as here, made in a way
that emphasized their verticality. The United Shoe Machinery Building
(V A 4) is the best Boston example.

The top here is a massive metallic stepped pyramid that recedes to a narrow,
flat section from which a curious spire ascends, like something misplaced from
a space-age pagoda. The whole shaping of the top was thought by some to be
an appeasement for its domination over the Trinity Church tower nearby. If so,
it reads instead like damning with faint mockery. The base, polished granite with
a large stripped Classical portico and a public meeting hall to one side, is of some
programmatic but little formal interest. In between the top and bottom there are
vertical stripes, some solid and faced with stone, others open and of glass and
metal. The solid stripes and the window stripes are of equal dimension, revealing
nothing about the structure inside and altered only at the corners, where wider
piers form thick corners of no structural and little compositional consequence.

All such distinctions are eschewed in the John Hancock Tower. It takes a form
at once more commanding and more austere. In the film *2001* a large, oblong,
gray and shiny slab appears, full of portent and surrounded by worshipers. The
Hancock Tower, of similar shape, is not gray and it certainly has no worshipers,

but it does appear that the architects, in their professed intent to take a minimalist approach out of deference to neighboring Trinity Church, have produced a building that borders on the occult.

The third John Hancock building is all mirror. The glass is of a special manufacture in exceptionally large sheets, held in place by mullions that are detailed to be a minimal intrusion in the reflective surface. These walls are made in a way that is so close to the limits of available technology that it has taken some years to make the glass secure. The whole reads as a very lightly gridded sheet of reflection, the sky and a few adjoining buildings in it tinted slightly green by the color intrinsic to the glass. The reflective sheet is 60 stories high, rising sheer from a bare granite plaza, the detailing so tightly restrained that the whole surface seems almost to slip into the elegantly formed drainage slot at its base. It would seem that there is no weight in this world, just as there is nothing to come up against except your own reflection and haunting memories of the fragility of glass.

The building is unsettling up close at its base, but from afar it is icily magnificent, the surfaces changing as the day changes, each side rendered in the color of the sky it faces. The drama of the reflecting surface is heightened by the parallelogram shape of the prism, which provides unexpectedly differing reflections on adjoining surfaces. On the short ends a sharp incision in the walls, glazed on one side, picks up yet another shaft of reflection, often sharply contrasting: gold when the rest is gray, dark when the rest is gleaming bright. The building adds to the skyline not so much an object as a spectacle of changing light, an intensified comment on the qualities of the sky itself.

The parallelogram plan places the bulk of the tower on an angle to the rectangular grid of Back Bay, creating a triangular plaza that exposes fully the south side of Trinity Church. The angle also skillfully makes it so that when you approach Trinity Church from Copley Square, the bulk of the Hancock Tower disappears in perspective behind the narrow, faceted shaft of the end elevation, which in turn dissolves the reflection of Trinity Church into a Cubist collage; reminding us that an early Hancock press release issued when the tower was still under hot dispute had the gall to pronounce that "the building will reflect the architectural character of the neighborhood." The dispute had to do with putting up a structure of this size on this site at all, a proposition which required overturning the existing height limitations and design guidelines and which was done in defiance of the Boston Redevelopment Authority's own architectural advisory board and the opposition of the Boston Society of Architects. The contest was not the first one to occur over this site. At the turn of the century the Hotel Westminster was built on this corner above the then-established height limit of 90 feet; its owners were required to remove the errant top.

If, despite its scenic splendor and elegant detailing, you still feel disoriented, adrift in reflected space, then go directly to the side entrance on Copley Square, pay your money and ride to the top of the building, where an entire floor is devoted to outlook. From here, there is a splendid panorama of Boston and an excellent taped exposition of the city's development, narrated by the late Walter Muir Whitehill, whose knowledge of Boston and its development was itself monumental. There is also a model of Boston in 1775, over which recorded narration, folk songs and programmed light bulbs enact the major events of that year in a miniature *son et lumière.*

IV A 8 · PRUDENTIAL CENTER

Boylston Street to Huntington Avenue, Exeter to Dalton and Belvidere streets

Charles Luckman & Associates designed the following:
Prudential Building: 1959–65
Hotel Sheraton–Boston: 1962–65
Prudential Apartments (The Fairfield, The Gloucester, The Boylston):
1964–68
Lord and Taylor: 1968
101 Huntington Avenue: 1970
Saks Fifth Avenue: 1971
addition, Hotel Sheraton–Boston: 1977

The Prudential Center was meant to be a great new center for Boston, splendid evidence of what large-scale development in the hands of modern Boston architects could bring to the city's future. To the *Progressive Architecture* Design Awards jury in 1954 it was all that, with a level of excellence that surpassed all competitors. That scheme, devised by Boston Center Architects, a group including Pietro Belluschi, Carl Koch, Hugh Stubbins, and the Architects Collaborative, led by Walter Gropius, was not the one that was built. What was built has been the work of Charles Luckman & Associates of Los Angeles. Worse deals have seldom been made.

Rather than the 40-story slab of the Boston scheme (pretty big at that), we have a 52-story Prudential Insurance Company tower, an energetically ugly, square shaft that offends the Boston skyline more than any other structure. Not the least of its offenses was the provocative challenge it offered its competitors, the Hancock Insurance Company, which subsequently felt compelled to exceed the Prudential's 52-story height by a few feet. The Prudential Tower, capped at the top like an unimaginably large newel post, is clad in various shades of green glass placed in a stagger pattern between narrowly spaced, vertically continuous mullions. The narrow spacing and alternating pattern so befuddle the mind that there is no way to use the parts of this surface to imagine the scale of the building; they create instead an overall texture of indeterminate size and color, mostly gray and unwieldy.

The Prudential Tower rises from the middle of a vast parking podium, atop which are lower wings for shopping arcades and to either side of which are subsequent buildings by the same architects, distinguished by their banality. On the Boylston Street side, a five-ton figurative sculpture by Donald Delue embodies the "Quest Eternal" in a form as graceless as the buildings themselves.

But all this is so much unseemly icing on the cake. The earlier scheme, like this one, was cut off from its surroundings in Back Bay by Boylston Street and the access ramps to the underground parking areas. What is really at stake here is the isolation of a segment of the city from all that is around it, an isolation that to a somewhat lesser extent was implicit also in the earlier scheme. That isolation is not simply willful; it was the natural course of events for a project this vast, under one ownership, incorporating the whole of the former Boston and Albany train yards, which themselves had been an impenetrable barrier between Back Bay and the South End.

And the project was intrinsically complex, involving an extraordinarily large parking structure and bridging both the rail line and a new turnpike right of way that cut diagonally across the site. Size and complexity notwithstanding, the project, in abler, more sympathetic hands, need not have been so alien. This alienation results from a limited vision—one which sees Boylston Street, for instance, as the outer limit of available land rather than as a living street of activities to be joined with; which sees architecture as the disposition of acres of low-maintenance surfaces enlivened by planters; which does not understand the dimensions of use and therefore produces too much open space, with plazas and terraces too windy to use and sealed passages too broad to seem lively. It is, finally, a drawing-board vision limited to the imaginative resources of one office and unable to receive the stimulus of new and livelier conceptions.

IV A 9 · JOHN B. HYNES CIVIC AUDITORIUM
Boylston Street, SE corner Dalton Street
Hoyle, Doran & Berry, 1963–65
· TENNIS AND RACQUET CLUB
939 Boylston Street, NE corner Hereford Street
Parker & Thomas 1902–03

The Hynes Auditorium is a major civic rallying place with a powerful absence of distinction.

Architecture in the late fifties and early sixties of the twentieth century was in a pretty confining state. The Classical vocabulary (base, column and entablature) and its associated devices for controlling the shape and appearance of buildings (basement, portico, arcade, attic and so on) had been effectively discredited, leaving those who were dependent on formula solutions bereft of a guiding hand. The imagery of the modern, on the other hand, was dependent for its life on real invention, rooted in the conditions of the specific problem—the functions to be accommodated, the paths of motion required and the means of construction, preferably innovative. But this is pretty demanding stuff for both architects and clients, and more often they turned, as here, to simple packaging. To connote civic importance they made occasional desperate attempts to embellish, here in the faceted-stone-and-gold-colored-metal pattern that makes an expansive blank billboard on the face of the building.

Inside is a vast multipurpose hall used for everything from auto shows to opera, even though acoustics that would be fine for a Buick are not altogether suitable for a baritone and nothing is done to make being there an event in itself.

Opposite, the Tennis and Racquet Club stands as simple evidence of the civility that this building lacks. It is quiet, cultured and very calm about housing an array of courts, locker rooms and lounges—hardly a conventional construction program.

IV A 10 · COLONNADE HOTEL
120 Huntington Avenue, SE corner Newton Street
Irving Salsberg & Associates, 1971

Motel as hotel. The Colonnade has a perfectly pleasant set of public spaces along the sidewalk under three floors of parking structure. Above this, rooms are stacked in an orderly row. The whole is held aloft by a long row of round-faced concrete columns, which rise from the sidewalk to the top of the building with concrete spandrels at the parking levels and with glass and metal spandrels filling the space in between columns to make hotel-room walls on the floor above.

Whereas Ralph Harrington Doane attempted in the Motor Mart Garage (IV A 2) to fit cars into an iconography ultimately based on person size, here dwelling space, albeit transient, is fitted to the rhythms of a parking structure.

Simple, pertinent perhaps, and articulated enough to establish a modicum of interest. The debt to I. M. Pei's work is obvious and identifies this building with the Christian Science Church Center plan, of which it was a part.

IV A 11 · PERKINS SCHOOL
St. Botolph Street, NW corner Cumberland Street
Henry H. Atwood, 1891
reuse: Graham Gund, 1980

This comely little block of a school has been converted to condominiums and it's altogether admirable. Retention of the small-scale yellow-brick institutional building gives us insight into the comfortable nature of neighborhoods in the 1890's. It asserts its presence, but in a way that is far from overpowering. In the renovation, windows have been redone and some skylights added to make usable living spaces of the former classrooms and take advantage of large attic spaces. The quiet care and craftsmanship of the original structure has been respected and changes have been made with a similar directness and invention using the materials and skills of the present.

IV A 12 · CHRISTIAN SCIENCE CHURCH CENTER
Huntington Avenue, Belvidere Street to Massachusetts Avenue
Mother Church: Franklin I. Welch, 1893–94
Extension: Charles E. Brigham and Solon S. Beman, Brigham, Coveney & Bisbee, 1903–06
Sunday School, Church Administration Building, Church Colonnade Building, Landscaped Open Space: I. M. Pei & Partners, with Cossuta & Ponte Associated Architects, 1968–73

For a religious group that is barely 100 years old, this is an impressive Vatican; testament not only to the power of Mary Baker Eddy's ability to move souls, but to her board of directors' ability to manage real estate. Not only the 10-plus acres that are visibly a part of the church center, but 22 acres of land in the vicinity have been brought under their control and formed the basis for a master plan drawn up by I. M. Pei.

The original Mother Church is a pleasant, quietly Romanesque church of rough-textured granite situated at the intersection of Norway and Falmouth streets, a location of no particular prominence. The church building is ingeniously inserted into the acute angle formed by these streets, with the apex filled by a large square tower that terminates an axis bisecting the site. Entries are slipped behind arcades in the severe walls that parallel the streets. These walls are intersected by others that return to the rectilinear geometry announced by the tower, making the church polygonal. As the rectilinear walls recede from the streets, small outside stairs slide up under arcades to make modest additional

IV A 12 · *The Mother Church, with Anthony Caro sculpture in foreground and Church Administration Building at right, Christian Science Church Center*

entries. With its granite walls pierced by a few openings and a tower that helps to resolve the angles of the site, this building is reminiscent of William Preston's nearly contemporary First Corps Cadet Armory (IV C 5) on Columbus Avenue, though the church is more modest in scale and a good bit more cramped in execution.

Mrs. Eddy's attachment to this first building was apparently sufficient to require that the very much larger church addition her followers needed only ten years later be considered merely an extension of the original. Brigham seems to have taken this task literally but not figuratively. The newer building is still referred to as the Extension, but against all odds—it far overshadows the earlier one in both size and style. Brigham, you may recall, was the architect who some years earlier had added the vast yellow-brick extension to the Bulfinch State House (I B 4).

The Mother Church Extension is organized on the same axis as that which bisected the streets and the plan of the first church, but it changes materials from rough stone to smooth and is very much grander, if not pretentious. It too is ingeniously planned, with a high, voluminous Renaissance dome as its center-piece. The dome has ribs that spring from the piers of an open arcade encircling the drum, and the whole bombastic enterprise sits atop a very large cube be-decked in Renaissance forms. From it a variety of architectonic devices are appended, including apses, arcades, octagonal and square entry blocks and, most notably, an astonishing new portico on the side opposite the original church. The apses, arcades and entry blocks adjust the cube to the angles of the site and are of relatively modest scale and pleasingly picturesque demeanor. The limestone portico, which was added in 1975, commands the large, newly formed open space in front of it with 42-foot-high columns, their capitals carved, amazingly enough, in allegiance to the Corinthian order found on the walls behind. The new capitals are less taut than the earlier ones; they seem rather like very large souvenirs. The space behind these columns is elegantly sheathed in glass. The interior of the Extension is a vast billowing space that emanates from the speaker's dais under the dome.

The Pei plan has removed from the premises any lingering threat that this site might be considered a backwater, but instead has created an open, landscaped forecourt along Massachusetts Avenue for the new portico to dominate and a vast reflecting pool and a tree-shaded promenade paralleling Huntington Avenue. The Mother Church Extension sits at the intersection of these two viewing spaces, very much in evidence. The Huntington Avenue space, terminated at the west by the fan-shaped Sunday School, bordered on the northeast by the Church Colonnade Building and marked at the southeast corner by the 28-story Church Administration Building, is part of a large pedestrian precinct into which Norway and Falmouth streets, which shaped the original church, have been absorbed. Even so, the geometry of their intersection still tends to control the place, as reflected in the buildings and their disposition.

The reflecting pool, 670 feet long by more than 100 feet wide, tops an underground parking garage and is used as a basin for cooling water from the air-conditioning system. It is large enough so that its surface is often vigorously rippled. The edge is a beautifully made, precisely placed round rim of red granite. From a distance the water has no visible containment; it rolls over its edge smoothly, as though reenacting the carving of the stone. The pavement is raised near the edge of the pool, forming walking paths that are slightly removed from the plaza and a bit more special.

A triple row of linden trees forms a promenade on the south; well-endowed planters and long concrete benches along the Huntington Avenue side of the pool provide places for gathering, patrolled by green-blazered security guards. The paving throughout is dark-burned brick edged with black granite and precast concrete. The concrete units articulate the plaza in large patterns, incorporating within their molded forms the gutters for these areas. At the intown end is an

IV A 12 · *The Mother Church, Christian Science Church Center*

IV A 12 · *Church Colonnade Building, Christian Science Church Center*

ever-so-restrained circle of paving that becomes in summer a thoroughly wonderful playground when a ring of closely spaced water jets spreads a high doughnut of water across the shallow dish. On a hot day the place turns into a field of scurrying bodies dashing back and forth, reveling among the jets. The paving here is a very carefully modulated series of levels that control the water, providing for varying degrees of wetness. At the outer edge on the east, the ring steps up to become a great semi-circular bench for onlookers, guardians and picnickers. When the water is off, however, there's less to recommend it.

It is, of course, possible to contend that all this is a brilliant scheme for keeping the residents of the South End distanced from the Mother Church, happily shaded and at play on the opposite side of a moat—but that would not be altogether fair, even though there are in fact no places to sit on the church side.

The new buildings of the church-center complex are large, austere and very carefully crafted. They are composed of grids and colonnades of a regular pattern framed in large masses of concrete that serve as attics, cornices or endpieces. The buildings are executed in the flawlessly formed and finished concrete for which the Pei office is renowned, colored here to match closely the limestone that covers the upper parts of the Mother Church Extension and cast in sections carefully stacked upon each other in a manner reminiscent of the severe granite-slab buildings of the waterfront.

The Sunday School at the far west end of the Huntington Avenue site is a simple quadrant of a circle in plan. It does a brilliant job of shielding the back of Horticultural Hall and the entrance to the garage, deflecting attention to the Mother Church and recalling an amphitheater all at once. The two short ends of the Administration Building slab tower to the east are configured with blank, faceted bays and are recollective in giant scale of the familiar Back Bay protru-

IV A 12 · *Christian Science Church Center Sunday School*

sions. The top of the Colonnade Building has a startling reinterpretation of entablature, with small glass-walled rooms between each pier as it reaches the heavy projecting cornice. They make inhabited glass dentils on the underside of the sloping concrete. Supporting this heavy top and marking time along the edge of the pool are four-story piers (not columns) of concrete. These oblong concrete piers are set at an angle to the building, so that the aspect is very different depending on which way you approach the building. Each one of the angled piers is penetrated at its base by a person-sized opening with an arch under a projecting block of concrete that holds sparkling light fixtures on each of its four faces. These give measure to the building and make it more penetrable at eye level.

On the northwest side of the Colonnade Building and both long sides of the Administration Building, a grid of concrete elements stands forward of the face of the glass. The wall becomes thick with shadow and reflected light as the elements cut off much of the sun, and vertical perforations in the grid pass reflected light and allow air heated by the sun to dissipate. The spandrels of the wall behind are slightly hollowed, so that the sunlight that does strike their surfaces produces further elaboration in the rich texture of light on this wall. They make a basic unit in the grid that is nearly square and of a size that can easily be imagined as the surround for a person. Leonardo da Vinci's diagram of a man inscribed in a circle could be lodged within one, only slightly larger than life. The elements of this wall are pieces of concrete in sizes consonant with the human body; in this it is scaled carefully, measured to man. Yet it is the inert figure spread-eagled in an ideal configuration that one imagines there, not the messy, errant folk we see around us.

IV A 13 · CHURCH PARK APARTMENTS
199–255 Massachusetts Avenue, Norway Street to Westland Avenue
The Architects Collaborative, 1973

This was one of the parcels of redevelopment associated with the Christian Science Church Center master plan. And obediently it plays an austere background for the splendor of the church as an uneventful slab of building that reduces the church surroundings to seemly uniformity. The apartment building demonstrates clearly that what is good for an affluent institution willing and able to control its grounds and their inhabitants and dedicated to the belief that error is illusion is not so good for mere developers collecting rent from their tenants. Church Park Apartments could not have been appropriately made in the full image of the church buildings and its developers could not have afforded to build or maintain them to comparable standards. Yet it has been constrained by its proximity into some vision of abstinence that is finally hermetic and dreary; a building that should be part of the city and accommodate the diversity of interests and living conditions that that implies is instead all diagram—concrete structure and stretches of glass.

Perhaps the architects or urban designers had some vision of the rue de Rivoli dancing in their heads. After all, Church Park is long, continuous, with housing above shops along a major street. And it is opposite not the Louvre, to be sure, but an institution of note. But the rue de Rivoli offers a lively passage with engaging storefronts, and courts behind that give identity to groups of residences. Its forms are studded with ornament and handsomely proportioned. And its sidewalks are not wider than people need or than the city can maintain. Here the building has been set back unnecessarily; the space might have been better used for bigger shops projecting forward on the ground floor to shield the lower-level apartments from the street.

IV A 14 · ST. GERMAINE STREET
between Massachusetts Avenue and Dalton Street
Various architects, c. 1894
reuse: Sasaki Associates, 1977

Another in the series of projects spawned by the Christian Science Church Center, this one organized by a private developer, though with property purchased from the church.

Stepping into St. Germaine Street is like stepping into a mild-mannered fairy tale. It's a whole street rehabilitated to the same standard: brick-paved sidewalks, cast-iron fences set in granite curbs to surround well-tended landscaping, buildings all of a type and planting boxes, many of them luxuriant, in nearly every window. The original builders, even while constructing a number of these at one time with a limited set of patterns, thought that they ought to carry distinguishing marks, so they varied the patterns slightly. One has the impression that even the minor variations introduced by the original builders made this environment more complicated than the present developer wished it to be, so the design sets about making everything else constant, dampening the errant (and often trivial) individuality of the buildings.

The result is a pleasant scene that keeps hovering on the edge of credibility. If a fully managed, right-thinking society is where we're going, then here we are. And the speculative builders of the turn of the century had it right all the while. It certainly seems a lot more livable than Church Park Apartments and presents an environment that could be conducive to neighboring; the street space between buildings, closed at each end, is small enough to be a collective room, and the forms that make it are all related to the size of people.

Part of all this was provided by the city, which supported the project with the installation of brick sidewalks, new street lamps and some landscaping. The developer undertook reconstruction of the exteriors of these buildings in a way that has obviously called for a high level of craftsmanship. If this can prevail on St. Germaine Street, perhaps the day will come when our everyday world will become crafted and ornamental as well, but with freer, more legitimate differentiation of parts and a manner not quite so much like a movie set—with perhaps some real invention.

IV A 15 · SYMPHONY HALL
NW corner Massachusetts and Huntington avenues
McKim, Mead & White, 1892–1900
· HORTICULTURAL HALL
NE corner Massachusetts and Huntington avenues
Wheelwright & Haven, 1901

The real corner of two major streets. This pair is one of the great urbanistic sets in America, bracketing Massachusetts Avenue with authority at the point where it bends.

Symphony Hall, which is bereft of the full decorative program apparently intended for it, is nonetheless a majestic red-brick gable-roofed volume closing the view down Massachusetts Avenue from the north. It stands distinct in form, its Renaissance ancestry evident even though the major portico on the south now faces the upper part of a highway underpass and the most active entrance is under a hanging marquee on the Massachusetts Avenue side.

IV A 15 · *Symphony Hall from Huntington Avenue, with Horticultural Hall at right*

Inside is a magnificent high box of space made to fill with sound. At one end the orchestra is framed by a full-height proscenium, the background provided by an immense organ. "BEETHOVEN" is inscribed in a shield at the top center of the frame. Narrow balconies band the other three sides of the rectangular space, shallow enough even at the far end so that from almost all seats the full volume can be seen and its splendid reverberations heard. A sloping wood floor, comparatively hard seats and a heavy coffered ceiling presumably add life to the acoustics of the place, which are so renowned that they have set what would now be called "the standards for the industry." No velvet here.

The side walls make a splendid set for the scene of arriving at the symphony. The two levels of balcony that stretch along the sides are so narrow that each person registers coming through the many doors. Above the balconies the wall is animated by an alternating pattern of pilasters and arches, with niches that hold aloft life-size sculptures clad not in gowns and tails but togas.

Horticultural Hall, which is now used for purposes more varied than originally intended, is a similar grand and simple brick volume more than amply endowed with decorative motifs, including lions' heads, swags and brackets with bundles of flowers carved underneath. It has a pronounced entry on the long Massachusetts Avenue side facing Symphony Hall. As the later of the two, it clearly followed the McKim, Mead & White lead, but with neither servility nor bombast. These buildings should be a lesson to us all.

B/THE SOUTH END

What is now termed "the South End" is a second-generation application of the term. The original South End was the southern half of the Shawmut Peninsula and is now the central business district of Boston. That's why Old South Meeting House (I A 3) is in what seems to be the center. The area now called the South End is stretched out along the neck, the strip of land connecting the Shawmut Peninsula with Roxbury, augmented on either side by landfill.

The area became subject to extensive development in the middle of the nineteenth century, in response to the pressures on real estate in Boston proper. A bit of building took place in the 1840's, much more in the 1850's, and a flood of homes, new streets and improvements occurred in the 1860's and 1870's as the area gained brief fashionability. Its prosperity was undercut by the social preemi-

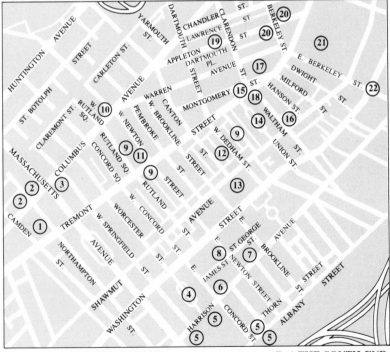

IV / THE SOUTHERN SECTOR   B / THE SOUTH END

nence of Back Bay and the beginnings of movement farther out along railroad lines into surrounding communities. The South End quickly became a haven of rooming houses, and by the beginning of the twentieth century it began a process of economic decline that only recently has been turned around. Its resurgence is due to the combined but opposing forces of gentrification and community-development programs put together out of the shambles of the Great Society by local minority groups.

Although it was developed only slightly earlier and is also dominated by row houses, the character of the South End is very different from that of Back Bay. To begin with there was no grand plan, no Commonwealth Avenue stretching from the Public Garden to the Fens. The South End was developed by the city, not the Commonwealth, and the models for its layout were English, not French. Where Back Bay has long rows of houses stretched out along a group of parallel streets, most houses of the South End are on short, often discontinuous streets that run perpendicular to the main thoroughfares of Columbus Avenue, Tremont and Washington streets. The South End is a collection of distinct places, many of them very handsome, loosely bonded together by a common building type, the coherence of which is threatened both by the dereliction it has suffered and by the heavy hand of institutions such as Boston City Hospital and the Boston Housing Authority that have appropriated land around its edges.

IV B 1 · PIANO CRAFT GUILD
791 Tremont Street, between Northampton and Camden streets
c. 1853
reuse: Gelardin/Bruner/Cott with Anderson, Notter Associates, 1972

The Chickering piano factory is reputed to have once been the second largest building in the United States. It was saved from extinction in 1972 and converted to artists' studios and apartments by an energetic group of architects who also served as developers, with financing from the Massachusetts Housing Finance Authority. Fundamentally, the Piano Craft Guild is a simple brick industrial building, but one built with pride. It's a wonderful combination of straight-forward factory architecture and an easygoing interest in formal composition. The middle is marked by an octagonal tower, half of it projecting forward of the main building wall, becoming a full cupola above the cornice line. With this dramatic device to make a center, the compositional intensity tapers off to either side and around the corners. What's nice is that it doesn't ever altogether give up.

Decorative motifs are used selectively here in a hierarchy that is most compli-cated at the central entry and almost nonexistent at the sides. But rather than the usual practice of slapping the decorations on the front of a building only to abandon them along the unadorned sides, brick banding here acknowledges the transition.

The central block has handsomely articulated piers topped by arches at two levels. The wings at either side have piers that rise all the way to an arcade at the top. Around the corner no piers or arches are used; there's only a plain brick wall and a banding that serves as a cornice, curving very gracefully into the corner to become the top of the arches on the front face.

Internally, the renovation is more informative than proud. From the central entry you go up left to the main office or down some stairs to the right into a

IV B 1 · *Piano Craft Guild*

IV B 2 · *Newcastle Court*

two-story art gallery. Just beyond is the community laundry: art and domestic service as social glue in a building for artists (though many non-artists now live here). The exhibition gallery has been carved out of the original first floor and basement. Massive granite-block basement piers are spanned by large wooden beams and struts, all clearly revealed, as is the inside wall of the foundation. All the new additions, in today's commercial vernacular of cheap building, are very spare, with minimal use of gypsum board, simple wood moldings and plain light fixtures. Then it's all surfaced in white in a way that's completely conventional. Compared to the thoughtfulness and pride of the original, the detail is a disappointment.

The interior courtyard has also been reclaimed with a few private outdoor spaces, but mostly it has been given over to an open field that serves as a breathing space for the whole building, surrounded by high wings on three sides and with a low wing across the back, where the steam engines used to be.

IV B 2 · SARANAC BUILDING
609–27 Columbus Avenue, NW corner Northampton Street
Rand & Taylor, Kendall & Stevens, 1896
reuse: Don Stull Associates, 1973
· NEWCASTLE COURT
Columbus Avenue, NE corner Northampton Street
reuse: Don Stull Associates, 1973

The Saranac Building is a good, solid apartment block. This, like the Piano Craft Guild, is organized by a central feature, but much more subtly. At the center the façade projects forward slightly and has a higher cornice. Each end also steps forward. This formal overlay of center and end pavilions is cliché, but it provides for middle, end and in between—both left and right—as recognizable places of entry. For a block of flats that would not otherwise be distinguishable one from another, this is helpful.

The overlay pattern is slightly out of synch with the apartment layout, so there are really four types of entry here. The organization is clearest in the end block: Apartments are on either side of the stair, their spaces clearly marked by the window pattern. The next entry along the façade has bay windows on either side, similarly marking the apartments with clarity. The third entry has a bayed unit on only one side; the other apartment it serves is visually a part of the center marked across the top by an ornamental band in two colors of brick. It's all carefully considered, and the pattern gives structure as well as an image of respectability to the place.

At the back the blocks of units are separated to allow small light wells in between, and the construction is direct and unpretentious, with wood porches that speak more directly of the lives inside.

Down the street at Newcastle Court, on the other hand, a single, large light-providing court is turned to the front and made into a gracious entry. This is an altogether fine building, sensibly organized. The court provides ground that can be commonly shared.

Entry to all apartments is from this controlled space—controlled, that is, by the porches and decks overlooking it at various levels. At the street an overhead balustrade held up on skinny cast-iron columns declares that the court space is semiprivate. The well-tended landscaping sets the tone inside, and an absence of entries on Columbus Avenue leaves room for planting along the street, where an impressive set of vines has taken over much of the frontage.

Bays on either side of each wing are stone-trimmed at the bottom, and each face is a distinct brick plane. The cornice breaks out around the bays, mimicking the indentations on the corners below. This gives the silhouette an extra little fillip that's just right.

IV B 3 · HARRIET TUBMAN HOUSE
566 Columbus Avenue, SE corner Massachusetts Avenue
Don Stull Associates, 1974

The South End is made up of buildings in large blocks, whether they're rows of repetitive single units, as along Tremont Street (IV B 9), or masses all organized at once, as at Saranac (IV B 2). The Tubman House captures that spirit. It does not look like its neighbors in any literal way, yet in a deep sense this building belongs here. It is a large, massive block faced with oversized brick of a purplish color. The façade is broken into at various places to let on that its interior is surprisingly open and light, with multistory spaces opening into each other and passages cutting through the space diagonally. It is, in fact, a genuinely believable building, one whose architect, with a constrained budget, formed the elements of a complicated program, including an important set of neighborhood social services, into a real presence in the street pattern. It works more successfully on Columbus Avenue than on Massachusetts Avenue, where the set-back position exposes the unprepared end of the neighboring row houses and a rather barren park in place of what might once have been stoops.

Nonetheless, Harriet Tubman's namesake is a building of interest and magnitude that makes no apologies for its new spirit. A fundamental respect for the place and the brio of its layered façade serve well in a community that deserves signs of affirmation.

IV B 4 · WORCESTER SQUARE
between Washington Street and Harrison Avenue

The South End summarized. A handsome residential square confronts a burgeoning institution at one end, while the other faces a devastated street. Boston City Hospital was placed at the end of Worcester Square in 1861. The central pavilion of the hospital, set in a garden, was an ennobling termination of the view from the square. The original building has been engulfed by subsequent additions (IV B 5), but the hospital entry still presents an ordered, reasonably scaled closure for the square, shielding the rest of the health-care behemoth from view. The influence of the hospital spills over into the square, however, where the lower floors of the end buildings have been made over into eating places for staff and visitors.

Down the center of the street is a fenced grass plot with big shady trees. The walls of the square are almost uniform, undulating with round bays and animated by high stoops and steps descending to the street. On one side of the park, many of the mansard roofs have been replaced by a continuous band of windows boldly providing light for renovated top-floor apartments. Like Union Park Square (IV B 14), Worcester Square is bracketed at each end by a narrower stretch of street before it meets the cross streets. The end lots face Washington Street rather than the square—unfortunately so, since Washington Street, blighted by a later elevated railway, is now a bad scene in every respect. Even the once impressive mansion at 1682 Washington Street has not been able to hold its own against the dereliction into which much of the South End has slipped. Its wonderfully proud and inventive swooping cornice and a bay almost oriental in form now forlornly front the el.

IV B 5 · BOSTON CITY HOSPITAL
intersection of Worcester Square and Harrison Avenue
Gridley J. Fox Bryant, 1861–64
· AMBULATORY CARE FACILITY
corner Massachusetts and Harrison avenues
Hugh Stubbins & Rex Allen Associates, 1977
· NURSING EDUCATION AND DORMITORY
Harrison Avenue between Massachusetts Avenue and Northampton Street
Samuel Glaser & Partners, 1974–75
· MECHANICAL PLANT
Albany Street between Springfield and Concord streets
Hugh Stubbins & Rex Allen Associates, 1977
· THE MASSACHUSETTS HOMEOPATHIC HOSPITAL
Albany Street, NE corner Concord Street
William Ralph Emerson, 1875–76

If Massachusetts General Hospital (II A 16) started life as a monument to the Age of Reason, Boston City Hospital began more like a French hospice, a row of mansard-roofed buildings surrounding a garden. In the center of the garden was a domed pavilion situated and styled like a patriarch. As with Mass General, events overtook the serene and paternalistic vision, and an array of buildings in a very different image arose in its place.

With a little bit of effort you can still catch glimpses of one of the original structures. It's nicely made with a mansard roof curved in profile, essentially a domestic structure, though larger than most.

The new Ambulatory Care Facility is less difficult to find, since it spans Massachusetts Avenue, its bottom two floors open to accommodate the thoroughfare. The bulk of the building makes a gate at this edge of the city. Beyond this, originally, was the tip of South Bay; now it's filled land for industry and transportation. Farther south, Massachusetts Avenue becomes incoherent, so this is effectively the southern boundary of a recognizable Boston. It's a location (and there are few such) where it really made sense to impose a wall across the street. Unfortunately, the building simply isn't up to its role as an urban gateway.

The upper part of the Ambulatory Care Facility is long and sleek, with alternating horizontal bands of glass-and-metal panels that extend across the road and onto an adjoining entry plaza, their architect seemingly unaware of the civic occasion taking place below. The only architectural acknowledgment of the Massachusetts Avenue axis is in the alignment of one of two pairs of giant ventilating nostrils in the high mechanical attic. They make a rather rudely diagrammatic ending for such an important road. More wittily, the glass corridors above the street have large photographic murals that are visible at night. One shows people about eight feet tall staring down at the cars passing underneath. At least the graphics people knew that something special was happening.

Entry to this part of the hospital is across a dreary plaza. An automobile circle wends its way through sloping mounds of brick holding the ventilating ducts. The whole, one supposes, is meant to be sculptural, but its barren hostility, though easily maintained, stands in marked contrast to the gardens and entry courts of the first buildings.

To the west a tower and a slab rise to form a nursing school and a recreation-and-residential complex. The tower, a dramatic element in the skyline, and the lower family-housing unit are executed with the same carefully studied concrete details. In the lower, ten-story building, the fine-grain articulation combines with porches and windows to make a quite satisfactory relation to the older apartment blocks across the way, buildings that are lower but have parts of similar size. In the higher building the same detail begins to look finicky, without any pattern that relates to the much greater height.

The details of this complex are thus thoughtful but circumscribed. They relate nicely to the problems of constructing a stack of floors with bands of windows to let in light, but the building lacks any emotional content.

If you approach the hospital from the south or along Albany Street, the most notable City Hospital landmark is the mechanical plant. It's an amazing structure, colossal, bright and glassy. From it a huge yellow duct as thick as a truck wends its way overhead across streets and between buildings to carry utilities to the new buildings, avoiding entanglement with existing underground services. Perhaps unwittingly, it establishes a pertinent visual simile for technological medicine: enshrined pumps and monitors connected to the body by tubes.

Still another notion of the healing arts is evident in what was once the Homeopathic Hospital off East Concord Street between Albany Street and Harrison Avenue. The building is an odd assortment of towers, turrets, bays and dormers, all rendered with the wood, brick and brownstone motifs of the late 1870's but with an imagination clearly nurtured by images of pleasant places to be in, with air, light and personality. It was deemed in its time to be one of the very best hospital buildings. Now it is inadequately equipped, an anomaly in search of a suitable use.

East of the main complex are many large buildings, allied in their pursuit of health services and occasionally linked together by bridges, answering to different institutional masters and totally bereft of any unifying imagery. There are sedate brick ones and shiny blue ones, sculpted concrete ones with brick infill, delicate concrete ones and lumpy concrete ones and, of course, stacks of parked cars. If there's a common aura, it's one of urgency and desperation, not healing.

IV B 6 · CHURCH OF THE IMMACULATE CONCEPTION
761 Harrison Avenue, NE corner Concord Street
Patrick C. Keeley, 1861

A powerful white granite surprise in a neighborhood of brownstones, with even more surprise inside. The sheer scale and simplicity of this church would make it special anywhere but in Italy.

It is cast in a broad temple form with giant order pilasters that measure out the full height of the side walls, and with tall arched windows between the pilasters. This spacing returns around the front, only to be interrupted by a curiously shrunken center pavilion with an awkward Palladian window as its centerpiece. These features mark it as midcentury American; it's ambitious, inventive and sometimes gauche. The entry itself is up broad stairs and through three large arched doors, set within a pilastered colonnade.

The interior, on which Arthur Gilman is thought to have worked, is awesome. A broad coffered barrel vault down the center springs from arcades to either side —arcades that sit lightly, even tenuously, atop tall, cylindrical shafts. The tops of these shafts bear profusely carved composite capitals that seem intended to make up in intensity for the absence of much visible supporting surface above them. The side aisles are groin-vaulted and brightly lit by the high windows that march along the sides.

Next door a stern brick building, contrasting with the expansiveness of the church, housed Boston College in its infancy and adolescence before it took to the suburbs.

IV B 7 · JOSHUA BATES SCHOOL
731 Harrison Avenue
Arthur H. Vinal, 1884

This is a very nice brick block schoolhouse by the former City Architect. It has a central entry pavilion that is set off-center and skewed, with a complicated arrangement of arches for the windows.

Many architects of this period delighted in using symmetrically arranged parts in a loosely composed manner, with an eye on the Romanesque forms championed by Richardson. They used asymmetry to accommodate specific uses or functional irregularities in the overall organization of the building—or sometimes just to bring the composition to life. The resulting forms, as here, reflect the impulse to generalized order combined with a keen eye for the special.

This was a public elementary school until only a few years ago, when it was turned into studio space for artists.

IV B 8 · FRANKLIN SQUARE HOUSE
11 East Newton Street, between James and Washington streets
John R. Hall, 1868
reuse: Boston Architectural Team, with Archplan, 1976

A cross between the Chickering piano factory (IV B 1) and the Old City Hall (I A 8), and not as good as either. Big and blunt, the French Second Empire stylistic dressing simply isn't vigorous enough to hold its own on a building that's really full factory size and built with clenched-teeth determination.

Originally the St. James Hotel, then the New England Conservatory of Music, it more recently has been converted into housing for the elderly, with corridors moved away from their original position in the middle of each wing where they divided the interior into two rows of rooms. The corridors are now on one side of the structure overlooking a large central court.

IV B 9 · 676–92 TREMONT STREET
between Rutland and West Newton streets
c. 1860
· 715–25 TREMONT STREET
between Rutland and Concord squares
Glazer, De Castro, Vitols, 1975
· RUTLAND SQUARE
between Tremont Street and Columbus Avenue
c. 1865–75
· UPTON STREET
between Tremont Street and Shawmut Avenue
c. 1860

Much of Tremont Street has been either transformed at the base into commercial space or torn down. The block where Nos. 676–92 stand has been reworked and brought back to reasonable condition. It shows the basic pattern that was dominant in the South End: continuous rows of houses facing the long streets, their faces bowed at each unit, their mansard roofs interrupted by dormers, their broad entrances at the top of high stoops. Much of the character of the place comes from the repetition of this type of housing in differing circumstances; facing broad, long streets, as here, or short, narrow ones, such as Upton, or Rutland Square.

Along Tremont Street these grouped houses formed a long row of inhabited walls with many windows and frequent entries. At the cross streets, where the sparsely windowed side walls of these row houses are exposed, they made a natural transition, a gate of sorts, to the intersecting streets.

Recent efforts to recover this frontage for housing by building new low-cost structures have been mostly dreary (along Columbus Avenue they are appalling). The set west of Rutland Square, Nos. 715–25, are made with some effort but not nearly enough. Most especially, they suffer from a negative sense of the street —a failing that is both social and architectural. The bottom floor is all blank security screens. There is no conception of how these units might relate to their setting in a positive way. Without that, there can be no sense that the civic world is anything but residue.

IV B 9 · *Rutland Square*

Rutland Square, on the other hand, is one of the more scenic bits of the South End. It's only one block long on both sides of a fenced-in elliptical green whose shade trees make a contained room beneath. Houses of three stories plus an attic define the walls of this space. The entrances are recessed slightly into the building and the basements are not very high, so there's only a rather gentle stair between sidewalk and house. These factors combine to make a special place that is quite a bit lower in scale and more intimate than many South End streets.

Several houses, including Nos. 13, 15 and 23, have an unusually frolicsome exterior treatment. They are stuccoed in a lighthearted combination of medieval and rococo motifs. Their entrance pediments are fundamentally rococo in inspiration, their windows are formed as arches on what are essentially Gothic colonettes and there's some half-timbering above. Many of these bays are made with narrow casement windows that give them a quite lovely sense of delicacy. The rooms behind these bays are often curved, to make oval chambers inside.

For some reason, at the midpoint of each side of the street the pattern changes from low stoops to the more typical South End form: high basement plus three stories and an attic. It's a much more intimate street at the south end than at the north, where these high stoops push out against you as you walk along the street. Here at the north the buildings seem to be peering down at you rather than offering a welcome shelter or haven off your path.

Upton Street is a short street closed at each end. On each side are high buildings, four stories on top of a high basement. Stoops go up with cast-iron brackets running along the stairs, while cast-iron fences capture tiny bits of yard.

The result is that Upton Street is a high, narrow space but very urban and very proud, with little variation in the way the buildings are made, except for tiny details here and there. A continuous wall of alternating round bays and flat entries makes the entire street undulate on both sides until it comes to its ends at Tremont Street and Shawmut Avenue. A very coherent street with a real sense of public space.

IV B 10 · UNION UNITED METHODIST CHURCH
485 Columbus Avenue, between West Rutland Square and West Newton Street
A. R. Estey, 1877

The street of Rutland Square closes visually at the north in the tower of Union United Methodist Church, its very simple Gothic Revival spire set at an angle so that the aspect is exceedingly picturesque. The angle of the church tower is set by Columbus Avenue, and the termination of Rutland Square is just a bend; West Rutland Square proceeds beyond to end again in a vista of the Christian Science Administration Building (IV A 12).

Union United Methodist was designed by A. R. Estey, the architect who brought us Emmanuel Episcopal Church (III B 3) on Newbury Street. He was best known for his suburban churches in the Gothic and Romanesque modes. This is quite a nice church, in rural parish style with a steeple at the corner entry and a two-pitched roof above the nave. The south transept comes out to Columbus Avenue and its face merges with that of a chapel at the rear.

IV B 11 · SOUTH END BRANCH LIBRARY
685 Tremont Street, between Rutland Square and West Newton Street
Mitchell/Giurgola Associates, 1967–71

This is a fine building that was intended to deal with its Tremont Street context without blindly imitating the existing pattern. It is, after all, too small, but what it lacks in bulk its architects tried to make up in genuinely useful open space. They placed the mass of the building on the West Newton Street end of the site and attempted to form the rest of the site into a cloistered park, with thick brick piers forming a passage around the perimeter, covered by a wooden trellis and edged by benches.

It's fundamentally an all-brick one-story library with a second-floor community meeting room standing in its midst. The brick box of the meeting room is set on columns that rise from the main reading room. A set of clerestories and skylights lets light into the upper spaces of the library; and a huge window for the upper part of the meeting room is a principal feature of the building's form. The interior shows very close consideration of natural lighting and of the way that the building's parts are made known, more so than most new buildings in Boston. The clerestories are equipped with hinged panels that enable the library staff to alter the direction of the light, letting it flow either into the central reading spaces or into the stacks around the edges.

The care that went into the design of the exterior, however, particularly in the open spaces, has been largely undone. The trellis has since been removed, and the benches, which enjoyed a rather subtle relationship with both sidewalk and courtyard, have been replaced by very clunky standard-government-issue park benches with wooden slats on ugly concrete frames. They now sit in the middle of what was designed as a passage, and face unequivocably back into the courtyard. In this way the effective size of the open space is enlarged, but most of its quality is destroyed. There is now no sense of protection or enclosure at all. And the brick piers, with nothing to support, have come to seem pointless.

IV B 12 · VILLA VICTORIA

· Torre Unidad

· Viviendas la Victoria
**bounded by Shawmut Avenue and West Brookline, Tremont and West
Dedham streets**
John Sharratt and Associates, 1969–76

Villa Victoria is a paradox. It is one of the earliest successful efforts by a local community group to gain both physical and economic control over a segment of the city scheduled for redevelopment. Yet their successful efforts to resist relocation have resulted in a place that is very different from its surroundings. In this case the sense of the place has been relocated while the residents' stayed put and gained some measure of political and economic power in the process. The group responsible for development was primarily Puerto Rican, hence the Hispanic names.

There are at present four parts to Villa Victoria, and it's still growing. The most evident is a 16-floor apartment tower for the elderly that protrudes above everything else in the South End and, I suppose, makes its gesture of power in the neighborhood with some deliberation. A second element, opposite the tower, is a long 6- to 7-story row of apartments above shops. Both these are dark-purplish brick with dark metal window frames surrounding large inset panes of glass and metal spandrels. The tower is bulky but not unpleasant; the long building is set above a concrete arcade that shelters shops underneath and creates a terrace above. Slight variations in the disposition of windows give a substructure to their façades. The two buildings face across a concrete plaza that was intended to be a recollection of the traditional plaza in Puerto Rico. Both buildings are easier to take than the town houses that make up the third element of the project, for they both are believable even if not cheerful extensions of the urbanity of the South End, of necessity recast in new forms.

The row-house units, which you might expect to be more like their South End predecessors, are instead less like them. This results from a number of factors, not least that they are made with the much smaller volumes of space that can now be afforded for a family in a project built with government subsidy. The subsidy in turn brings with it uniform regulations that are abstracted, often at odds with the nature of the place itself. Most of the houses are three short stories aboveground, while the most vivid streets of the South End are four and a half tall stories. The lower buildings here cannot give shape to streets and squares as powerfully as the earlier ones did.

Further, the row houses are designed to look like individually made suburban houses all strung together. The regular rhythmic agreements that characterize the fabric of the South End, and make it a distinct place with enduring quality despite economic neglect, are forsaken here for a nervous palette of bright colors and interrupted roof lines that make an effort to give each house a crude but distinct identity. These devices, which in another situation might be welcome deviations from a project norm, are here precisely the factors that separate Villa Victoria from its South End surroundings and make it a place apart, a place adrift. The first segment of the complex to be completed, was, happily, a well-handled renovation of town houses along Tremont Street that maintains the continuity of that street form and partly shields the enclave behind.

All this is problematic because the distinct project character of this complex can be seen as a positive attribute—a welcome sign of the community's ability to shape space to its own ends. And if other, more affluent developers—Prudential Insurance (IV A 8), for instance—make their mark by abandoning traditional patterns, why should a minority group bear the burden of attempting to heal and protect the physical fabric of the South End, which earlier Boston Redevelopment Authority schemes were prepared to abandon totally?

The coherence of the South End environment is a resource that should not be wasted. Whether built for the affluent or for the poor, new work answering to differing demands and made with differing means should nevertheless be made in ways that gain strength by supporting and extending the essential character of existing places. Otherwise we all march to nowhere.

IV B 13 · BLACKSTONE SCHOOL
380 Shawmut Avenue, SW corner West Dedham Street
Don Stull Associates, 1976

At once tough with itself and gentle with its surroundings, this building wraps around its own play space facing Blackstone Square.

Walls of brick-colored concrete block are used to join the ground and to make stair towers and other parts that are particular. They form a shaped and perforated base, above and behind which sheets of window and rust-colored metal siding make the standardized parts of the building. Along Shawmut Avenue the buildings are set back behind walled courts. Masonry walls bounding these courts remain person-sized along the street, interrupted periodically by panels about the height of a normal entry porch. Large and small geometric cutouts are placed playfully in these street walls so that children can look out and passers-by can look in. At the corner the masonry returns to the building and rises up into a small tower announcing the entry.

Tough industrial materials were chosen, no doubt in anticipation of the trashing and neglect that have been endemic to inner city schools, and the result, though thoughtful, is grim.

IV B 14 · UNION PARK SQUARE
between Tremont Street and Shawmut Avenue
c. 1851–60

The South End's answer to Louisburg Square (II B 1). The park itself has a fence around it and two splashing fountains, beds of flowers and great trees within. It's one of the most beautiful open spaces in Boston, an elliptical room made by the continuous wall of town-house façades surrounding it. The space was laid out by the City Engineer in 1851, then developed by various individuals in subsequent decades—evidently in groups of three or four, judging from details in window heads, balusters and cornices.

On the southwest flank of the square and at both ends, the town houses each have a round bay the full height of the façade and a flat stretch of wall for the entry. The entry is slightly recessed, with a dramatic set of steps reaching out to the ground. At the curved end these town-house units step out in a fabulously undulating sequence, the bottom a diagonal progression of sloping stairs, the top an alternation of square corner and curving bay that makes a distinguished silhouette. The flamboyance of this edge is matched by a sudden outbreak of rococo inspiration in the window heads of Nos. 42–52.

IV B 14 · *Union Park Square*

Midway on the northeast side is a flat-faced set (Nos. 19–31) with wooden bays at the second floor over the entries. Several of these bays have pilasters, colonettes and wood-paneling details that are more like the furniture of the time than like parts of buildings. They add an intimacy to the space, like big sideboard cabinets pinned to the wall.

The first floors are uniformly quite high, a good seven feet off the ground on top of a full basement, permitting a view of the park over the cars and gardens. The stairs that climb up to them are dramatic. It's easy to imagine running up or down these stairs, or pausing at the top to survey the scene.

In Union Park Square the space between the façade and the sidewalk is typically enclosed by a stone base, either in granite or brownstone, and a cast-iron fence that connects with the front steps. Three basic types of handrail can be identified: the standard cast-iron baluster linked to the fence, the carved brown-

IV B 14 · *doorways, Union Park Square*

IV B 15 · *St. Cloud Hotel*

stone baluster when brownstone is the base, and a wonderful looping display of cast-iron volutes that slide down granite stringers to greet the street.

IV B 15 · ST. CLOUD HOTEL
567 Tremont Street, NE corner Union Park Street
Nathaniel J. Bradlee, 1870

Nathaniel Bradlee designed many of the South End's row houses. Here he altered his style slightly to lend an especially elegant air to an apartment house with two full-floor flats on each floor, paired around a central stair. Servants' quarters here as elsewhere were in the mansard, though living in the corner tower room must have given princely ambitions to some.

The building was faced with marble, with projecting bays added at either end of the Tremont Street façade. These bays, together with slight projections in the main wall, arcaded windows at the fourth floor and steep pyramidal roofs at the top on each corner, make a twin-towered façade, demonstrating once again the power of illusion.

IV B 16 · 281–91 SHAWMUT AVENUE
SW corner Hanson Street
c. 1880

In the block of Shawmut Avenue that runs between Waltham and Hanson streets is a very instructive set of row houses done up in an entirely different style. They're all flat, fronted with Flemish or Dutch gables as their only decoration. The stoops descend not quite so steeply as elsewhere in the South End.

They're instructive because that one change in the façade gives the whole street a different sense. There's nothing projecting toward the street; everything that goes on in these houses goes on behind the front wall, so the separation of public and private space is very sharp here.

Just north, at the intersection of Ringgold and Bond streets with Hanson Street, there's a particularly intimate streetscape. The streets come together here, with views closed in every direction by buildings just one block away. One street ends in the Boston Center for the Arts (IV B 17), the others end in row houses to either side. Then in the middle a little open park has been partly converted into a concrete playground of the parks-department sort.

IV B 17 · CYCLORAMA
· BOSTON CENTER FOR THE ARTS
541 Tremont Street, between Berkeley and Clarendon streets
Cummings & Sears, 1884 (and later revisions)

Once the simulated scene of the Battle of Gettysburg, the Cyclorama building is now the centerpiece of an enterprise hopefully called the Boston Center for the Arts, which for ten years has been accumulating the momentum to bring this place and its surroundings back to life.

The original castlelike entrance to the Cummings & Sears building disappeared during one of its several transformations, and the vast surrounding mural has been removed, suitably enough, to Gettysburg. The space inside remains a beautiful shallow dome of exhilarating width. Stripped of its scenic clothing, the direct ingenuity of the place is fascinating. It is spanned by steel trusses arching radially from a rim of brick buttresses to a compression ring at the center. Over the middle another network of radiating metal ribs forms a shallow conical skylight hovering above the spidery trusses.

The present front is of little intrinsic interest. The chief feature outside is not a part of the present, rather no-account façade. It is instead a kiosk of notably vigorous scale and silhouette that marks the whole complex of renovated and soon-to-be-renovated buildings that are part of the projected center. The kiosk is in fact the salvaged lantern from a building in Roxbury, now demolished. It was designed by Gridley J. F. Bryant of Old City Hall (I A 8) fame and has lately come to be the serving station for a summertime outdoor café.

IV B 18 · 550–62 TREMONT STREET
opposite Clarendon Street, between Waltham Street and Union Park Square
c. 1850–60

An exemplary row of town houses with very subtle swelling bays and a mansard roof that is slightly curved at the bottom so that it joins the wall very gently above a banded brick cornice. The principal floor is up almost a whole level, and the front yard, ground floor and, in some cases, first floor have been absorbed into a commercial space added on to the front. A real estate office at No. 558 has been especially carefully restored, its windows bedecked with awnings—a way of dealing with the heat of the sun that was typical of row houses in the South End (and elsewhere) in the era before we decided to waste our petroleum reserves on air conditioning.

IV B 19 · APPLETON STREET
· LAWRENCE STREET
· DARTMOUTH PLACE
between Berkeley and Dartmouth streets
c. 1870–80

Appleton Street is a handsome little street, at first appearing to be very consistent, though in fact made up of three different building forms; one set alternates flat surface and round bay and is placed high up off the street for privacy, another set has simple flat fronts and is also high off the street with occasional added bays, and a third set is closer to the ground, with chamfered bays. All are set slightly back from the street to allow for little bits of greenery.

Lawrence Street, to the north, and Dartmouth Place, to the south, are another pattern altogether. They are like Acorn Street on Beacon Hill (II B 3), with houses close up against the sidewalk on the south, and the north sides bordered by gardens to the rear of dwellings in the next street. The backs of these houses, even more than the fronts, show adjustments and revisions and the signs of personal patterns of use and care. These are intimate little streets with large trees overhanging from the adjoining gardens.

Dartmouth Place is made especially intimate by being closed at the east end by the backs of houses that face Clarendon Street. The houses at its other end have bays that project up through the cornices to form little towers on the faces of the mansard roofs. The buildings, which are nearly identical, have been renovated in various ways over time, sometimes with asphalt brick, sometimes with rustic siding, once with large multiple-pane windows and so on.

These streets run parallel to those of the Back Bay and were a part of the landfill operation, but separated from the fashionable section by railroads. The special pattern of Lawrence Street and Dartmouth Place results from fitting three rows of houses within the basic grid established for two rows in the more affluent Back Bay.

IV B 20 · PAINE MEMORIAL BUILDING
49–55 Berkeley Street, NE corner Appleton Street
1872
reuse: Boston Architectural Team, 1974

· BERKELEY RESIDENCE CLUB
40 Berkeley Street, SW corner Appleton Street
Kilham, Hopkins, Greeley & Brodin, 1952

These two buildings are eighty years apart and equally distant in conception. The Paine Memorial Building is all show and a pretty good one at that; the Berkeley Residence Club is a respectable rendition of building for function from a period when architects took pride in being "direct." Walter Kilham coined the phrase "plain American" in admiration of the granite State Street Block (V B 9), and his firm here emulates that spirit in brick.

The Paine building appears as though it could once have been two buildings, or one plus a later meeting-hall extension that is bonded to the original by a common mansard roof. In any case, all its parts are crafted in careful pursuit of our affection. On the Berkeley Street façade, well-formed triplets of windows are disposed at either side of a central tower that evidently holds the stair and is lighted by an oversized window still bearing a Star of David from the period when it served as a synagogue. The Appleton Street face bears less incised decoration but is no less studied, with its own central pavilion and an entry off-center. One can easily imagine this as a place of community life, even though it has now been converted into condominiums.

The Residence Club is a more sober place concerned more with ideas about building and amenity inside than with emblems of ennoblement. Its fundamental form is a gray brick slab set close to the Appleton Street side of the site to allow a garden to the south. The entry space is carved into the block at the lower floor with curved forms that accommodate the movement of entering.

Bricks and concrete, the stuff of building, and the actions of people using the building were all that counted here. The traditional symbols of entrance were deliberately abandoned in order to be single-minded in the service of their clients' real needs. Unfortunately, such architecture leaves us without the essential fiction that the street may be a place of public importance.

IV B 21 · CASTLE SQUARE HOUSING
400–90 Tremont Street, between Berkeley Street and Shawmut Avenue
Samuel Glaser & Partners, 1967

The Castle Square Housing project is a telling case of mismatch between the level of attention and concern that the norms of the architectural profession encourage and the reality of the living conditions that public architecture must support.

Along Tremont Street, around a courtyard, are seven-story buildings, still quite modest in scale, but spoiled by pockets of grayness and litter, much of them invited by the niches and recesses that articulate the structure, and aggravated by the bland color of the concrete. The buildings show in great detail just how they're made. The concrete frame is very directly expressed, and the concrete floor comes all the way out to the edge, with the brick infill clearly demonstrated. A combination of high windows to light the ceiling and low windows opening out to the view is perhaps a too-subtle differentiation of usage: in most cases, window shades cover the upper windows.

A concrete colonnade running along Tremont Street is very carefully made, architecturally—an articulated structure that reveals different kinds of shop-front bays along its length and has a concrete frame between the buildings' fronts and the sidewalk itself. This colonnade leads into a court in the south end of the project, 120 feet square. It's very simple and pleasant, with a day-care center on one side and connections with the other spaces of the project. A terrace at the upper level, associated with housing for the elderly, allows people to enjoy the more active court below without having to participate in it.

Beyond, four-story walk-ups with balconies are arranged in a variety of court-yard patterns. The balconies get a great deal of use and attention. These lower units have brick walls forming their courtyards and wood-slat fences to make private yards for individual apartments. But these wood-slat fences simply aren't built to survive, and they make the more public spaces seem derelict.

However, these lower spaces that are less controlled architecturally offer some hope. The housing here is organized in a series of rows alternating between public walk and private backyard, with a piece of untended greenery in the middle. An area between the building and the sidewalk is claimed by tenants for their own uses. It's a wonderful shabby collection of all sorts of fencing and all sorts of gardens—some filled with flowers, some with vines and vegetables, some with laundry. Despite its ramshackle quality, it is rich in signs of human life and of hope.

IV B 22 · DOVER STATION
E. Berkeley and Washington streets
Alexander Wadsworth Longfellow, 1901
alteration: Robert Swain Peabody, c. 1909

Over the intersection of Berkeley and Washington streets is the Dover station of the elevated Orange Line. It's a wonderful piece of copper façade dangling from the sturdy steel support structure that keeps the rail lines aloft. The whole rail platform widens at this point just over the crossing of the streets to accommodate people getting on or off, and the great copper front with its domestic-looking windows and dropped center bay accompanies them down the stairs to the sidewalks.

IV B 22 · *Dover Station*

The elevated rail line is not long for this world and will be a good riddance, but for now it traces the route of the original neck of land joining Boston to the Roxbury highlands.

C/BAY VILLAGE AND THE THEATER DISTRICT

What is now known as the South End was originally connected to the center of Boston across the neck along Washington Street. As more land was filled, Shawmut and Tremont streets paralleled Washington's path into town. The last landfill project in the area extended Columbus Avenue out from Park Square to Roxbury in 1860. Bay Village, the area just east of Columbus, was already filled and developed in the 1820's when the Back Bay was still a tidal basin. It remains an anomalous containment of houses and streets from the period, a Beacon Hill on the mud flats.

The theater district occupies the oldest, most solid land along the neck. It was until recently picturesquely known as the Combat Zone, characterized more by the boisterous scene on the streets than by the more subdued drama inside. In recent years the city has made a considerable effort to create an alternative image based on the concentration along Tremont Street of Boston's legitimate theaters (and a number on Washington Street that have turned illegitimate). Beyond Kneeland Street, Washington Street itself has been almost completely taken over by Tufts New England Medical Center.

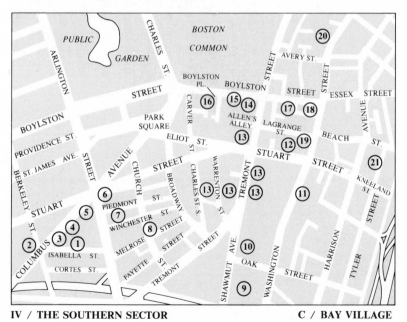

IV / THE SOUTHERN SECTOR   C / BAY VILLAGE

IV C 1 · ISABELLA AND CORTES STREETS
between Berkeley and Arlington streets

· **Hotel Isabella**
34 Isabella Street
A. S. Drisco, 1885

· **40 Isabella Street (former Hotel Clifford)**
1867
reuse: Payette Associates, 1976

Isabella Street is a handsome street of four-story buildings in brick with stone lintels augmented by metal bays of various decorative allegiances. When they were built these apartments, or flats with each unit all on one floor, were dubbed hotels in the terminology of the time. Hotel Isabella, at No. 34, is a particularly energetic example, with brick decorative patterns employing angles, slits and notches within the brick bonding, and rough granite blocks for the spring points of segmental arches or simply for lintels. The fundamental principle of this building is clear: If it's possible to do something more than one way, do it.

No. 40 Isabella is really the back of 25 Cortes Street, which was modestly and neatly turned into a new front by Payette Associates. It serves as their office entry off a pocket of parking. They've simply added a vinyl canopy of appropriate size to grace the rear and announce their presence. More flats line Cortes Street, mostly with bays of various handsome and comfortable-looking sorts and some with names like Elisabeth, Gordon and Devon emblazoned in their tops or above the door.

IV C 2 · 209 COLUMBUS AVENUE
SW corner Berkeley Street
H. W. Hartwell & W. C. Richardson, 1890–92

Hartwell & Richardson turn here from the Romanesque of their mentor, H. H. Richardson, to decorative forms more like those used by Louis Sullivan in Chicago. The elevations are elegantly detailed, panelized in vertical bays of two and three windows and in horizontal bands on top, bottom and in between. A balustraded cornice across the very top has been stripped off. The mass of the building is a direct consequence of its site, filling the odd obtuse angle of the intersection of Columbus Avenue and Berkeley Street, but not for a moment revealing the angle in either elevation.

The piers in the middle-range panels are clustered colonettes, which lets the architects have it both ways, upping the scale by joining several floors together and yet retaining small sizes near the windows themselves. Decorative panels abound, with serrated brick edges and cast foliage, making the whole surface a series of frames with each of the elements frayed at the edge and elaborated. The two-story base of the building is red sandstone, with broad openings at the ground floor that reflect steel beams above and arched entries at either end. A grander, more commanding arch in the center on the Columbus Avenue side shelters the main entry.

At some point later than the original building, but not much later, a large marquee was hung around the lower floor, held up by lion heads dutifully gripping chains in their teeth.

IV C 3 · FIREHOUSE
200 Columbus Avenue, corner of Isabella Street
Carlin & Pozzi, 1970

A very respectable, straightforward job, this is a clear example of construction logic governing design. The concrete structure of columns and beams is clearly exposed. The areas between concrete are filled with either brick, glass or rolling doors in the engine hall below, and with brick and T-shaped windows in the sleeping rooms on the upper floor. The alarm center is a separate little cockpit set to one side of the big doors, with a strip of glass between jaws of concrete. Inside, the parts of the building—pipes, conduit and mechanical apparatus as well as structural frame—are all forthrightly laid out and carefully organized as elements of the building's order. It's all very admirable and incredibly dry. Two fire stations in New Haven, designed by the same architects, follow a similar logic but with a lot more verve.

IV C 4 · BACK BAY RACQUET CLUB
162 Columbus Avenue, between Berkeley and Arlington streets
T. M. Clark, 1886
reuse: Payette Associates and Graham-Meus, 1979

The Back Bay Racquet Club has recently moved into a very fine old building and given it the spirited attention it deserves. The original building is more conventional than Clark's later Copley Hotel Annex (III C 6) and perhaps even more gracefully done. The façade is five stories, the bottom one with two big columns creating three large bays in the middle, opening the space for commercial advantage. The next three floors of openings are absorbed within three brick arches, and the top floor is expressed as an attic with groups of three segmental arched windows.

Between the arched windows and the rectangular façade, panels of molded brick contain insignia. These and the window sash have been maintained, the latter with delicate, subtly arranged muntins in the upper floors. The whole façade is graciously scaled and carefully studied.

The inside has been thoroughly restructured. The ground floor has a brightly colored and well-detailed reception area, office, bar and café fronting three racquet-ball courts at the back. The middle one is glass-walled for a clear view of the action. Above, the floor spacing has been ingeniously rebuilt with courts on staggered floors opposite a crosswise corridor. From each corridor you look into courts at the same level and below.

IV C 5 · FIRST CORPS CADET ARMORY
130 Columbus Avenue, SW corner Arlington Street
William G. Preston, 1891–97

The First Corps Cadet Armory is one of the outstanding landmarks in Boston, for which, unfortunately, there has been great difficulty finding an appropriate continued use. For many years it was used as part of the library of the University of Massachusetts, which was spread throughout this area but is presently located at Columbia Point, Dorchester. Now the armory is being remodeled inside as an exhibition and convention hall for the Park Plaza Hotel (IV A 1), apparently without benefit of either architect or skill; its beautiful, airy steel-bar trusses are now smothered behind a flat slab of acoustic ceiling. One can only hope the intensely wrought balcony ringing the space will remain undesecrated, along with the fantastic coiled steel brackets that support the balcony at the stair-hall end.

The most remarkable feature of the exterior, and intentionally so, is a hexagonal fortress tower of granite blocks, so placed that it takes advantage of the peculiarities of its angled site. With one side on each of the streets that intersect at an acute angle, the segment in between faces the intersection, which the tower commands with unquestioned authority. A magnificent winged-lion-head gargoyle and a very tall flagpole salute the Columbus Avenue corner.

The stonework is massive in the extreme and very carefully thought through as a series of patterns. The upper part of the corner tower flares out in silhouette and is punctuated by the obligatory corner turrets. The main hall of the building is a great gable roof, low along the street, with four dormers set into it and bastions at the corners that make it a distinct piece of its own, joined to the castellated scenery of the tower and head building.

The fortress style in which all this was cast not only presented military overtones consonant with the unfortunate imperial adventurism of the times, but in purely architectural terms it provided opportunities to respond to the site and accommodate specific configurations. As Richardson had so eloquently shown, the medieval vocabulary has within it the opportunity—almost a demand—for invention of forms accommodated either to the movement of people within or to the peculiarities of the site; accommodations that were harder to come by within the rectitude of Classical form. The tower here and the marvelous stair along Arlington Street that slips out of the building in a series of descending roofs are instances in point. The stair, a distinct form bulging the face of the building as in so much of the work of Richardson, invests the massive bulk of the armory with a sense of the actions of people moving within it. Emerson's Boston Art

IV C 4 · *Back Bay Racquet Club*

IV C 7 · *35–37 Winchester Street*

Club (III B 18) and the original Christian Science Mother Church (IV A 12) by Welch are comparable buildings.

The rear façade of the armory shows how carefully they made even the backs of buildings. The simplicity of the building and its organization are evident, as is the persistent carving craftsmanship with which it was formed. The major roof and the back wall have a grand, sturdy thoughtfulness, with long coursings of rusticated stone, windows set in great arches, chopped sills that wash water down over the walls rather than collect it and so on.

At the Arlington Street end, the scenic head building ends in a beautifully sculpted corner that shows signs in every detail—from the little crockets growing out of the base to the very top where it swells in termination—of the architect's constant attention to the three-dimensionality of the building itself and to its location on the site.

IV C 6 · BOSTON DOWNTOWN CENTER (University of Massachusetts)
100 Arlington Street, SE corner Columbus Avenue
Parker, Thomas & Rice, 1926

Originally built for the Boston Consolidated Gas Company, this was taken over in the 1960's by the University of Massachusetts. On completion of their Harbor Campus at Columbia Point, the university designated this building as a downtown center to be used mainly for adult-education classes.

It provides light to the interior in the same way that the Park Plaza Hotel (IV A 1) across the way does, with a solid wall on Stuart Street and indentations around courts at the upper floors along Arlington Street. The windows are designed as an arcade at the top in a gesture of apparent civility that sets the building somewhat apart from the neighboring hotel. The arches of the bottom are pleasant, but odd—with round openings framed by moldings that make a slight point at the top. There's vivid, knowledgeable carving, but it's tame in a way that fuses subtle invention in the details with absolute decorum in the whole, like a man in a three-piece suit wearing a tie emblazoned with small, exquisitely drawn dragons.

IV C 7 · 35–37 WINCHESTER STREET
off Arlington Street
Hardy, Holzman & Pfeiffer, 1967

Freewheeling revisionism. This pair of town houses is a spirited reinvestment in the traditional brick-walled street frontage of Bay Village without looking at all like the older buildings. It carries the thread of the older street fabric and some chunks of the older cornice, yet its new, freely arranged windows and doors make clear the nature of new conditions: an increased interest in privacy at the street level and a freer plan within. The two have recently been differentiated in color; from the beginning they were given prominent markings by two splendid large blocks with street numbers vigorously inset.

IV C 8 · *Bay Village streetscape, with the Prudential (left) and John Hancock towers*

IV C 8 · BAY VILLAGE STREETSCAPE
bounded by Piedmont, Tremont and Arlington streets and Charles Street South
c. 1825

Tight streets, low buildings, a fine persistent scale of structures—these attributes are so consistent here that they close out the sense of the large city looming all around. Streets either have buildings at their end or twist so that, from within, all views out are blocked at eye level. Melrose, Fayette and Church streets are best.

The buildings are modest, none of particular note—granite base, brick walls, trim at the sills and heads of windows, flowerpots, street trees, roof gardens and so on. Humble means that create an ensemble with personality.

The area was developed on speculation mostly by Ephraim Marsh, who owned much of the land, which must originally have been marginal if not squishy, located as it was on the edge of the Back Bay mud.

IV C 9 · JOSIAH QUINCY COMMUNITY SCHOOL
885 Washington Street, SE corner Oak Street West
The Architects Collaborative, 1976
· QUINCY TOWER
5 Oak Street West, between Washington and Tremont streets
Jung-Brannan Associates, 1976

The Quincy Community School is a thoroughly remarkable place, one that required invention, courage and persistence on the part of all parties concerned. And there were many parties concerned: several community groups, the Boston Redevelopment Authority, the School Committee, the Tufts New England Medical Center and the architects, to mention the most central. The result is more than a school, it's community spaces, a health clinic, a parking garage, several elevated playgrounds, an extraordinarily lively indoor street and the most brightly enlivened schoolyard fences, perhaps of all time.

A diagonal path cuts across the site and forms the spine of the building. To the southeast are schoolrooms stacked around stairs over the clinic and community spaces. To the northwest are lecture hall, gymnasium and garage. Over it all clamber a series of playgrounds ascending in terraces from street level on the northwest corner to high rooftop on the south.

Stairs and ramps of various sorts attend this ascent, dimensioned with generosity and shaped with ad hoc ingenuity. The walls of these and of the terraces themselves are poured concrete. Odd bits of angled concrete wall and round, fat bollards substructure the terraces in ways that are unfathomable but which may work well as supports for schoolyard hanging out. The walls of the school and the adjoining residential tower are split-face concrete block, all buff-colored. Steel pipe rails and fence stanchions are a very brilliant yellow, and the sides of the high, upper-level playground screens carry a most astonishing array of porcelain-enamel murals with inscriptions in Chinese, Spanish and English woven among child-style drawings by Maria Termini, all reds and greens and purples emblazoned on the same yellow background. Dramatically cheerful, indeed; this school's presence is made known by the play space it provides.

But the greatest cheer is provided by the interior street cutting through the lower levels of the building. It works as a genuine extension of the city path, with community services and recreation spaces visible on either side, soft clerestory light from above and pockets of space along its edges, which result from the diagonal cut. Each set of schoolrooms is connected by a set of stairs that exit onto terraced stoops alongside this inner street. At the end of the school day it's an incredible scene, with parents waiting inside along the street corridor and children spilling out of the stairs on a slightly raised level where they can see and be seen for parental sorting. The coming together of all this is wonderful—the scale and size of things inside the place, the light and banners and intriguing diagonal views, and the easy sense with which people use the space as extension of their community. In 1978 the school was selected for the prestigious Harleston Parker Award.

The tower by Jung-Brannan that stands by its side, with housing for the elderly of the Chinese community, is less remarkable.

IV C 10 · DON BOSCO TECHNICAL HIGH SCHOOL
300 Tremont Street, NE corner Oak Street West
1927
Addition: Halasz & Halasz, 1975

Here is another set of school spaces half-buried under their own terraces. These architects also had to deal with a diagonal force on the site, in this case the alignment of the original building with a street that has since been removed, in part to make room for the building's expansion. The terraces that form the top of this addition are much more sedate than those of the Quincy School, forming an approach to the main spaces of the complex rather than a playground. It's a pleasant, relaxed approach, with terraces gently interlocking, considerable shrubbery and several changes of direction before you reach the entry. The entry is the first time that the new work reveals itself as a building rather than simply as a terraced forecourt for the original school, a rather dreary factorylike building got up in a bit of Renaissance garb.

Most of this terrace space is over the swimming pool, and a pyramidal skylight at one corner makes a direct visual connection between the two. Inside, the terrace level becomes the mezzanine level for the gym, and a set of windows just beyond the entrance looks down to the gym floor. To one side of the gym a large series of stairs descends again to the lower level, with doors opening in off Oak Street and a passage leading back to the swimming pool.

There is in this building a subtle, controlled interweaving of spaces that is more urbane than that of the Quincy School, even if less bright and lively. It's a place for adults to walk through, conscious that they're in a place different from the street. There is a fine level of design craftsmanship throughout, all exercised directly in the materials of building.

IV C 11 · *Tufts New England Medical Center*

IV C 11 · TUFTS NEW ENGLAND MEDICAL CENTER
Kneeland to Oak streets along Washington Street and Harrison Avenue
· DENTAL SCHOOL AND PROGER BUILDINGS
SE corner Kneeland and Washington streets
The Architects Collaborative, 1978
· PEDIATRIC HOSPITAL ADDITION
crossing Washington Street
Perry, Dean, Stahl & Rogers, 1982

The Medical Center is an awesome group of buildings that is part of a very ambitious plan for the area which has been underway for many years and which has met with almost as many years of resistance from neighborhood groups. The Chinese community in particular has seen itself being blockaded by vast concrete structures.

The first buildings were constructed with an overall uniformity of materials and structure, yet with a concerted effort to make differences in building massing and wall treatment when special arrangements or particular services justified them. The changes do help to break down the apparent size of the concrete buildings somewhat, but only marginally and then for reasons that remain obscure. The differences in building form escape any lay explanation; they are not explicable to an observer on the street. But then, neither is medicine. Here at least you can see it from the street and it's coherent, not the remote jungle of disparate buildings that so many medical centers in Boston are. Come to think of it, the new buildings of the complex wear the look of tidy professional specialists of different physiques, all dressed in hospital whites.

Usually, however, we endure the hospital regimen in order to leave it. These buildings, though carefully designed for their purpose, cast a permanent and dominating stamp on a whole sector of the city, just as the cost of medical care hovers relentlessly over the economy. In being a part of the city with planned functional linkages to the adjoining community, as in the Quincy School (IV C 9), Tufts New England is well on the right path. What's needed, though, is a fresh vision of the city. "A nice place to visit, but I wouldn't want to live there" won't do.

Most grievously, the center, like Boston City Hospital (IV B 5), crosses over a major street separating one part of the city from another. Only here it's Washington Street—the neck—that is bridged. The original topography of the neck connecting Boston's peninsula to the mainland had been obscured, first by landfill and buildings that removed Back Bay to the west, then by the railroads, industrial development and the Massachusetts Turnpike that filled South Cove to the east. But Washington Street remained as a visible path to the south. Now any sense of that initial relationship is irretrievable.

IV C 12 · JACOB WIRTH'S
31–39 Stuart Street, between Tremont and Washington streets
Greenleaf C. Sanborn, 1844–45

Sawdust on the floor, black jackets, white aprons, bow ties, lots of dark-brown wood and a bit of brass. It's a turn-of-the-century German restaurant that's for real, not one of your touched-up phonies. Jacob Wirth's has changed little since

IV C 12 · *Jacob Wirth's restaurant*

IV C 13 · *Charles Playhouse*

the 1890's, when it expanded from the ground floor of one row house to two and extended out the back.

The change of level between the two houses and the brick bearing wall between them serve to separate the bar and part of the kitchen from the main eating areas. Beyond these inherent differentiations there's little else: coat hooks on the wall, bowl-shaped lamps on chains and a well-carved and mirrored backdrop for the bar.

The original buildings are the only remaining examples in this area of the bow-front Greek Revival houses that were the dominant type in this locale. Along the street the two buildings are joined by a storefront with a bold lintel, cast-iron columns, a fine big gold molded-letter sign and a great black clock hanging out over the sidewalk. Good solid stuff.

IV C 13 · *detail, Saxon Theatre*

IV C 13 · *Wilbur Theatre, corner of Tremont and Stuart streets*

IV C 13 · *Shubert Theatre*

IV C 13 · CHARLES PLAYHOUSE
76 Warrenton Street, off Stuart Street
Asher Benjamin, 1839–43
renovations: Cambridge Seven, 1957–66

· SAXON THEATRE
219 Tremont Street, near NW corner Stuart Street
John Galen Howard & J. M. Wood, 1903

· WILBUR THEATRE
250 Tremont Street, near SE corner Stuart Street
Clarence H. Blackall, 1914

· SHUBERT THEATRE
265 Tremont Street, between Stuart Street and South Cove Park
Thomas James, 1910

· MUSIC HALL
268 Tremont Street, between Stuart and Oak streets
Clarence H. Blackall, 1925

A handy set of comparisons for a week out on the town. This group of theaters runs the gamut from genuine Greek Revival to Baroque put-on, with some hearty homage to Rome and a reminiscence of Palladio in between. But none of these theaters abandons the Classical mode. They show, rather, the range of moods and the variety of interpretations that nineteenth- and early-twentieth-century Classical allegiance allowed.

The Charles Playhouse was not, to be fair, designed as a theater. It was first a Universalist church, then a Jewish temple and finally a Scottish church until claimed recently for a theater. Clearly, however, it always served as a place for congregating, and its severe temple front, achieved with only two wooden Ionic columns and some well-studied proportions, indicates both the civic seriousness with which church-making was endowed and the economy of means with which importance could be conveyed in the early half of the nineteenth century.

Six decades later John Galen Howard adopted, in essence, the same scheme for the civic front of the Saxon Theatre, but in accordance with the spirit of its expansive times, he reached beyond the severity of the Greek Revival to the extravagance of imperial Rome as a source for his execution of the scheme. Here there is no pediment. The two half columns in the middle are echoed by quarter columns adjoining the side blocks at either end, and the order is Composite, not simple Ionic. The spacing is much wider, which offers more scope for three great arched openings that elaborate the wall's surface. The terra-cotta ornament is positively lush, with extravagant garlands around the windows, theatrical masks at the top of the keystones and an altogether surprising outbreak of foliage in the upper reaches of the column flutings. The façade, though mutilated by later renovations in the lower register, remains filled with the sense of its original title, the Majestic. There is really no better, more richly scaled and engaging imperial façade in Boston. Few are as large in size, and those that are, like the City Hall Annex (I A 15), lack wit.

The interior is equally, if differently, remarkable. It's an opulent, complicated design that gathers proscenium and balconies in a series of concentric curves— lavishly adorned fluid bands that envelope the space and serve as well to meet the demands of lighting and acoustics.

Clarence Blackall, in the Wilbur Theatre, uses the same three-part entry scheme, with altogether different consequences. The Wilbur even has the three theatrical masks again: smiling, grimacing and mouth agape. But there are no giant order columns or pilasters; here the material is brick with stone trim. The materials as well as the manner are within a conservative Boston tradition of building that is closer to London than to Rome. Restraint and intimacy prevail both outside and in. Or at least intimacy prevails inside, for despite their small scale and refined demeanor, the ornamental surfaces inside probably would not seem restrained to everyone. But then the Wilbur did not mean to address itself to everyone. The tone throughout is elite intimacy, Beacon Hill in theater dress. The foyer spaces are comparatively small, the theater itself closely compact, with a very deep balcony that makes the theater seem smaller than its twelve hundred seats would suggest. The main intermission space is a chamber below street level with a fireplace at one end and chairs sitting about as in a large drawing room.

The Shubert Theatre makes its civic front with only one bay, a beautiful pairing of rectangular openings on either side with a larger arched opening in the center—the pattern that we have come to call Palladian and to identify with stair landings in Georgian architecture and garden loggias of the Renaissance. It's an especially felicitous use of traditional form in this case, marking the upper levels of the public foyer.

At the Music Hall the façade is not the point, nor is it really the front of the building. It simply provides the opportunity to have a marquee and to enter a long series of spaces that lead eventually to a vast theater turned at right angles to the entrance, its orchestra, stage and recently extended backstage reaching all the way back to Stuart Street. No restraint here; the multilayered lobby spaces are themselves a fantastic stage, exuberantly displaying the audience to itself among the paraphernalia of the Baroque. It makes a splendid place to gather.

IV C 14 · LITTLE BUILDING
80 Boylston Street, SW corner Tremont Street
Blackall, Clapp & Whittemore, 1916

Ten years later than the Berkeley Building (III B 7) and considerably less grace-ful in its detailing, the Little Building is of similar type, fit neatly into the city.

Along Boylston Street the building reads as a solid block facing the Common, an appropriately sturdy piece of the wall of buildings that fronts the south edge of that green. The façade is neatly organized in piers of terra cotta with metal window infill. The windows are set flat but recessed at the third floor. Above that each bay has a simple large window on the front face and two double-hungs on either side, angled back to reveal the thickness of the piers. The piers make reference to Gothic shafts, and there's a much adorned terra cotta screen-wall at the attic. The surface is filled nicely with light and dark, even in the absence of much sun on either the north-facing Boylston Street side or the narrow Tremont Street side.

On Tremont Street the architects make a point of the heavily indented configu-ration in which projecting wings are formed around three narrow light courts above a continuous band of street-fronting commercial space at the lower two floors. Each court is cut back and made slightly wider at the back, allowing light into the corners and making the courts seem more spacious than they really are.

Inside there's a two-story arcade through most of the building, with a mezza-

IV C 14 · *Little Building*

nine ringing it to provide access to upper-level shops and offices. This arcade confirms the expressed importance of the bottom two levels and continues the order established outside, with two levels denoted as public space. Like the outside, it is dressed in neo-Gothic detail. The inside arches contain a series of historical paintings, now much obscured by the clumsy lighting troughs installed to illuminate them. The building absorbs a considerable drop in the sidewalk level between Boylston Street and the lower end along the Tremont Street side and it also accommodates the nonrectangular lot shape by drawing people in off Boylston Street through a vaulted passage that curves and slopes down before opening into the two-story-high arcade space that is organized parallel to Tremont Street.

IV C 15 · COLONIAL BUILDING, COLONIAL THEATRE
100 Boylston Street (theater address: 106 Boylston), between Tremont Street and Boylston Place, opposite the Common
Clarence H. Blackall, 1899–1900
theater interior: H. B. Pennell

The Colonial Building fronts the Common with a well-studied façade that has a row of shops along the street, a narrow, well-fashioned, but very unassertive theater marquee and entrance slipped among the shops and a handsome two-story loggia stretched across the top of the building, with columns modeled and standing free of a double-height inset wall that sustains the illusion of lighter, more open upper levels. The building combines the standard mix of shops below and offices above with a large and distinguished theater tucked in behind, a not inconsiderable planning feat.

The Colonial Theatre, for all its modesty on the street, is a magnificent place inside, lavishly adorned in emulation of the spirit of the Boston Public Library and displaying the work of many distinguished artists and craftsmen of the period. This is the theatrical conclusion to an extraordinary decade of metropolitan achievement. During the previous ten years, Boston had developed a park system and initiated a subway that were models for subsequent efforts throughout the nation, and had built Symphony Hall and the Public Library, both standard-bearers for American culture. Blackall himself had introduced, in the Winthrop Building (I A 12), the use of steel-framed construction, implement of the city's subsequent transformation; and across the Common, the State House (I B 4), while still dominant in the skyline, had been enlarged several-fold by Charles Brigham's grandiose extension to the rear. To the stimulus of all this, Blackall and Pennell responded with white-glove formality, embellished with paneling, gilded ornament, framed pastoral murals and floral stencils. The whole is suitably more frivolous than the decorative schemes that adorn its civic peers.

IV C 16 · WURLITZER COMPANY
100 Boylston Street (Colonial Building), between Tremont Street and Boylston Place

· BOSTON MUSIC COMPANY
120 Boylston Street

· STEINERT BUILDING
162 Boylston Street, SE corner Boylston and Carver streets
Winslow & Wetherell, 1896

These three are the most visible survivors of a fine period when this section of street facing the Common was referred to as Piano Row, in deference to the concentration of establishments concerned with music. They note, as well, a period when visual refinement was thought to be an accompaniment to, rather than in competition with, the musical arts.

The Wurlitzer façade is a bit of a paste-up. The Wurlitzer sign and the organ improbably lodged above the door were brought to this façade from elsewhere on the block, but it is in any case a splendid remnant of shop-front elegance that deserves more protection than the Wurlitzer Company has been able to give it. The whole sweep of the front face is designed as an elegant oversized fanlight for a modest front door, set slightly in from show windows on either side. The windows are exaggeratedly fine in detail, all of the spindly parts delicately embellished with fruit and garland motifs among a miniaturized panoply of colonettes and architrave.

The Boston Music Company plays differently with a similar theme. It too has a center entrance, but this one has a vigorously molded pediment at the center with a fanlight that reaches up into the bottom of its triangle. To either side the window surfaces are angled back from the outer edges toward the center, to give prominence to the door and its pediment. Each of these walls is glass reaching the full height of the bay, with small-paned glass above eye level and an arched pattern of muntins marking the center. Very refined and sparkly, offering a sense that buying sheet music is roughly akin to visiting an Edwardian tailor.

The Steinert Piano Company still occupies its building, which is by comparison much tamer, a rather staid Classical sort. It does have an appealing entrance, a lot of pianos inside and a concert hall on the upper floors.

IV C 17 · *Young Men's Christian Union*

IV C 17 · YOUNG MEN'S CHRISTIAN UNION
48 Boylston Street, between Tremont and Washington streets, corner Tamworth Street
Nathaniel J. Bradlee, 1875

Boylston Street of another generation—pre–steel frame, pre–Classical opulence, pre–adult entertainment. King's *Handbook of Boston* of 1885 tells us that the aim of the union was to "provide for young men a homelike resort, with opportunities for good reading, pleasant social intercourse, entertainment and healthful exercise." To this end the building and its 1882 extension included "the largest reading room in Boston" and a gymnasium that was then "the largest and most complete in the country."

The building gives us a good view of Ruskin's influence in America, conceived as it is in both Christian purpose and Ruskinian Gothic form. It's also very handsome, even bereft of the top of its tower, which originally made the entrance a landmark along the street. The façade is thickly layered, the windows set so far back in the heavily carved wall that they seem to be an altogether separate layer, their simple double-hung sash entirely subordinated to the carved, pointed arches, piers and stringcourses that carry the image. The entrance itself is richly elaborated with colonettes bracketed from the wall, a carved balustrade and male heads—one young and eager, one older and wiser—staring out from the wall overhead. Both now seem a little harried.

IV C 18 · BOYLSTON BUILDING
2–22 Boylston Street, SW corner Washington Street
Carl Fehmer, 1887

The masonry face of this building is hung from iron-frame construction, but hardly reveals that technical innovation. It has, however, a noble façade that neatly works as a strong, clear face to the open space that it fronts. The space is a remnant of the old Boylston Market, which this building replaced. The large, repetitive paired arch pattern of the second floor is now sadly blanked. The ground floor, with broad iron lintels, leaves opportunity for the individual identity of shops within its fabric, an opportunity that is poorly exploited at the present moment. This is a building that has much to reclaim.

The style here is Richardsonian Romanesque tamed by Renaissance refinement, a step on the path that led McKim, Mead & White only a few years later to the Boston Public Library (III C 4). The building has some of the love for layered masonry surface that can be seen in the adjacent YMCU Building (IV C 17), but none of its Gothic excrescences, save for a set of very restrained and curious puppy-ear turrets on each corner that break the massiveness of the silhouette ever so slightly; apologizing, perhaps, for untimely rationality.

IV C 19 · HAYDEN BUILDING
681–83 Washington Street, SW corner Lagrange Street
H. H. Richardson, 1875

Overlooked for years, this modest and clumsy little building has recently been discovered to be Richardson's first commercial work and is now the subject of much veneration in landmark circles. Like the Crowninshield House (III A 19), it offers evidence that greats don't always do great work.

It's all right, and it does have a string of arches that bind the third and fourth floors together, as well as a continuous band of unadorned rectangular windows for the attic story, and it is made of roughly cut stone; but so what? To claim, as others have, that it is "an early, long unrecognized prototype for the modern skyscraper" because similar elements recur in the Marshall Field Warehouse in Chicago is to fetch significance from a rather great distance.

What the Hayden Building utterly lacks is the confident, inspiriting vision of wholeness that made Richardson's later work so commanding.

IV C 20 · SAVOY THEATER
539 Washington Street, between Avery and West streets
Thomas Lamb, 1928

· MODERN THEATER
523 Washington Street, between Avery and West streets
Clarence H. Blackall, 1914

The Savoy Theater has now become the home of the Boston Opera Company. With a little more funding, this may yet prove to be the salvation of two great institutions.

The Opera Company has been adrift for many years, seeking a place ample enough for the adroit imaginings of its director, Sarah Caldwell, who brought it to world fame in a series of temporary quarters some years after the Boston Opera House in Back Bay, a splendid brick building in the manner of Symphony Hall (IV A 15), was torn down.

Ironically, the Savoy, which suits opera splendidly, was first a movie house, one of the grandest anywhere. It too resulted from the efforts of a great show business personality. It was first known as the B. F. Keith Memorial Theater, named for an energetic and successful promoter of vaudeville who had founded the company that built it and determined much of the character of its surrounds. Its great hulk of theater space is set back between Washington and Tremont streets and is reached by long passages from each street, the passage from Tremont Street crossing an alley en route. Inside, its auditorium bears the usual Classical trappings, with giant order pilasters, elaborate ceilings and balconies of amplitude.

The Washington Street façade of the Savoy is very narrow, only the width of the passage leading back to the auditorium. But it is a whipped-cream confection of a sort unparalleled in Boston's architecture. It oozes florid ornament above and around its few openings, simulating the limited but flamboyant ornamentation of Spanish and Latin American Baroque. The façade is terminated at the top by a freestanding triumphal arch barely distinguishable among the vines, urns and similar emblems of profusion that encrust the surface and inhabit the openings.

Revivers of the Modern Theater, just down the street, are still getting their act together, but it too, we hope, will soon recover its much more modest splendor. The Washington Street front is a single arch of triumphal proportions set in the lower two floors of a handsome six-floor Ruskinian Gothic structure. The latter was originally a warehouse purveying wool carpets made in Pennsylvania.

IV C 21 · CHINATOWN
concentrated on Harrison, Tyler and Hudson streets between Kneeland and Beach streets

The commercial section of Chinatown in Boston is not large, but it is certainly intense. Tyler Street is the most dramatic, with a vivid, magnificent collection of Chinese signs that transforms the street into a place of an oriental character not unfamiliar to those who frequent Chinese restaurants. Beach Street is made more by the people and shops that inhabit it and has the sense of a living community doing business with itself. It does not need the commercial flamboyance of the more obvious symbols of Chinatown. On all these streets, even the flashy ones, there is an intensity of use that signals the presence of a close-knit community. In this, it is startlingly different from the half-empty commercial spaces and sleazy operations that border it to the north.

D/SOUTH STATION

The area east of Washington Street and a little bit south of Essex Street is nearly all landfill, much of it placed by the South Cove Associates, who undertook in 1833 to fill the cove from what is now Harrison Street and Chinatown almost to the yards of South Station. The bulk of this land was to be used for terminal wharves and warehouses associated with the Boston & Worcester Railway, and the primary focus was the United States Hotel, then the biggest in the country, but now vanished.

The scheme floundered but the land remains, cut through recently by the spaghetti of roads exiting from the Southeast Expressway as it prepares to go underground, and by the tunnels leading to the Fitzgerald Expressway. The swath cut by these highways separates the small-scale activity of Chinatown from the isolated orderly group of warehouses generally called the Leather District—candidates, one supposes, for the next wave of renovation.

Beyond South Station lies the Fort Point Channel, and across the channel is another massive group of warehouses stretching out along Summer and Congress streets. What port remains lies farther east along Northern Avenue.

View from the Federal Reserve Bank (V A 1) *over Fort Point Channel to South Boston and the harbor beyond*

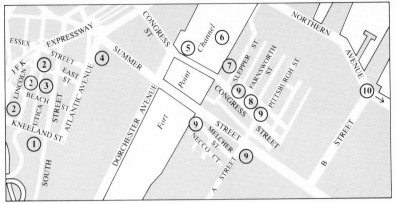

IV D 1 · BOSTON EDISON COMPANY POWERHOUSE
Kneeland and South streets
Wadsworth/Hubbard & Smith, 1932

The most visible landmark in the area is the twin-stacked powerhouse that greets your arrival off the expressway. Its massive bulk has been well dressed in subtle Renaissance scaling devices that are probably lost on just about everybody. It would appear that the original plan anticipated adding more turbines, for on the south side the brick dressing abruptly stops. The metal panels that fill in are a surprisingly subtle mauve-rose color, carefully hued to sustain the aura of the brick without literally mocking it—not the sort of delicacy one ordinarily expects from a public utility.

Opposite, on the northwest corner of South and Kneeland streets, is one of the few remaining diners in town, located, appropriately enough, opposite the railroad yards. It's not in altogether good repair, but it's still shiny and distinguished by blue glass, blue-and-green tile inside, some nice glass blocks, a corner entry and a sign designating it the Blue Diner.

IV D 2 · 179 LINCOLN STREET
between Kneeland and Beach streets
c. 1910
· 116–28 LINCOLN STREET
between Beach and Tufts streets
Franklin E. Kidder, 1888
· LINCOLN BUILDING
70–80 Lincoln Street, between Tufts and Essex streets
Willard T. Sears, 1894

These are three warehouse and office buildings on Lincoln Street that bear special note; the two at either end are more recent and more like each other, probably intended from the first for office and manufacturing use. The one in the middle is best.

No. 179, at the Kneeland Street end of the block, has recently been renovated

IV D 3 · *detail, 145 South Street*

IV D 1 · *Boston Edison Company Powerhouse*

for the Teledyne Corporation with dark glass and dark-metal frames as infill for the two lower floors, emphasizing the building's principal features: carved-stone entries gracefully proportioned, with polite but not very inspired Renaissance detailing.

The middle building at No. 116 is a thoroughly splendid Richardsonian Romanesque structure nearly as good as the Hartwell & Richardson building at No. 5 Causeway Street (II A 12). Its three middle floors are held within a row of piers that are topped by an arcade, the capital of each pier executed in a different Romanesque motif. The bottom has been messed up by later commercial fronts of no distinction.

Arches are essential to the charms of the Lincoln Building as well; only these are formed closely around your head as you enter the building. The general mass of the building is brick, but a stone band around the base provides all the fun. The base alternates between narrow stretches of solid wall and big, thick columns that stand in the round, obviously carrying the full weight of the building above them, while the light metal-and-glass storefronts slide around behind them. The arches form entries in the solid walls, each arch springing from the tops of fine little marble columns just about your size. This building is no contribution to the history of architecture, but it gives plenty of pleasure on the street as you pass.

IV D 3 · 121–23 SOUTH STREET
between Tufts and Beach streets
Rand & Taylor, with Allen Frink, 1880's
· BEEBE BUILDING
129–31 South Street
Rand & Taylor, 1888
· 137 SOUTH STREET
c. 1885
· 145 SOUTH STREET
NW corner Beach Street
J. H. Besarick, 1885–87

A row of tall brick commercial structures that experiments with the structural and decorative possibilities of the 1880's. They have similar structural bay sizes, and are all built out to the limits of the street, with lots of glass and split levels at the base. At the street floor, windows open into stores and offices half a level down, and stairs, often iron, lead up to glass-walled offices half a level up. Together they make a marvelous ensemble, varied and well built, each part invested with imagination, yet all of a piece—a true city wall.

The most routine composition is the Beebe Building at No. 129. It has a very straightforward drawing-board organization of piers and windows, with smaller openings in a brownstone band at the second level and the obligatory attic top for the sixth floor.

By comparison, No. 121 is a brilliant stroke. A building of only one structural bay, it has a single beautiful arched window that controls the whole elevation.

The building at No. 137, of similar size, is also only a single bay, but the architect here was preoccupied with accommodating the elevator in the elevation. The lower floors are fully open on the right and closed with a single window on the left. Then, through a sneaky migration of the window alignments as they climb, the top becomes a beautiful, evenly spaced brick arcade. In between, brownstone spandrels are carved with relief patterns.

The most accomplished of these warehouses is that by J. H. Besarick on the corner of Beach Street. It is a simply wonderful brick building with a scheme similar to that used by Preston less successfully in the Chadwick Lead Works (V B 19). This one begins with a cast-iron-and-glass base under a thick, continuous, cast-iron lintel. Thick indeed, for above it sit five stories of brick. The first level of brick is an almost evenly spaced alternation of window and pier, every second pier resting above the cast-iron columns and very slightly larger than the others to bear the weight of the main structure above. Spanning between these piers is a projecting brownstone lintel. From it, the supporting piers rise three floors to hold a row of large round arches. The brick of the spandrels, meanwhile, slopes back from the front surface of that lintel so that windowsills and heads and the intermediate brick panels between windows are all in a plane behind the structural piers, thus letting their vertical scope dominate the building. At the top, a simple set of regularly spaced windows and piers makes the attic.

All this, which is wonderful enough, is made both softer and more compelling by an angled corner that provides entry below and a small display of plasticity at the level of the arches, where the arched opening is replaced by a solid wall held on brick corbels and pierced by a round window trimmed in brownstone.

IV D 4 · SOUTH STATION HEADHOUSE
SE corner Summer Street and Atlantic Avenue
Shepley, Rutan & Coolidge, 1898

Not much of South Station is left, but what is forms a powerful landmark. Since the rail lines came in along the shore to one side of the city, the design problem here was to bring people out of the trains into a grand hall and then out one end of the hall, on the diagonal, to face the heart of the city. The public front of the building is focused on the corner of Summer Street and Atlantic Avenue, opening into what was once Dewey Square and is now a vast desolate intersection of roads.

IV D 4 · *South Station, with the Federal Reserve Bank* (V A 1) *to the left*

The main entrance to the station does splendidly, even under the present adverse conditions. The scale is grand, indeed, with a two-story base surmounted by three stories of colonnade made by full, round columns that stand in front of the masonry wall and windows. These columns support a thick architrave and a cornice topped by an intermittent balustrade. The whole building curves majestically around the corner, the entry marked by a pedimented front that steps forward in front of a Baroque curving screen wall. At the apex of all this is the hooked silhouette of a very aggressive eagle.

The inside was never as good, and it has yet to recover from years of wear and neglect, courtesy of the decline of the railroads. There's a pleasant enough main hall facing what used to be a train shed, but it has never related very well to the ceremonial entry on the corner. Outside on the Atlantic Avenue face, there is one remaining glass-and-metal canopy, in itself a treasure to be protected. There are only a few left of these once-ubiquitous rain shelters, which cast such a beautiful softened light on the walls of buildings and provide solid cover without forcing the building's walls to be contorted into meanly scaled solid canopies. A glass marquee like this has to do with the idea of the city, not just with waiting for taxicabs.

Fortunately South Station and its surroundings are being reclaimed. The new bland black-glass office box beyond the headhouse is not at all bad as a way to let the triumphant attitude of the station's frontispiece continue to command our sense of the place.

IV D 5 · BOSTON TEA PARTY MUSEUM
Congress Street Bridge at Fort Point Channel

Following a standard tourist map or hopping the Boston Tea Party Shuttle, which departs from the Freedom Trail, will get you to the site of the Boston Tea Party ship, moored in Fort Point Channel at the Congress Street Bridge.

It's clear, I suppose, what this is all about. If not, the little museum will tell you—and will even provide crates to dump into the water. No Indian dress is required.

The peripheral benefits are great. The ship has riggings enjoyable to behold, and the Fort Point Channel is a small museum of bridges. The one on Northern Avenue is a trussed rolling bridge that on appropriate occasions rotates on its center point to clear the channel for ships on either side. The Congress Street Bridge itself is a Baskerville, with a giant concrete counterweight hanging overhead, waiting to engage the very large gear system that lifts the bridge up. The piers of this bridge are handsomely made of stone, with cast-iron light brackets and big sturdy pipe rails. A third bridge, at Summer Street, is a wonderfully preposterous metal plate truss on wheels that just slides sideways out of the way.

IV D 6 · FORT POINT CHANNEL
between Congress and Summer streets

Fort Point Channel is what remains of the segment of the inner harbor that rounded the eastern tip of the Shawmut Peninsula at Fort Point and continued into South Cove, separating Boston from the peninsula that became South Boston. This latter was extended even more dramatically than the Boston Side by vast areas of fill, providing for warehousing, wharves and a naval base.

The east face of the channel now offers a varied collection of fine vantage points for viewing the city and the harbor, as well as an important place of instructional resort in the museums recently ensconced there.

The wharf in front of the museums is a wonderful place in the summer, bustling with the activity of visitors and given a slightly surreal air by a giant wood-slat milk bottle that commands the space. This odd food stand originally belonged to the Sankey milk company in Taunton, Massachusetts, and was barged to this location in 1977 by the H. P. Hood Company to herald the Children's Museum. It now dispenses frozen-yogurt lunches and other delectable snacks.

IV D 6 · *Fort Point Channel*

The area around the milk bottle has been made into a pleasant little plaza with wood timbers and boardwalk, a bit of granite, a few trees, benches and flagpoles. Farther along, a restaurant spills out of the warehouse onto a large terrace facing the towers of downtown.

The Boston Tea Party ship in the center of the channel, generally festooned with flags and festive signs, and the foot-and-auto traffic of the bridge combine with an occasional tugboat and barge to make a thoroughly lively scene. On those occasions when the Northern Avenue Bridge opens, the harbor comes into view with sailboats and East Boston beyond.

On the other side of the channel near the State Street Bank (V A 11) was Fort Hill, site of the installation of cannon that originally guarded the harbor and gave the channel its name. The hill was later leveled to fill in Atlantic Avenue. In the foreground on the Boston side of the channel, the James Hooking Lobster Company's industrial waterfront shacks are topped by a gilded, man-sized lobster weathervane.

Toward the Northern Street end of this walk is the Victoria Street Station Restaurant, a chain eatery constructed here, as elsewhere, out of old railroad cars and cabooses. It is totally upstaged, however, by the floating crane lodged in the channel in front of it. The crane arms extend from a wood-sided house that has windows of various sorts disposed about its walls in an array one can only presume to be functional. With its metal-roof shacks, cylindrical stack and great crane arm extended, it has a chunky forcefulness that makes the tidied-up train cars all jammed together for Victoria Street Station look like the appurtenances of a powder room.

IV D 7 · CHILDREN'S MUSEUM
· TRANSPORTATION MUSEUM
Museum Wharf
Congress Street at Fort Point Channel
M. D. Safford, 1889
reuse: Cambridge Seven and Dyer Brown Associates, 1975

For some years the Children's Museum, housed somewhat remotely in the suburb of Jamaica Plain, has been one of Boston's great creative institutions. Now it has joined with the new Transportation Museum in the takeover of a fine old woolens warehouse along the edge of Fort Point Channel.

The renovation is excellent: direct, unpretentious and informative. The thick, heavy timber structure has been cleaned and exposed inside, with metal brackets joining the great beams of lumber when needed. Through the structure are threaded the predictable elements of renewal—painted ducts, carpeting, suspended lighting and metal rails, the latter especially nicely done. But the wonderful instructive exhibits are the thing.

Outside, the severe brick façade retains some of its shuttered openings; others remain blank as they were before renovation, and a few are filled with large areas of plate glass. Nothing much is done to pronounce the building's new use, save for a few bold painted signs offering directions, some handsome wooden doors and a readily accessible gift shop. Drama is reserved for the elevators, which are housed outside in a sparkling fresh, trussed metal cage that stands next to the

IV D 7 · *Museum Wharf*

entry, looking very like the elevator mechanisms of the adjacent Congress Street Bridge. It's a great device, the form as direct as the warehouse itself, the ascending and descending box of the elevator an emblem of the activities inside. The views its glass walls provide of the channel and the city towers beyond offer splendid evidence before our eyes of the history that is unfolded in exhibits inside the Transportation Museum on the upper floors.

The Children's Museum is ever inventive; a place, as they say, for children of all ages. For our purposes a visit to the Ruth Harmony Green Hall of Toys with its great collection of doll houses offers a chance to get inside, to imagine being behind some of the façades of Beacon Hill and Back Bay.

The Transportation Museum has a range of historical displays about the city's growth (excellent background for using this book) and a good number of photographs that show bits of the city that have now been totally transformed.

IV D 8 · CONGRESS STREET FIREHOUSE
334 Congress Street
1891

The final segment of the museum complex is the Boston Fire Museum, housed in the Congress Street Firehouse, a pleasantly cranky building of 1891 that bears close study.

The long box of a building has been fronted with a scaled-down, powerfully stable composition, a fundamentally triangular organization called out by the peculiar combination of chimney and pediment that tops the upper-floor windows. The parts are all deftly used granite and brick, save for a section of wall that is covered in proud red tile shingles and made to look like a mansard roof.

The creative perversity of its elevation is worthy of the hand of Clarence Luce, who designed the Sunflower Castle (II C 5) on Mt. Vernon Street; or even, if you like, a Post Modernist.

IV D 9 · *253 Summer Street*
IV D 8 · *Congress Street Firehouse*

IV D 9 · BOSTON WHARF COMPANY BUILDINGS

332 Congress Street
M. D. Safford, 1891

348 Congress Street
M. D. Safford, 1894

354 Congress Street
M. D. Safford, 1900

368 Congress Street
M. D. Safford, 1901

253 Summer Street
M. D. Safford, 1901

285 Summer Street
M. D. Safford, 1903

311 Summer Street
M. D. Safford, 1904

259 Summer Street
M. D. Safford, 1905

As you cross the Summer Street Bridge into South Boston, there is a large electric sign on top of the buildings ahead saying "BOSTON WHARF COMPANY" and "INDUSTRIAL REAL ESTATE." As you proceed down Summer Street, six- and seven-story warehouses shape a canyon around the elevated street. Most bear a round medallion with the initials BW and a date. They were designed by M. D. Safford during a period of fifteen years. Together these buildings form a fascinating log of subtle changes in the design of a simple building type and of the ingenuity with which new variants could be developed when the site required.

To trace the full development of the type, go first to 332 Congress Street, which has a front made up of cast iron and brick. It is accordingly more frame and fill than any of the others, which are all brick. This wall is made of iron posts and double-hung windows with only a very narrow little brick spandrel that bears no implication of weight whatever. Stampings in the bottom of the posts announce that these were made in the New Bedford Iron Foundry of New Bedford, Massachusetts. The thin elegance of this cast-iron front was abandoned in subse-

IV D 9 · *348 (left) and 354 Congress Street*

quent buildings, probably as it became apparent that cast iron was not as resistant to fire as its earliest boosters had hoped.

The next warehouse in the sequence, at 348 Congress Street, is entirely faced in brick, with the familiar rusticated base, paneled middle and attic top, the arched windows here capped by a cornice. It is interestingly made, with an expression of the thick iron lintels that hold the wall above lower floors of glass, these in an English basement arrangement, that is, with the main floor up half a level over openings into the semicellar. The bays are also clearly expressed, with wider piers and a band of cast decoration that forms the double-hung windows between them into panels. The bays are marked off into three different sizes: one window's width over the entrance, two windows' width in the space remaining to the pier and four windows' width for each of the other structural bays. Direct and uncomplicated, the straightforwardness of this structure is disturbed only by the very prominent cast volutes placed as keystones in the center of the flat-arched brick lintels of the second- and third-floor windows.

The adjoining building at 354 Congress Street, built six years later, is somehow more serious. Its bays are now worked out to three windows with wider spaces between, and the entry is absorbed into a bay only slightly narrower, with two windows above. The material here is yellow brick trimmed with stone. The keystones now are much more literal and the stringcourse below the attic is shallower. Neither keystone nor stringcourse cast the little bits of sparkling shadow that characterize the earlier building.

This sequence of warehouses records the gradual transformation from an open-framework cast-iron sensibility with plasticity in the parts, to a more solid masonry sense with plasticity in the whole.

For a special treat, however, go inside the building at 368 Congress where there is a splendid full-height atrium made with white glazed brick, segmental arched windows and an open steel-framework elevator. The tall central space is roofed with glass and bridged by balconies that have rails made of woven wire, like large-scale, elegantly made chain-link fencing. Straight industrial vernacular but very fine, very intelligent—an enviable space.

A year later, at 253 Summer Street, more strenuous demands were placed on Safford's ingenuity by the odd configuration of the site, bordered on one side by the Fort Point Channel and on the other by the sharp curve of Melcher Street. The result is a magnificently strange, oddly shaped building that is easily recognized from across the channel as light models its curved surface. It is the first of the Boston wharf buildings that comes into view and the one you're most likely to remember. The vocabulary of form here shifts again, this time to a more straightforward expression of the frame, its major vertical members reaching directly from sidewalk to attic as a giant order marked by a strong stringcourse above the ground-floor base and moldings that form capitals and architrave beneath the attic. A wide, overhanging copper cornice emphasizes the curve as it swings effortlessly with the street. The Necco Candy Company, when it was housed here, depicted the building on their letterhead—with a nonexistent park in front.

Summer Street is essentially a raised causeway. This can most readily be seen at its intersection with A Street, which is a full floor below. Here again, the site placed certain demands on Safford's ingenuity, and he (or his designer) seems to have taken delight in fussing with the opportunities provided, very likely as welcome relief from the persistence of the warehouse-building task.

The A Street elevation of 311 Summer Street is a treatise on wall openings. The largest three-window openings are spanned by segmental arches, the yellow bricks buttressed at either end by trapezoidal blocks that absorb the angle thrust of the curved arch and transform it to the rectangular matrix of the brick, looking meanwhile like perky little ears. Contrasted to these are single-width windows, similarly formed and evenly spaced—except for one set that is syncopated with the stair landings. Next to the stair, incising a slot in the building, are very large openings that run up the face of the building to make loading portals. Because of the two levels of street, the base of the building is two stories high on this side, the pattern of the upper-sidewalk level carried around the corner with simple flat lintels. A great Tuscan cast-iron column holds the corner aloft at the Summer Street sidewalk to make an entry for the building. At the other A Street corner, facing an alley, the yellow dress brick keys into the ordinary red brick of the rear of the building, built essentially in the same way.

The last building in the set, at 259 Summer Street, dates from 1905 and shows the architect in full command of the vocabulary. Its shape is determined by the inside curve of Melcher Street and it forms an eloquent mass in the light. Among the set it has the richest decorative detail, with red brick trimmed in granite for stringcourses, lintels and the like, and a very ornate, heavy copper cornice. It's the final flowering of a continuous program of building and experimentation in which a single building type was repeated and improved, with careful attention to the refinements of detail.

IV D 10 · NEW ENGLAND FISH PIER
212–34 Northern Avenue
Henry F. Keyes and Monks & Johnson, 1914
reuse: Mintz Associates, 1980

The real waterfront. This grand scheme for fish processing was built to be the largest pier in the world devoted solely to the fish business. Two long rows of unloading, processing and storage space stretch 735 feet out into the water on either side of a loading area. The proud New England Fish Exchange sits proudly at the open end.

IV D 10 · *New England Fish Pier*

The space in between is generally occupied by semitrailers. The buildings on either side are of no particular interest, save two great arches midway, which provide access to the waterside. There, fishing boats unload into wooden crates, conveyors and motorized carts. It's still a real working scene and Massport is anxious to keep it that way. The fish is crated and processed inside, then shipped out by truck. (In truth, half the fish is now shipped in by truck from Maine and Canada, then redistributed from here.) Some of it stays, however, in the No Name Restaurant, a former hole in the wall near the east arch whose anonymous fame has caused its recent, still-crowded, expansion.

The New England Fish Exchange Building, freestanding at the end, was the scene until very recently of bartering between captains and merchants as boat cargoes were unloaded at the dock. The auction held inside its high central space was somewhat laconic but nevertheless genuine, offering real ties with a period when commerce was personal. The building is threatened now by its spectacular view and destined by renewal schemes to become more profitable; yet another scenic, overstuffed restaurant, no doubt. The auction area will be moved elsewhere on the pier.

This brick-and-stucco block of a building is distinguished by a rather perverse Classicism that makes it seem halfway between triumphal arch and warehouse. A large arch from grade level at the center fills half the front façade, holding deeply recessed areas of glass that open to the bartering hall inside. The brick trim surrounding the arch is keyed at the top by a wonderful large carved stone head of Neptune, fish embracing his ears, starfish and barnacles lodged in his beard.

V/ THE HUB
OF BUSINESS

45 MILK STREET

Entry, International Trust Company Building
(V A 13), *45 Milk Street (detail)*

A/THE FEDS

Federal Street and Congress Street have remained true to their names, lined mostly with buildings that reflect the presence in Boston of national systems, governmental or corporate. Accordingly, these buildings bear the stamp of national architectural developments more than many other sections of Boston. The recent ones are tall and slick, the middle-aged are pompous and overtly federal, the older bear traces of adventure—wrinkles left from the days of stylistic inquiry.

At one end the area converges on the State House and Government Center beyond; at the other it ends indecorously in the barren gash above a sunken expressway, with the new Federal Reserve Bank gleaming from the other side.

left to right: First National Bank of Boston (V A 6), *Keystone Building* (V A 3), *United Shoe Machinery Building* (V A 4), *Union Warren Savings Bank* (V A 5)

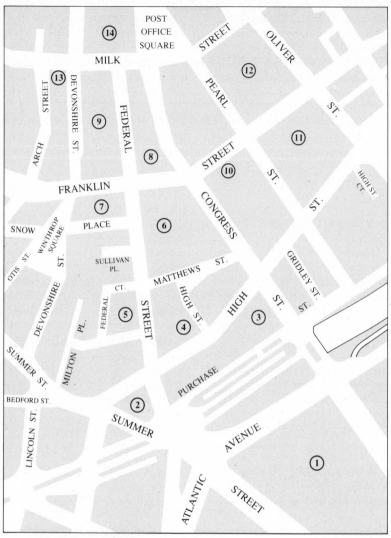

POST
OFFICE
SQUARE

⑭

STREET

OLIVER

MILK

⑫

⑬ DEVONSHIRE ST.

ARCH STREET

PEARL

ST.

FEDERAL

⑨

⑪

⑧

STREET

HIGH ST. CT.

⑩

ST.

FRANKLIN

CONGRESS

ST.

⑦

SNOW

WINTHROP SQUARE

PLACE

⑥

GRIDLEY ST.

OTIS ST.

SULLIVAN PL.

ST.

DEVONSHIRE ST.

MATTHEWS

CT.

HIGH ST.

HIGH

ST.

ST.

FEDERAL PL.

STREET

⑤

HIGH ST.

④

③

DEVONSHIRE

MILTON PL.

SUMMER ST.

PURCHASE

BEDFORD ST.

②

LINCOLN ST.

SUMMER

AVENUE

①

ATLANTIC

STREET

V / THE HUB OF BUSINESS   **A / THE FEDS**

V A 1 · THE FEDERAL RESERVE BANK
Atlantic Avenue, between Congress and Summer streets
Hugh Stubbins & Associates, 1977

The Federal Reserve, like its friend John Hancock III (IV A 7), borrows glamour
from the sky around it. The bright sheen of its aluminum panels changes as the
sky changes, its color ranging from a cool white to the pink tones of the low sun.
But whereas the Hancock comes unwaveringly to the ground, confounding its
relation to adjacent buildings with angled mirrors, the Fed looks as if it were two
buildings, one occupying the street space on a par with its neighbors, the other
pretending not to start until well above the street and all its trappings.

But the lower building doesn't really belong to the streets around it so much
as to some image of continuous parkland. The undulating little bits of English

park that front the building only mock the place around them. Dewey Square and Summer Street opposite South Station were once densely urban, crowded places filled with the excitement of city. They are now barren wastes of road presided over by this gleaming emblem of our inflation, the space its lobby opens to empty of everything but contrived significance. The chief function of the green space seems to be to provide an opportunity for the lobby to pretend it's part of an uninterrupted sylvan expanse, with its wall an assembly of clipped glass panels that have no intervening solid structure.

Around and about the building are the fruits of an extensive art-acquisition program that is not a part of the building itself or integral to its conception, but an addendum of select paintings and sculpture chosen by an adroit consultant. They're worth attention.

V A 2 · FIDUCIARY TRUST BUILDING
175 Federal Street, SW corner Federal and High streets
The Architects Collaborative, 1975

This rather nicely sized speculative office building occupies a nearly impossible site. It has a dark-brown glass and metal skin, which is cleanly detailed, and the cantilevered polygonal form is undoubtedly ingenious.

In having no clear, recognizable shape, however, No. 175 misses the fun of jousting with its neighbors, most of which stand resolutely rectangular on sites of irregular orientation. For all its ingeniousness this oddly shaped prism closes the end of Federal Street like a bathtub stopper that doesn't fit. It's well finished and cared for (though reflections in the dark glass are a bit wobbly), but it gives you nothing to hang on to: no thickness of material, no elements of structure or support, no forms to measure with your eye.

V A 3 · KEYSTONE BUILDING
99 High Street, SW corner of Congress Street
Pietro Belluschi & Emery Roth, 1968

Well mannered in the street, rather blunt from afar, the Keystone Building is mercifully unencumbered by plaza. Its travertine walls come down directly to the sidewalk in a simple colonnade and reside there comfortably. A quiet but simply scaled entry opens gently off the street; commercial space rings the periphery in the time-honored fashion, most of it occupied by a bank. There are no great emptinesses and there is no great excitement. Here business as usual seems a relief. The building walls are made with a system of demure bow windows covering the surface of the building. These forms, like those of the State Street Bank (V A 11), are meant, presumably, to be similar in scale to traditional building forms in Boston. But they are abstracted, and their unrelieved repetition from bottom to top and around the corners on all sides of the building makes them simply a wrapping for the building rather than elements of a coherent visual structure.

From farther afield the rippling white, perforated walls of the Keystone Building appear more aggressive, though in the skyline the building's uneventful volume tends not to hold the mind and it looms less than it might.

V A 4 · *United Shoe Machinery Building*

V A 2 · *Fiduciary Trust Building at 175 Federal Street, flanked by 100 Summer Street (V C 1) on the left and the Federal Reserve Bank (V A 1)*

V A 4 · UNITED SHOE MACHINERY BUILDING
NE corner Federal and High streets
Parker, Thomas & Rice (Henry Bailey Alden, associate architect), 1929

Quiet Deco. The walls are alternating vertical bands of brick and window, more relaxed and appropriate here than in many more strenuously styled buildings of the period, such as the Post Office (V A 14).

Although the lower walls follow the streets in their irregular angles and curves, the overall mass steps back on the east and west sides in obedience to the zoning regulations of the time. This forms a polygonal tower with wings that reach out to make a court for light on the south. At the top a truncated pyramid of tiles centers the building.

At the ground floor and filling in the lower levels of the light court, commercial

V A 4 · *detail, United Shoe Machinery Building*

fronts with fine cast-metal detailing are set into a limestone frame that bands the base. A modest entry leads into a handsome vaulted passage, connecting the adjoining streets.

It's thoughtfully detailed, intelligently planned; a well-bred instance of the ziggurat office-tower type. The tiled tower roof makes it a visible landmark from afar, and the carefully detailed entries and shop fronts make polite and engaging walls for the street. Four giant steps in the building bond bottom to top to make an understandable whole.

Maybe an Art Deco revival will be good for us.

V A 5 · UNION WARREN SAVINGS BANK (originally Massachusetts Blue Cross/Blue Shield)
133 Federal Street, between High and Franklin streets
Paul Rudolph, and Anderson, Beckwith & Haible, 1961

A collector's item, this building is a singularly studious work in which you can find comment on the condition of modern architecture as it entered the sixties. The best architects were confidently searching for forms of expression that would be rich in visual texture and appropriately scaled, but rooted still in the basic elements of construction. The building is structure embodied, structure shaped to give it measurable, discernible form—to be seen in sunlight and to be wondered about. It comes from a period when architects still thought they could control the building process, not just clothe it. And they knew their heritage.

The patrimony of Louis Sullivan is evident here: a strongly expressed base with exposed columns, a richly textured wall surface that is decisively upright, windows and piers interspersed in a rhythmic sequence that is more than a literal interpretation of solid and void, structure and skin. The modernist critique of Sullivan is evident, too. The top ends not in a crowning slab but with a strong change of texture; the corners are dramatically open, not thickened to be a frame.

The architects have also drawn from Boston's patrimony. The building's precast-concrete elements bear resemblance to the early granite-skeleton build-

V A 5 · *Union Warren Savings Bank (left), with First National Bank of Boston (V A 6) at right*

ings such as those by Alexander Parris at Faneuil Hall Markets (I D 5) and others along the waterfront, though these are fussier.

For all that, like too many serious scholars, the building earns more respect than affection.

V A 6 · FIRST NATIONAL BANK OF BOSTON
100 Federal Street, SE corner Franklin Street
Campbell, Aldrich & Nulty, 1971

All the jokes about pregnancy that this building has engendered are as inapt as the building itself. The bulge, tapered top and bottom, that makes this building unforgettable carries with it no promise of a redeeming future.

The polished red-granite face of the structure is inescapable, rising vertically from a plaza, then sloping out overhead until it becomes a vertical plane again. Its shiny sloped faces reveal little of the structural effort required for this trick, and the space thus formed is hardly comfortable. We look in vain for what has been gained. Perhaps there is an advantage in that the obtuse form that imposes itself on our perceptions dramatizes the building's incongruous size.

A small plaque informs us that this was the site of the Long Lane Meeting House, in which Massachusetts delegates ratified the United States Constitution. This historical note is an example of the corporate establishment's quaint habit of reminding us of what used to be present in the sections of town that they have long since usurped.

V A 7 · 111 FRANKLIN STREET
between Federal and Devonshire streets
Thomas M. James, 1930

This is the kind of building that makes movies from the thirties seem credible —those in which captains of industry could stand in their wood-paneled suites staring pensively into the street below at dark-suited men and women scurrying about—not too far below and through a real window, not a wall of glass.

The mass of the building fills one end of the block. From the streets nearby, the building is all wall, the lower sections embellished with intricate but uninspired terra-cotta reliefs and bronze panels that depict a great deal of physical industry surrounded by plenty. Abundant floral motifs are mechanically repetitive, and the sweaty actions portrayed are notably not of a sort to be found inside.

On the skyline Babylon prevails. The top steps back symmetrically at floors 11, 13, 17, 20 and 21, with a great copper roof at the peak summing it up.

Circulation for the building is of the urbane T-shaped sort beloved at the time, with a passage through the building at the middle of the block intersected by the main corridor off Franklin Street leading through the center of a bank of elevators. This main passage, suitable for the aforementioned captains, begins in a vestibule lined with a frieze that intermingles waves and whales, then proceeds down a corridor paced off by black pilasters with yellow-marble infill to the elevator doors, which are truly splendid. Embellished with tooled flower patterns, they have inset bronze panels that step up symmetrically on either side, just like the building mass above.

V A 8 · LOEB, RHODES, HORNBLOWER & CO.
70 Federal Street
Stahl Associates, 1968

A Brahmin in tailored stevedore's clothes, this building is a true descendant of the granite-slab skeletal buildings of the waterfront. Here the material of the day is concrete—Le Corbusier's Domino House Project should probably be cited in a paternity suit—but the spans are similar to the older local buildings, making a light net of concrete columns and slabs that distributes the load of the structure evenly enough to bear on the foundations of a previous masonry bearing-wall building.

The concrete frame is thoughtfully but simply detailed, with a slight relief where spandrels join columns. This lets the force of the slender round uprights counteract the apparent thickness of the floor slabs. The glass wall between slabs is set back from the edge, sliding freely behind the columns to leave the structure eloquently unencumbered. The whole is very lean and understated: polite, rational and charged with energy.

V A 8 · *70 Federal Street (right) adjacent to National Shawmut Bank* (V A 9)

V A 9 · NATIONAL SHAWMUT BANK
67 Milk Street, between Federal and Devonshire streets
The Architects Collaborative, 1971

Among behemoths, this is well mannered. Its tower is quiet in color, unassuming in shape, tautly clad in exposed concrete aggregate panels with flush windows, and it comes down to the street in a way that shapes the public space. There's elegance in detailing and proportion and a genuine concern for its place in the urban fabric.

No. 67 fills the entire block, high on the end near the massive Post Office (V A 14), lower on the Franklin Street end where it meets the general height of older buildings along that street.

All this works well as seen from afar, or as it might be seen in a model. Up close on the street below, the scale of the building is dramatically different from its surroundings, especially on the lower (banking hall) block, where these architects also succumbed to an infatuation with great sloping surfaces overhead. Here, though, they're glass and the principal visual excitement is in seeing the parked cars of Federal Street reflected in glass sloping outward up high where ordinarily a cornice might be found.

V A 10 · NEW ENGLAND TELEPHONE HEADQUARTERS BUILDING
185 Franklin Street, between Congresss and Pearl streets
Cram & Ferguson, 1947

Another of the retardataire Art Deco office buildings by the Cram & Ferguson firm, this is kin to the second John Hancock Building (IV A 7) and to the Post Office (V A 14) down the street. It is less interesting than either, though it does capture the eye. The upper floors step back forcefully to cut a ziggurat figure against the sky, but the radar-tower crown that now complicates the silhouette from Post Office Square is probably a more pertinent, even if not more gracious, image. The lobby has a remarkable cyclorama of murals depicting the benefits of telecommunications.

V A 11 · STATE STREET BANK
225 Franklin Street, between Pearl and Oliver streets
Pearl Street Associates (that is, F. A. Stahl & Associates, Hugh Stubbins & Associates, Le Messurier & Associates), 1966

The State Street Bank is made with precast-concrete window frames, each a distinct unit. They're carefully studied, nicely proportioned, of a size to imagine yourself into. These frames are quite believably related to old Boston; quite comparable to the windows of older buildings nearby. In this they are appealing. But assembled in sheets across the face of a large building, with no intermediate structure exposed, they lose all dimension. The units become texture and their extent becomes arbitrary; there could be more or there could be fewer. On the skyline we're left with a rather amiable but vague block.

At the lower levels the mass of the building is broken into several elements to provide a closer relation to the scale of buildings around it. The windows are spaced apart in a subtly alternating rhythm, and the lower mass is fitted rather carefully to the differing street grades. But even here the modern doctrine that high buildings should stand on piers above the ground led the architects to hang these lower portions out over the sidewalk, and their cantilevered masses seem more aggressive than sheltering. With walls it could have come to the ground in a more approachable way.

The architects evidently cared about Boston and the scale of the buildings that make up its fabric, but to know this we must think it; the building gives us little chance to sense their concern or to feel that the building is a companion to the street. Even so, think of the glass-sheathed peers of its period and you will recognize that this is a noble effort.

V A 12 · *Old Federal Reserve Bank with the First National Bank of Boston* (V A 6)

V A 12 · OLD FEDERAL RESERVE BANK
Pearl Street, between Franklin and Milk streets
R. Clipston Sturgis, 1922
reuse and tower adjunct: Jung-Brannan Associates, 1981

High Renaissance detail in Federalist proportions; a chilly, delicate little number that is much more reticent than its successor (V A 1).

The detailing is austere, strictly delineated Renaissance, but the window spacing and the general sense of polite containment have much more to do with Beacon Hill than with Roman bravura. The lower part of the building is treated as a high base with a very gentle, nicely scaled band of paired Tuscan pilasters alternating with arched windows. Above are stacked windows marching at a brisk pace. It's all very light-handed and unimposing, yet filled with a solid sense of authority. It should suit itself well to the financial district hotel that it's now been converted into—an inspired reclamation proposal that has taken shape in a grotesque and disfiguring mansard. A rather nervous high tower has replaced a lower pompous but refined 1953 addition designed by Paul Cret.

In the middle of the Pearl Street side of the earlier building there is a small, modestly triumphal entry. Nearby are plaques with decorative borders that include images of coins. One of these plaques bears text from a letter written by Alexander Hamilton in 1781: "The tendency of the national bank is to increase public and private credit. The former gives power to the State for the protection of its rights and interests, and the latter facilitates and extends the operation of commerce among individuals. Industry is increased, commodities are multiplied, agriculture and manufactures flourish and herein consists the true wealth and prosperity of the State."

And we all lived happily ever after.

V A 13 · INTERNATIONAL TRUST COMPANY BUILDING
45 Milk Street, between Arch and Devonshire streets
William Gibbons Preston, 1893, 1906

Faneuil Hall (I D 1) and the Somerset Club (II B 16) were enlarged by doubling their widths and adding a story. William Gibbons Preston here followed suit, modifying a building of his own design. The original structure fronted Devonshire Street and remains intact. To make the present Milk Street elevation, the Devonshire Street scheme was simply applied in the perpendicular direction, with the original narrow end elevation becoming one of three bays across the face of a building now square. A new, more fanciful Classical entry was placed in the narrow middle bay on Milk Street. The story added at the top was a low one with alternating windows and volutes. It's not clear whether the projecting cornice of the original was replaced and then later removed or whether the present, rather blunt attic top was intended. Wonderfully sculpted allegorical figures by Max Bachman bring life to Commerce and Industry on Arch Street, while Security and Fidelity are more staid on Devonshire Street.

Compare this to the original's contemporary, the Ames Building (I A 11), just a short walk away. The sense of robust sculpted wall is similarly Richardsonian but with details around the entrance that are more Roman than Romanesque. It's a very telling example of this moment in history, when masonry structure was being replaced by steel and architects' sensibilities were struggling with a flood of influences: These included new and larger forms of building organization and construction, unprecedented building heights, the evident attractions of vigorous modeling, as seen in Richardson's work, and an emerging demand for Classical refinement and civic grandeur. That demand was popularized by the Columbian Exposition in the same year that the original half of the International Trust Company Building was constructed.

In 1889 the architects of the Ames Building got it all together, largely by ignoring both steel frame and enthusiasm for the Classical. They worked with

V A 13 · *International Trust Company Building, 45 Milk Street*

what they knew. Preston, in the International Trust, doesn't quite get it all together. Prolific as he was, he attempted here to ingest too much. Compositionally, the building lacks the coherence of the Ames Building, despite a strong similarity. The sturdy vivacity of its forms earns our interest and affection, but in sum its parts don't quite suit each other.

V A 14 · *Boston Post Office and Federal Building*

V A 14 · BOSTON POST OFFICE AND FEDERAL BUILDING
Post Office Square, between Water and Milk streets
Cram & Ferguson and James A. Wetmore, 1930–31

Imagine, if you will, that Clark Kent was a postmaster. You will then understand much more readily the nature of this building and its Superbuilding aspirations. Admittedly, it does not fly, but it has a mighty chest, a very upright stance and the most muscular shoulders in town.

It's an interesting building, though. It fills the block at street level, while at the upper levels its C-shaped plan allows natural light to penetrate the office wings. The arms of the C reach out toward Post Office Square; the middle of the back of the C rises several stories to form a focus for the building mass. The basic scheme is similar to that of the United Shoe Machinery Building (V A 4).

The main entrance off the square opens into a concourse filled with postal windows. From there an extraordinary stair leads up through the heart of the building to a second large corridor that can be entered directly, uphill, off Devonshire Street. Despite subsequent alterations and the general tenor of General Services Administration maintenance, the interior still holds a sense of pride in detail and that particular mix of urbanity, cultivation and optimism that Art Deco embodies—a supposition that all the new world would call for was a change of manners.

The exterior is massive indeed, visually dominated by sheer shafts of stone that reach from pavement to sky with slight modulations of surface at the top. Between these shafts of stone, which clothe a steel-frame structure, attenuated slits hold vertical bands of window and metal spandrels. This motif was destined to reappear in Cram & Ferguson's work seventeen years later for the second John Hancock Building (IV A 7) in Back Bay and the New England Telephone Headquarters Building (V A 10) down the street, in neither case with as much panache as here.

All in all, it's a very heavy presence, designed at a time when the enthusiasm for authority could still lead to the use of fasces as decorative elements on Federal buildings; here as clever little cylindrical motifs to round the corners at the top. It's worth noting, too, that three hundred years before this building was built, the first settlers drew water from a spring near the northwest corner of the site.

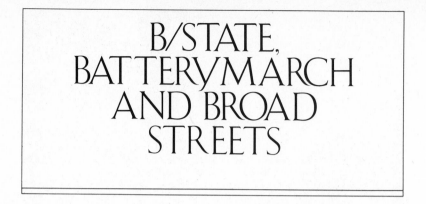
The balcony of the Old State House (I A 1) commands not only the space in front of it, which was the site of the Boston Massacre and later of the first reading in Massachusetts of the Declaration of Independence, but the path extending out through Long Wharf and the harbor to the sea beyond. Because the Old State House stands up the hill a bit, its relationship to the water is more easily recognized than is Faneuil Hall's (I D 1), even though the latter once stood right at the water's edge.

The Old State House has, from the first, served as a destination point and the center of the city. Not surprisingly, it has also attracted to its proximity the financial center of town.

To accommodate the money trade, the Exchange Coffee House was built, around 1810, across from the southern face of the Old State House. It was eight stories high—then Boston's tallest—and topped with a dome roughly akin to the one that can now be seen atop Quincy Market. Inside there was a hall for bartering, an eating place and a number of rooms for lodgers. Apparently its

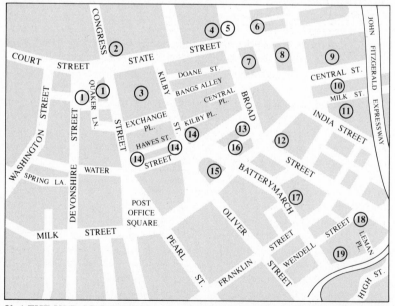

V / THE HUB OF BUSINESS   B / STATE, BATTERYMARCH AND BROAD STREETS

State Street Block (V B 9), *Flour and Grain Exchange Building* (V B 11) *and Custom House* (V B 8)

grandeur was wasted on the bartering crowd, which is reported to have still preferred to do business on the sidewalks outside. Exchange Place off Congress Street may recall this activity.

By the end of the century, however, the Exchange needed a big hall and a big bold building; Peabody & Stearns provided both in the Boston Stock Exchange (V B 3). Now it too has been replaced, or rather demeaned into the quaint face for an even bigger structure. Trading happens differently now: You will look in vain for the whole hall filled with the frenzied scurrying of traders and messengers known to us from Wall Street films. At best you'll find an array of desks topped with computer terminals and a rather lethargic group of keypunch operators.

Across State Street at No. 60 (V B 2) is an even more accessible version, where the windows of a brokerage house open onto TV monitors that dispense stock quotations to the passer-by. But for a glimpse of old-fashioned bartering, make an early visit to the New England Fish Exchange on Fish Pier (IV D 10), where captains still auction their daily catch. Hurry, for that tradition may die any minute, too.

The State Street pier was the earliest and longest pier into the water, and alongside it the proud Custom House (V B 8) was built, in 1837–47. The area to the south, as far as Fort Hill, was expanded into an important harbor and warehousing district in the early part of the nineteenth century by the construction of India Wharf (I E 3) and Central Wharf (V B 10) and by the developments of the Broad Street Association. All seem to have involved the hand of Charles Bulfinch in one way or another. Later many of these brick buildings, the docks and the water itself were replaced by granite structures often of great size and ponderous appearance, as in the State Street Block (V B 9).

The harbor is now elsewhere, screened by the overhead highway, but India Street, Broad Street, Wharf Street and Water Street carry still the names associated with it, and the Cunard (V B 5), Board of Trade (V B 7) and Flour and Grain Exchange (V B 11) buildings have ornaments that are unmistakably nautical.

V B 1 · THE BRAZER BUILDING
27 State Street, SE corner Devonshire Street
Cass Gilbert, 1896

· THE WORTHINGTON BUILDING
33 State Street, SW corner Congress Street
Carl Fehmer, 1894

Close runners-up in the claim to be the first steel-frame building in Boston. Together with the Winthrop Building (I A 12), which bears the distinction, they form an extremely interesting chapter in the development of downtown Boston. This pair stands noticeably at the entry of the financial district as approached from the north on Congress Street. Their size, very modest by comparison to their new neighbors, and the intensely cared-for masonry walls in which they are dressed make them seem charming now: dollhouse office buildings divided by a minute alley, a dark slot left from the street pattern of colonial Boston.

An inscription over the entrance to 27 State Street declares that this is the site of Boston's first meeting house, built in 1632 and used until 1640 for town meetings and sessions of the colony's general court. The Brazer Building is an inventive structure of irregular shape, done up with one eye staring fixedly at the Italian Renaissance. It has an elegant base, and the first two floors are made up of fine, high arches. Then come seven floors of windows crowned by two floors that are articulated quite differently. Instead of the usual mansard or Classical cornice motifs, the top here is something like a loggia. It's treated more openly than the bottom, with a series of piers filled in by a remarkable collection of reeds and pilasters, and medallions with glass in between. This is a rare example of a building top that conveys a sense that it's a special place of its own rather than a garreted attic. (In this regard it is a precedent for the New England Merchants Bank [I C 3] across the street.) At the skyline an aggravated copper cornice alternates between spiky floral motifs and shell forms, giving a rather jagged silhouette.

The middle floors, compared to this pseudo-loggia, are tiresome. However, the exposed corners on State Street are curved, each with round windows on the axis of the bend. The special reflections from these curved glass corners give the whole building a twist.

The entry inside has been remodeled in dreary commercial-office-lobby style with no relief from the drab off-white-and-brown marble. Somehow, and happily, two mosaic ceiling pieces from the original interior have been preserved.

The Worthington Building is more foursquare and solid, influenced, no doubt, by contemporary developments in Chicago, but unwilling to risk very much. It's high and narrow, a sibling in size, shape and structure to the Winthrop Building on Washington Street, but no match whatever in elegance and adventure. Just compare the bottoms.

V B 1 · *Worthington (left) and Brazer buildings*

V B 2 · *60 State Street*

V B 2 · 60 STATE STREET
NE corner Congress Street
Skidmore, Owings and Merrill, 1977

The structure of 60 State Street is interesting. Its outer frame is a grid close-spaced enough to behave like a bearing wall. Its shape is that of two adjacent tubes rigidly connected.

But it's an awesomely inarticulate building, the architectural equivalent, perhaps, of minimalist art. The pink granite face reluctantly concedes that it has reached the street with openings that are only slightly higher than those up above. One minimal overhanging marquee announces the First National Bank of Boston, another No. 60 itself.

The windows are absolutely simple rectangular frames set between triangular piers faced with pink granite. Each pier has a slot in the apex that presumably holds tracks for the window-washing equipment. But it's a rather unsettling detail, literally exposing the thinness of the casing at just the point where we most wish to believe in its strength.

Aside from this slot and the irregular angles that the building makes as it fronts the street, there's nothing much to engage your attention here, just an expanse of assertive but uninformative material. It adds little to the Boston streetscape except from a distance, when the slim faceted faces of the tubes stand tall—even as their thirty-eight stories cast a numbing shadow over the outdoor spaces of the Faneuil Hall Markets.

A great ventilation duct, also encased in pink granite, occupies the plaza but is no great help; it offers no gesture of concession or generosity to the people who might use this particular spot. For contrast, see the base of the Boston Public Library (III C 4).

V B 3 · BOSTON STOCK EXCHANGE BUILDING
53 State Street, between Congress and Kilby streets
Peabody & Stearns, 1889–91

Granite and big and confident. Peabody & Stearns did a number of buildings along this street, of which this was the first. It comes at the tail end of the Romanesque enthusiasm, and it's not hard to understand how, in the absence of any passion here, their next one down the block, the Cunard Building (V B 5), could be in a wholly different mode.

The Stock Exchange Building is a ponderous brown block. The bottom two floors and basement have large windows set between massive piers in a thick trabeated wall. The capitals of these piers have some spirited carving, but otherwise the building's face is made up mostly of identical windows framed in various ways. The structure is rounded at one end, but it's otherwise uneventful. You enter off the sidewalk at the middle of the building and go upstairs inside rather than out. At the rounded corner adjoining Kilby Street, doors open onto stairs going down to a nicely visible basement shop.

The copper-topped light fixtures near the entry are perhaps the most engaging part of the building. Each of these fixtures is housed in a diminutive domed temple. These are held out overhead by an elaborate system of brackets incised into the heavy stonework at the bottom to respect the sidewalk line.

First this building lost its grand trading hall inside. Now it's lost its innards altogether and will remain simply as the face for a gargantuan tower block behind.

V B 4 · THE RICHARDS BUILDING
114 State Street, between Merchants and Chatham rows
c. 1859
addition of upper floors, 1889

The Richards Building is a perfectly astonishing cast-iron-front building, the most richly layered building in Boston. Unfortunately, it was ruined at the bottom in the fifties by a very careless restoration, if you can call it that, but its upper levels are still magnificent. For four floors the sequence of the arcades is a triplet of arches with one colonette between each, a thickened pier with two colonettes, a pair of arches over the entry, another thickened pier and then another triplet on the other side of the entry.

The building is marvelous because it has all this metal arcading actually set forward of the main building face. The thicker piers between windows make it resemble very deep masonry with a thin structure of columns out in front. There's a great deal of thickness and relief in this wall, plenty of space for the mind to play in.

At the top two floors, two curious two-story rounded bays project forward and the arcading is omitted to reveal the back plane of the façade. These, it appears, date from a later addition. At the very top floor there's another step back to give access to a little balcony.

V B 5 · CUNARD BUILDING
126 State Street, at foot of Broad Street
Peabody & Stearns, 1902

Built to be the headquarters for the Cunard Steamship Line, this building breaks out in nautical motifs at every opportunity. However, since the initial conception of the building was quite severe, it doesn't get swamped. Instead, its steel frame is fairly directly expressed, with a two-story base marked only by a change in window size and a stringcourse that terminates in Neptunelike figures at either end.

Whereas most of the wall is direct, bordering on bland, the top is a splendid urban device. Four boldly configured Palladian windows absorb the vertical piers and turn them into a wall, capped by a molded metal cornice. As an end to Broad Street, it's terrific: legible, graceful and strong. Up close, the little turret bays on each end of the nearby Richards Building are much more engaging and fun, but viewed from a distance, they seem fussy compared to this syncopated arcade.

The entry, off center because the building has four bays, sports a well-carved inscription on the lintel and a pair of bronze stanchions rising to hold lights on either side from brackets concocted of anchors and dolphins. Lions of the British Empire are embedded in the upper cornice.

V B 6 · 150 STATE STREET
between Butler and Commercial streets
renovation: C. Howard Walker, 1918

Boston has a few tiny office buildings embedded in the main fabric. This one is a renovation of an earlier four-story building, most likely made Tudor for the British Consulate, which once occupied it.

An absolute anachronism, it sits on the street of ponderous buildings with a gable at the top, a little half-timber work, and very high, square, double-hung windows that stretch all the way across the second floor and consume large parts of a very slightly projecting bay at the third and fourth floors.

It's a very charming bit of somewhere else, too small to do any harm—even painted yellow and ochre.

V B 7 · BOARD OF TRADE BUILDING
131 State Street, between Broad and India streets
Winslow & Bradlee, 1901

If our century could start like this, why hasn't it turned out better? This is not one for the history books, but it's a very civilized bit of urban building. All the elements are brought together in a way that suggests that the world is settling down a bit and will soon be under control.

Of course, the Renaissance trappings are a bit excessive, and you might be forgiven for thinking the whole thing a bit crass, but it's all here: steel frame absorbed into the design, H plan for getting light into the offices, windows of a size to stand by and at the base a handsome triple arcade filling the block out to the edges of the street with a gracious entry.

The building is mostly brick with stone details of considerable skill and wit. Most notable is a recumbent group of allegorical figures above the arcade. Most amusing are carved remembrances of the sea trade that caused Boston to prosper. Piers in the rusticated base have helmeted masthead figures carved in stone and the prow of a ship spilling over with abundance as it comes rowing, remarkably enough, through waves that suddenly erupt from the stone.

V B 8 · THE CUSTOM HOUSE
State and India streets, McKinley Square
Ammi B. Young, 1837–47
tower: Peabody & Stearns, 1913–15

There's an adage floating about that if you want to get away with building a bad building, you should hire a good architect. Lance Laver, writing about the John Hancock Tower, has observed that if, on the other hand, you hope to get away with a really outrageous one, you should hire a great architect.

The addition to the Custom House is clearly outrageous. And it would seem that Peabody & Stearns got away with it. They may not have been all that great, but they were certainly prestigious enough, with offices atop their earlier Stock Exchange Building (V B 3). Peabody had been voluntary head of the City Park

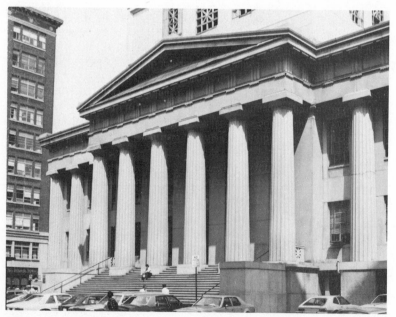

V B 8 · *Custom House*

Department, president of the Boston Society of Architects for many years and national president of the American Institute of Architects in 1900–01.

The original Custom House, by Ammi B. Young, is one of the finest examples of Greek Revival architecture in America, a very solid Doric-ordered granite building with engaged columns all around, each a single shaft of granite, and projecting pediments front and back. It stood on the edge of the water, originally surmounted by a dome that was, of course, not very Greek, but certainly handsome.

Then, seven decades later, an astonishing thirty-story office tower was built over the dome. Oversized windows in the tower base still let light into the space underneath the dome. Four corner pylons, starting at this attic base, extend up the sides of the tower to the beginning of the top, a four-faced Ionic treasury superimposed over the office windows. From its top some great winged-beast scrolls make the transition to another base, this one for a huge clock face. Above this, in turn, there's another cornice and the steep pyramidal top.

To place this phallic object on such a respectable Greek temple was unthinkable. The tallest building in Boston for many years, it's still the most peculiar on the skyline, with a strong, clear, very memorable silhouette. And the older building that is its base remains the most vividly Doric structure in town, worth a trip in itself.

V B 9 · STATE STREET BLOCK
1 McKinley Square, State to Central streets
Gridley J. Fox Bryant, 1858

Those who prefer an architecture that's stern and direct will take solace in the State Street Block opposite the Custom House.

Big enough as it stands, it originally had sixteen additional bays extending toward the water. It filled an inlet that used to reach to the Custom House. Bigger and later than most of its mates along the waterfront, the State Street Block has been eulogized by Walter Kilham as "plain American." Actually, it's less plain that its predecessors. It shows Gridley J. F. Bryant's developing susceptibility to French interpretations of the Renaissance, a tendency that culminated in the Old City Hall (I A 8), with a little help from Arthur Gilman.

The block is a carefully formed granite warehouse with just a few trappings. The overall wall treatment consists of a rusticated granite with keystones over every one of the segmental arch windows. Occasional vertical slabs of granite serve as pilasters marking the corners and the central pedimented section and at each floor there are bold projecting stringcourses. So even though it's a flat building, it has quite a strong profile. In the center facing the Custom House, the cornice arches improbably to make a low, round gable. Locked in the center of the large arched windows this provides is a bulging granite globe.

To appreciate this building as it was intended, you have to wish away the steep mansard roof and replace it with a shallow hip roof. But don't wish too hard: These mansard additions are among the few remaining examples of a once-common nineteenth-century form of expansion. Many of them have fallen prey to the preservationists' wrecking ball, the rest to neglect.

V B 10 · CENTRAL WHARF
Milk Street, between India Street and Fitzgerald Expressway
attributed to Charles Bulfinch, 1816

A walk from the Board of Trade Building (V B 7) to the State Street Block
(V B 9) to the Central Wharf buildings on Milk Street represents two forty-year
steps backward in time, and the buildings measure this well.

The Board of Trade is an urbane structure for office work; the State Street
Block is at once a warehouse and a prideful monument to the economic power
stored within. The Central Wharf buildings are the last remaining of a row of
fifty-four similar brick buildings that stretched out to where the Aquarium
(I E 4) now stands. Their purpose was to receive goods unloaded from ships
docked alongside them. Where they now face the gray granite of the State Street
Block, they once opened out to the riggings of schooners. They were a major
development probably designed by Bulfinch, certainly with great clarity and no
extraneous pretensions.

V B 11 · FLOUR AND GRAIN EXCHANGE BUILDING (Boston Chamber of Commerce)
177 Milk Street, SE corner India Street
Shepley, Rutan & Coolidge, 1889–92

It wasn't ever the tallest, it wasn't designed by Bulfinch, it wasn't the scene of
any great declaration, but the Flour and Grain Exchange is a landmark nonetheless by dint of sheer silhouette (and some pretty good stonework).

Though designed by the same firm and about the same time as the Ames
Building (I A 11), this one is a very different type. It's a building of particulars,
constructed for the Chamber of Commerce with (originally) a large trading hall
on the third floor, marked by bands of three-story arches and double-hung
windows. All very lovable and unexpected. After all, it's rather odd to have a
stone Teutonic castle standing along India Street in Boston, in what used to be
the harbor.

What makes it tangibly marvelous is the top. The main entrance corner, at

V B 11 · *Flour and Grain Exchange Building*

V B 12 · *50–54 Broad Street*

Milk and India streets, is surmounted by a mammoth conical roof, its bottom rim serrated by dormers. Each dormer has a steep triangular stone face in the plane of the wall below, and each ends in a very pronounced crocket.

On the India Street side, the curve of the structure does not just run into the straight wall; it actually curves back slightly first. This articulates, in a quiet way, the curved part as an independent pavilion under its own conical roof. The same sort of bulging occurs at the expressway end of the elevation, which curves under a smaller conical roof. In between cones, the wall is capped by a high balustrade. It's a very carefully controlled composition.

Where curve meets straight on Milk Street, there's an amazing stone cartouche: a globe with all sorts of emblems upon it, an eagle perched atop and two cornucopias below, one for exotic fruit, one for coins; the ensemble stacked above what appear to be packing crates.

Fantasy and power meet here in connubial bliss.

V B 12 · 50–54 BROAD STREET
SE corner Milk Street
c. 1863

Straight granite with style. The builders of this square block were determined to make it distinguished. It has a rough granite arcade at the base, with keystones just slightly pronounced, and a three-story rusticated granite wall above with regularly spaced windows, each capped by a bracketed slab. At the top a band of little arches holds the cornice, while the roof swoops back from sight in an elegantly curved mansard. Dormers and chimneys along the edge remind us that the roof is there.

This is an altogether solid building, yet it has, in tough granite, the kind of dandy refinement that you might expect to find on Main Street in Disneyland. At the corner the ground-floor arcade is open on both sides to allow a diagonal entry. Below the door the name set in tiles reveals that this was at some intermediate time the Columbia Spa, "spa" being a rather quaint New England term for something midway between corner drugstore and grocery, but equipped with a soda fountain.

V B 13 · 45 BROAD STREET
SW corner Water Street
Carl Fehmer, 1876

A fine brick building with stone trim; a study in the artful crafting of walls. Each of the elements in its multicolored face is distinct and detailed to highlight the other.

The brick wall of the upper floors is interrupted by very handsomely made, rough-textured brownstone lintels and banded with precisely carved yellow stone strips that make up the sills. The lintels have a curved, bracket-shaped bottom, but the windows are set far enough back in the wall so that their wooden frames slip behind the brick and ride up behind the lintels, avoiding the conflict between shaped lintel and rectangular window frame. The result is a crisp set of shapely hollows in a beautifully textured wall.

The walls themselves follow directly the lines of the angled adjoining streets, save at the corner, which cuts across between them. The ground floor has numerous openings, once for shops, now for corporate consultants, all strung under a continuous lintel.

When the same architect built the Worthington Building (V B 1) twenty years later, he invested far less attention in the pieces, and the result is much stodgier.

V B 14 · LIBERTY SQUARE

· 44 KILBY STREET
NE corner Water Street
c. 1870

· 54 KILBY STREET
1873

· 55 KILBY STREET
NW corner Water Street
Sturgis & Brigham, c. 1880

· 60–62 CONGRESS STREET (Hornblower and Weeks Building)
NE corner Water Street
Andrews, Jacques & Rantoul, 1907

The intersection of Water, Kilby and Batterymarch streets is called Liberty Square, not for any of the reasons you would suppose, having to do with Colonial Boston. It earned the term through association with a wild feast and celebration held in the area to commemorate the French Revolution.

Perhaps the absence of a direct line into Boston's history accounts for the neglect it has suffered. It is certainly one of the yet-to-be-discovered sections of town. With its coherent shape and an array of nineteenth-century buildings,

V B 14 · *55 Kilby Street, Liberty Square*   V B 14 · *60 Congress Street*

Liberty Square could become something really distinctive. All it needs is some attention and enthusiasm.

The square is dominated by the Samuel Appleton Building (V B 15), but there are three smaller buildings from the 1870's whose walls are filled with invention. These are brick, with carved stone trim and lintels, syncopated window spacing and brackets. At 44 Kilby Street the lintels of the second floor are punctuated by some strange carved faces with twisted foreheads and heavy eyebrows; while at the third floor a curious brick corbel holds up the edges of the building as it bends. At No. 54 the rhythmically spaced windows are focused on a handsomely configured relief panel with the date 1873.

Facing the square on the west side of Kilby Street at No. 55 is a building by Sturgis & Brigham with a decisive split personality. The entrance has a curiously warped arch and lintels—akin to those above the second-floor windows across the street at No. 54—which forcefully establish the center. The next two stories look like the commercial equivalent of a good sharp-edged Italianate villa with felicitously proportioned windows. But then the top three stories are suddenly a rather mushy Romanesque. Was one building built atop the other?

Around the side the building changes scheme again and butts up against another at the other end of the block. There, at 60 Congress Street, a similar volume is treated much more formally and of a piece, with lusty Renaissance detailing on a wall that is high, narrow and elegantly proportioned.

V B 15 · SAMUEL APPLETON BUILDING
110 Milk Street, Batterymarch to Oliver streets
Coolidge & Shattuck, 1924
reuse: Irving Salsberg, 1981

Boston has an inordinately large number of round-ended buildings, because it has an inordinately large number of converging streets; the one follows the other as the Classical solution to a tapering lot. The Appleton Building is the most singleminded of these, a very simple three-stage drum. Its nearest kin are the Sears Block (I C 5) with its tea kettle apex and the Flour and Grain Exchange (V B 11), its corner heightened by a dormered conical roof. There are no such frills here. On either side the huge bay simply turns into flat walls bordering Batterymarch and Oliver streets as they diverge.

When you stand back facing the building on axis, the shape is astonishingly powerful. Yet because of the way it sits in the street, high and remote, it is practically unnoticeable as you pass around the bottom. The high stone base is full of windows coming down almost to eye level, but their metal grills prevent them from engaging your attention.

Yet tarry awhile and stand back, for the composition of this wall is subtle and instructive. As in their earlier building at 7–11 Beacon Street (I B 9), Coolidge & Shattuck have considered carefully what this building is about. While adopting a Classical vocabulary of detail, they have invented a pattern of openings that at once gives a measurable scale to the stone skin and clearly signals that all that stone is hung on a frame.

The three stages of the drum are nearly identical. They consist of alternating piers and windows equally sized, the windows interrupted by a spandrel at the third floor. The fourth floor in each stage is banded by two carved stringcourses, again with piers and windows alternating between them, but this time only half as wide. The syncopation that this produces creates strong horizontal bands around the building. It also reveals that the stone piers above are hung on a frame, since only a small segment of the wall continues all the way to the ground, far too little to carry such weight.

A tremendous carved entrance on the Liberty Square axis is now inert. The Milk Street entrance is far less auspicious; a set piece of neo-Classical design with the parts articulated only slightly. The entrance portico has swags at the top and a little aedicular piece around the central window. It incorporates a big flagpole and a helmeted figure with vines sprouting out of his ears, and once held copper light fixtures hanging off brackets as pendants on either side.

Neglected for many years, the Appleton Building deserves the recognition and attention it is now receiving and merits special care in renovation.

V B 16 · 22 BATTERYMARCH
between Milk and Water streets
Ball & Dabney, 1893

A bit of cultivated elegance in an area not otherwise noted for it. It's self-conscious and graceful but all to the point, for No. 22 started as the Exchange Club, a gathering place for successors of the eighteenth-century merchants who used to meet daily at the Exchange Coffee House (p. 266). The early traders may have preferred to do their bartering in the streets, but their late-nineteenth-century counterparts thought it more suitable to do their socializing in style.

The building, in brick and stone, is laden with Renaissance detail. The face on Batterymarch Street has, in addition, two extremely graceful light fixtures similar to the ones at the Boston Public Library (III C 4), arching out on either

V B 15 · *Samuel Appleton Building*

V B 17 · *Batterymarch Building*

side of the entrance. All the proportioning is careful, and the carved details are executed with a great deal of scholarship.

The resolution of the angles made by the intersection of Batterymarch with Milk Street and an alley at the rear are absorbed in curved panels at the corners, complete with curved glass in all the windows.

V B 17 · BATTERYMARCH BUILDING
60 Batterymarch Street, NE corner Franklin Street
Henry Kellogg, 1927

The Artillery Company's march from the Commons to Fort Hill gave its name to this street. But by the 1920's Fort Hill was long gone and Batterymarch needed a new destination. Art Deco to the rescue, with this richly colored bit of scenery at the bend in Batterymarch Street. The elements used in the Board of Trade Building (V B 7) are used here in similar but even more promising ways in that the specific shapes and forms are drawn from the nature of the building rather than applied to it. It is a hopeful building, a wonderful testament to the twenties.

At the ground floor the building fills its block with commercial space all around the edges. From the third level up, three slabs of offices run perpendicular to Batterymarch Street, connected in their middles by a slab that runs the length of the building. The offices thus surround two light courts on each side of the building. An open Art Deco arcade above a two-story base connects all the parts.

Viewed down Batterymarch Street, the building appears to be made entirely of brick piers, those at the corner stopping short of the top so that the front of each slab has a tapering head. It's very elegant in the limited framed view that Batterymarch Street provides, but less so when seen across the large formless parking lots that were unanticipated in the urbanism of the time.

At ground level the building is a beautiful dark-brown stone-glazed brick. The color gradually changes as your gaze moves toward the top, becoming lighter and lighter until it's almost whitish, a Deco form of homage to the sunlight, or to the absence thereof in the street below.

V B 18 · BROAD STREET
between Franklin and High streets
c. 1860

Along the south end of Broad Street is a row of granite structures that shows the contrast between granite used in plain slabs directly presented and granite fashioned into elements of architectural convention. There is, however, no substantial difference between the two in volume or building type. Between Franklin and High Street, the row of granite structures is interrupted by Moon Lane, a remnant of eighteenth-century street that has twisted the brick wall of its neighbor into a beautiful curved pocket of space.

V B 19 · CHADWICK LEAD WORKS
184 High Street, between Batterymarch Street and Leman Place
William Gibbons Preston, 1887

William Preston, architect of the Museum of Natural History (III B 5) and the

V B 19 · *detail, Chadwick Lead Works*

Cadet Armory (IV C 5), can be seen here working in a Richardsonian Romanesque mode. The façade of the Chadwick Lead Works is directly related to
Richardson's Marshall Field Warehouse in Chicago, of almost the same year,
and we should be glad of it. The three-story arched windows and continuous
band of alternating windows and piers at the top make for a noble, clear form
that organizes the whole with great ease and makes a fine bit of urban scenery
at the end of High Street.

   True, the wide arches of the middle and the narrow windows of the top press
together rather abruptly here in the absence of Richardson's intermediate two
floors of smaller arches, but it's grand anyway and for compensation we get
sections of terra-cotta ornament, a carved gargoyle and occasional grotesques.
To make sure that the building comes alive, the lower spandrel in each arch
curves back from the face of the building at its center to reveal the edge of the
arches at either side. Then at the second level the center post bends back to
support the middle of a straight spandrel above that is in line with the reveals.
Subtle transitions were the stuff of this architect's art. J. H. Besarick used similar
devices in his warehouse at 145 South Street (IV D 3) of the same period.

   At the rear of the building, visible from the back and from various vantage
points in the neighborhood, is the shot tower. It's a nice little brick tower with
a prim hip roof, just high enough to allow the molten lead poured from inside
its top to cool into shot before reaching the floor at the bottom.

C/SUMMER TO WINTER STREETS

The path from the Common to the water that is now Summer and Winter streets appears on the earliest maps of Boston. It traced the high land between hollows on either side, which only later became building sites. Until well into the nineteenth century Summer Street, a fashionable address, was lined with fine houses and shady boughs. The area was converted to commerce in the second part of the century, leveled by fire in 1872 and rebuilt almost instantly. Summer, Bedford and Franklin streets and the cross streets adjoining still contain the best record of Boston's late-nineteenth-century commercial appearance.

Summer changes to Winter at Washington Street. The intersection of Summer, Winter and Washington streets has been, since before 1900, what the real estate

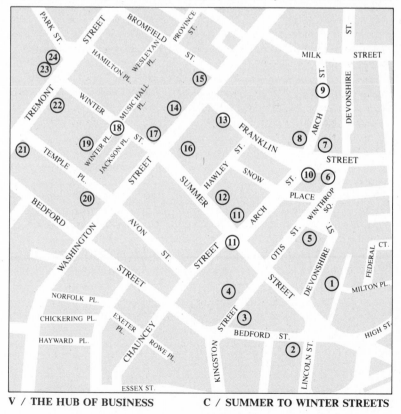

V / THE HUB OF BUSINESS   C / SUMMER TO WINTER STREETS

people call a "100 percent corner," the recognizable center of commerce. Here three department stores vied for their customers' allegiance. Two have become the giants of Boston commerce, Filene's expanding north along Washington Street and Jordan Marsh moving south, with plans to extend still further into a large addition designed by Mitchell/Giurgola Associates.

In 1979, Washington Street was closed to through traffic, embellished with an arcade (V C 14) and remade in the image of a pedestrian shopping precinct. It is ideally suited for the commercial stroll, packed with people and shops and visually closed at each end by slight bends in the street. These bends recollect the original path, which closely followed the rise and fall of the land.

Winter Street has also been closed to traffic and repaved as a walk, and the first stretch of Summer Street south from Washington has been nearly filled with wood-slat benches. The whole area is now officially called Downtown Crossing.

To the north, on Washington Street, the Old South Meeting House (I A 3) jostles into view, its surprisingly attenuated spire contending still with the high buildings all around. A little beyond are the Old State House (I A 1) and Old City Hall (I A 8). To the east, Summer Street descends gradually to South Station (IV D 4) and the Federal Reserve (V A 1), then crosses Fort Point Channel and proceeds on to South Boston. To the west, Winter Street ends in the Common, with the Park Street subway station (V C 24) and the commanding elegance of the State House (I B 4) standing above on Beacon Hill. The gold-domed State House makes up in visual intensity for the disappearance of Trimountain, the indigenous landmark of the peninsula that was radically transformed as Bostonians built their city upon a hill.

V C 1 · 100 SUMMER STREET
NE corner Devonshire Street
Skidmore, Owings & Merrill, c. 1970

The simple, well-tailored unassertiveness of this metal-panel-and-glass building is a welcome relief. Its dark surface makes no pretense to being more than a carefully considered, straightforward cladding for a steel-frame structure. The windows are almost continuous, with the framework only lightly indicated in the spacing of panels that are hung in front of it. The resulting slick surface is given a slight change of texture by a switch from glass to metal at the spandrel. At the bottom of each spandrel a row of inset panels creates a small section of shadow that gives emphasis to the sheer, smooth glassiness of the building face.

It's unquestionably alien, but matter-of-factly so, in ways that make it more assimilable than many of its more stridently costumed peers. No doubt it's helped by the presence nearby of a whole set of good solid scene-stealers: South Station (IV D 4), the Bedford Block (V C 2) and One Winthrop Square (V C 5) easily slake our thirst for the glyptic charms of masonry.

At the ground level it's much less appealing, demonstrating once again that what is good from afar against the sky is not necessarily very engaging up close at the ground. A set of orange enameled-metal lollipops that shift in the wind above the entry plaza do little to help. Inside, the materials are flashier than they are solid, but there's a lively sense of activity, with shops entered off the lobby and a shaft of sun from the south that streams through high windows over the entrance.

V C 2 · BEDFORD BLOCK
SW corner Bedford and Lincoln streets
Cummings & Sears, 1875–76

Proud as they come and a landmark that holds this section of town in place. Made with red granite and white marble, now a bit grimy but expansive in scale and built in good chunks, this is a vividly memorable building.

The elevations are laid out with symmetrical care, with an abundance of Ruskinian Gothic window motifs, mostly collected in threes. Their large openings are spanned by thick red-granite lintels, sometimes assisted by relieving arches faced with alternating red and white slabs. On the Bedford Street side especially, the façade maintains a remarkable equivalence between large glassy openness and solid stone presence. On the Lincoln Street side, it is thicker, with the bottom floor fashioned in a manner that is wonderfully blocky and carved, free of the constraints of any rigorous system, ending in a separate entrance at No. 15. The back sides are brick, also carefully made and worthy of study.

But it's the corner tower that stays in the mind, gesturing to the angular space where Bedford and Summer streets intersect. The corner is chamfered simply enough, then made imageable by two projecting walls that corbel slightly forward at the fourth floor to carry a solid cubic tower once capped by a pyramidal roof. The block of the tower displaces the mansard roof at the corner to house a very large window where once there was a clock. "BEDFORD BUILDING" is emblazoned across the top face of this tower in letters appropriately granitic.

V C 3 · *detail, Procter Building*

V C 2 · *Bedford Block*

V C 3 · PROCTER BUILDING
100–06 Bedford Street
Winslow & Wetherell, 1897

Few buildings deserve to be likened to jewels, but this one is faceted, crested with filigree and most notably ornamental. It is as enthusiastic about terra cotta as the Bedford Building is about stone. And it's tiny.

Cream-colored and lavish, the Procter Building brightens an otherwise dull corner. Each of its windows sports some form of cap, the principal ones being marked by conch shells in arches. Pilasters that measure the pace of the second floor are each topped at the third by a finial. The frieze and cornice, like the copper openwork above them, glitter with patterned sun and shadow, and the frieze resolves into human faces at each bend of the building.

V C 4 · 19–43 KINGSTON STREET
between Summer & Bedford streets
Various architects, 1875–90

Along the west side of Kingston Street, there is an uncommonly coherent group of commercial buildings dating from 1875 to 1890. Hovering, one presumes, on the edge of destruction, they form an ensemble that is both pleasing and instructive. They present an abbreviated encyclopedia of ways to organize four windows in walls of brick and stone, all standing high above two stories of commerce that are mostly fronted with glass.

Given how few choices there were to make, it's cheering to see how varied these are. They're comparable in size, variety of detail and uniformity of type to houses built during the same years in Back Bay. Take your pick.

V C 5 · *One Winthrop Square, with 111 Franklin Street (V A 7) and 89–93 Franklin Street (right)*

V C 5 · ONE WINTHROP SQUARE
Intersection of Devonshire and Otis streets
W. R. Emerson & Carl Fehmer, 1873
reuse: Childs, Bertman, Tseckares Associates, 1974

The teaming of Emerson & Fehmer was evidently inspired, for this looks like the work of neither one. There is a striking clarity here, but it almost confounds explanation. Stylistically it's inconsistent; as a way of transferring weights to the ground, its visible pattern is perverse, being heavy at the top, and it commits the academically unpardonable sin of having a column in the center. Withal, it's quite splendid.

The lower three floors have very wide openings and large pieces of granite; the piers at the second and third floors are carved into clusters of pilasters that make the wall seem like a high colonnade, especially at the center, where giant order pilasters frame the openings over the entry. The fourth and fifth floors, unquestionably errant, give the building its compelling visage. At either corner these floors are designed as tower pavilions, with hipped roofs above and walls that are more solid than those in the frame underneath. Between these very solid corners, the fifth floor hides behind a dormered mansard roof. The entry is marked at the cornice by a very shallow, round pediment divided in the middle by a projected bracket. At the ground the entry is framed by freestanding columns that join with a heavy lintel to form a porch. This in turn intercepts the pesky central column and holds it above the entry. This little feat of derring-do is a later modification of the original design.

The building has been meticulously adapted from publishing plant to offices, including the transformation of the open space in front into a pleasant little park. The open space that is now the square was for many years the hectic scene of trucks loading up for the delivery of newspapers fresh from presses inside. The lusty bronze statue of Robert Burns that is now there was evidently imported from the Fenway, where his vigorous stride and broken-branch walking stick would seem more at home.

V C 6 · 89–93 FRANKLIN STREET
corner Devonshire Street
N. J. Bradlee & W. T. Winslow, 1873

The southwest corner of Franklin and Devonshire streets is made by a building of astonishing shape: a free-form version of the round-corner building. For later versions see the Flour and Grain Exchange Building (V B 11) and the Samuel Appleton Building (V B 15).

This one sways first with the Franklin Street memory of the Tontine Crescent, then swoops around the corner and back on itself to negotiate the turn into Otis Street, which branches off Devonshire Street.

It's an incredibly supple act, made possible by the flexibility of brick and some finely hewn stone trim. The wall is banded in five stages. The bottom is simple and open in mercantile fashion. The three middle floors are a fast-paced alternation of window and brick panel enlivened by stone stringcourses that step up around the windows to form window heads and flatten out to form sills. The top band, above the cornice, is a row of small arches. Along Devonshire Street the wall pattern is more syncopated, with ingenious deference to the need for chimneys.

V C 7 · BOSTON SAFE DEPOSIT BUILDING
100 Franklin Street, between Arch and Devonshire streets
Shepley, Rutan & Coolidge, 1908–11

A very accomplished building—it's simple, restrained and powerful. The white stone surface is unencumbered by rhetoric, modulated instead by the graceful forming of large arched openings into the banking hall of the tall lower floor. The mass of the building follows the curve of Franklin Street, with narrow light courts inset off Devonshire and Arch streets. Windows on the upper levels of the Franklin Street façade are regular to the edge of dull, rescued from oblivion by missing a beat at each end.

The arches of the ground floor are beautifully scaled. The windows are set back in the depths of these arches, starting from a base on Arch Street that is just about waist-high. These shapely niches make you feel that you can be, are wanted to be, a part of this building, yet the cast-metal grills that fill these windows assert the security of the bank inside and establish a distance between outside and in that is both seemly and comfortable.

The banking hall inside has recently been mucked with, but is still very spacious and grand. A corridor across the back of the building from 60 Arch Street to 201 Devonshire Street links the elevators to the street in a handsomely vaulted space that curves like the building and accommodates a change in level between the two streets.

On either side of the Franklin Street entry there are, inexplicably, cast conquistador figures holding lamps off the wall in a flurry of twisted passion of the sort that has been transmuted everywhere else into serene assurance.

V C 8 · 74 FRANKLIN STREET
NW corner Arch Street
Cummings & Sears, 1878

In the years just before designing this, Cummings & Sears built the New Old South Church (III C 3). Here they cast their eyes away from the medieval to make an especially nice commercial block that seems at once a descendant of the State Street Block (V B 9), a cousin of Bradlee's St. Cloud Hotel (IV B 15) and a precursor of the Renaissance enthusiasm that emerged in countless buildings during the next decades.

The Arch Street face of the building block is designed as though the two ends were pavilions. In these, the windows are framed by pairs of pilasters except at the top, where they're topped by low-haunched arches, with stones shaped to fill out a rectangular panel. In between the simulated pavilions, the granite window frames are very businesslike. There is no mansard; the top ends with a cornice originally surmounted by a balustrade.

In the original scheme the center pier on Franklin Street went directly to the ground and a broad bank of stairs was recessed into the front bay on the left;

V C 9 · *detail, Arch Street*

V C 7 · *Boston Safe Deposit Building*

two levels of stores occupied the corner. Today, the whole lower space is filled with a Bailey's ice cream store and its addicts.

V C 9 · ARCH STREET
between Milk and Franklin streets

Arch Street is so named because its southern extremity once passed through the arch in the center of the Tontine Crescent (I A 5). The curve in the south face of Franklin Street still reflects the layout of Bulfinch's brilliant but short-lived exercise in urbane collective form.

The northern, more recent section of Arch Street, from Franklin to Milk streets in particular, is a confrontation of opposites, each seeking an answer to the ever-more-massive buildings our century has seemed to require. On the west is the soaring ramp for a parking garage five stories above, an in-town port for suburban cars. The stack of cars is here absorbed in the midst of the city, high above the sidewalk and its ordinary commerce.

On the east is an office building from the first decades of the century, now being linked to 45 Milk Street (V A 13) in an ambitious reuse project. It's a straightforward frame structure with a shallow light court and generous windows set into a brick wall. Its unrecorded architect devoted almost all his attention to spanning the windows. Each of the stone lintels is coursed as a flat arch, so the face of the building is enlivened by an array of well-groomed eyebrows. At the bottom a new code is established where the building meets the street. Here the frame is expressed as a colonnade. At the center, three piers that bear no weight from above are adorned with pressed metal flutes and Ionic falsies. From this distance in time, in our era of mannerisms, it seems the architect was both serious and witty. Or was he merely incompetent?

V C 10 · COLUMBIAN NATIONAL LIFE INSURANCE BUILDING
77 Franklin Street, SE corner Arch Street
Parker, Thomas & Rice, 1912

The ten stories of this building are wedged into a narrow trapezoidal site among much lower neighbors. Two decades after the Columbian Exposition that popularized it, the Classical vocabulary has here been fully adapted for high buildings. Despite its peculiar shape and somewhat exaggerated pretensions, the elements of the design are handled with considerable grace and assurance.

The Classical orders are used here for what they are: a means for giving measure to the surface of the building. A rusticated base encompassing large windows shapes the public ground floor, and giant order Corinthian pilasters reach above it three floors to an architrave that relates approximately to the height of earlier adjoining buildings. The five stories above, measured by flat relief in the piers, echo but do not repeat the carefully modulated scale of the forms below. The top floor is made to seem lighter and continuous by a slight change in the spacing of windows and the addition of carved panels between them. A several-layered cornice gives definite shape to the top. Yes, this would be a plausible place to buy insurance.

V C 11 · CHARLESTOWN SAVINGS BANK
65 Summer Street, SE corner Chauncy Street
The Architects Collaborative, 1976
· UNION WARREN SAVINGS BANK
50 Summer Street, NW corner Arch Street
Sasaki Associates, 1976–77

Where Arch Street intersects Summer Street, two banks built in 1976 conspire to dissipate the street. Charlestown Savings Bank, the bigger, rose-granite-and-glass one at 65 Summer Street, has its corner lopped off to open a great cave to the banking hall inside, all smooth and cool. The division between inside and out is made by a slick glass screen framed with tiny, bright-metal trusses and supplemented by a lot of conditioned air.

The Union Warren Savings Bank, the small red-brick one at 50 Summer Street, is chopped off and configured on the corner. It has spare windows, a layered neon logo and a simple high white space inside that is distinguished mostly by a huge red air-handling duct. Along the Arch Street side, its lower level keeps a little more in tune with its neighbors.

Here the contrasts of Boston's architecture are all played out again: on one side the single, urbane, expensive Establishment gesture, a little bit classier than thou; on the other side the building of parts, albeit cheap ones and few, seeking our affection. The latter says we offer personal service, the former says we *are.* One relates in scale to the brick-housed merchant of the early 1800's, the other to the polished-granite banking halls of the 1910's. Neither shows much interest in its neighbors from the 1870's.

Usually we see little buildings replaced by big ones. Union Warrren does the reverse. A street of big, proud four- and five-story buildings has been unsettled on the north by a two-story brick model. If it were blown up to full scale, it still, alas, would be clumsy. The Charlestown Savings Bank on the south chips the corner off Chauncy Street and not only diminishes the excitement of the street as it disconnects one block from another, but in this case does us the particular disservice of exposing more of the embarrassing 1950's brick façade of Jordan Marsh. The latter roughly resembles an ocean liner rendered with oversized Georgian motifs.

V C 12 · 40–46 SUMMER STREET
between Arch and Hawley streets
1873

Adjacent to the Union Warren Savings Bank, at 40–46 Summer Street is a very cheerful bit of cast-iron-front building dating from immediately after the 1872 fire. It's built, clearly, on two lots, with a superposition of columns that makes up in airiness what it may lack in Classical correctness. The front of the building has very wide openings on the bottom near the street and diminishing window sizes as it reaches the top: the inverse of what masonry has led us to expect. The whole surface of the building is made to engage our attention with delicate columns lacing the front. At the top they step forward impudently to be sure that we see them and enjoy their prim roundness.

V C 12 · *detail, 40–46 Summer Street*

V C 13 · LINCOLN FILENE PARK
corner Franklin and Washington streets

The park at the intersection of Franklin and Washington streets is the sunniest spot along the busiest shopping street downtown. With the Filene's extension on one side, a Woolworth's topped by a parking garage (V C 9) on the other and the Washington Street Arcade (V C 14) across the way, it is more than amply supplied with consumers in need of a pause. The park does surprisingly well by them.

Surprisingly because like the new buildings around it, the things which make it have no intrinsic formal interest whatever. Paradoxically, that's partly why it works so well. The simple parallel rows of planting tubs and wide seat-width walls are so totally unassuming that they provoke improvisation: Those who find a way of sitting or leaning or lounging about on them can have the sense that they have found the park themselves and are making do with it, improvising their own claim on the space rather than assuming some place and posture preordained for them.

The area of the park is shaped by planters into small spaces descending Franklin Street. These allow small groups of people a certain amount of privacy and offer the additional choice of being close up to where the Washington Street throng passes within reach or somewhat more remote.

In full use on a warm Saturday, the whole collection has something of the aspect of a picnic on the rocks—with people perched about at various levels, resting in attitudes of improvised and unstable comfort. The scene is well peopled, but it lacks the natural interest of rocks.

V C 14 · WASHINGTON STREET ARCADE
Washington Street, between Milk and Winter streets
Arrowstreet, 1976

It may not have the grandeur of a nineteenth-century glass train shed, but the

Washington Street Arcade has some of the same mechanical ingenuity. The constraints set on this design might well have boggled the imagination, or at least hobbled it. Not so here.

To meet the requirements of an arcade which could be superimposed on the front of an existing building, which could be prefabricated for simple, fast construction and which could be supported on those limited points where underground service vaults and utility lines would not be disrupted, Arrowstreet created a light-hearted unit design. Its modular structure deftly accommodates irregularities in building design and street alignment on the west side of Washington Street as it provides almost continuous covered shelter for shoppers along the face of the buildings.

The steel frameworks, each cantilevered off a single steel column, are happily a mite frivolous, but their forms at least begin with the realities of assembling bits of steel into an overhead support without intervening much in the busy sidewalk below. The curving plexiglass surface captures reflections of the sky and bends them down to us in the street, muting the chaotic diversity of shop fronts behind a gleaming and continuous surface. Underneath, the relation of pedestrian to shop is unchanged, save for the shelter provided and a division in the sidewalk formed by a row of columns. This latter quite coincidentally tends to create something approximating an express lane for hurried pedestrians along the outside, with window shoppers gravitating to the inside.

What comes next is a bit more worrisome, as evidenced in the Barnes and Noble storefront. The gleaming uniformity of the arcade obscures the identity of shops, and the tame signs on its surface (all that are allowed by the Boston Redevelopment Authority) are no match for merchandisers' ardor. At Barnes and Noble the second floor has been turned into a giant billboard, obliterating the carefully formed and crafted detail of the building behind it, detail specifically

V C 14 · *Washington Street Arcade*

designed to give human measure to the building face. A continuous row of such billboards along the second floor, should it happen, would transform Washington Street into the visual equivalent of an automobile-oriented commercial strip— just when it's been made into a pedestrian street.

V C 15 · WASHINGTON BUILDING
381–87 Washington Street, between Bromfield and Winter streets
Bowditch & Stratton, 1904

The first fifteen years of the 1900's witnessed a transformation of Washington Street, with high steel-frame buildings and terra-cotta facings replacing the earlier brick, granite and cast-iron structures. The Washington Building is one of the earliest of the newcomers. It lacks the single unifying vision of Filene's (V C 16) across the way and the uniform system of Gilchrist's, now The Corner (V C 17). Both of these were built a few years later, and they represent the major divergent trends that have worried the rest of the century: one leading to ever-greater simplifying abstractions, the other following the dictates of building systems into more repetitive forms. The Washington Building reflects an earlier stage when the use of terra-cotta panels had not yet been assimilated and architects were still wondering what to do with them.

The shapes imagined here are really quite peculiar, a collection of banded spandrels and fluted verticals that intertwine at the junctions and terminate in volutes at the cap. Even at that, the terra cotta all sits above a three-story wall that is entirely metal and glass, well suited to the arcade (V C 14) added seventy-two years later.

V C 16 · FILENE'S DEPARTMENT STORE
NE corner Washington and Summer streets
Daniel H. Burnham & Co., 1912

We have been treated to the blandishments of beautifully lighted, atmospherically tuned interior spaces for so long that we take them for granted. We forget that shopping needs light, which in 1912 wasn't quite so easy to come by, especially in large, thick buildings. Daniel Burnham didn't forget.

Indeed, he was so taken with the huge areas of glass that are used here to light this department store that he made them the point of the building: He framed five floors of terra cotta and glass like a picture with massive corner piers, attic floor and cornice, then pinned it to the wall of the street. Alas, alack, no one wants much natural light in department stores anymore (at least not yet) so the windows are mostly blocked, lifeless and dirty. The whole appears now like a big, dumb graphic design that's become sooty.

The grand full-height frame is terra cotta too, sporting medallions, pilasters, swags and like trappings of Burnham's grand Classical ambitions. There are particularly nice terra-cotta–framed balcony windows at each corner of the third floor, which invite you to imagine being in them.

Sight closely along the Washington Street edge and you'll see the most surprising thing of all: This giant wall is bowed just slightly to follow the alignment of the street. A quiet, sweeping gesture if ever there was one.

From recent appearances, it might have seemed that this grandiloquent building would come to a dark and humiliating end. However, with the energy crisis rekindling interest in natural light, and the world of architectural fashion flaming with interest in the grand and Classical, there is hope for it yet.

V C 17 · THE CORNER
431 Washington Street, NW corner Winter Street
Bigelow & Wadsworth, 1912
reuse: Add, 1977

Formerly Gilchrist's Department Store, built at virtually the same time as Filene's across the street but in a very different mode. Organizationally, each upped the ante for consolidated shopping and used considerable innovation in doing so. Each is surfaced in terra cotta, and together they form a testament to the wondrous malleability of that material, as well as to the pecularities of their architects' imaginations.

Whereas Burnham makes his building into a mammoth singular statement, Bigelow & Wadsworth have built a system building that could as easily be a few bays bigger or smaller without changing anything. Whereas Burnham presses the terra cotta into Roman Imperial service, Bigelow & Wadsworth form the terra-cotta panels in a manner that seems more like the Gothic on Anglican Church pews. And whereas the pomp of Burnham's decorative motifs seems of a piece with the arrogant spirit of Teddy Roosevelt, the enigmatic figures at the bottom and top of each Bigelow & Wadsworth pier give rise to perplexing speculation. Are they wit pure and simple? If so, why so painful? Do the human heads at the top cover their ears in despair of the city? Do the grotesque animal figures at the bottom grimace in pain at the weight on their shoulders, or are they waiting to pounce on some hapless passer-by, leaving the weight of the piers dangling in midair?

Since Henry Bigelow was also the architect for the marvelously urbane Boston Athenaeum (I B 8), one must assume that this was intentionally droll.

More recently the department store was converted to a complex set of individual boutiques on several levels with passages cutting through from both Washington and Winter streets. The new signs and trappings are spirited and flashy, but dead straight.

V C 18 · 12 WINTER STREET
SW corner Washington Street
Henry Preston, 1878
reuse: A. H. Bowditch, 1912

· STOWELL'S JEWELRY
24 Winter Street, between Washington and Tremont streets
c. 1908

· LOCKE-OBER'S
Winter Place, between Winter Street and Temple Place
c. 1832, plus numerous revisions

Winter Street is a fine short and narrow street, running from Washington Street to the Common, that has been turned into a pedestrian walk as part of the

V C 17 · *The Corner*

V C 19 · *Provident Institution for Savings*

Downtown Crossing. It has building walls on either side that shape the space clearly, and the kiosk of Park Street station (V C 24) closes the view to the west, though with hardly any grace.

The corner building on the south at Washington Street was originally built by Henry Preston, then completely reclothed in terra cotta, presumably in 1912, as a means of keeping up with Gilchrist's (V C 17) across the street.

At No. 24, Stowell's Jewelry has fostered a marvelously ornate façade of copper and simulated marble skillfully painted on. The motifs of this building are of Classical derivation, but of a size and intricacy that has much more to do with cabinetry and show windows than with the stuff of building.

Winter Place, which might be mistaken for an alley, leads south to the entrance of Locke-Ober's restaurant. Its ground-floor room, visible from the street but until recently open only to gentlemen, is a magnificent period piece, with dark wood, heavily carved wainscoting and moldings, gold wallpaper, carved hatracks and fleshy paintings, shiny brass fittings, a mirror behind the bar and a chandelier with a central globe surrounded by little light bulbs poised at the end of delicate metal tendrils.

Upstairs in the main dining areas, the dinner may well be worth the price of admission, but the architecture isn't—unless you have a party big enough and foresighted enough to preempt one of the several small chambers available. These are intimate, at least.

V C 19 · PROVIDENT INSTITUTION FOR SAVINGS
30 Winter Street at Winter Place, between Washington and Tremont
streets
Shepley, Bulfinch, Richardson & Abbott, 1973
· 37 Temple Place
between Washington and Tremont streets
1833
renovation: James Purdon, 1933

Saving Providently, it would appear, leads to incremental additions of increasing magnitude. From Temple Place to Winter Street, there is a built record of this institution's growth since 1854, when it bought the 1833 Greek Revival Perkins House on Temple Place and had it converted to banking quarters by N. J. Bradlee, who removed the Doric portico.

In 1933 the brick structure was again considerably modified and extended to include neighboring properties. In doing so, the architect, James Purdon, created a seamless match between new and old, modeling the extended building on details from the older one (the round bow on the right) and transforming the interior into a big banking hall, while retaining the earlier parlor for the president's office. On the outside the extension is so seamless that it distorts the character of the original house and expropriates its historical properties for its own purposes.

The most recent addition, fronting on Winter Street, is a more forthright office building of the type to be found in bigger blocks along Congress and Federal streets. Despite these affinities, the Provident makes genuine efforts to fit in its quaint place. The lower floors are coincident with the height of adjoining storefronts, with insets and bays that break the lower surfaces into a scale quite consistent with the buildings that it adjoins. The segments of the building that you're easily aware of here in close quarters are small and well peopled. The taller, more routine elements of the office structure are mostly screened from view by the walls of the adjoining narrow streets.

On Winter Street the façade of the building is open at the bottom to make its columnar structure clear. But the volume of the upper floors projects out above on both sides supported on brackets. The angle of the sloped bracket is repeated in the stone coursing at either end of the façade, all the way up the face of the building. It's a design device that is optically bewitching, a simple refinement that in these close quarters is just unsettling enough to command attention and to dispute the rigidity of the stereotypical office block.

V C 20 · BLAKE BUILDING
59 Temple Place, SW corner Temple Place and Washington Street
A. H. Bowditch, 1912

The Blake Building is as lyrical as Bowditch's earlier Old South Building (I A 14) is stodgy. In its present state it is a study in modulated planes, transparencies and reflections. Even the fifties storefront on the corner is infested with its spirit, though the original storefronts are on the south end of the Washington Street side.

The framework is clad in terra cotta, the piers articulated as clusters of colonettes. At the bottom these disappear behind the glass planes of the first two floors, their visual force sublimated into little explosions of Gothic fantasy of the sort that are normally found hovering over the heads of saints on a cathedral. At the third and fourth floors, beautifully crafted bays, with glass on three sides and the top, make a transition to the gridded terra-cotta skeleton of the building above. The front face of these bays is a large sheet of glass in the forward plane of the windows below; the sides and top facet back to slip behind the colonettes of the framework. This allows the vertical thrust of piers and window mullions to rise uninterrupted to a set of segmental arches at the top that bind the whole building block together. The crowning cornice, alas, has been undone.

V C 22 · *St. Paul's Cathedral*

V C 20 · *Blake Building*

V C 21 · 141 TREMONT STREET
SE corner Temple Place
c. 1975

Conspicuously hardheaded; the building's shiny glass planes are set out to the front surface of the structure and framed with ribbed precast panels bearing no visible joints. Nothing is modulated save at the edges, where the sheets of glass wrap the corner. Not pretty, not phony. A world made like this would have no need for observers.

V C 22 · ST. PAUL'S CATHEDRAL
Tremont Street between Temple and Winter streets
Alexander Parris, 1820

An Ionic temple front built at the same time that Parris was supervising construction of Charles Bulfinch's Ionic portico for the Massachusetts General Hospital pavilion (II A 16). Science and Religion could be embodied similarly then. St. Paul's is more notably Greek, with a thicker architrave and blank panels in the pediment waiting to be transmuted into heroic figures. Perhaps the intentions were too fleshly for the deacons.

St. Paul's now seems a wonderful anomaly: sandstone Greek columns on a granite temple for Episcopalians, standing amid the towers of commerce. The building is not very friendly, but it is engagingly clear, witness to the conviction that motivated the successors to Bulfinch.

Inside there's a very broad vaulted ceiling and a comparable clarity of volume. The half-domed chancel at the end, with coffering as in the Pantheon, is a revisionist work by Ralph Adams Cram, who worked on the interior in the 1920's.

It's all grand, simple and perfectly scaled.

V C 23 · LAFAYETTE MALL
Tremont Street and the Common

· PARK STREET SUBWAY STATION KIOSKS
Tremont and Winter streets at the Common
Wheelwright & Haven, 1897

The hard edge of the Common becomes the soft edge of downtown. This overlapping of domains makes for an ever-active scene. The most pleasant place along the mall is around the Brewer Fountain, replica of a Parisian fountain with the requisite undulating sculpted silhouette, nudes and dolphins, two bowls for successive stages of splash and a granite-framed collection pool at the bottom. The fountain, paving and surrounding steps have recently been refurbished handsomely to designs by Arrowstreet.

At the Park Street end, two kiosk entries for the subway station bracket the mall. They mark out a parenthesis of space that forms an arena in good weather for musicians, proselytizers and tired passers-by. Between these severe blank blocks and Park Street, the paved plaza is heavily trafficked by patrons of the subway and the hawkers who seek their attention. For all that, the two little copper-roofed, granite-faced buildings, protected by the National Register of Historic Places, are inescapably dull.

V C 24 · PARK STREET SUBWAY STATION
Park and Tremont streets, underground
Wheelwright & Haven, 1897
renovation: Arrowstreet, 1978

Would you like to have a new kind of subway station? One that is neither dingy, gray and obscurely confusing nor white, antiseptic and primly efficient? A station that is colored pale pumpkin, festooned with lights, with red, green and varicolored tiles underfoot? A station perhaps just a tiny bit gaudy? This stop on the Green Line, readily distinguishable from all others, is just such a place.

A plethora of rather tinny light fixtures hang from the ceiling, their red-and-green shields tracing out the paths to points of exchange between the Green Line above and the Red Line below. The floor surfaces are tiled in beguiling patterns, mixing deep earthy colors in bands that frame columns, mark out bays with some subtlety and rise occasionally to support benches and kiosks and other station paraphernalia. This floor is a great invention, with colors and patterns that do not demand but do reward our attention. The design energy embedded here is what matters most, what bears the most wear and what is most easily recognized when hanging from the strap of a passing trolley.

What has happened here is that the architects have added intensity to the place without being able to make substantial alterations in its structure of tunnels and passages. Earlier plans for the stop had included replacing the kiosk entries with a much larger, more dramatic opening to the sky above, an opening that would have let natural light and sun down to the platform and established much clearer relationships between the trains below and the place above. This, which was the best idea, the one that would have given a large sense of order to the whole, was frustrated by the landmark status that has been accorded the structures (V C 23) at the present entrance. This was a considerable loss, for the slightly manic quality of the station underground comes in part from its lack of connection to the world above.

VI/BEYOND
THE HUB

Courtyard, Isabella Stewart Gardner Museum

A/THE RIVERSIDE LINE

Were this book to continue, as your explorations well might, it would follow two paths out beyond the hub of the city. One would be a radius cutting out from the center through the adjoining suburbs, along the Riverside branch of the MBTA Green Line. The other would strike a wide circumference following the Emerald Necklace Park system established by Frederick Law Olmstead, the foremost landscape architect and planner of the nineteenth century. Both routes would provide valuable insights into the natural topography of the Boston area and a view of the suburban pattern that accompanied the late-nineteenth- and early-twentieth-century development of the center city. The Emerald Necklace route also includes some of the most distinctive of Boston's institutions.

The Riverside Line can be boarded conveniently at many spots within the Hub: Government Center, Park Street, Boylston or Arlington Street, Copley Square, and Auditorium are all stops within the area covered by this book. Kenmore Square, the first stop outside it, is where the regular pattern of Back Bay ends. Here Beacon Street crosses Commonwealth Avenue to befuddle our sense of orientation. During baseball season the crowds jam on or off the train, headed to or from Fenway Park, the baseball stadium that is worth a visit even by those immune to the charms of our national sport.

Fenway Park is quintessentially Boston. From behind home plate, the Hancock and Prudential towers stand in full view, and the odd, improvised, irregular shape of the field, the stacks of green bleachers (for 33,532 spectators) and the surrounding industrial walls all echo the intimacy and irregularity of the city's dominant street pattern.

After Kenmore Square the train comes aboveground, running alongside the Muddy River through the Riverway park system. The second stop above ground is Longwood in Brookline. Directly opposite the stop are the Longwood Towers, a very strong and beguiling set of tall apartment buildings of 1925, rationally organized apartment wings with a large underground garage and an active crenelated silhouette, twisted occasionally by large octagonal bays. Nearby and also visible from the stop is Christ Church of 1862, a chapel of Romanesque derivation that is a distinct and impressive feature on the landscape. Beyond Longwood Towers to the northeast is Longwood Mall, a large green with great ornamental trees. David Sears, one of the first major developers of Brookline, planned this area as a picturesque suburb. By 1849, Sears is reputed to have landscaped the streets and squares of his estate with fourteen thousand trees of various exotic types. These included European sycamore, English and Dutch elms, Norway maples and assorted oaks imported from England. The few that remain from this original assortment are in the Longwood Mall. The purple-leaf European beeches here are considered among the finest in the Boston area.

In the immediate vicinity and along Hawes and Colchester streets are a number of marvelous houses big and small that proclaim the idiosyncrasies of their owners, architects and remodelers. Farther to the east along Monmouth Street and in Monmouth Court is a group of truly exceptional row houses. The best of them, at 69–77 Monmouth Street, were designed by George Tilden sometime around 1870. They are willful and inventive, full of the craft of building with bricks, stone and wood, but playfully. Each of the houses has a distinct identity, yet the whole is an organized, easygoing and amusing composition. J. Pickering Putnam's block of the same years but around the corner on Monmouth Court is less differentiated but does have a magnificent roof, a mansard that is very steep at the top and swoops down in a shallow curve between an astonishing array of dormers—heavenly mansions on the roof.

Another block over is Beacon Street, with rows of more mundane town houses and apartments that follow the Beacon Street trolley line demarcating the areas of higher density that grew up next to the tracks. Next out along the Riverside line is Brookline Village, now made evident by the presence of the Hearthstone Plaza Building directly adjacent to the tracks on the south. This complex of cinema, shops and offices designed by Imre and Anthony Halasz in 1969 uses skillful massing and spare detail to connect shopping, parking, pedestrian passage, access to the transit stop and a bridge across the wide and busy Route 9 artery, all on a small angled redevelopment site. The older part of the village is well described in a brochure by Margaret Henderson Floyd, titled *Brookline Village Walking Tours*.

The rest of the trip on the Riverside line is an exercise in watching the city fabric unravel. At Beaconsfield there is a mix of single family houses and apartment groups, some quite recent, one a conversion of an old factory building. At Cleveland Circle a playground lies between the rail line and the wooden porch backs of the brick three-decker flats near Beacon Street.

After Cleveland Circle the train passes by two great waterworks stations opposite the Chestnut Hill Reservoir. The earliest, a great picturesque Romanesque brownstone pile with vast windows and doors to see the machinery through, was designed by Arthur Vinal, the Boston City Architect in 1887, and was added to by his successors Wheelwright & Haven in 1889. The other, of similar bulk and impressiveness but of Classical demeanor, was designed by Shepley, Rutan and Coolidge in 1900.

If you were to disembark from the train at the Chestnut Hill station, you would be near the Longwood Tennis Club and a fine selection of turn-of-the-century wooden shingle-style houses along Devon Road and Norfolk Street to the south; or, along Hammond Road to the north, a good row of ambitiously pretentious houses, interspersed with more recent innovative efforts, such as the solar house of 1979 by Lawrence A. Linder at 10 Woodman Road.

As the train passes from Chestnut Hill to Newton Center, it goes through the Hammond Pond Park. Here it is possible to see, finally, something that approximates the original landscape—wooded, with great chunks of irregular stone outcroppings. One can imagine the early parts of Boston being built from something more or less like this.

The final stop, for our purposes, is Newton Center, where one can sense still the character of villages that surrounded Boston in the 1880's and 1890's. The Richardsonian suburban railway station still remains, with massive brownstone

Newton Center Baptist Church

and pudding stone walls, a great slate hip roof enlivened by eyebrow dormers and a wooden bracketed train shed along the tracks.

At the upper level opposite the station is a quite nice bit of English townscape dominated by a yellow brick block with a large slate roof and copper cornice. Farther north is what's left of the green: not much, now that parking has taken over.

On the southwest corner of Beacon and Center streets is a Baptist Church of 1885 designed by H. H. Richardson. This is deemed second-rate by Richardson scholars, but its exaggeratedly high polygonal tower and broad, low hovering gable mark their place with such energy and spirit that they bring this excursion to a fitting close.

B/THE EMERALD NECKLACE

To follow the path of the Emerald Necklace park system involves starting near Kenmore Square in a car and moving south and counterclockwise to the east along a network of parkways and drives. The starting point of the park system was initially Charlesbank Park, the first major park along the waterfront, located near the Charles Street Jail in an area which has now become dominated by the ramps and diversions of Storrow Drive as it passes under and connects with the Cambridge Street Bridge. The Esplanade now connects this area with Charlesgate at the end of Back Bay, where the Muddy River entered the Charles River Basin. As Back Bay was filled during the last half of the nineteenth century, the marshes became controlled and limited to the Back Bay Fens, a park laid out by Olmstead. The river wends its way back and forth across the Fens, which are a marvelously low-key park with tall marsh grasses, victory gardens and occasional recreational structures. Park Drive and the Fenway border its circumference. Beyond the park on either side are rows of apartments and flats, with a few grand town houses clustering near the intersection with Boylston Street. The Fenway side is replete with gates and sculpture, most notably at Westland and Boylston streets. But the most worthy structure in the park is an altogether beautiful stone bridge designed by H. H. Richardson in 1880 for the place where Boylston Street crosses the river.

The Fenway, opposite the Boston Museum of Fine Arts

Boston Museum of Fine Arts, Huntington Avenue entrance

At the opposite end of the Fenway and within sight of each other are two great Boston institutions, very unlike each other yet each a repository of the arts. The Boston Museum of Fine Arts is one of the nation's great museums. Its Indian and Chinese collections are exceptional (remnants, in part, of the clipper-ship trade), and there are ample opportunities to study the works of nineteenth-century America. The building, designed by Guy Lowell in 1907, is a second home; the first (now gone) was built in Copley Square. The building spans the area between Huntington Avenue and the Fenway, and its two sides are very different. On the Huntington Avenue side, the long, sprawling building is focused sharply on a central temple-front pavilion at the entrance, a front unparalleled for its antiquarian precision and formal sterility. The Fenway front, on the other hand, is a long, almost undifferentiated colonnade that stretches in front of window, wall and porch alike, with only a slight recession at the entry. To the southwest I. M. Pei & Partners have added a stone-clad, glass-topped wing that is neither recessive nor assertive, a comfortable cohabitant, despite its obviously subservient position.

Farther west along the Fenway is the Isabella Stewart Gardner Museum. Where the BMFA is distinguished but predictable, with rows of rooms, a grand central stair and permanent displays organized into clusters of rooms holding works of obvious stylistic affinity, the Gardner Museum is altogether different —a personal fantasy palace brought into being through one woman's determined, if quirky, patronage of the arts. From the outside the Gardner Museum is a large but unprepossessing, mildly ungainly box with a broad overhang. It sits matter-of-factly by the side of the road with a walled garden behind. The chief (and perverse) feature of the façade is a preposterous chimney that starts in the middle of the face but forks into a great Y just before the top floor to embrace a projecting bay. It's Venetian Gothic, we are told, but don't necessarily believe, designed by Willard T. Sears in 1902. Inside, however, we believe... The building surrounds a four-story glass-roofed courtyard with walls of pink stucco, detail most decidedly Venetian and a beautiful landscaped and mosaic-tiled terrace at the bottom. In the rooms that frame the courtyard above, the works of art are arranged as a private collector would arrange them (indeed, as Isabella Stewart Gardner did), with the personal pleasures of juxtaposition, the exercise of secret comparisons and pleasurable associations.

Beyond the Gardner Museum the Fenway loops away from Huntington Ave-

*Isabella Stewart Gardner Museum
courtyard*

nue toward the north, becoming Riverway as it follows the path of the river, which is here lined with trees, walks and bridges. The road leads back again to the southwest, crossing Huntington Avenue near Brookline Village, as it becomes the Jamaicaway.

In the triangle between Huntington Avenue and the bend in the parkways lies a collection of hospitals that is itself worth an extended analysis. The group includes Beth Israel Hospital, Children's Hospital, Boston Hospital for Women (Boston Lying-In), Peter Bent Brigham Hospital and the Harvard Medical School. All manner of building is found here, reflecting several generations of thoughts about and hopes for the nature of medical services and for the nature of architecture. Recently the hospitals of the area have formed a coordinated planning group that hopes to bring some semblance of purpose to the scattered plans of these various institutions, which each impinge on the other. But for the present the area is rather like a jungle populated by large, exotic and unrelated species.

The Jamaicaway moves southward toward Jamaica Pond along a broad, hilly stretch with several ponds that divide the rather densely packed, but often very pleasant, residential areas of Jamaica Plain from the extravagantly large estates, preserves and land tracts of the southern reaches of Brookline and Newton.

Jamaica Pond itself is a pleasant sailing basin with paths around its edges (used now for running) and a pavilion opposite Pond Street that is characteristic of the pleasantly breezy buildings that were built around the turn of the century in outlying park areas. A short distance beyond Jamaica Pond is the Arnold Arboretum, a large, beautiful acreage that is part of the Boston park system, though administered by Harvard University and funded by gifts and a private endowment. The arboretum is magnificently planted with a great variety of trees and bushes, and it publishes maps and guides, including a calendar of what you may expect to enjoy during the various seasons of the year, ranging from "forsythias, Cornelian cherry and daphne" in early April to "witch hazels, conifers, bark patterns and snow scenes" in midwinter.

The parkway, now the Arborway, leads on south and east toward Franklin Park, the final link in the chain of green. In between you get a real sense of the hilly landscape of the area, especially in crossing Washington Street on an overpass that affords a view through the valley to Boston along the roads and transit and rail lines that make up the southwest corridor. Franklin Park and the Forest Hills Cemetery are contiguous. Together they form a large landscape preserve. The park is characterized by large, rolling bucolic hills and meadows, occasional playing fields and, at its eastern extremity, the Franklin Park Zoo. The Emerald Necklace ends in Franklin Park, with the loop around the city incomplete.

Persistence in completing the loop would lead you down Columbia Road, through Upham's Corner with its small brick commercial center, a Masonic Hall and the Strand Theater, which has a marvelously misplaced white triumphal arch, and on toward Columbia Point, jutting into Dorchester Bay.

Columbia Point has a strange and ironic history as modern Boston's place of last resort and architectural experiment. The story starts with the placement here in the 1950's of a very large and repetitive brick public-housing project. It was doomed to failure as a decent place to live—isolated from any surrounding city, its buildings a monument to bureaucratic indifference, the spaces between buildings devoid of any genuine amenities. It was, quite obviously, a ghetto. Fail it did, on a massive scale, creating one of the most frequently troubled areas in the city.

In 1974 the state added another mammoth project to the area, this one a campus for the University of Massachusetts at Boston. It is a fortresslike collection of brick buildings on the south side of the point, which were designed to form a campus with distinct buildings but uniform overall character. It's an extraordinary, and mostly overbearing, assembly of brown-brick structures that create a multilevel world of their own—parking underneath, various bridges and glass linkages above and a continous underlying structural rhythm, though not one that swings much. Students commute here and stay in isolation.

On the far northeastern edge of Columbia Point, with the most dramatic view of the harbor, is the John F. Kennedy Library, by I. M. Pei & Partners, which was opened in 1979. The library too is here as a place of last resort. It was first planned in Cambridge, as part of the Kennedy School of Government at Harvard University, but the enlightened citizens of the already-crowded Harvard Square area saw the prestigious library as the source of a constant stream of additional visitors and traffic and opposed its construction. So the library was constructed at Columbia Point amid a lot of stirring talk about Kennedy's love for the sea and the sweeping vision of the New Frontier. Alas, the powerful motivating force of those Camelot years seems now so far away and lost that it appears only mildly strange to see it encapsulated in a large pristine jewel box oriented to the scenic view.

From here, though, as from nowhere else in the areas covered by this book, the vast flat extent of the sea can be seen beyond the shallow hills of the harbor islands; the majestic and terrifying emptiness that was crossed both by those who implanted the first buildings of Boston near Spring Lane and by those who swelled its population in the nineteenth century. For more than two centuries the sea dominated the economic life of Boston. Only with the opening of the rail lines and the pressures of overcrowding did the imagination of Boston turn toward the land. Nearly a century ago the Emerald Necklace of parks and parkways gave tangible form to this new imagination and did so with the scope and grace that derive from an integral and far-reaching vision.

INDEX

References in boldface type indicate pages where the specified subjects are discussed in full.

Aalto, Alvar, 184
Abbey, Edwin Austin, 167, 170
Abbot Lawrence Mansion, 24
Acorn Street, 73, **94**
Adams, Samuel, 23
African Methodist Episcopal Church, 113
Alberti, Leon Battista, 18
Alfred Wisniski Square, **82**
Algonquin Club, **141**
Allen, H. B., 151, 153, 154
Allen & Cullen, 145
Allen & Kenway, 177
Ambulatory Care Facility (Boston City Hospital), **209–10**
Ames, Frederick, 13–14, 133, 134, 182
Ames, Oliver, 13, 182
Ames Building, **13–14**, 29, 37, 182, 193, 264–65, 274
Ames Mansion, **182–83**
Ames Monument (Sherman, Wyo.), 14
Ames-Webster House, **133–34**
Amory, Thomas, 24
Amory-Ticknor Mansion, 23, **24**, 117
Anderson, Beckwith & Haible, 259
Anderson, Lawrence, 20
Anderson, Notter Associates, 10, 41, 58, 59, 63, 67, 68, 69, 206
Andrews, Jacques & Rantoul, 276

Andrews, Robert D., 24
Appleton Street, **219**
Arborway, 304
Architects Collaborative, The, 40, 196, 202, 228, 230, 257, 261, 288
Archplan, 212
Arch Street, 285–86, **287**
Arlington Street, 124, 187, 299
Arlington Street Church, 10, **143–44**
Arnold Arboretum, 14, 304
Arrowstreet, 180, 190, 296
"Art" (Pratt), 167
Artists for the Preservation of the Fenway Studios, 181
"Asaroton" (Harries), 47, **48**
Ashley, Myer & Associates, 179
Atlantic Avenue, 51, 62, 246
Atwood, Charles, 136
Atwood, Henry H., 198
Avery, George, 173, 174

Bachman, Max, 264
Back Bay, 110, 121–141, 161, 187, 223, 299, 302
Back Bay Fens, 302
Back Bay Racquet Club, **225**, 226
Back Bay Station, 161
Back Bay West, 173–84
Back Street, 73

Bailey's ice cream store, 287
Ball, H. B., 23
Ball, Thomas, 12, 123, 190
Ball & Dabney, 278
Baptist Church (Newton Center), 301
Barnes, Edward Larrabee, 36, 53
Bartholdi, Frédéric Auguste, 129
Bates Hall, 169
Batterymarch Building, 157, 278, **279**
Batterymarch Street, 266–80
Bay State Junior College, 107
Bay Village, 223–239
Bay Village streetscape, **228**
Beach Street, 239
Beacon Hill, 4, 21, 22, 25, 32, 33, 37, 90–117
Beacon Hill West, 110–17
Beaconsfield, 300
Beacon Street, 299, 300
Beal, C. R., 150
Bedford Block, 282, **283**
Bedford Building, 283
Bedford Street, 281
Beebe Building, **242–43**
Bellingham Place, **108**
Bellows, Aldrich & J. A. Holt, 100
Belluschi, Pietro, 18, 127, 196, 257
Belluschi, Tony, 41
Beman, Solon S., 198
Benjamin, Asher, 86, 94, 100, 113, 233

Benjamin Franklin statue (Greenough), 11
Benjamin Thompson Associates, 48
Bennett, J. E., 152
Bennett, John, 109
Bergmeyer, Moritz, 66, 69
Berkeley Building, 142, **147–49, 234**
Berkeley Residence Club, 220
Besarick, J. H., 135, 177, 242, 280
Beth Israel Hospital, 304
B. F. Keith Memorial Theater, 239
Bigelow, Henry Forbes, 29
Bigelow & Wadsworth, 292
Blackall, Clapp & Whittenmore, 234
Blackall, Clarence H., 14, 15, 16, 171, 233, 235, 236, 238
Blackstone Block, 34, 43, **45–48**
Blackstone School, **216**
Blackstone Street, 47
Blake Building, **294,** 295
Blaxton, William, 4
Blue Diner, 241
Board of Trade Building, 194, 268, **271–72,** 274
Bond, Richard, 66
Bonwit Teller, **146–47**
Boston & Albany Railroad, 187
Boston & Providence station, 187
Boston & Worcester, Railway, 240
Boston Architectural Center, 20, **179–80**
Boston Architectural Team, 212, 220
Boston Art Club, 13, 155, 156, 226–27
Boston Athenaeum, 20, 22, 28, **29–30,** 96, 176, 292
Boston Bar Association, 28
Boston Bicycle Club, 156
Boston Blue Print, 160
Boston Center Architects, 196
Boston Center for the Arts, **218–19**
Boston City Hall, 20, **34–36,** 37, 41, 42, 43

Boston City Hospital, **209–11,** 231
Boston College, 122, 211
Boston Company Building, **18–19**
Boston Consolidated Gas Company, 227
Boston Downtown Center (University of Massachusetts), 227
Boston Edison Company Powerhouse, **241,** 242
Boston English High School, 107
Boston Evening Clinic, **178–79**
Boston Fire Museum, 247
Boston Five Cents Savings Bank, **19–20,** 34, 42
Boston *Globe,* 6
Boston Hospital for Women (Boston Lying-In), 304
Bostonian Society, 6
Boston Library Society, 8
Boston Massacre, 5, 266
Boston Music Company, **236**
Boston Opera Company, 238
Boston Opera House, 238
Boston *Post,* 12
Boston Post Building, **12**
Boston Post Office Building and Federal Building, 43, 258, 262, **265**
Boston Public Library, 24, **76–77,** 146, 161, 162, **166–70,** 178, 180, 235–36, 238, 278
Boston Public Library Addition, **170–71**
Boston Redevelopment Authority, 16, 33, 51, 84, 195, 216, 228
Boston Safe Deposit Building, **285–86**
Boston Society of Architects, 176, 193, 195
Boston Stock Exchange, 267, **270,** 272, 279
Boston Stone, 48
Boston Tea Party, 6
Boston Tea Party Museum, **244–45**
Boston Tea Party ship, 244, 245, 246

Boston Tea Party Shuttle, 244
Boston *Transcript,* 12
Boston Transcript Building, 12
Boston University, 28, 122
Boston University School of Theology, 96
Boston Wharf Company Buildings, **248–50**
Bosworth, Welles, 184
Bourne, Frank, 110
Bowditch, A. H., 292, 294
Bowditch & Stratton, 291
Bowdoin School Building, 108
Bowdoin Square, 73
Boyden, E. N., 137
Boylston Building, **237–40**
Boylston Market, 238
Boylston Street, 121, 142–60, 161, 187, 299, 302
Bradlee, Nathaniel J., 218, 237, 285, 286, 294
Bradlee, Winslow & Wetherell, 12
Bradlee & Winslow, 131, 271
Bramante, Donato d'Agnolo, 170
Branner, Peter, 22
Brazer Building, 43, 126, **268,** 269
Brewer Fountain, 296
Brigham, Charles E., 24, 26, 178, 198, 199, 236
Brigham, Coveney & Bisbee, 198
Brimmer Street, 110, 114–15
Broad Street, 266–80, **279**
Broad Street Association, 267
Brookline, 299, 304
Brookline Village, 300, 304
Brookline Village Walking Tours (Floyd), 300
Brooks, Phillips, 161, 165
Brooks Brothers, 142
Bryant, Gridley J. Fox, 10, 12, 26, 61, 88, 108, 123, 127, 209, 219, 273
Bulfinch, Charles, 7, 8, 22, 23, 24, 25, 32, 41, 42, 45, 49, 53, 55, 73, 78, 82, 86–88, 95–96, 97, 99–100, 101, 103, 109, 267, 274, 287, 295

Bulfinch Pavilion, **87–88,**
107
Bulfinch State House, *see*
State House
Bullerjahn Associates, 96,
100
Bunker Hill Movement, 81,
109
Bunting, Bainbridge, 121
Burnham, Daniel, 291, 292

Cabot, Edward Clarke, 29,
176
Cabot & Chandler, 175
Caldwell, Sarah, 238
Cambridge Seven, 56, 233,
246
Cambridge Street, 73
Cambridge Street Bridge,
302
Canal Street, 73, **83**
Cancelleria, 170
Capital Bank Building, **41**
Carlin & Pozzi, 225
Carl Koch & Associates,
66, 67, 76
Caro, Anthony, 199
Castle Square Housing, 221
Catalano, Eduardo, 37, 184
Causeway Street, 73
Center Building, 45
Central and Long Wharf
views, **57–58**
Central Wharf, 8, 49, 55,
56, 267, **274–75**
Chadwick Lead Works,
243, **279–80**
Chandler, Joseph E., 4, 74
Chapman, William, 24
Charlesgate Park, 182, 302
Charles Hilgenhurst &
Associates, 191
Charles Luckman &
Associates, 196
Charles Playhouse, 231,
233
Charles River, 82, 110, 182
Charles River Basin, 182,
184, 302
Charles River Square,
110–11, 112, 116
Charles Street, **112–13,** 114
Charles Street Jail, **88–89,**
302
Charles Street Meeting
House, The, **113,** 114

Charlestown, 3, 81
Charlestown Naval Yard,
81
Charlestown Savings Bank,
288
Chart House Restaurant,
59
Chester Harding House,
28–29
Chestnut Hill Reservoir,
300
Chestnut Street, 94, **98–99**
Chickering piano factory,
206, 212
Children's Hospital, 304
Children's Museum, 187,
245, **246–47**
Childs, Bertman, Tseckares
Associates, 133, 158, 284
Chinatown, **239,** 240
Christ Church, 299
Christ Church (Old North),
80–81
Christian Science Center,
193, **198–202,** 227
Christopher Columbus
Waterfront Park, **59–60,**
62
Churchill, Chester Lindsay,
192
Church of St. John the
Evangelist, **109**
Church of the Advent, 110,
114–15
Church of the Covenant,
150
Church of the Immaculate
Conception, **211**
Church Park Apartments,
202–3
City Hall Plaza, **33–34,** 35,
40, 43
City Signs and Lights
Project, 190–91
Civil War, 27
Claflin Building, **28**
Clark, Thomas W., 158
Clark, T. M., 225
Cleveland Circle, 300
Clough, George A., 4, 39
Codman, Stephen, 83
Codman & Despredelle, 147
Collins, John, 33, 34
Colonial Building, **235**
Colonial Theatre, **235–36**
Colonnade Building, 202
Colonnade Hotel, **197–98**

Columbian Exposition, 264,
287
Columbian National Life
Insurance Building, **287**
Columbia Point, 305
Columbus Avenue, 223
Columbus Plaza Elderly
Housing, **61–62**
Commercial Street, **64–65,**
81
Commercial Wharf, 49, 60,
61, **62–63**
Commercial Wharf North,
63–64
Commercial Wharf West,
62, **63–64**
Committee on Civic
Design, 187
Common, 21–22, 32
Commonwealth Avenue,
121–41, 173, 187, 299
Commonwealth Avenue
Mall, 121
Congregational House, **29,**
194
Congregational Society, 78
Congress Street, 43, 255
Congress Street Bridge,
244, 245, 247
Congress Street Firehouse,
247
Coolidge, Cornelius, 94, 97,
99, 105
Coolidge & Carlson, **110–
11**
Coolidge & Shattuck, 30,
277
Coolidge House, 175
Copley Plaza Hotel, 161,
162, **171–72**
Copley Plaza Hotel Annex,
183
Copley Society, 157
Copley Square, 161–72, 299,
303
Copley Square Plaza, **172**
Copp's Hill, 73, 81
Copp's Hill Burying
Ground, **81**
Copp's Hill Terrace, **81**
Corner, The, 291, **292,** 293
Cortes Street, **224**
Cossuta & Ponte
Associated Architects,
198
Coulton Building, 142,
149–50

Cram, Ralph Adams, 115, 180, 193, 295
Cram & Ferguson, 147, 193, 262, 265
Creek Square, 47
Cret, Paul, 263
Crowninshield House, 134–35, 238
Cugini, Gerald, 65
Cummings, Charles A., 152, 154
Cummings & Sears, 131, 137, 152, 165, 218–19, 283, 286
Cunard Building, 268, 270, 271
Cunard Steamship Line, 271
Custom House, 33, 267, 272–73
Custom House Block, 58–59, 62
Custom House Tower, 57–58
Cyclorama, 218–19

Dallin, Cyrus E., 80
Daniel H. Burnham & Co., 291
Daniel Webster painting, 46
Dartmouth Place, 219–20
Delivery Room, 169–70
Delue, Donald, 196
Densmore, LeClear & Robbins, 41, 191
Densmore & LeClear, 191
Desgranges & Steffian, 112
Desmond & Lord, 18, 39
Despredelle, 147
Dewey Square, 257
Dinsmoor, William, 95
Doane, Ralph Harrington, 17, 177, 190, 198
Dock Square, 51
Domino House Project, 261
Don Bosco Technical High School, 229–30
Don Stull Associates, 38, 207, 208, 216
Dorchester Bay, 305
Doric Hall, 27
Dover Station, 221–22
Downtown Crossing, 282, 293
Drisco, A. S., 224

Driscoll Building, 159
Durgin Park Restaurant, 50
Dyer Brown Associates, 246

Ebenezer Hancock House, 48
Eddy, Mary Baker, 198, 199
Edward Everett Hale statue (Pratt), 123
8, 10 Fairfield Street, 175–76
80 Commonwealth Avenue, 127–28
87 Mt. Vernon Street, 95
88 Exeter Street, 158–59
89 Mt. Vernon Street, 95
89–93 Franklin Street, 284, 285
"Emancipation Group" (Ball), 190
Emerald Necklace Park, 182, 299, 302–5
Emerson, William Ralph, 106, 155–56, 209, 226, 284
Emery Roth & Sons, 18
Emmanuel Episcopal Church, 145, 214
Endicott Street, 82
Engine and Hose House No. 33, 180–81
Esplanade, 110–17, 177, 184, 302
Essex Street, 240
Estey, A. R., 145, 214
Exchange Club, 278
Exchange Coffee House, 266, 278
Executive Office Building (Washington, D.C.), 11
Exeter Street Theatre, 158
Exeter Towers, 157

Fairfield Street, 173
Faneuil, Peter, 23
Faneuil Hall, 33–34, 38, 43, 45–46, 51, 103, 264, 266
Faneuil Hall Markets, 12, 33–34, 43–45, 48–50, 64, 88, 191, 260, 266
F. A. O. Schwartz, 142
F. A. Stahl & Associates, 262
Faxon, J. L., 155

Federal Reserve Bank, 240, 244, 255, 256–57, 258, 263, 282
Federal Street, 255
Fehmer, Carl, 182, 237, 268, 275, 284
Fenway Park, 299
Fenway Studios, 181
Fiduciary Trust Building, 257, 258
Fields Butcher, 48
15 Beacon Street, 30–31
50–54 Broad Street, 274, 275
50–58 Brimmer Street, 115–16
51, 53 Mt. Vernon Street, 97
54 Kilby Street, 276–77
54, 55 Beacon Street, 100–101
55 Kilby Street, 276–77
56, 57 Beacon Street, 100–101
57 Hancock Street, 108
57 Mt. Vernon Street, 97
Filene's Department Store, 190, 282, 291–92
Firehouse, 225
First and Second Church in Boston, 125–27
First Baptist Church, 20, 129–30, 134, 150
First Corps Cadet Armory, 199, 225–27, 280
first Harrison Gray Otis House, 8, 25, 45, 86–87
first John Hancock Building, 147, 187, 193
First Lutheran Church, 127
First National Bank of Boston, 43, 255, 259, 263
First Spiritual Temple, 158
Fisher, R. A., 115, 116
Fitzgerald Expressway, 51, 73, 240
5 Causeway Street, 83–84, 242
550–62 Tremont Street, 219
Fletcher, Robert, 28
Flour and Grain Exchange Building (Boston Chamber of Commerce), 55, 267, 268, 274–75, 277, 285
Floyd, Margaret Henderson, 300

Forest Hills Cemetery, 305
Fort Hill, 246, 267
Fort Point Channel, 240,
    244, **245–46**, 282
14 Walnut Street, **97–98**
40 Isabella Street (former
    Hotel Clifford), **224**
40–46 Summer Street, **288**,
    289
41 Brimmer Street, **115**
42, 43 Beacon Street, **102–
    103**, 178
44 Kilby Street, **276–77**
45 Broad Street, **275–76**
45 Milk Street, **287**
45 Newbury Street, **150–51**
421, 423 Marlborough
    Street, **183**
425, 427, 429 Marlborough
    Street, **183**
Franklin, Benjamin, 12, 13,
    46
Franklin Park, 304–5
Franklin Park Zoo, 305
Franklin Place, 8
Franklin Square House, **212**
Franklin Street, 8, 41, 281
Freedom Trail, 75
French, Daniel Chester, 167
French Revolution, 276
Frink, Allen, 242
Frog Pond, 21
Fulmer & Bowers, 41

Gardner, Isabella Stewart,
    303
Gardner Building, **59**
Garrison, William Lloyd,
    136–37
Gelardin/Bruner/Cott, 206
"Genius of America, The,"
    21
George Washington statue
    (Ball), 123
Gibbs, James, 144
Gilbert, Cass, 268
Gilchrist's Department
    Store, 291, 292, 293
Gilman, Arthur, 10, 11, 89,
    123–24, 127, 143, 211, 273
Glazer, De Castro, Vitols,
    212
Goodhue, Bertram, 115
Goodspeed's Bookshop, 7,
    28
Goodwin Place, **108**

Government Center, 16,
    32–42, 255, 299
Government Center
    Garage, **42**, 43, 73, 83
Government Center
    redevelopment project,
    17, 33
Graham, Thomas P. R., 16
Graham Gund Associates,
    180
Graham-Meus, 225
Granary, 22
Granary Burial Ground,
    22–23, 29
Great Fire of 1872, 8, 12
Greenough, Richard S., 11
Gropius, Walter, 40, 196
Gund, Graham, 184, 198
Gwathmey/Siegel, 145

Haas, Richard, 179, 180
Haddon Hall, 124, **125**, 182
Halasz, Anthony, 300
Halasz, Imre, 130, 300
Halasz & Halasz, 62, 63,
    130, 150, 151, 229
Hall, John R., 212
Hall of Flags, 27
Hamilton, Alexander, 263
Hammett & Joseph
    Billings, 9
Hammond Pond Park, 300
Hancock, John, 23, 46
Hancock, The, **109**
Hancock Place, 120, 130,
    146, 161, 162, 163, **193**,
    194–95, 228, 256, 272,
    299
Hancock Street, 109
Handbook of Boston
    (King), 12, 237
Hanover Street, **75–76**
Harbor Tower Apartments,
    53–54, 55, 60
Hardenbergh, Henry, 171
Hardy, Holzman & Pfeiffer,
    227
Hark Beef, 48
Harries, Mags, 47, 48
Harriet Tubman House,
    208
Harrison, Peter, 7
Harrison Street, 240
Hartwell, H. W., 103, 158,
    224, 242
Harvard Bridge, **184**

Harvard Graduate School
    of Design, 40
Harvard Medical School,
    304
Harvard Square, 305
Harvard University, 304
Hayden Building, **238**
Health, Welfare and
    Education Service Center
    for the Commonwealth
    of Massachusetts, **84–85**
Hearthstone Plaza
    Building, 300
Hemenway Building, **12–13**
Hereford Street, **173**
Herter, Albert, 27
High Spine, 187–204
Holmes, William, 77
Holy Ghost Chapel of the
    Paulist Fathers, 24
Home Owners Federal
    Savings Bank, 18
Homes Savings Bank, 37
Horticultural Hall, **203–4**
Hotel Bostonian, 48
Hotel Cambridge, **183**
Hotel Charlesgate, 174, **182**,
    183
Hotel Isabella, **224**
Hotel Sheraton, 196
Hotel Vendome, 121, 128,
    132–33
Hotel Victoria, **155**, 159
Hotel Westminster, 195
House of Representatives, 27
Howard, John Galen, 233
Howe & Bainbridge, Inc.,
    65
Hoyle, Doran & Berry, 41,
    197, 262
H. P. Hood Company, 245
Hub, 51, 299
Hugh Stubbins &
    Associates, 176, 256, 262
Huntington Avenue, 161,
    303–4
Hutchinson Building,
    17–18, 190
Hyatt Hotel, 184

I. M. Pei & Partners, 33,
    53, 162, 193, 198, 303, 305
India Street, 51, 55, 268
India Wharf, 51, 55, 267
India Wharf Harbor views,
    55

"India Wharf Project" (von Schlegell), **54–55**
Institute of Contemporary Art **180–81**
International Trust Company Building, **264–65**
Irving Salsberg & Associates, 197
Isabella Stewart Gardner Museum, 303, 304
Isabella Street, **224**

Jackson, F. H., 177
Jacobs, G. N., 130
Jacob Wirth's, **231–32**
Jamaica Plain, 304
Jamaica Pond, 304
Jamaicaway, 304
James, Thomas, 23, 24, 233, 260
James Hooking Lobster Company, 246
J. C. Hilary's, 160
John B. Hynes Civic Auditorium, **197**
John F. Kennedy Federal Building, 34, **40–41**
John F. Kennedy Library, 305
John Hancock Mutual Life Insurance Buildings, 146, 147, 161, 162, 163, 187, **193–95**, 228, 256, 262, 265, 272, 299
John Hancock Tower, 120, 130, 146, 161, 162, 163, **193, 194–95**, 228, 256, 272, 299
John Sharatt and Associates, 61, 215
Johnson, Philip, 162, 170
Jordan Marsh Department Store, 282, 288
Joshua Bates School, **211**
Josiah Quincy statue (Ball), 11, 12
Josiah Quincy Community School, **228–29**, 230, 231
Jung-Brannan Associates, 228, 229, 263

Kahn, Louis, 30, 42
Kallman, McKinnell & Knowles, 34, 35

Kallman & McKinnell, 19, 20, 33, 42
Katherine Gibbs School, 123
Keely, Patrick C., 211
Kelley, James T., 140
Kelley, S. D., 137, 152, 173, 183
Kellogg, Henry, 279
Kendall & Stevens, 207
Kenmore Square, 39, 122, 299, 302
Kennedy School of Government at Harvard University, 305
Kepes, Gyorgy, 109
Kessler, S. J., 128
Keyes, Henry F., 250
Keystone Building, 255, **257**
Kidder, Franklin E., 241
Kilham, Hopkins, Greeley & Brodin, 220
Kilham, Walter, 273
Kilham & Hopkins, 159
King's Chapel, **7**, 25
Kirstein Business Branch, Boston Public Library, 7, **8**, 104
Kitson, Henry Hudson, 132
Kitson, Theo Alice Ruggles, 132
Knoll Showroom, 142, **145**
Koch, Carl, 196
Koch, Ruth Chamberlain, 67

La Crêpe Restaurant, 159
La Farge, John, 165
Lafayette Mall, **296**
Lamb, Thomas, 238
Langer, Suzanne, 54
Laver, Lance, 272
Lawrence Street, **219–20**
Leather District, 240
Le Corbusier, 261
Leif Ericsson statue (Whitney), **181–82**
Le Messurier & Associates, 262
Lever House (New York City), 193
Lewis, G. Wilton, 173, 174, 175
Lewis, W. Whitney, 138
Lewis Wharf, **66–67**

Liberty Mutual Insurance Company, **192**
Liberty Square, **276–77**
Lincoln, Abraham, 190
Lincoln Building, **241–42**
Lincoln Filene Park, **289**
Linder, Lawrence A., 300
Little Building, **234–35**
Locke-Ober's, **292–93**
Lodge, The, 152
Loeb, Rhodes, Hornblower & Co., **261**
Logan Airport, 55
Logue, Edward, 33
Longfellow, Alexander Wadsworth, 221
Longfellow, Henry Wadsworth, 80
Long Lane Meeting House, 260
Long Wharf, 53, 58, 266
Longwood, 299
Longwood Mall, 299
Longwood Tennis Club, 300
Longwood Towers, 299
Lord and Taylor, 196
Louisburg Square, 39, **91–92**, 93
Louis Philippe (king of France), 46
Lowell, Guy, 303
Luce, Clarence, 114, 247
Lynch, Kevin, 33

McGinnis, Walsh & Sullivan, 78
McKim, Charles, 165, 170
McKim, Mead & White, 140, 141, 162, 166, 173, 178, 180, 203, 204, 238
McLaughlin Building, **66,** 82
McNeely, James, 109
Magic Pan Crêperie, 151
Maginnis, Charles D., 163
Maginnis & Walsh, 23
Margin Street, 73, 82
Market Street, 73
Marlborough, The, **183**
Marlborough Street, 121
Marsh, Ephraim, 100, 228
Marshall Field Warehouse (Chicago, Ill.), 83, 238, 280
Marshall Street, 47

Mason family, 97
Massachusetts General
    Hospital, 8, **87–88**, 107,
    209, 295
Massachusetts Historical
    Society, 8
Massachusetts
    Homeopathic Hospital,
    209–11
Massachusetts Housing
    Finance Authority, 206
Massachusetts Institute of
    Technology (MIT), 146,
    161, 162, 184, 187
Massachusetts Turnpike,
    161
May, Henrietta, 77
Meacham, George F., 122,
    156
Mercantile Wharf, 49, **61**
Merrimac Street, 73
Mill Creek, 47
Mill Pond, 26, 42
Ministries Building
    Addition, **22**
Mintz, Sy, 48
Mintz Associates, 61, 250
Mitchell/Giurgola
    Associates, 214, 282
Modern Theater, **238–39**
Monadnock Building
    (Chicago, Ill.), 14
Monks & Johnson, 250
Monmouth Court, 300
Moon Lane, 279
Moore, F. H., 152
Moses Pierce-Hichborn
    House, **74–75**
Motor Mart Garage, **190**,
    198
Mt. Vernon Square, **114**
Mt. Vernon Street, **97**, 115
Muddy River, 182, 299,
    302
Mullett, A. B., 11
Museum of Fine Arts, 146,
    161, 162, 302, 303
Museum of Natural
    History, 146, 161, 279
Museum Wharf, **246–47**
Myer, Jack, 33
Mystic River, 82

National Peace Jubilee, 161
National Shawmut Bank,
    261–62

New Bedford Iron
    Foundry, 248
Newbury Street, 121,
    142–60, **156–57**, 173
Newcastle Court, **207–8**
New England Aquarium,
    55, **56–57**, 274
New England Conservatory
    of Music, 212
New England Fish
    Exchange, 250, 251, 267
New England Fish Pier,
    250–51, 267
New England Merchants
    Bank Building, **36**, 37,
    43, 46, 53, 268
New England Mutual Life
    Insurance Building, 147
New England Telephone
    and Telegraph Company
    Building, 40, **41**, 42
New England Telephone
    Headquarters Building,
    262, 265
New Old South Church,
    152, **165–66**, 286
Newton, George F., 16
Newton Center, 300–301,
    304
Nichols House, **97**
19–43 Kingston Street, **284**
90 Commonwealth Avenue,
    130–31
90–102 Mt. Vernon Street,
    93
97 Newbury Street, **151**
No Name Restaurant, 251
North and South Market
    Buildings, 43, 45, 49–50
North Bennet, Street
    Bathhouse, **78**, 79
North Cove, 73
North End, 73–89
Northern Avenue Bridge,
    246
North Square, **74–75**
North Station, 51, 73, 83
North Street, 73, 75
Nursing Education and
    Dormitory (Boston City
    Hospital), 209

Ober, J. F., 128, 132
Old City Hall, **10–12**, 16,
    39, 124, 143, 146, 212, 219,
    273, 282

Old City Hall Annex
    (Boston School
    Committee Building), 15,
    16–17, 39, 233
Old Corner Book Store, 6
Old Federal Reserve Bank,
    263
Old South Building, **16**,
    294
Old South Meeting House,
    6–7, 25, 127, 166, 205,
    282
Old State House, 2, **4–6**, 8,
    25, 27, 39, 43, 58, 266,
    282
Old West Church, **86**, 113
Olmstead, Frederick Law,
    182, 299, 302
1 Beacon Street, **30–31**
One Center Plaza, 34, 39
1–5 Joy Street, **105**, 106
1–12 Arlington Street, **123**
1–23 Pinckney Street, **106**
One Winthrop Square, 282,
    284–85
100 Summer Street, 258,
    282
101 Huntington Avenue, 196
109 Newbury Street, 152, 154
111 Franklin Street, **260**
113–23 Newbury Street,
    152–53
115–125 Commonwealth
    Avenue, **131–32**
116–28 Lincoln Street,
    241–42
121–23 South Street, **242–43**
128–34 Newbury Street, **154**
137 South Street, **242–43**
137–41 Newbury Street, **153**
141 Tremont Street, **295**
143–45 Newbury Street, **153**
145 South Street, **242–43**,
    280
147 Newbury Street, **154**,
    155
150 State Street, 271
165 Commonwealth Avenue,
    137
165 Marlborough Street,
    135
167 Commonwealth Avenue,
    137
170–74 Portland Street,
    83–84
172 Commonwealth Avenue,
    135–36, 177

175 Berkeley Street, 146, 187, **193–94,** 262, 265
176, 178 Commonwealth Avenue, **136**
179 Lincoln Street, **241–42**
180 Beacon Street, **128–29**
195 Commonwealth Avenue, **139–40,** 182
196 Marlborough Street, **138–39,** 175
199 Commonwealth Avenue, **140,** 152
199 Marlborough Street, **137–38**
Otis, Harrison Gray, 25–26, 87, 93, 96, 102
Otis Place, **115–16**

Paine Furniture Building, **191–92**
Paine Memorial Building, **220**
Park Drive, 302
Parker, J. Harleston, 193
Parker, Thomas & Rice, 19, 147, 181, 193, 227, 287
Parker & Thomas, 197
Parker House Hotel, **18**
parking garage, 287, 289
Park Plaza Hotel, **189–90,** 226, 227
Park Square, 142, 187, **190–91,** 223
Park Square Building, 190, **191**
Park Street, **23–24,** 299
Park Street Church, **22,** 23, 143
Park Street subway station, 282, **296**
Park Street subway station kiosks, **296**
Parris, Alexander, 43, 48, 49, 88, 102–3, 105, 109, 178, 260, 295
Patrick Andrew Collins Memorial (Kitson & Kitson), 120, **132**
Paul Revere statue (Dallin), 80
Paul Revere House, **74–75**
Paul Revere Mall, 78, **79–80**
Payette Associates, 224, 225
Payne, William, 4

Peabody, Robert Swain, 221
Peabody & Stearns, 12, 48, 96, 125, 133, 140, 150, 154, 187, 267, 270, 272–73
Pearl Street Associates, 262
Pei, I. M., 33, 35, 184, 198, 200
Pemberton Hill, 39
Pemberton Square, **39**
Pennell, H. B., 235, 236
Perkins, G. Holmes, 28
Perkins House, 294
Perkins School, **198**
Perry, Dean, Stahl & Rogers, 230
Perry, Dean & Stewart, 192
Peter Bent Brigham Hospital, 304
Phillips Brooks statue (Saint-Gaudens), **165,** 172
Piano Craft Guild, **206–7,** 212
Piano Row, 236
Pinckney Street, 100, **107**
Plaza Hotel (New York City), 162, 171
Pond Street, 304
Pope, Fred, 151
Portland Street, 82
Post, George B., 189
Power House, 69
Powers Court, 70
Pratt, Bela, 123, 167
Preston, Henry, 292, 293
Preston, William Gibbons, 28, 30, 131, 132, 146, 147, 199, 225, 243, 264–65, 279
Price, William, 80
Prince Building, **67–68**
Prince Macaroni Company, 67–68
Procter Building, **283–84**
Provident Institution for Savings, **293–94**
Province House, 9
Province Street, **9**
Prudential Apartments, 196
Prudential Building, 157, 196
Prudential Center, 161, 187, **196–97,** 216
Prudential Tower, 196, 228, 299
Public Garden, 110, **122–23**
Purdon, James, 293, 294

Putnam, J. Pickering, 125, 139, 154, 182, 300
Putnam & Cox, 8, 104
Puvis de Chavannes, Pierre, 167, 169

"Quest Eternal" (Delue), 196
Quincy, Josiah, 11–12, 34, 43, 48–49
Quincy Market, see Faneuil Hall Markets
Quincy Market Building, 44
Quincy Tower, **228–29**

Ramsey, Gilbert Miles, 48
Rand & Taylor, 109, 207, 242
Rantoul, William, 178
Rapson, DeMars, Kennedy & Brown, 184
Raymond Cattle Company, 158
Revere, Paul, 23, 37, 75, 81
Revivers of the Modern Theater, 239
Rex Allen Associates, 209
Richards Building, **270–71**
Richardson, H. H., 13, 14, 83, 129, 134, 138, 150, 151, 155, 161–65, 211, 224, 226, 238, 242, 264, 280, 300, 301, 302
Richardson, W. C., 103, 158, 224
Ritz-Carlton Hotel, 123, 142, **144–45**
River House, **112**
River Street Place, **114**
Riverway, 304
RKO General Building, **41–42**
Robert Burns statue, 285
Rogers, Isaiah, 4, 58, 62, 63
Rogers Building, 147
Rollins Place, **108**
Rotch & Tilden, 125, 182
Roth, Emery, 257
Rouse Company, 43
Roxbury Mill Corporation, 121
Rudolph, Paul, 84, 125, 126, 259
Ruskin, John, 161, 237, 283

Rusty Scupper Restaurant, 64
Ruth Harmony Green Hall of Toys, 247
Rutland Square, 212–13

Safford, M. D., 246, 248
St. Botolph Club, 140
St. Cloud Hotel, 217, 218, 286
Saint-Gaudens, Augustus, 165, 167
St. Germaine Street, 203
St. James Hotel, 212
St. Leonard's Church, 77–78
St. Martin's-in-the-Fields, 144
St. Paul's Cathedral, 295
St. Stephen's Church, 8, 75–76, 78–79, 80, 113
Saks Fifth Avenue, 196
Salem Street, 73, 76
Salsberg, Irving, 277
Samuel Appleton Building, 277–78, 285
Samuel Glaser & Partners, 42, 209, 221
Samuel Glaser Associates, 40
Sanborn, Greenleaf C., 231
Sankey milk company, 245
San Sebastiano at Mantua (Alberti), 18
Saranac Building, 207–8
Sargent, John Singer, 167, 170
Sasaki, Dawson & Demay, 172
Sasaki Associates, 59, 203, 288
Savoy Theater, 238–39
Saxon Theatre, 232, 233
Schrafft's Restaurant, 147
"Science" (Pratt), 167
Scott's Lane, 47
Seafood Grotto, 159
Sears, David, 103, 299
Sears, Willard T., 183, 241, 303
Sears Block, 38–39, 277
Sears Crescent, 33, 38
second Harrison Gray Otis House, 8, 87, 95, 96
second John Hancock Building, 146, 187, 193–94, 262, 265

Senate Chamber, 27
Senate Reception Room, 27
Senate Staircase Hall, 27
Sentry Hill Place, 108
Sert, Jackson Associates, 184
7–11 Beacon Street, 30–31, 277
70 Federal Street, 261
70, 72 Mt. Vernon Street, 96
70–75 Beacon Street, 117
74 Franklin Street, 286–87
77 Newbury Street, 150–51
715 Boylston Street, 159
715–25 Tremont Street, 212–13
739 Boylston Street, 159
777 Boylston Street, 159–60
Shaw, Jessie, 93
Shawmut Peninsula, 3, 4, 81, 205, 245
Shepley, Bulfinch, Richardson & Abbott, 84, 147, 163, 293
Shepley, Rutan & Coolidge, 13, 14, 29, 163, 243, 274, 285, 300
Shubert Theatre, 232, 233–34
Shurcliff, Arthur, 79, 182
6 Joy Street, 105
16 North Street, 48
60 State Street, 43, 269–70
60–62 Congress Street (Hornblower and Weeks Building), 276–77
61 Beacon Street, 100–101
63, 64 Beacon Street, 100–101
69–77 Monmouth Street, 300
676–92 Tremont Street, 212
Skidmore, Owings & Merrill, 30, 144, 269
Smibert, John, 45
Smith, O. F., 183
Snell & Gregerson, 23, 135
Society for Human and Spiritual Understanding, 158
Society for the Preservation of New England Antiquities, 163
Somerset Club, 102–3, 264
South Boston, 245
South Cove, 245

South Cove Associates, 240
South End, 205–22
South End Branch Library, 214
South Station, 51, 240–51, 257, 282
South Station Headhouse, 243–44
Spring Lane, 3
S. S. Pierce store, 12
Stahl Associates, 261
Stahl/Bennett, 22, 38, 132
State, War and Navy Building (Washington, D.C.), 11
State House, 21, 22, 23, 24–27, 39, 199, 236, 255, 282
State Office Building, 25
State Street, 58, 266–80
State Street Bank, 246, 257, 262
State Street block, 49, 267, 273, 274, 286
Statler Office Building, 189–90
Steffian Bradley Associates, 157
Steinert Building, 236
Stimson, Louise, 77
Storrow Memorial Drive, 110, 302
Stowell's Jewelry, 292–93
Strand Theater, 305
Stratton, E. B., 154
Strickland & Blodgett, 123, 144
Stubbins, Hugh, 176, 184, 196
Sturgis, John, 114, 115, 133
Sturgis, R. Clipston, 24, 263
Sturgis & Brigham, 114, 137, 150, 161, 175, 276, 277
Suffolk County Court House, 39–40
Sullivan, Louis, 84, 224, 259
Summer Street, 257, 281–96
Sunflower Castle, 114, 247
Sunoco gas station, 68–69
Swan, Hepzibah, 99
Swan Boats, 122, 123, 147
Symphony Hall, 203–4, 236, 238

Teledyne Corporation, 242
Temple Place, 294

Tennis and Racquet Club,
  197
10 Woodman Road, 300
Termini, Maria, 229
Thayer, S. J. F., 103
Third Baptist Church, 113
third Harrison Gray Otis
  House (American
  Meteorological Society),
  8, 87, 96, **101–2**
third John Hancock
  Building, 120, 130, 146,
  161, 162, 163, **193–95**, 228,
  256, 272, 299
13–17, 18 Chestnut Street,
  99
32 Hereford Street, **178**
33–39 Hancock Street, **109**
34 Hancock Street, **109**
35–37 Winchester Street,
  226, **227**
36 Pinckney Street, **107**
37 Temple Place, **293–94**
303 Commonwealth
  Avenue, **178**, 179
311 Summer Street, **248–50**
315 Dartmouth Street, 133,
  134
326–28 Dartmouth Street,
  135
330 Beacon Street, **176**
332 Congress Street,
  248–49
346 Beacon Street, **177**
347 Beacon Street, **177**
348 Beacon Street, **177**
348 Congress Street,
  248–49
354 Congress Street,
  248–49
358–92 Beacon Street,
  177–78, 190
363 Beacon Street, **177**
368 Congress Street,
  248–49
Ticknor, George, 24
Tilden, George, 300
Tontine Crescent, 8, 39,
  285, 287
Town Cove, 4, 51, 64
Transportation Museum,
  187, **246–47**
Tremont Street, 4, 208, 212
Tremont Temple, **16**
Trimountain, 4, 282
Trinity Church, 20, 134, 161,
  162, **163–65**, 166, 194, 195

Trinity Rectory, **151**
Tudor, The, **103–4**
Tufts New England
  Medical Center, 223, 228,
  230–31
12 Fairfield Street, **175–76**
Twelves, Robert, 6
12 Winter Street, **292–93**
20 Fairfield Street, **175**
20–36 Commonwealth
  Avenue, **123–24**
21 Fairfield Street, **175**
22 Batterymarch, **278–79**
22, 30 Bromfield Street,
  9–10
22–30 Marlborough Street,
  127
24 North Street, 48
24 Pinckney Street, **106–7**,
  156
25 Beacon Street, **104–5**
25 Exeter Street, **140**
25, 27 Commonwealth
  Avenue, **124–25**
27 Chestnut Street, **100**
29A Chestnut Street, **100**,
  101
29B Chestnut Street, **100**,
  101
200 Clarendon Street, 147,
  187, **193**
209 Columbus Avenue, **224**
210 Portland Street/5
  Causeway Street, **83–84**,
  242
246–52 Newbury Street,
  174
247 Commonwealth
  Avenue, **178**
253 Summer Street, **248–50**
254–80 Newbury Street,
  174
259 Summer Street, **248–50**
269 Newbury Street, 174–75
270 Clarendon Street, **128**
270 Dartmouth Street,
  155–56
281–91 Shawmut Avenue,
  218
285 Summer Street, **248–50**
295–97 Beacon Street,
  137–38
Tyler Street, 239

Union Club, 24
Union Oyster House, **46, 47**

Union Pacific Railroad, 13
Union Park Square, 209,
  216–18
Union United Methodist
  Church, **214**
Union Warren Savings
  Bank (50 Summer
  Street), **288**
Union Warren Savings
  Bank (133 Federal
  Street), 255, **259–60**
Union Wharf, **69**
Unitarian Universalist
  Association, 105
Unitarian-Universalist
  Church, 113
United Shoe Machinery
  Building, 41, 194, 255,
  258–59, 265
United States Hotel, 240
University of Massachusetts
  at Boston, 305
Upham's Corner, 305
Upjohn, Richard, 96, 150
Upjohn, Richard M. (son),
  150
Upton Street, **212–13**

Van Brunt, Henry, 115
Victoria Street Station
  Restaurant, 246
Villa Victoria, **215–16**
Vinal, Arthur H., 180, 211,
  300
Vinci, Leonardo da, 202
von Schlegell, David, 54, 55

Wadsworth/Hubbard &
  Smith, 241
Walker, C. Howard, 271
"Walk to the Sea," 33
Ware, William Robert, 115
Ware & Van Brunt, 115,
  125, 126
Warner, Olin L., 136
Washington Building, **291**
Washington Mall, 36, **37**
Washington Street, 4, 73,
  82, 240, 281–82
Washington Street Arcade,
  282, **289–91**
Water Street, 268
waterworks stations, 300
Webster, Daniel, 47
Welch, Franklin I., 198, 227

Wesleyan Association
Building, **9–10**
West Cedar Street, **94**
West End, 73–89
West Hill Place, **110–11**,
112, 116
Westland Street, 302
Weston & Rand, 128
Wetmore, James A., 265
Wharf Street, 268
Wheelwright & Haven, 108,
203, 296, 300
White, Kevin, 53
White Building, **87**
Whitehall, Walter Muir,
195
Whitney, Anne, 181

Wilbur Theatre, 232,
233–34
Willard, Solomon, 16, 23,
39, 81, 109
William Lloyd Garrison
statue (Warner), **136–37**
Willow Street, **94–95**
Winslow, W. T., 285
Winslow & Wetherell, 236,
283
Winter Place, 293
Winter Street, 281–96
Winthrop, John, 3
Winthrop Building, **14–15**,
30, 171, 236, 268
Women's City Club, **103**
Women's Educational and

Industrial Union, **147**,
148
Wood, J. M., 233
Woolworth's, 289
Worcester Square, **209**
Worthington Building, 43,
268, 269, 276
Wright, Chester, 78
Wurlitzer Company, **236**

YMCA Building, 149, 150
Young, Ammi B., 272, 273
Young Men's Christian
Union, **237**, 238

ABOUT THE AUTHOR

DONLYN LYNDON writes about architecture as an architect who has been actively engaged in practice and teaching since 1960. He earned his A.B. and M.F.A in Architecture at Princeton University and was a founding partner of Moore Lyndon Turnbull Whitaker (MLTW), a firm that has won many design awards and has been widely publicized in the United States and abroad. A fellow of the American Institute of Architects, former resident at the American Academy in Rome, and partner in Lyndon/Buchanan Associates, Lyndon has designed buildings in Massachusetts, Rhode Island, Vermont, New Hampshire, Mississippi, Oregon, and California. He wrote *The Place of Houses* (1974) with Charles Moore and Gerald Allen, and his articles have appeared in leading architectural journals throughout the world

As a teacher, Lyndon has headed the Architecture departments at the University of Oregon and MIT, and is presently Professor of Architecture at the University of California at Berkely. The material for this book was collected during eleven years of residence in the Boston metropolitan area.

PHOTOGRAPHER'S NOTE

With one exception, these photographs of present Boston buildings were taken from the street level, the point of reference of most passers-by. Often we can admire, or despair, only from the exterior, and therefore the view from the street matters a great deal. This is particularly true in cities such as Boston that have large numbers of students as four-year dwellers, and an equally large number of tourists visiting more quickly without benefit of degree.

I have always thought that buildings spoke to me; their power as markers informs my urban passages. I have tried to portray the feeling of jubilation brought to me by this edificial discourse in Boston. These photographs of Boston buildings are dedicated to Wendy MacNeil in appreciation for discussions about photography, and to Pamela Daniels in admiration for her astute insights and sanguine observations about Boston.

—ALICE WINGWALL